The Future Was Here

Platform Studies
Nick Montfort and Ian Bogost, editors

The Future Was Here

The Commodore Amiga

Jimmy Maher

The MIT Press   Cambridge, Massachusetts   London, England

MIT Press books may be purchased at special quantity discounts for business or sales promotional use. For information, please email special_sales@mitpress.mit.edu or write to Special Sales Depart-ment, The MIT Press, 55 Hayward Street, Cambridge, MA 02142.

This book was set in Filosofia and Helvetica Neue by the MIT Press. Printed and bound in the United States of America.

Library of Congress Cataloging-in-Publication Data

Maher, Jimmy, 1972–
The future was here : the Commodore Amiga / Jimmy Maher.
   p.   cm. — (Platform studies)
Includes bibliographical references and index.
ISBN 978-0-262-01720-6 (hardcover : alk. paper)
1. Amiga (Computer). 2. Multimedia systems—Social aspects. I. Title.
QA76.8 A177M35   2012
006.7—dc23
2011038518

10   9   8   7   6   5   4   3   2

To my wife, best friend, and most tireless supporter, Dorte. Without you, this book would still be just a dream.

Contents

How can someone create a breakthrough game for a mobile phone or a compelling work of art for an immersive three-dimensional (3D) environment without understanding that the mobile phone and the 3D environment are different sorts of computing platforms? The best artists, writers, programmers, and designers are well aware of how certain platforms facilitate certain types of computational expression and innovation. Computer science and engineering have likewise long considered how underlying computing systems can be analyzed and improved. As important as scientific and engineering approaches are, and as significant as work by creative artists has been, there is also much to be learned from the sustained, intensive, humanistic study of digital media. We believe it is time for humanists to consider seriously the lowest level of computing systems, to understand their relationship to culture and creativity.

The Platform Studies series has been established to promote the investigation of underlying computing systems and how they enable, constrain, shape, and support the creative work that is done on them. The series investigates the foundations of digital media—the computing systems, both hardware and software, that developers and users depend on for artistic, literary, and gaming development. Books in the series will certainly vary in their approaches, but they all will also share certain features:

- A focus on a single platform or a closely related family of platforms.
- Technical rigor and in-depth investigation of how computing technologies work.

- An awareness of and discussion of how computing platforms exist in a context of culture and society, being developed based on cultural concepts and then contributing to culture in a variety of ways—for instance, by affecting how people perceive computing.

Acknowledgments

Although my name is on the jacket of this book, its contents reflect many others' contributions.

I must first of all thank Nick Montfort and Ian Bogost, who envisioned and brought into being the Platform Studies series to which this book belongs and provided the example of *Racing the Beam: The Atari Video Computer System* to show how exhilarating and useful this way of approaching digital culture can be. Nick and Ian not only entertained the first pitch from an unproven author and researcher but also helped me to formulate a workable scheme for the book as a whole and delivered invaluable feedback on my first chapters before leaving me in the able hands of Douglas Sery, the MIT Press acquisitions editor who shepherded this book through to completion. Along the way, the press's anonymous manuscript readers also provided useful advice and feedback, helping me to make this book the very best that it could be.

My research put me into contact with a number of former Amiga developers who gave generously of their time and opinions. I thank in particular Joe Decuir, badge number 3 at "Hi-Toro" and one of the principal minds behind the Amiga's hardware design. Joe went through the whole manuscript looking for oversights and inaccuracies—and, yes, he did find a few. Dallas Hodgson, one of the programmers behind Deluxe Paint IV and V, and Eric Graham, mastermind of the Juggler demo, SSG, and Sculpt-Animate, also provided invaluable insights, as did the programmer of the first Amiga virus, who for obvious reasons wishes to remain anonymous.

Much of the Amiga's history survives thanks to the efforts of the Netizens who have archived software and even entire books and magazines that are now very difficult to find in their original forms. These digitized treasures from the past were key to much of my research. The magnificent Ultimate Amiga Emulator (UAE) similarly gave me access to virtually any model or configuration of Amiga I could imagine through the magic of emulation. Indeed, some of the deepest software explorations in this book would have been virtually impossible if I had been restricted to real Amiga hardware, without access to the additional tools UAE provides the digital archaeologist. UAE was created by Bernd Schmidt, but it includes contributions from a list of programmers far too long to include here. I would be remiss, though, not to mention Toni Wilen, longtime maintainer of the Microsoft Windows version of UAE that I use.

The current Amiga community is smaller than it once was, yet it remains a rather shockingly friendly and helpful bunch, something I relearned time and time again when drawing upon their experience and expertise in online resources such as the Amiga Addicts Sanctuary. Ernie Wright and Bob Eaton were particularly wonderful in helping to seek out and recover software from aging floppy disks, a process that was complicated by my living in Denmark.

Finally, I must once again thank my wife, Dorte, who saw me through the long process that has finally resulted in this book and through a transitional time in my life that saw me moving to an unfamiliar country and contending with a new language as well as all the other challenges that accompany immigration. Dorte is the very picture of my imagined reader: one very smart cookie, but not schooled in computer science or engineering. She read the whole manuscript, telling me where I overexplained and underexplained and prompting much revision and improvement. Tak, min skat. Du er den bedste kone i hele verden.

What do you do with your computer today?

Perhaps you store and view your albums of photographs there after transferring them from a digital camera or scanning them in from the original prints or negatives. Perhaps you go further, processing and manipulating these photos with an application such as Adobe Photoshop. Perhaps you integrate your computer with a video camera to create films or presentations for sharing with friends or associates or with the world via services such as YouTube. If you own a Macintosh, perhaps you have tried your hand at music creation via Apple's GarageBand, and if you are a professional musician or even a serious amateur, you have likely made use of Pro Tools to mix, edit, and even perform your compositions. Musician or not, you have almost certainly collected some MP3 files containing your favorite music, and perhaps you have moved beyond compact disks (CDs) entirely, using your computer as your CD rack and stereo in one. If you are younger than a certain age—and, increasingly, even if you are not—you are almost guaranteed to spend at least a little bit of time most days gaming, whether you do it via simple but addictive casual games such as *Zuma* or immersive audiovisual extravaganzas such as *Crysis*. If you are technically informed, and particularly if you choose to compute on an *open-source platform* such as Linux, perhaps you volunteer some of your time and expertise to one of the many open-source software projects, such as the Mozilla Firefox Web browser that now rivals corporate giant Microsoft's Internet Explorer in popular acceptance and that is enabled by the participation of thousands of volunteers spread all over the world. And of course you surf the World Wide Web, enjoying crisp, realistic pictures alongside the text you find there even on the lowest-end computers. It is very likely that you use your computer for more than one of these common applications (or the many others available) at the same time: surfing the Web while you listen to music, for instance, or sneaking in a quick game of solitaire while you chat online with a friend. None of these scenarios is extraordinary as I write these words; they are everyday life in the second decade of the twenty-first century.

If we glance back more than a quarter of a century to early 1985, however, we find a world with a very different perception of computing technology. *Personal computers* (*PCs*) in those days came in two general categories: the boring, beige, very adult box, personified by the products of IBM, and the friendly, fun, childish game machine, personified by the Atari Video Computer System (also known as the 2600) and the Commodore 64. The former category of machines generally booted, after an unpleasant beep or two, into a green or amber display boasting little more than a blinking command prompt. Once one had learned the requisite string of esoteric commands and keystrokes, one could do many useful, businesslike things with the beige box: drafting and editing letters and reports, updating spreadsheets and databases, keeping track of accounts receivable and payable. But it all was done in that same depressing green or amber text and always felt like the work it was. The game machines were much more fun. With them, the family could gather around the television to play early, graphically spare, but surprisingly compelling videogames such as *Space Invaders* and *Pac-Man* as well as more conceptually rich games such as *Impossible Mission* or the early textual interactive fictions from Infocom. Talented programmers took these machines to places never dreamed of by their designers. But their blocky displays, painfully slow tape or floppy-disk-based storage, and extremely limited memory and processing power could not be completely overcome. They stood—and still stand today—as fascinating technical and artistic platforms, but platforms of limited real-world utility nevertheless. The IBMs of the world, meanwhile, placed little emphasis on the aesthetics of their platforms and essentially none on the even more amorphous concept of fun, feeling such concerns had little bearing on their businesslike focus.

The one outlier in the computing world of early 1985 was Apple's recently introduced Macintosh line, which promised to be the "computer for the rest of us" and to make productivity fun by replacing the command line with a mouse-based *graphical user interface* (*GUI*). The Macintosh certainly deserves the credit that is so often bestowed upon it for introducing a new, user-friendly paradigm to computing, a paradigm that even the IBM world would finally—albeit only after years of dismissive snorting—embrace. As elegant, intuitive, and, yes, revolutionary as the Macintosh's *operating system* (*OS*) and accompanying applications were, however, the machine was profoundly limited in many ways, being saddled with a tiny black-and-white display and, in its initial 128-kilobyte (KB) version, starved for memory. The early Macintosh made a wonderful platform for paper-document authoring and processing, but its suitability for other applications was at best limited, and its extremely high price rather belied its populist advertising campaign. Thanks perhaps to these factors, Macintosh sales, after an initial surge, had gone quite flat by 1985.[1] Although they would recover somewhat with the introduction of higher-powered models and eventually color, the Macintosh would remain for years largely a desktop-publishing tool, a niche it created and one for which it was superlatively suited.

It was into this environment that the Commodore Amiga 1000[2] arrived during the latter half of 1985. It is interesting to look back upon the considerable press that greeted that arrival. Virtually all of this press excitedly regurgitated the same set of technical specifications—and small wonder, for these specifications were very impressive indeed in 1985: a palette of 4,096 colors, screen resolutions of up to 640 × 400, four-channel digital stereo sound, true preemptive multitasking, and the user's choice of a GUI similar to that of the Macintosh or a more traditional command prompt. All of these features were powered by a 7.16 megahertz (MHz) Motorola 68000 microprocessor and a set of sophisticated custom chips to relieve the central processing unit (CPU) of much of its normal burden and thus vastly increase the system's overall processing potential. These chips even included a unique pair of powerful custom coprocessors useful for fast animation as well as other tasks. Yet these numbers and bullet points are not the most intriguing aspect of the press notices. Before, after, and among the technical details, one can see the writers grappling with more abstract questions, groping to understand what these features, delivered together in this package, *meant*.

Byte Magazine, among the most sober and respected members of the technology press at the time, was, if one can draw a conclusion from its devoting thirteen pages to a description of a pre-release version of the machine, tremendously excited by the Amiga. But it remained relatively restrained in its conclusions, mentioning "a complexity of hardware design that we have not seen before in personal computers," and stating that "the Amiga will probably have a great effect on other personal computer companies and the industry in general."[3] So many others, though, were inspired to take off on flights of rhetoric (or hyperbole) unusual to find in mere product reviews. *Creative Computing*, always the technology dreamers to complement *Byte*'s realists, invoked Marshall McLuhan's famous "the medium is the message" slogan and called the Amiga nothing less than "a new communications medium—a dream machine."[4] *Compute!* not only proclaimed the Amiga "a pivotal machine that will shatter the traditional boundaries and prejudices which for years have divided the microcomputer marketplace" but also called it "the first true personal computer," meaning it could become an important part of the owner's daily lifestyle rather than existing as a mere toy or tool.[5] Electronic Arts (EA), a young, innovative, and artistically ambitious software publisher, stated that "for the first time, a personal computer is providing the visual and aural quality our sophisticated eyes and ears demand" and was inspired to dream of the time coming soon when "the home computer will be as important as radio, stereo, and television today" as a medium for bringing the world into the home.[6] The premiere issue of *AmigaWorld* echoed these sentiments, saying the Amiga "is the first to go beyond the clunky graphics and animation heretofore seen on personal computers, and in so doing, merits the admiration of the refined eye and ear."[7] All of these sentiments can be summed up in the phrase found on the cover of that magazine: "The Future Is Here."

Of course, not everyone understood the Amiga's transformative potential. Said a representative of one business-oriented franchise store that had elected not to carry the Amiga: "What's important is doing basic jobs in a simple, straightforward way. There are products now that address every need of the business person. Why add another one unless there is a compelling reason[?] And in this case, that compelling reason doesn't exist."[8] The lack of vision or understanding of the potential for computing technology beyond the spreadsheet and the word processor is disconcerting, particularly in retrospect, but is also in its own way prophetic. The Amiga, built by a company known as a manufacturer of toys in the business computing world, would have an uphill struggle to win respect from that quarter.

Nevertheless, it is remarkable that so many genuinely visionary perspectives of the Amiga existed in so many places, even if their expression was sometimes delivered in rather muddled language. There is a term they all were groping toward, one that had not yet entered common English usage under its modern meaning: *multimedia*. The term itself was not precisely new even in 1985, having cropped up from time to time, albeit often in a hyphenated form ("multi-media") in reference to artistic works and performances. It even enjoyed a brief cultural vogue of sorts during the late 1960s, when "multimedia happenings" incorporating (at a minimum) live music and visuals were common. The Exploding Plastic Inevitable shows put on in 1966 and 1967 by Andy Warhol and the Velvet

Underground were an early example of this genre, and Pink Floyd was perhaps its most long-lived practitioner, embellishing their musical performances for decades with projected visuals, lasers, elaborate lighting effects, smoke, and such physical props as enormous inflatable pigs that hovered over the audience.

The term *multimedia* came to be commonly associated with computing technology, however, only in 1989, when the arrival of reasonably good graphics cards, affordable sound cards, and *CD read-only memory (CD-ROM)* drives first began to transform the heretofore bland beige world of IBM and Apple. It became a favorite in those companies and others' marketing literature and was soon one of the buzzwords of the era. The hype that surrounded it for a number of years did little to lend it a coherent meaning because it seemed to be applied to virtually everything new and shiny in the world of computers. Commodore did attempt to provide a usable definition in 1990: "[Multimedia is] a method of designing and integrating computer technologies on a single platform that enables the end user to input, create, manipulate, and output text, graphics, audio, and video utilizing a single-user interface."[9] Tony Feldman put it more elegantly and succinctly in a 1994 book on the subject: "Multimedia is the seamless integration of data, text, images of all kinds and sound within a single, digital information environment."[10] The word *digital* is key here; a multimedia computer entails the *digitization* of the *analog* world of image and sound into the world of discrete numbers inside the machine."[11] The birth of the multimedia age begot nothing less than a revolutionary change in the way that all forms of media are stored and transmitted, marking the end of the analog era and the beginning of the digital, the end of an era of specialized devices capable of dealing with only one form of media and the beginning of our era of smart, programmable devices that can deal with many media.

My central claim in this book is that the Amiga was the world's first true multimedia PC.

Although earlier computers existed in isolation from the world, requiring their visuals and sound to be generated and live only within their memory, the Amiga was *of* the world, able to interface with it in all its rich analog glory. It was the first PC with a sufficient screen resolution and color palette as well as memory and processing power to practically store and display full-color photographic representations of the real world, whether they be scanned in from photographs, captured from film or video, or snapped live by a *digitizer* connected to the machine. It could be used to manipulate video, adding titles, special effects, or other post-production tricks. And it was also among the first to make practical use of recordings of real-world sound. The seeds of the digital-media future, of digital cameras and Photoshop and MP3 players, are here.

The Amiga was the first aesthetically satisfying PC. Although the generation of machines that preceded it were made to do many remarkable things, works produced on them always carried an implied asterisk; "Remarkable," we say, ". . . for existing on such an absurdly limited platform." Even the Macintosh, a dramatic leap forward in many ways, nevertheless remained sharply limited by its black-and-white display and its lack of fast animation capabilities. Visuals produced on the Amiga, however, were in full color and could often stand on their own terms, not as art produced under huge technological constraints, but simply as art. And in allowing game programmers to move beyond blocky, garish graphics and crude sound, the Amiga redefined the medium of interactive entertainment as being capable of adult sophistication and artistry. The seeds of the aesthetic future, of computers as everyday artistic tools, ever more attractive computer desktops, and audiovisually rich virtual worlds, are here.

The Amiga empowered amateur creators by giving them access to tools heretofore available only to the professional. The platform's most successful and sustained professional niche was as a video-production workstation, where an Amiga, accompanied by some relatively inexpensive software and hardware peripherals, could give the hobbyist amateur or the frugal professional editing and postproduction capabilities equivalent to equipment costing tens or hundreds of thousands. And much of the graphical and musical creation software available for the machine was truly remarkable. The seeds of the participatory-culture future, of YouTube and Flickr and even the blogosphere, are here.

The Amiga brought many developments from the world of the larger *institutional computer* to the *personal computer* for the first time. For instance, programmers and artists experimented extensively with three-dimensional (3D) modeling and ray tracing on the Amiga, popularizing and democratizing these techniques that had heretofore been confined to universities and corporate research facilities. The result was a revolution in the way that animations and cartoons were developed as well as in the aesthetics of videogames. And the Amiga's most well-known application, Deluxe Paint, was a direct heir to the pioneering research conducted at Xerox's Palo Alto Research Center (PARC), written by someone who had worked closely with the PARC researchers. Even its OS had more in common with sophisticated institutional OSs such as Unix than it did with the primitive PC OSs of its competition. The seeds of the future, of desktop systems that no longer seemed like toy versions of their larger cousins, that, indeed, would soon make most of the room-filling colossi of old obsolete, are here.

As the first mainstream PC OS to support *multitasking*, the Amiga's OS ("AmigaOS") redefined the way we interact with computers. The idea of a single-tasking computer today is almost unthinkable, but that was the norm prior to the Amiga. With the Amiga, one all of a sudden could run multiple applications simultaneously, moving data among them via the system clipboard; one could listen to music while one worked on a letter or report; or one could play a game while waiting for a long download to complete. This new mode of working and even thinking, which has become particularly marked among the young today, has prompted reams of psychological analysis of both an approving and a concerned character. The seeds of the multitasking future, of surfing the Internet while chatting with a friend while playing a game while listening to music, are here.

And the Amiga impacted the culture of computing in another significant way: in drawing together a community of users who shared code and labor in an effort to further and sustain the platform. If there was one article of faith among Amiga users, it was that Amiga's corporate parent, Commodore, was incompetent and unworthy of the technology it had managed to acquire. Through projects such as Fred Fish's extensive disk library of *free software*, which he distributed to all and sundry for the cost of shipping, these users attempted to bypass Commodore's bumbling interference and assume de facto ownership of the platform. Their efforts prefigure the later Internet-enabled efforts of the free-software community that began to gather around the Linux OS in the early 1990s. (A fair number of the old Amiga guard wound up as Linux converts.) The seeds of the open-source future, of high-quality, freely distributed, community-developed software, are here.

I have just made a series of rather bold statements, and most are certainly worthy of the further qualifications that will come later in this book. Although the Amiga could acceptably display photographic images on screen, for instance, their fidelity was certainly not what we are accustomed to today; and although multitasking worked well enough in many scenarios, the Amiga's lack of virtual memory and memory-protection technology could make the platform a crash-prone house of cards in others. The Amiga was far from a perfect creation even in its time. The critical disk operating system (DOS) component of AmigaOS was clunky and ill matched, for instance, and the platform's interlaced video modes with their omnipresent flicker were a constant annoyance and distraction to everyone not engaged in the video production that they enabled. These points become especially important to make when one confronts a certain narrative about the Amiga that has become the dominant one in many computing circles, which almost deifies the platform as a perfect creation and lays all of the blame for its ultimate downfall at the feet of Commodore's mismanagement. Although Commodore did the Amiga very few favors, I believe many of the reasons for the Amiga's downfall can be found not in external factors, but within its core design—ironically, the very same design that made it such a remarkable machine in 1985. I address these issues, like so many others I have introduced here, at greater length later in this book. For now, I just want to state that I believe the Amiga deserves a place alongside such earlier computing platforms as Colossus, the Digital Electronic Corporation Programmed Data Processor 1 (PDP-1), the Keyboard Input Monitor 1 (KIM-1), the Commodore Personal Electronic Transactor (PET), and the Apple Macintosh as a pioneering machine and a signpost to the future.

This book is an attempt to situate the Amiga within its historical and cultural context, to explain what made it unique and why it is important, and to do so in a fairly technically rigorous way. Each of its chapters examines one important historical facet of the platform. At the core of each chapter, I examine one or two specific programs, companies, or communities in considerable detail and, by the end of the book, use them as exemplars to draw a holistic picture of the Amiga platform and the communities of practice that surrounded it. I explain the ways in which the machine's technical qualities made it useful or even ideal for various purposes and how engineers, programmers, artists, and others harnessed these qualities to push back boundaries and transform the culture of computing. My position here is certainly not one of strict technological determinism; although the Amiga's hardware design made it remarkable, most of the credit for the vibrant, creative culture that sprang up around this platform must go to the people who saw the potential in the hardware and made it sing. Indeed, most of the superior technical specifications that made the Amiga so remarkable upon its 1985 release were surpassed by competing platforms as early as 1989. The unique spirit of creativity and innovation that surrounded the platform for years after that date are thus more a cultural than a technical phenomenon. Another important goal I have for this book, therefore, is to credit and properly document the work of some of these visionaries who played such a role in shaping the world we currently live in. I also hope to offer some more general insights into the technical, cultural, and economic factors that bear on the life cycle of a platform and its ultimate fate. Finally, although many of the problems and restrictions that the engineers, programmers, and artists whose work I analyze in this book are no longer with us today, the fundamental principles of computing upon which their work was based certainly are. I therefore hope you will gain through these "worked examples" not only an appreciation of the cleverness these engineers, programmers, and artists brought to bear upon their work, but also an increased understanding of those fundamental principles and how they can be applied to accomplishing practical tasks even on modern platforms with their own sets of strengths and weaknesses.

In a study of this nature, a certain level of technical depth is absolutely necessary. I can promise, however, that I expect of you only a basic level of computer literacy and perhaps sometimes a willingness to read slowly and carefully. As you may have noticed already, technical terms and acronyms not in everyday modern English usage are printed in *italics* when an understanding of them first becomes critical to an understanding of the text as a whole. Although the more esoteric and Amiga-specific terms are also clarified in the main text, all of them can be found in the glossary at the back of the book. Most of the chapters contain one or more detailed case studies that attempt to convey some of the experience of an Amiga user programming a demo or game, creating a piece of art, or solving a problem. You should follow along with these "worked examples" in whatever depth suits your knowledge and interest level. On this book's accompanying Web site (http://amiga.filfre.net), you will find a variety of resources that should help you to do just that, as well as more general materials that should also aid in your appreciation of each chapter. These materials include images and movie clips as well as programs that you can download and run on a real Amiga or an Amiga emulator.[12] Programmers will also find some C and assembly-language *source code* there that may be of interest, although a knowledge of those programming languages is certainly not a prerequisite to understanding the contents of this book.

It is difficult indeed to come to a full understanding of a multimedia computer such as the Amiga through a traditional linear text alone. I therefore encourage you to make active use of the Web site to put yourself in the shoes of the multimedia pioneers who used the Amiga and to use the book that you hold in your hands now as a guide, but not the sum total of your journey into this important corner of computing history. Although Amiga's pioneers were sketching the future, they always seemed to manage to have a great deal of fun also. The Amiga remains such a beloved platform to so many at least in part because programming and working with it could be such a sublime pleasure, in a way that has perhaps been lost to the enormously complex computing platforms of today. Remember this as you explore the Amiga's history and technical workings, and remember to have some fun of your own exploring this book, its accompanying Web site, and whatever other resources they prompt you to uncover.

During the 1980s, when Internet access was not yet commonplace and the World Wide Web did not yet exist, trade shows assumed enormous importance to computer hardware and software producers. Here they could announce and demonstrate their latest and greatest to the public and, even more important, to industry insiders and the technology-related press. Perhaps the most important stop on the technology-show circuit was also the first of the year: the Winter Consumer Electronics Show (CES), begun in 1967 and held every January from 1978 to the present in Las Vegas. The list of technologies debuted at the CES through the years is impressive, including as it does the videocassette recorder (VCR, 1970), affordable digital watches (1976), the CD (1981), and the digital video disk (DVD, 1996), just for starters. Early PC manufacturers also made good use of the show and its attendant publicity. Many of the first affordable home computers debuted there in the late 1970s, as did Atari's landmark *Pong* home videogame in 1975 and video computer system (VCS) game console in 1977, the massively popular Commodore 64 computer in 1982, and the Nintendo Entertainment System in 1985—all harbingers of major cultural and economic changes in the world of home computers and videogames. Virtually all computing magazines devoted space—often considerable space—to the products, opinions, and rumors they found at CES. A company that failed to make an appearance or that appeared toting old or disappointing products to display could find its name tarnished for the remainder of the year. Conversely, a company that brought a fresh, compelling product there could generate major momentum that could carry it right through that year and beyond.

The 1984 edition of Winter CES was fairly typical of its era. Although there were no obvious bombshells like the Commodore 64, many new machines and products were on display, and the industry press covered them in the usual detail. Coleco had a new computer, the Adam, and Commodore had a new machine, which it called at that time "the 264";[1] both were greeted with justified skepticism by the savvy press, and, indeed, both were destined to be commercial failures. More intriguing were some of the first IBM PC compatibles, the beginning of a landslide that would eventually steal the business-computing leadership role away from IBM. Also present, as usual, were seemingly endless quantities of games and other software from companies large and small. If nothing else, the 1984 Winter CES demonstrated that just months after the bottom had dropped out of the home-videogame-console market, the home-computer market, while decidedly weakened by that related industry's failure, was facing nothing like the same sort of apocalypse.

In one corner of the show floor a tiny company called "Amiga, Incorporated" had on display its line of peripherals for Atari's aged 2600. The display garnered little interest from the public or the press; Amiga seemed like just another console bandwagon jumper left high and dry by the videogame crash. There was, however, a private space behind the Amiga booth into which only selected members of the industry and the press were invited. In this space was the prototype of an entirely new computer that Amiga called the "Lorraine." The motley mass of breadboards and exposed wiring looked like a mad scientist's experiment, but the graphical demonstrations it produced were nothing less than jaw dropping even to jaded industry veterans. Some in fact refused to believe that the Lorraine was the source of the graphics and persisted in attempting to peak under the table on which the prototype rested to find their "real" source.[2] Most impressive of the Lorraine demos was an animation of a large rotating red-and-white-checkered soccer ball that bounced fluidly over a static background and even cast a realistic shadow behind it.

The idea of demonstrating a computer's graphical capabilities using a bouncing ball was hardly a new one in 1984. Charly Adama in 1949 or 1950 wrote a simple bouncing-ball demo for the Whirlwind, the first computer capable of real-time processing; this demo later served as direct inspiration to the creators of *Spacewar!*—generally regarded as the first real-time videogame.[3] Bouncing balls continued to crop up regularly at trade shows during the early years of the PC era in such places as demonstrations of the MOS Technologies video interface chip (VIC) for graphics that would eventually find a home in the popular Commodore VIC-20.[4] Nevertheless, the Boing demo took on a life of its own as the most enduring symbol of the Amiga, as one of the most famous graphical demos ever created, and as a lovely piece of minimalist digital art in its own right. And the computer that ran it should be recognized as one of the most important products ever brought to Winter CES.

Lorraine, Paula, Denise, and Agnus

The man universally considered the "father of the Amiga" was a bearded, soft-spoken hardware engineer named Jay Miner.[5] Even had Miner never worked on the Amiga, his place in the history of computing would be secure, for during his tenure at Atari from 1975 to 1979 his was one of the key engineering minds behind the first videogame console to achieve widespread popularity in homes, the Atari Video Computer System (later rebadged the "Atari 2600").[6] After completing that project, Miner became lead designer of Atari's first general-purpose home computers, the Atari 400 and 800. In these machines, we can already see the emergence of a design philosophy that would come to fruition in the Amiga.

In most PC designs of this era, the *CPU* is not just the *central* processing unit, but really the *only* processing unit. Absolutely every task the computer performs must be performed by the CPU, including not only the processing of whatever program the user is actually running, but also all of the little maintenance tasks that generally go unremarked by the user: updating the screen, handling data transfers to and from disk or tape, scanning the keyboard and other peripherals for the user's inputs, just to begin the list. In Miner's Atari machines, however, many of these tasks are offloaded from the CPU to one or more of three *custom chips* that can then do the job relatively autonomously while the CPU simultaneously works on other tasks. Two chips, the Alpha-Numeric Television Interface Circuit (ANTIC) and the Color Television Interface Adaptor (CTIA), take over much of the responsibility for generating the machine's display, and another, the POKEY chip (whose name derives from a combination of the terms *potentiometer* and *keyboard*), generates sound and performs many input/output functions. Thanks to these custom chips, the MOS 6502 microprocessor at the heart of the machine can devote many, many more of its cycles to the core task of running the user's programs.[7] Although most of the Atari machines' direct competitors used this same CPU, the Atari's unique design delivered a considerable performance advantage for most applications—particularly for applications, such as games, that made extensive use of graphics and sound. In fact, the Atari 400 and 800 offered by far the most impressive graphics and sound in the nascent home-computer industry at the time of their late 1979 release. They offered, for instance, a potential palette of 256 colors at a time when few other machines could display even 16.

The machines did not, however, achieve commercial success to match their technical superiority. The Atari VCS, after a couple of years of only sporadic sales, was finally gaining major traction that 1979 holiday season and was on the way to becoming a full-fledged cultural phenomenon. In the face of this fact, coupled with the promising new standup arcade machine division Atari had just launched, the 400 and 800 became a horrendously mismanaged afterthought for the company. For instance, Atari did not just fail to encourage the third-party software development that any computer depends on for popular acceptance but actually threatened to sue some developers who attempted to create software for the platform for infringing on Atari's intellectual-property rights.[8] Perhaps surprisingly in light of such bizarre corporate logic, the machines were in no way a complete failure—Atari would eventually sell two million of the 400 and 800 and their successor models by 1985,[9] and these machines would attract a fanatically loyal core of users—but they would remain second-tier players in comparison to the 6502-based competition from Apple and Commodore. The 400 and 800 would not, alas, be the last Jay Miner–designed machines to fail to sell in the numbers their technical superiority would have seemed to ensure.

By the time the Atari 400 and 800 debuted, Miner, disenchanted like many of the company's pioneers by the changes that had followed Atari's acquisition by Warner Communications and founder Nolan Bushnell's departure, had already left Atari and the home-computer industry to design chips for pacemaker medical devices. He was still working in that field in 1982 when an old colleague from Atari, Larry Kaplan, contacted him to ask if he would be interested in designing a new videogame console for a startup company Kaplan was putting together with the support of a group of venture capitalists and investors. In spite of being outdated even by the technological standards of 1982, the Atari VCS in that year was at the height of its popularity. Videogames were hot, and investors searched for a piece of the proverbial action with an eagerness that reminds one somewhat of the dot.com bubble of the late 1990s. Kaplan had thus had little trouble finding investors—mostly dentists, as it happened—to contribute to his scheme of producing the next-generation videogame console to take the market-leading place of the aging Atari VCS. Now he needed Miner's talents to design said console for his company, which he had named "Hi-Toro." Miner agreed, but with two conditions: this proposed game machine must be at least expandable into a full-fledged PC, and it must be built around an exciting new microprocessor, the Motorola 68000.

The 68000 was something of a wunderkind of the computing world in 1982. First introduced in 1979, the 68000 was, as is still normal today in the world of microchip production, initially quite expensive and thus saw its first applications mainly in high-end *Unix*-based *workstations* such as those produced by Sun Microsystems.[10] By 1982, its price had come down enough that designers such as Miner (not to mention his peers at companies such as Apple and Atari) could seriously consider incorporating the chip into consumer-level, general-purpose computers.

Microprocessors and the computers that employ them are often described in terms of their bit count, which represents not only the largest number they can natively understand, but also, even more important, the amount of data they can move in a single operation, a critical factor in such multimedia scenarios as fast graphical screen updating. A 32-bit processor running at the same clock speed as an 8-bit processor is, all else being equal, effectively capable of four times the throughput. A simple thought experiment might best explain why. Imagine watching two men digging separate holes side by side. Both work at exactly the same speed. After a time, though, you notice that one of the holes is four times as deep. A further look at the two men reveals the reason: one man is working with a shovel four times as large! This man, of course, represents the 32-bit processor, whereas the other represents the 8-bit processor.

Thirty-two-bit processors have been the most common type in home and small-business computers since the early 1990s, but in recent years they have been slowly giving way at last to a new generation of 64-bit machines. The home-computing market of 1982, however, was still dominated by the 8-bit MOS 6502-equipped Apple II and Commodore 64, and the business-computing world had just been shaken up by the release of the soon-to-be industry-standard IBM PC, equipped with an Intel 8088 that is something of a hybrid between an 8-bit and a 16-bit processor. The new 68000 was likewise a hybrid—but a hybrid between a 16-bit and a 32-bit processor. It is capable of transferring data to and from main-system memory only 16 bits at a time, but it performs many internal operations like a full 32-bit processor.[11] Consumer-level 68000s could be easily clocked at up to 8 *MHz*, a figure that could be matched among the competition only by the even newer and more expensive Intel 80286. The 68000 also boasted an extensive instruction set designed specifically to support programming in *high-level languages* such as *C* rather than the tedious *assembly code* that was the norm of the time[12] and was capable of addressing no less than 16 *megabytes* (*MB*) of memory, an unheard of figure at a time when few computers sold with more than 64 KB onboard. Its extensive system of *interrupts* also made it a natural choice for the *event-driven programming* paradigm of the new generation of GUI-equipped PCs that would begin shortly with the Apple Lisa and Macintosh and continue with the Atari ST and, of course, Miner's own Amiga.

Changes came quickly at Hi-Toro after Miner came onboard. Kaplan suddenly grew disillusioned with the venture and left just weeks after founding it. His role as business and financial leader was assumed by a new arrival from Tonka Toys, Dave Morse. Concerned about the resemblance of the name "Hi-Toro" to the named used by the Japanese lawnmower manufacturer, "Toro," the company's investors asked for a new one. The name "Amiga," from the Spanish word meaning "female friend," was chosen based on its friendly yet elegant and "sexy" sound, not to mention the fact that it would be listed before both Apple and Atari in telephone and corporate directories.[13] While Miner was doing preliminary design work on the new machine with another former colleague from Atari, Joe Decuir, the newly christened Amiga, Incorporated designed and released a few hardware peripherals for the Atari 2600 as a way of bringing in some income and disguising its real plans from rivals.

A team of young and precocious engineers and programmers was soon assembled around Miner and set to work developing the machine that would become the Amiga. Miner, fully a generation older than most of his charges, presided over this brilliant but idiosyncratic group as a sort of benevolent father figure. He was a fair, warm, tolerant man as well as an innovative engineer, and the former qualities perhaps contributed as much as the latter to giving the Amiga its finished character. Speaking of his management philosophy, he said, "Allowing people to be different is terribly important. Who cares, as long as you get the work done?"[14]

These early years of an independent Amiga, Incorporated have come to occupy a storied place in Amiga lore, serving the platform as a founding myth in which a group of visionaries gathered together to create the perfect computer. R. J. Mical, an early employee who became one of the principal architects of AmigaOS as well as a coauthor of the Boing demo, solidified the story by repeating it in unabashedly sentimental presentations at Amiga meet-ups and trade shows beginning just a few years after the historical events themselves. Mical said of the company's hiring policy, "We were looking for people who were trying to make a mark on the world, not just on the industry but on the world in general. We were looking for people that really wanted to make a statement, that really wanted to do an incredibly great thing, not just someone who was just looking for a job."[15] The most memorable anecdotes from this period have become indelible parts of Amiga lore: Miner drawing circuits with his beloved cockapoo Mitchie always at his feet;[16] hardware engineer Dave Needle wandering through the office in fuzzy bedroom slippers;[17] Mical and fellow program-mer Dale Luck dancing to Led Zeppelin in the middle of the night to stay awake while waiting for their software to compile;[18] Miner and others mortgaging their houses to keep the lights on and the dream alive for a few more weeks.[19]

In keeping with a tradition inherited from Atari of naming machines in development and even their internal components after women at or around the office, the machine was christened the "Lorraine," after company president Dave Morse's wife. The Lorraine, like Miner's previous design for Atari, was built around three custom chips that take much of the load off of the CPU.[20] Each of these chips, *Denise*, *Paula*, and *Agnus*,[21] performs very specific tasks: Denise managing the display, Paula manag-ing sound and input and output to disks and other peripherals, and Agnus managing the other two and ensuring that they do not conflict with the CPU. Agnus also provides a home for two unique *coprocessors*, the *copper* and the *blitter*; these coprocessors gave the Lorraine remarkable anima-tion capabilities, in ways that I explain later in the book.

The Lorraine's hardware design was fairly well along, and an OS was also in the works when the Great Videogame Crash of 1983, which almost brought an end to the videogame industry, suddenly gave Amiga's inves-tors reason to bless Miner's dogged insistence that the Lorraine be a viable basis for a full-fledged computer as well as a videogame console. Over-saturated with too many incompatible consoles and too many uninspired games, many of them from industry leader Atari itself, the console market collapsed that year, an event forever symbolized by Atari's ignominious dumping of trailer loads of its *E.T.* cartridges into a New Mexico landfill. Undaunted, Amiga simply began describing the Lorraine as a computer rather than a videogame console and continued full speed ahead with a sigh of relief that Miner and his team had designed its circuits from the start to interface with a mouse, keyboard, and disk drive as well as a joy-stick and television. The Lorraine's planned coming-out party at Winter CES was drawing near, and there was still much to do. In fact, the show was assuming ever greater importance, for Amiga, Incorporated was quickly running out of money and desperately needed to demonstrate something to the potential additional investors who might keep it afloat long enough to complete the Lorraine.

Enter Boing

The Lorraine was made ready in time for the show, but only barely and only for a fairly generous definition of "ready." The machine that the

Amiga team brought with them was a cobbled collection of circuit boards and wires that failed constantly. The hardware technicians brought piles of chips and other spare parts with them and learned to repair the machine on the fly during demonstrations. The software situation was also problematic because Amiga's team of programmers had had access to the prototype for just a few days before the show began and thus precious little time in which to prepare and test demonstrations of the machine's capabilities. Mical and Luck worked furiously at the show itself to improve upon the software the team had brought with them. They created the first version of the Boing demo in Amiga's little rented back room on the CES show floor in an all-night hacking session fueled by "a six-pack of warm beer."[22]

The experience of programming on that Lorraine prototype was very different from that of programming a production Amiga. Although the custom chips' specifications and operation were mostly the same, the Lorraine had neither an OS nor any of the tools and utilities available to an Amiga programmer a couple of years later. In fact, the Lorraine did not even have a keyboard or, indeed, any user interface at all; it could be operated only by uploading a program from a remote terminal connection.[23] Mical and Luck wrote the Boing demo as well as many AmigaOS libraries and tools on a high-end development computer known as the "SAGE IV," manufactured by the small company Sage Computer.[24] Like the Lorraine, the SAGE had a 68000 CPU and ran an OS known as "Idris" that was a sort of stripped-down version of the institutional Unix OS, also a major inspiration behind AmigaOS. Because the SAGE used the 68000, it was possible to write a C program on that machine, compile it into an *executable* the 68000 that could run using a customized C compiler, and transfer it over to the Lorraine via a cable for execution.[25]

There is some confusion in the existing documentation of that Winter CES as to the exact state of the Boing demo when it was presented there. Quite a number of histories speak of the demo as being essentially in its final state there, and various interviewees who were present mention being able to hear clearly the booming noise of the demo from out on the show floor. Luck, however, stated in an interview that the version of the demo presented there had the ball bouncing only up and down, not left to right, as in the final version, and, further, that the demo had no sound at all at the time.[26] I tend to accept Luck's recollection; as one of the programmers of the demo, he certainly ought to know. Further, one wonders how the Amiga team would have been able to digitize the real-world sounds that were the source of the demo's "booming"—a very cumbersome process in 1984—amid the confusion of CES. Certainly, though, both the sound and the left-to-right motion had been added to the demo by the time it was presented (behind closed doors once again) at the Summer CES show in Chicago in June 1984. My belief is that those who speak of *hearing* the Boing demo in January are likely conflating memories of two separate CES appearances.

Whatever the state of the Boing demo there, Amiga's Winter CES appearance more than succeeded in its main purpose of attracting favorable press exposure and, most important, moneyed interests to a company that desperately needed both. By the time the Lorraine and the Boing demo made their next appearance at Summer CES, two of the "big four" North American PC manufacturers of the time, Commodore and Atari, were deeply interested in acquiring the company and its technology. Atari injected some much needed funding into Amiga while negotiations proceeded and looked likely to win the prize as a result, but it was mired in complications of its own in the wake of the Videogame Crash of 1983 and was in the process of being sold by communications giant Warner to a private investment group headed ironically by Commodore's recently ousted founder Jack Tramiel. A last-minute deal finalized on August 15, 1984, therefore made Amiga a fully owned subsidiary of Commodore. Bitter recriminations and a fruitless lawsuit from Atari followed, but those issues were for Commodore's management to deal with. Properly funded at last thanks to Commodore's relatively deep pockets, the Amiga team could concentrate on packaging the mad scientist's experiment that was the Lorraine into a mass-produced computer.

The Commodore Amiga 1000 that debuted in a lavish presentation at New York's Lincoln Center on July 23, 1985, was not quite everything the team behind it had dreamed of. Like most commercial products that must conform to economic as well as technical realities, it contained plenty of compromises that were painful for its engineers to behold. Everyone agreed, for instance, that the machine's standard 256 KB of *random-access memory* (*RAM*) was hopelessly inadequate, barely enough to boot the OS; users hoping to do any sort of real work (or play, for that matter) simply had to expand it to at least 512 KB. And the machine lacked internal expansion slots; seriously expanded Amiga 1000s would inevitably end up looking almost as homemade and chaotic as the old Lorraine prototype, with peripherals daisy chained across the desk from the single expansion port. Nevertheless, the Amiga 1000 was a surprising product from Commodore, previously the producer of lumpy, almost endearingly unattractive case designs such as the "breadbox" Commodore 64. By far the most stylish Amiga model that would ever be produced, the Amiga 1000 still looks sleek and attractive even today. And it bore, literally as well as figuratively, the imprint of the unique personalities that had created it; on the top of the inside of its case were stamped the signatures of the entire team, including a paw print from Mitchie.

Virtually the entire Amiga team also attended the debut. And another old friend was there. Near the end of his presentation of the machine, Bob Pariseau introduced an "old standby,"[27] the Boing demo, by now rewritten yet again to run politely under AmigaOS. When Commodore demonstrated the Amiga 1000 on the influential PBS television show *Computer Chronicles*, the Boing demo was likewise in prominent evidence.[28] In fact, the demo now had an additional appeal as a demonstration of AmigaOS's multitasking capabilities; demonstrators delighted in showing the ball bouncing and booming merrily away in one virtual screen, while one or more other programs ran in another. The Boing ball had by now become so identified with the Amiga that it very nearly became the machine's official logo, even appearing on pre-release versions of Amiga hardware. One can clearly see, for instance, a Boing ball on the external floppy drive of the machine in Commodore's official video of the Lincoln Center debut. Very shortly before the debut, however, Commodore suddenly decided to replace the Boing ball with a rainbow-colored checkmark that bore a strong resemblance to Commodore's logos for its successful eight-bit machines such as the Commodore 64, thus situating the Amiga as a continuation of Commodore's earlier efforts rather than as an entirely new creation.[29]

Before delving into the technical details of the Boing demo, I need to introduce (or reintroduce) the concept of *binary* representation because this concept is essential not only to understanding the material that immediately follows, but to understanding much of the technical material in this book. After that, I provide some foundational information on the way the Amiga creates its display.

Thinking Binary

As every beginning computer literacy student learns, computers are ultimately capable of dealing only with binary numbers: a series of off-or-on switches, or *bits*, represented respectively as 0 and 1. In fact, these arrangements of bits must stand in for absolutely everything stored in a computer's memory, whether numbers, text, other forms of data, program instructions, or even addresses of other locations in memory. For convenience and simplicity, humans generally group these bits into larger units. The smallest of these units, representing eight bits, is the *byte*. A byte can store any unsigned number from 0 to 255, there being 256 possible combinations of the eight off/on switches that make up the byte; it can store, in other words, an eight-digit binary number.

We can quickly convert a 68000-processor byte from binary to decimal by making use of table 2.1. We simply add together the decimal counterpart of each binary digit that is a 1. Let us consider the binary byte 00001011. We can find its decimal equivalent by calculating $8 + 2 + 1 = 11$.[30] Numbers larger than 255 can be represented only if we devote more bits to the task: "bit 8" representing the decimal value 256, "bit 9" the value 512, and so on. Two bytes (16 bits) taken together are frequently called a *word* and can contain any unsigned number up to 65,535; four bytes (32 bits) are called a *long word* and can contain any unsigned number up to 4,294,967,295. A bit sequence might also represent something other than a number. The American Standard Code for Information Interchange (ASCII), used by the Amiga and virtually all other small computers,[31] encodes a unique byte-size bit sequence to every glyph in common English usage. The glyph *A*, for instance, is represented by the binary sequence 01000001, or the decimal number 65. ASCII thus provides a means of encoding text on the computer, with each character represented by a single byte. Program instructions are encoded in a similar way, using schemes specific to the microprocessor in use, with each bit sequence corresponding to a single assembly-language command.

A computer's memory is indexed not by bits, but by bytes, with every single byte in RAM having its own unique *address*. These addresses, numbered from 0 to the limit of the computer's memory, allow the OS and the programmer to keep track of what is stored where. Engineers and programmers generally try to align their data with word or even long-word boundaries for reasons of efficiency and simplicity, for microprocessors deal more quickly and efficiently with data aligned with these boundaries. Bytes are also grouped together in much larger units to represent the overall storage capacity of a computer or a subsystem thereof: 1,024 bytes equal a kilobyte(KB); 1,024 KB equal a megabyte (MB); 1,024 MB equal a gigabyte (GB); and 1,024 GB equal a terabyte (TB). Although commonly spoken of today, gigabytes and terabytes were of only theoretical import to Amiga engineers and programmers in the 1980s.

The Amiga's Display System

Before, after, and during the Amiga's debut, the aspect of it that received by far the most discussion was of course its remarkable graphical capabilities. As all of the machine's reviewers and promotional literature excitedly trumpeted, the original Amiga was capable of displaying 32 colors on screen at once from a palette of 4,096 colors in its low-resolution modes (320×200 and 320×400), and 16 colors from the same palette of 4,096

Table 2.1

Converting an eight-bit binary number to decimal

Binary Position	7	6	5	4	3	2	1	0
Decimal Value	128	64	32	16	8	4	2	1

in its high-resolution modes (640 × 200 and 640 × 400). Further, users gradually discovered that the Amiga was also possessed of two more modes that could be used to place 64 or even all 4,096 colors on the same screen. Although these numbers might not sound overly impressive today, they were remarkable at the time. Apple's massively hyped Macintosh, for instance, could display exactly 2 colors, black and white, and even the Amiga's most obvious competitor, the Atari ST, was limited to 16 colors out of 512 in low resolution and 4 colors out of 512 in high resolution. The IBM PC, meanwhile, was saddled with the primitive 4-color Color Graphics Adaptor (CGA) for nontextual displays.

With the previously given foundation in binary representation, we find that the Amiga's color-selection process works in a fairly straightforward way. Each of the 4,096 possible colors can be described as a mixture of 3 primary colors: red, green, and blue, with the relative proportion of each defined by a number from 0 to 15. These numbers form the color's "*red green blue*" (*RGB*) value. For example, pure white has an RGB value of red 15, green 15, blue 15; sky blue has a value of red 6, green 15, blue 14. Because each component can have a value from 0 to 15, each can be stored in 4 bits of memory; combined, then, we need 12 bits to store each color. Because it is easier for the CPU to deal with data aligned to word boundaries, two bytes (or a word) are devoted to the storage of each color, simply leaving the extra four bits unused. These words are placed into a table of *registers* used by Denise, numbered (as is normal in computer applications) not from 1, but from 0 and ending at 31. (In cases where the current screen is configured to display fewer than 32 colors, the latter parts of the table simply go unused.) Let us say, for example, that we have stored the RGB value for tan—red 13, green 11, blue 9—at position 15 in the table. When Denise receives a request to paint a particular pixel with color 15, she accesses register 15 to learn that this register represents tan and therefore sends that color to the screen. A program is free to modify the color registers at any time. In our example, we could change all on-screen occurrences of tan to black very quickly by changing register 15 to red 0, green 0, blue 0. As we are about to see, the Boing demo made good use of exactly this property.

Before we can appreciate the specifics of the Boing demo, though, we also need to understand how this table of colors is used to build the image seen on the monitor screen. This concept is somewhat more challenging. Although the image obviously exists on the screen of the monitor used to view it, it also exists within the memory of the computer itself. The latter image is in fact the original of the image that is mirrored to the monitor and is changed as needed by the programs running on the computer when they wish to modify the image on the screen. On the Amiga, the area of memory representing the screen display is called the *playfield*, a legacy of the machine's origins as a pure game machine. The playfield is translated into a signal the monitor can understand and painted onto the monitor by Agnus and Denise, working in tandem.

We can represent a 320 × 200 two-color display in memory using just 64,000 bits, or 8,000 bytes. Each bit stands in for one pixel, 0 being the first color on the color table and 1 the second, and we simply work our way across and down the screen, one row at a time. This is called a one-*bitplane* playfield. Of course, such a display would not be the most aesthetically pleasing. If we wish to add more colors, we must devote more memory to the task. Devoting 2 bits to each pixel will allow us to encode each as 1 of 4 colors, at a cost of (((320 pixels across × 200 pixels down) × 2 bitplanes) / 8 bits per byte) or 16,000 bytes of memory; devoting 3 bits gives us 8 possible colors at a cost of (((320 × 200) × 3) / 8) or 24,000 bytes. In its normal low-resolution modes, the Amiga can devote up to 5 bits to each pixel; in other words, it can generate up to a five-bitplane display, allowing each pixel to be any of 32 colors. These bitplanes are not, however, arranged together in a linear fashion; the Amiga is like all computers in that it hugely prefers to deal with data at least one full byte at a time, and writing and retrieving screen information in such odd quantities as just five (or for that matter three) bits at a time would be a huge performance bottle-neck and programming nightmare. Each bitplane is stored separately in memory, and only when the time comes to send the display to the screen is the whole collection combined together by Agnus, one overlaid upon another. Each set of five bytes—one from each bitplane—encodes eight pixels. An example is certainly in order.

Let us imagine a 32-color screen as it is stored in the Amiga's memory. Thirty-two colors requires five bitplanes. Let us further say that the following are the first byte of each of the five bitplanes respectively, beginning with the first: 11101000, 11000001, 00011101, 01011110, 00011010. To determine the color for the first pixel on the screen, Agnus pulls the first bit from each bitplane beginning with bitplane 5 and ending with bitplane 1, resulting in the five-bit binary number 00011—or decimal 3 (figure 2.1). (In other words, bitplane 5 holds the most significant digit of the binary number, bitplane 1 the least.) Agnus passes that value to Denise, who looks in color register 3, finding there whatever RGB value was last assigned to it. Finally, Denise sends that color to the screen for that first pixel. The pair then repeats the process for the next pixel, albeit drawing the second bit from each bitplane, ending up with binary 01011, or decimal 11, and therefore sending to the screen the color found in color register 11. After working through all 8 pixels in this way, Agnes and Denise move on to the next byte of each bitplane. And they continue this process, working across the screen and downward, until the display is completely painted. Throughout, Agnus is the hand that guides the paintbrush, and Denise is the paintbrush that paints the image to the monitor screen.[32]

Although the original Amiga can process five bitplanes for 32 colors in its lower resolution modes, it can manage only four bitplanes and 16 colors in its higher-resolution modes of 640 × 200 and 640 × 400. This limitation is purely one of system performance; Denise and Agnus simply cannot work through a five-bitplane high-resolution playfield fast enough to keep the monitor screen up to date. Four bitplanes, though, they can manage.

An alternative to the so-called *planar method* of screen representation employed by the Amiga is the much more intuitive *chunky system*, in which all of the bits needed for each pixel are grouped together; bits that do not line up conveniently with byte boundaries are simply left unused. (For example, representing a 32-color, 320 × 200 screen using a chunky system would require (((320 × 200) × 8) / 8) or 64,000 bytes—in fact, the exact same number that would be required to represent a 256-color screen of the same resolution.) Virtually all modern computers opt for the chunky representation.[33] The Amiga's designers chose a planar system in part due to considerations that no longer apply today. Memory at the time was

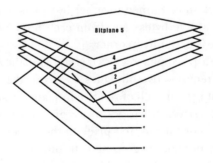

2.1 The encoding of a five-bitplane pixel

precious and expensive; the 37.5 percent total memory savings for a (for example) 32-color planar display versus a 32-color chunky display was vastly more significant than it would be today. The planar method also allows the creation of some impressive visual effects at limited processing cost through the manipulation of only one or some of the playfield's total bitplanes rather than of the playfield as a whole. In fact, the Boing demo itself does this, as we are about to see. Set against these advantages, however, must be the planar system's confusing memory layout, which can make many simple graphical programming tasks much more difficult than one thinks they ought to be. Jay Miner actually mentioned the choice of planar rather than chunky graphics as one of his major Amiga design regrets, although it is by no means certain that all of the programmers who took advantage of the planar system over the years would agree with him.[34]

Deconstructing Boing

Viewers looking at the Boing demo today may see a spare piece of digital art that is quite appealing aesthetically, but they may be hard pressed to understand why it stunned so many technically savvy show attendees. The key facet of the demo here is the sheer size of the ball. In an era when PC and game-console animation relied almost entirely on small, *Pac-Man*-like sprites, the Boing ball, about 140 × 100 pixels at its widest and tallest, was absolutely, unprecedentedly enormous. Further, it moved about the screen with complete fluidity; no jerkiness or hesitation could be seen as it realistically gained and lost speed over the course of each bounce. Its appearance and motion are so realistic that many viewers today might simply assume it to have been rendered with a 3D animation engine such as those that are used for many modern videogames. Such engines, though, were hardly more than dreams in 1984.

The biggest surprise I encountered in my analysis of the Boing demo's technical operation is its relative simplicity. Unlike later Amiga games and demos that rely on customized copper lists, hardware sprites, dual play-fields, and other advanced wizardry, the Boing demo operates in a fairly basic way while still taking clever advantage of some unique properties of the Amiga's hardware. It therefore provides an ideal subject around which to frame our first plunge into the technical details of an Amiga program in action. For this discussion, I am indebted to Antti Pyykko, who located and hosted an apparently early version of the demo executable that still has its debugging symbols, and to Harry Sintonen, who did an initial disassembly of this executable and inserted some useful commentary. To aid your understanding of its workings, I have reimplemented the Boing demo in a step-by-step fashion using the same techniques that Luck and Mical employed in the original. Doing so allows us to view and discuss each of its techniques in isolation as we gradually layer them upon one another. Video clips of each stage of the process are available on this book's Web site, as are executables and C source code for those readers with the knowledge and interest to explore this subject in even greater depth. I encourage you at a minimum to have a look at the short clip of the original Boing demo in action, also on the Web site, before reading on.

Stage One: Ball

One of the first decisions the creator of a graphical demo must make—not only on the Amiga, but on most other computing platforms as well—is what combination of screen resolution and number of colors to employ. In the abstract, of course, a higher resolution is always better than a lower, as are more on-screen colors, because higher numbers in both categories allow the display of sharper, more natural-looking images and more on-screen detail. However, having more pixels and more colors on screen not only consumes more memory but also taxes computing resources in another way: the 68000 and the custom chips must manipulate that additional memory and must do so quite rapidly to achieve the appearance of realistic animation. Programmers of games and other graphically intense Amiga software in the 1980s therefore generally chose the lowest resolution and bitplane count that would yield acceptable results. For performance and other reasons, colors and resolution often had to be balanced against one another. The Amiga's high-resolution modes, for instance, are limited to just 16 colors rather than 32, a considerable disadvantage that often outweighed their greater quantity of horizontal pixels. These considerations doubtlessly influenced Luck and Mical to choose the Amiga's lowest resolution of 320 × 200, with five bitplanes (numbered 0 to 4) for the machine's normal maximum of 32 colors. This mode was the most commonly used by programmers of games and demos during the platform's early years. Although an absurdly low resolution by the standards of today, it could be made to look more than acceptable by the standards of the Amiga's day when constantly in motion and painted in plenty of bright, striking colors.

Although the Boing demo runs in a mode that allows 32 colors, it actually shows just 7. Luck and Mical were not being wasteful; they made good use of the registers available to them. For now, let us set aside bitplane 4 entirely and thus deal only with color registers 0 to 15. As soon as the Boing demo begins, it maps these registers to the RGB values shown in table 2.2.

Having defined the color-register table, the Boing demo clears the playfield to the light-gray color in register 0 by filling all of the bitplanes

Table 2.2

The Boing demo's initial color-register table, colors 0 through 15

Color Register	Red Value	Green Value	Blue Value	Resulting Color
0	10	10	10	light gray
1	6	6	6	dark gray
2	15	0	0	red
3	15	0	0	red
4	15	13	13	reddish white
5	15	15	15	white
6	15	15	15	white
7	15	15	15	white
8	15	15	15	white
9	15	15	15	white
10	15	15	15	white
11	15	0	0	red
12	15	0	0	red
13	15	0	0	red
14	15	0	0	red
15	15	0	0	red

that make it up with 0s. Next, the ball itself is drawn into the newly blank playfield. A programmer working on the Amiga after it became an established computing platform would most likely have drawn the ball in one of the many available paint programs, such as EA's Deluxe Paint series (the subject of chapter 3), and then saved the image data for importation into her program. I in fact took this approach in re-creating the demo in preparation for this chapter. However, applications such as Deluxe Paint did not yet exist in early 1984, so Luck and Mical were forced to do things the hard way, drawing the ball programmatically in the demo itself using trigonometry functions.

Stage Two: Rotation

Regardless of how the ball is generated, the encoding behind the ball is not quite what it appears to be when viewed on screen. Figure 2.2 shows two versions of the ball. The first version shows the ball as it normally appears, but in the second the ball's normal color palette has been replaced with a new palette that consists of a series of unique, graduated shades of red and white. The actual data that form the image have been left completely unchanged.

2.2 The right-hand image of the Boing ball has had its normal palette replaced with a series of graduated hues of red and white

These images illustrate that what appear to be fairly large, solid blocks of color are actually not encoded as such. Each of the checks making up the ball is actually divided into six narrow slices, with each slice given over to a separate color number. The checks appear to be monolithic blocks of colors because the colors encoded into each of those registers happen to be the same. The ball thus uses 14 color registers, even though those 14 registers encode among them only three unique colors. It is on this fact that the ball's rotation animation relies.

The rotation is generated without manipulating the playfield that contains the image of the ball at all, but rather entirely by manipulating the color registers. The registers are cycled with every frame, thus changing the RGB values associated with the colors in the playfield, which itself goes unchanged. These changes produce the appearance of rotation and do so at minimal cost in system resources. Changing 14 color registers to generate each frame of the rotation animation requires the 68000 to alter just 28 bytes of memory, a fairly trivial amount even in the 1980s and vastly less than would be required to manipulate the playfield itself. Although the ball appears to move, a closer representation of what is actually happening internally can be had by picturing waves of color moving over a static surface. By frame 5 of the rotation animation, the color registers are as shown in table 2.3.

Only the first two registers, used for the background and the shadow of the ball, remain unchanged. The reddish white color that always occupies just a single register (register 14 on table 2.3) is always placed at the border between white and red checks and creates an impression of motion blur in the view that makes the ball's rotation look more believable. With frame 14, the color table is returned to its initial state to repeat the cycle

Table 2.3

The Boing demo's color-register table on the fifth frame of the ball-rotation animation, colors 0 through 15

Color Register	Red Value	Green Value	Blue Value	Resulting Color
0	10	10	10	light gray
1	6	6	6	dark gray
2	15	15	15	white
3	15	15	15	white
4	15	15	15	white
5	15	15	15	white
6	15	15	15	white
7	15	0	0	red
8	15	0	0	red
9	15	0	0	red
10	15	0	0	red
11	15	0	0	red
12	15	0	0	red
13	15	0	0	red
14	15	13	13	reddish white
15	15	15	15	white

again; thus, speaking in conventional animation terms, we can say the rotation animation is a repeating cycle consisting of 14 cells.

Stage Three: Bounce

We have now seen how one of the ball's two motions is accomplished by taking advantage of certain properties of the Amiga's display system. The second motion, the vertical and horizontal bounce, is implemented even more cleverly and once again while avoiding the difficult and expensive task of manipulating the contents of the playfield itself. Figure 2.3 illustrates the block of memory the Boing demo reserves as its playfield immediately after starting.

This block of memory totals 40,824 bytes, with 9,072 bytes going to each of the four bitplanes and an additional 4,536 bytes filled with 0s going unused at the beginning of the block when the demo begins.

AmigaOS conceptualizes its display system's view into the playfield via a software construct called a *viewport*. Contained within a viewport is a great deal of information about the current display and its relationship to the Amiga's memory, among which are pointers to the address in memory

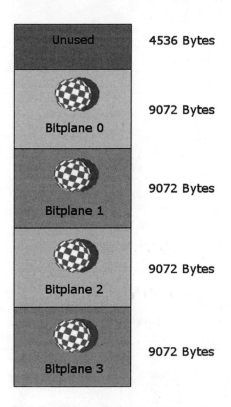

Unused	4536 Bytes
Bitplane 0	9072 Bytes
Bitplane 1	9072 Bytes
Bitplane 2	9072 Bytes
Bitplane 3	9072 Bytes

2.3 The Boing demo's display memory immediately after the demo starts

where each bitplane in the playfield begins. We might think of a viewport as a camera lens looking down into selected areas of the Amiga's memory and transmitting what it sees there to the monitor screen. Picture a camera set up on a tripod; its initial facing direction, height, and zoom correspond to the information the programmer passes to AmigaOS when she first sets up her playfield. Like a camera mounted on a tripod, though, a viewport can be moved about even after "filming" has begun, by specifying an X and Y adjustment from its starting location. This feature was included to allow the programmer to scroll through playfields much larger than the actual monitor screen. In the Boing demo, Luck and Mical moved their camera up, down, right, and left as necessary, shifting the ball about within the frame of the screen and thus creating the illusion that the ball itself—rather than the "camera" capturing the ball—was in motion. The technique is similar to those employed by many stop-motion-miniature and spe-cial-effects filmmakers. By carefully arranging the memory allocated to their playfield, Luck and Mical minimized the amount of memory they

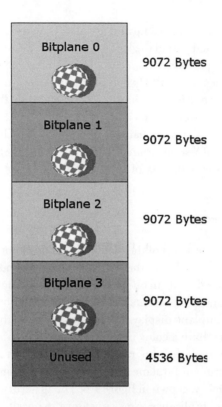

Bitplane 0 — 9072 Bytes

Bitplane 1 — 9072 Bytes

Bitplane 2 — 9072 Bytes

Bitplane 3 — 9072 Bytes

Unused — 4536 Bytes

2.4 The Boing demo's display memory
with the ball at the bottom of its bounce

needed. When the ball is at the extreme bottom of its vertical bounce, the
block of playfield memory now looks as shown in figure 2.4.

The viewport has now moved upward fully 100 lines, or half of a
screen, with the result that the ball now stands near the bottom of the
frame. The importance of the extra 4,536 bytes of memory that were left
unused before now becomes clear: if this buffer were not there—or not
filled with os to yield a blank background—Agnus would interpret whatever data happened to be contained in the 4,536 bytes before the previous
beginning of bitplane o as the first half of the contents of bitplane o. The
result would be ugly, random garbage on the screen. And if the bitplanes
were not contiguous in memory, the results would be similarly undesir-
able. Mical and Luck therefore took pains in the initialization stages of the
demo to make sure the bitplanes were contiguous, thus ensuring that the
viewport, when processing bitplanes 1 through 3, captured only the blank
regions that previously belonged to the bitplane above.

As the viewport is moved up and down, it is also shifted left and right to yield the horizontal part of the ball's motion. (To allow for this, each line of the playfield is 336 rather than 320 pixels wide.) The Boing demo once again accomplishes a seemingly complex animation in a way that places surprisingly little burden on the 68000 or even on the custom chips; changing the orientation of the viewport entails little more than changing a few numbers stored in a special area of memory, which define the viewport's current X and Y scroll as an offset from the playfield's starting location. And the actual contents of the playfield once again go completely unchanged.

Stage Four: Background

But there is of course a part of the playfield that does not scroll along with the ball in the finished demo: the latticelike background (figure 2.5).

This background exists in bitplane 4, which I have heretofore ignored. Each bit of bitplane 4 represents the most significant binary digit of one pixel of the five-bitplane display. Therefore, any pixel that contains a 1 in this bitplane must have a color in the range of 16 to 31. Look at the RGB values initially defined for this range of colors, shown in table 2.4. And consider this section of bitplane 4 shown as a collection of binary digits, as it exists in memory, shown in figure 2.6. The 1s here represent the lines of the grid, the 0s its absence. Now consider the possible results of combining bitplane 4 with the other four bitplanes. Comparing tables 2.2 and

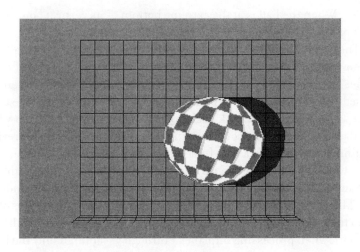

2.5 The Boing demo frozen during execution

2.4, we can see that the latter 14 colors in each range, those that are used to draw the ball itself, are identical. Thus, in the drawing of the ball, the presence or absence of a bit in bitplane 4 is effectively meaningless. A pixel containing either a 2 or an 18, for instance, will result in the same on-screen color red. The effect for the viewer, then, is of the ball overlying whatever exists in bitplane 4, obscuring it entirely. This important fact will remain true as long as these register ranges remain in synchronization, which indeed they do throughout the Boing demo's execution; colors 18 through 31 are cycled in exact parallel with colors 2 through 15 to generate the rotation effect. Therefore, I was able to ignore bitplane 4 in the earlier stages of this reconstruction.

But of course colors 16 and 17 do not correspond with colors 0 and 1. These four registers are not cycled but rather remain constant throughout the demo's execution and are not used to draw the ball itself but rather to draw the background. Nevertheless, registers 0 and 16 as well as registers 1 and 17 are linked in other ways. Consider a pixel that when decoded through the first four bitplanes results in color 0, or light gray. If that pixel is set in bitplane 4, the result is 16, or light purple, the color of the background grid. A pixel that decodes through the first four bitplanes to color 1, the dark gray used to represent the ball's shadow, will similarly decode to a darker purple if the corresponding bit in bitplane 4 is set,

Table 2.4

The Boing demo's initial color-register table, colors 16 through 31

Color Register	Red Value	Green Value	Blue Value	Resulting Color
16	10	0	10	light purple
17	6	0	6	dark purple
18	15	0	0	red
19	15	0	0	red
20	15	13	13	reddish white
21	15	15	15	white
22	15	15	15	white
23	15	15	15	white
24	15	15	15	white
25	15	15	15	white
26	15	15	15	white
27	15	0	0	red
28	15	0	0	red
29	15	0	0	red
30	15	0	0	red
31	15	0	0	red

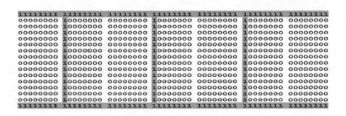

2.6 A snapshot in binary notation of part of the Boing demo's bitplane

representing the same shadow cast over a section of the grid. Bitplane 4 thus can be conceptualized as existing somewhat independently of its siblings, even though its appearance is of course affected by them. It is this independence that makes it possible to hold bitplane 4, the background, in place while its siblings, making up the ball, appear to move about. The adjustments necessary to accomplish this combination are once again made via the viewport structure.

In addition to panning over the playfield as a whole by adjusting a viewport's X and Y scrolling numbers, a programmer can also manipulate a viewport on a more granular level by adjusting the pointers that define the beginning of each individual bitplane. After calculating the appropriate X and Y scroll for the current position of the ball in its bounce, the pointer to bitplane 4 is readjusted to account for this scroll and effectively return the beginning of bitplane 4 to its original starting address. Thus, the background, encoded into bitplane 4, remains motionless while the ball appears to move. As you read the description of this process below, it is important to remember that what we conceptualize as a grid of rows and columns exists inside the Amiga's memory only as an unbroken stream of bytes, 42 of which (336 pixels per line / 8 pixels per byte) make a single line on the monitor screen. Thus, to adjust a bitplane's starting position upward by one line, we must subtract 42 from its current starting address; to shift it to the right by 16 pixels, we add 2 to the starting address.

Although relatively simple conceptually, the process is complicated by certain attributes of the Amiga's display system. Adjusting a viewport's X and Y scrolling values allows the programmer to move the beginning of the part of a playfield to be painted onto the screen to any arbitrary X and Y coordinate pair on that playfield. Directly adjusting the pointer that defines the start of a bitplane, however, is subject to more restrictions. Not only must the pointer begin on a byte boundary, but due to the 68000's architecture, which makes it prefer to read from and write to memory two bytes at a time, the pointer must contain an even-numbered address.

Therefore, a programmer can horizontally adjust an individual bitplane using this method only in increments of 16 pixels, far too coarse for an application like this one. Luck and Mical's somewhat memory-expensive solution to the problem was to create no fewer than 16 individual bitplane 4s, each containing a background grid that is the same as its siblings except for one important detail: the grid drawn into each of these bitplanes is staggered one horizontal pixel over from the one drawn into the previous bitplane. The scrolling adjustment is then done in two stages: first, the appropriate member of the set of 16 bitplane 4s is chosen, accounting for the fine adjustment, and then that member's pointer is adjusted to reverse the viewport's X and Y scroll, accounting for the coarse adjustment. An example may help to clarify the workings of the process as a whole.

Figure 2.5 shows the Boing demo at an arbitrary point in its execution. At this point, the ball has moved considerably from its initial state near the top center of the screen to a position closer to the bottom right. The viewport at this instant has an X scroll of -37, which has the effect of shifting the view to the left 37 pixels and thus makes the ball appear to have moved to the right; and a Y scroll of -54, which has the effect of shifting the view upward 54 lines and thus makes the ball appear to have shifted toward the bottom of the screen. Note that this Y scroll is given in the opposite of normal mathematical notation, with numbers increasing rather than decreasing in value as they move downward on the Y axis.

Dividing the X scroll of -37 by 16 yields a remainder of -5; therefore, the program selects from among the 16 possible bitplane 4s the one whose grid is shifted 5 pixels to the left (or 11 pixels to the right) from the grid of the starting bitplane 4 used as the initial background. The needed bitplane happens to be located at address 225,032 in memory. However, this value cannot be simply inserted into the viewport as the starting point of bitplane 4; the X and Y scroll of the viewport means that doing so would result in an effective bitplane starting address of (225,032 - ((42 bytes of memory consumed by each line × Y scroll of 54 lines) - (X scroll of 37 pixels / 16 pixel fine adjustment that is made through choosing the correct bitplane))), or 222,762. Therefore, the program instead places 227,302 into the viewport as the address of bitplane 4. When Agnus applies the X and Y scroll, the resulting effective starting point for bitplane 4 is 225,032.

This example and the numbers used in it of course represent just one frame of animation. For the next frame, the X and Y scroll of the viewport must again be adjusted as needed to reflect the appropriate next position of the ball in its bounce, and the correct bitplane 4 address must be calculated and inserted into the viewport to continue the illusion of a single, nonmoving backdrop.

I have now described how all of the visual elements of the Boing demo are accomplished, but there remains another component to discuss, one that is responsible for much of the demo's impact: the booming sound the ball makes as it bounces off the screen's "walls" and "floor." Just as explaining the visual elements of the demo required that I first provide some general background information on the Amiga's display system, explaining its audio elements must first entail an explanation of computer sound generation in general and of its specific implementation in the Amiga, where it, along with certain other more mundane tasks related to device management, falls to Paula.

The generation and storage of sound on a computer are a complex subject about which plenty of books much larger than this one have been written. A few basic concepts should suffice for our present purpose. What the human ear perceives as sound is a repeating cycle of air-pressure variations that travel to it through the atmosphere. These variations can be graphed as a series of waves showing changes in the sound's amplitude (or volume) on the Y axis over the course of time, which is represented by the X axis. A sound can be recorded and stored on a computer for later playback by *sampling* a sound wave's amplitude many times per second and storing the result as a series of numbers, a process performed by a specialized electronic component known as an *analog-to-digital converter (ADC)*. Two principal factors dictate the fidelity of the resulting recording to its source: the *sample rate*, or number of discrete *samples* taken per second, and the *sample resolution*, or the range of possible amplitude values. The latter is often given in bits; an eight-bit ADC, for instance, encodes each amplitude as a number between 0 and 255. In the case of both sample rate and resolution, higher is obviously better in terms of sound quality, albeit also more taxing on computer-processing power and storage. Multiple channels of audio can be encoded together, to be played through separate speaker channels or blended together into one. A CD, for instance, is recorded and played back at a sample rate of 44,100 samples per second, using 16-bit resolution, in two channels (for stereo sound). Digitally encoded sound is ubiquitous in the modern world, being found not only in computers and CDs, but in all manner of other consumer devices, from cellular phones to televisions to portable music players such as the Apple iPod. The Amiga, though, appeared at a time when the audio world was still largely an analog one, with CD players still a new, pricey technology embraced primarily by audiophiles.

Connected to Paula are four channels for sound output; this means that she can play up to four sounds at once, whether they be synthesized tones or digitized samples of real-world sounds. Each of these channels houses an eight-bit *digital-to-analog converter (DAC)*, a device that, as its name implies, performs the opposite function of an ADC in converting a string of digital numbers into analog voltage fluctuations to be sent on to an amplifier and from there to a speaker. The Amiga does support stereo sound; channels 0 and 3 go to the right stereo channel, 1 and 2 to the left. A programmer wishing to output the same sound to both speakers must thus send the sound simultaneously to two of the available four audio channels; no other facility for stereo mixing is provided. Playing a basic sound from a programming standpoint consists of filling a block of memory with eight-bit sample data and requesting that Agnus and Paula play said sample at a given sample rate through a given sound channel. They will then process the request autonomously; in a process akin to that of painting the display, Agnus fetches the sample data from memory and passes them to Paula one byte a time, who in turn passes them through her DACs and on to the external speakers. (Agnus plays the musical instrument; Paula *is* the instrument.)[35]

Step 5: Boom

The sounds of the Boing ball hitting the "floor" and "sides" of the screen are digitized samples of Bob Pariseau hitting the outside of a closed aluminum garage door with a foam baseball bat. An Apple II computer inside the garage was used to digitize the sound as it reverberated through the enclosed space, yielding a suitably big and echoing sound.[36] The right sound was found only after considerable experimentation.

Sound sampling technology was somewhat primitive in early 1984 but extant—although expensive. The exact details of the computing setup used to sample the sounds have been lost, but it is likely that the Amiga team used a hardware product called the DX-1 Effects II from Decillionix, which consisted of two hardware components, one to sample sound and one to play that sound back. (The latter component was imminently necessary because the Apple II to which the DX-1 was connected ironically had one of the worst internal sound systems of the early PC era.) Running on an eight-bit computer with as little as 48 KB of memory, the DX-1 was limited to recording extremely short, monophonic samples. It was not designed to be used to record and play back long sequences of sound in the manner of a conventional recording, but rather to furnish the programmer or musician with short bursts of sound, such as a single guitar chord or a thunderclap, that could be manipulated and incorporated into musical compositions or games. Although the Boing recording is rather lengthy by

DX-1 standards, Luck and Mical also indulged in some programmatic manipulation to stretch it even farther.

The sound data are housed in an external file that contains about 25 KB of eight-bit samples. Because each sample occupies one byte, the file contains about 25,000 individual samples, each encoding an amplitude in the range of 0 to 255. The data are thus in the perfect format to be fed (via Paula) through one or more of the eight-bit DACs and on to external speakers. Although the DACs are fairly strict in demanding sample data in eight-bit format, the programmer has more flexibility with other aspects of sound playback. Most notably for our purposes, she is free to play the sample data back at any rate she desires. A sample played back at a lower rate than that at which it was recorded results in a sound that is deeper and longer than its real-world antecedent; a higher playback rate has the opposite effect. (The effect is the same as that of playing a vinyl record album at a lower or higher number of revolutions per minute than its specified rate—for example, playing a 33-RPM record at 45 RPM.) When the ball bounces off the floor, the Boing demo plays its samples at a rate of approximately 14,000 per second, resulting in a deep tone that lasts slightly more than 1.5 seconds; when the ball bounces off a wall, it plays the samples at a rate of 22,375 per second, resulting in a somewhat higher tone that lasts just more than 1.0 second. (The rate at which the samples were originally recorded is unfortunately unknown.)

Although the sample data themselves are monophonic, the Amiga's stereo capabilities are nevertheless also used to good effect. When the ball bounces off the floor, the sound is fed simultaneously through two of the Amiga's four sound channels, one on the right and one on the left, so that the listener hears it from both speakers; when it bounces off a wall, the sound is fed through only one channel, on the appropriate side. The sound programmer is also free to vary the relative volume at which she plays sampled sounds, and Luck and Mical took advantage of this freedom as well. The floor-bouncing sound is played at maximum volume, the side-bouncing sound at about two-thirds volume. Luck and Mical were thus able to coax two distinct sounds out of the same set of sample data: a loud, dramatic, almost menacing sound when the ball hits the floor and a softer, shorter sound that emanates only from the appropriate speaker when it hits a wall. This difference contributes immensely to the sense of kinetic verisimilitude that is one of the demo's most striking features.

None of this process is terribly taxing to the 68000 because Paula and Agnus do virtually all of the work of sound playback. When the viewport X or Y scroll reaches a limit and is about to begin moving in the other direction, playing the bounce sound requires of the 68000 little more than that it request that sound playback begin on a given channel and supply some basic information: the location of the sample data in memory, the length of the sample data, the playback rate, the playback volume, and the sound channels to be used. Paula and Agnus then take over, leaving the CPU to focus on other aspects of the demo—or on other programs currently running. The fact that the demo as a whole does not unduly strain the hardware is one of its key attributes because this feature makes it ideal for running in tandem with other programs to demonstrate the Amiga's multitasking capabilities.

Lessons from the Boing Demo

As the first Amiga program that many future users ever saw, the Boing demo presaged a vast body of work that would follow from coders of Amiga demos, games, and creativity and productivity applications. It thus seems appropriate to end this detailed technical analysis of its workings with some higher-level precepts we can see demonstrated through those workings—precepts that so many of the Amiga programmers who followed Luck and Mical would take to heart. These precepts are also worth remembering and thinking about as you read further in this book, for they will be demonstrated in action again and again.

Effects can often be accomplished in unexpected ways that take good advantage of the machine's design and even design quirks. Moving an animated object the size of the Boing ball fluidly and believably about the screen in the obvious, straightforward way would have been extremely taxing even for the Amiga, a computer with almost unprecedented animation capabilities for its time. By taking advantage of the Amiga's viewport system, the workings of its palette selection system, and its planar graphics system, however, Luck and Mical accomplished the same effect while taxing the Amiga's hardware resources fairly minimally. Indeed, one of the factors that made the Boing demo such a favorite of marketing in the early days was that it left enough of the machine's horsepower unused that the demo could be shown running in parallel with other tasks, thus demonstrating in one shot not only the Amiga hardware's graphics and sound capabilities, but also AmigaOS's multitasking capability. In short, the obvious way to implement a visual or audio effect is very often not the best way, at least when performance is an overriding concern.

Animation is about creating a perception in the viewer's eyes, not about simulating reality. When one understands fully how the Boing demo operates, one must inevitably be impressed with the sheer cleverness of its implementation. Yet one perhaps also feels a bit disappointed when the whole bag of sleight-of-hand tricks stands fully revealed, and one realizes that the machine is not quite doing what it seems to be doing. And I suspect that the privileged insiders who saw the demo at early trade shows would have been even more disappointed to learn that the Lorraine was not "really" performing the animation feats it seemed to be. Nevertheless, the attributes that Luck and Mical took advantage of are as much a part of the Amiga as its (for the time) powerful CPU or unprecedentedly fast memory-shuffling blitter. Luck and Mical's only goal was to impress the viewer, not to simulate the physical reality of a bouncing soccer ball within the Amiga's memory.

Visual and audio assets are precious and expensive and should be conserved and reused wherever possible. By cycling the color registers rather than attempting to alter the appearance of the Boing ball in the playfield itself, Luck and Mical were able to reduce a 14-frame animation to just one. Similarly, they were able to use the same set of sound samples to create three distinct bouncing noises by adjusting the playback rate, volume, and stereo channel(s) to which those same data were sent. Such creative reuse of assets might never even occur to a programmer working on a modern machine, but on a machine with such limited resources as the Amiga it is sometimes essential. An Amiga programmer's mantra might be: use as few assets as possible, and maximize what you do use.

Aesthetic qualities are as important as technical qualities. Countless demos and games eventually followed Boing, many of them vastly more impressive in their technical sophistication, but few had anything like the same visceral or cultural impact. There is an elegance about the Boing demo's spare simplicity and even about the relatively relaxed pace at which it runs that for many users came to symbolize the machine on which it ran. Boing stands up today better than many other more showy and manic Amiga creations. Luck and Mical did not just blunder into such a pleasing final effect, as is demonstrated by their spending a great deal of time and energy to find just the right sound for the bounces. The Boing demo is certainly interesting and pleasing technically for those with the knowledge and desire to peek behind the curtain, but it is also interesting and pleasing aesthetically for the casual viewer, even one with no technical interest in it or knowledge about its place in computing history.

One must on occasion do things the "wrong" way to achieve the desired results. Boing flagrantly breaks the rules of "proper" AmigaOS programming and does so repeatedly. Luck and Mical often bypassed the OS entirely to poke and prod at the innards of the Amiga's display system, manipulating with abandon the color registers and many details of the current viewport configuration. Their constant changing of the pointer to bitplane 4—done behind the OS's back, as it were—would elicit horror from most systems programmers. Commodore's official series of programmer's bibles—documentation to which Luck and Mical actually contributed—is filled with admonitions against exactly these sorts of practices.

A Computing Icon

As time went on, the Boing demo was inevitably replaced in Commodore's promotional efforts by other more flashy and impressive demonstrations of the Amiga's audiovisual capabilities. Even as this happened, though, frustration was steadily mounting within the Amiga community at Commodore's perceived mishandling of and lack of respect for the Amiga and its original creators. Many perceived Commodore to have plainly demonstrated its shortsightedness in 1986, when it made the decision to close down Amiga's California offices, effectively fire the entire visionary Amiga team, and bring all future Amiga engineering to an in-house group accustomed to working only on simpler eight-bit machines such as the Commodore 64. Others would point the accusatory finger to an even earlier point, focusing on Commodore's ham-fisted early attempts to market the Amiga 1000, with the result that its cheaper but technically inferior 68000-based rival the Atari ST, which had been put together quickly at Atari when the company realized it would not be able to get Amiga's technology, gained the initial upper hand in hardware sales and software support. To the hardcore Amiga faithful, the Boing ball became a symbol of the original, pure vision of the Amiga that predated Commodore's clueless interference. From their perspective, Commodore's last-minute decision to replace the Boing ball with the rainbow-colored checkmark as the official Amiga logo thus took on a deep symbolic significance as the first step in Commodore's dilution of the Amiga vision. Some Amiga fans went so far as to re-replace the checkmark logo on their machines with the Boing ball, and Amiga stores did a thriving business in T-shirts, coffee mugs, hats, and other merchandise sporting the Boing ball rather than the official checkmark. Boing balls also turned up in countless Amiga-created pictures, animations, demos, and even games in what public-domain software distributer Fred Fish referred to as the "boing wars" in his notes for Fish Disk Number 54.

After Commodore's 1994 bankruptcy left the Amiga an orphan, the Boing ball assumed if anything an even greater importance to the dwindling Amiga community, who continued to hold out hope for new Amiga hardware and a return to what now looked like the comparatively successful golden age of the Commodore years. For them, the Boing ball came to symbolize this hope for a rebirth. Amiga, Incorporated, a new company with no relation to the first that went by this name, consciously attempted to evoke this hope when, having acquired the Amiga intellectual-property rights, it chose a modernized version of the Boing ball as its official logo fourteen years after Commodore had rejected that image.

Amiga, Incorporated has enlisted various partners in its attempted revival of the platform, but its efforts have yielded only sparse fruit and little interest outside of the existing Amiga faithful. The Boing ball therefore seems destined to continue its gradual passage from a living symbol to a piece of computing history. Its place in the latter is, however, secure forever.

As badly as Commodore mismanaged the Amiga's marketing and further development virtually from the moment it became available as a real product, the company's actions in the months before that were often thoughtful and even clever. One of these actions was holding the splashy if expensive Lincoln Center launch party; another was to get a prototype or two into the hands of legendary pop artist Andy Warhol and to convince him to appear at the launch along with Debbie Harry, former lead singer of popular rock band Blondie. Warhol made a portrait of Harry using an onstage Amiga, first capturing her image using a digitizer and then manipulating it with some simple patterns and flood fills. Although Warhol was obviously not completely comfortable with the machine and indeed had to be led by the hand through much of the act of creation by a Commodore representative, Warhol and Harry's presence added interest to the launch, giving it a cultural caché that transcended a mere computer industry event and winning it coverage in places that would otherwise have ignored it, such as the mainstream *New York* magazine. The Lincoln Center party stands as an almost singular event in Commodore history, a rare bit of elegance and promotional style from a company that generally seemed clueless about its own image and aesthetics in general. But Warhol's presence in particular was emblematic of more than just shrewd marketing; it reflected a real, deeply held belief in the Amiga as a new kind of artistic tool.

That is not to say, however, that Warhol himself always made the most convincing or even coherent spokesman. When *AmigaWorld* visited him at his studio shortly after the premiere, Warhol, doodling all the while with apparent interest if not skill on an Amiga, answered the magazine's questions disinterestedly and often monosyllabically. Only one subject seemed to truly interest him, and he came back to it again and again: how to get images onto paper looking as good as they did on the screen.[1] We might be tempted to dismiss this fixation as simply a legendary eccentric being eccentric, but perhaps it should not be dispensed with so readily. For the same "creative issue," *AmigaWorld* interviewed four respected contemporary artists about the potential of the Amiga as an artistic tool, and the same concerns arose again. Paula Hible: "What gets me is what do you get for your trouble after this? You get this thin sheet of shitty paper with a printout on it. I don't respond to that."[2] Warhol, Hible, and other artists might have been intrigued by the Amiga, but they nevertheless saw it as an adjunct tool to use in creating their traditional prints on canvas or paper. They were too trapped within their traditional artistic paradigms to recognize computers as a whole new medium of artistic exchange in their own right. Rodney Chang, the first Amiga artist to receive a listing in the *Encyclopedia of Living American Artists*, described the frustration of working in this new, not quite legitimate medium: "When I work on the monitor, I consider the work a completed piece in light; a first-generation image. The actual art is on the disk. However, to make a living at this, I have to produce a sellable hard copy. I can't use a printer because the fine arts quality is not there." One bizarre solution was to *paint* the image seen on the monitor using traditional oil and canvas, but, Chang stated, "that would make the monitor image only a design tool, even though I consider it the final product."[3] Such was life in this era as an art world whose values (and economy) revolved around physical "originals" struggled to come to terms with a medium defined in part by its reproducibility. Only years later would the advent of new-media art as a school of practice in its own right make monitor screens a common sight in galleries. Indeed, a common theme that emerged again and again in these early discussions of computer-created art was whether it is art at all, as if having its origin on a computer somehow invalidates the experience. The very question seems absurd today, as absurd as asking whether music created with the aid of synthesizers is still music, but such was the skepticism that still surrounded the idea of computer technology among all too many artists of the era.

To their credit, other authors writing in that unusually thoughtful, even philosophical issue of *AmigaWorld* do recognize the Amiga's transformative potential. Vinoy Laughner stated that the screen, rather than being a mere mechanism for viewing art that must ultimately be captured on paper, opens up new visual possibilities of its own because of the way it glows with light, and he noted that the Impressionists struggled end-lessly—and never entirely successfully—with capturing exactly this quality of light while working with oil and canvas.[4] And Scott Wright was down-right prophetic in predicting a future where PCs would provide everyone with the ability to become personal artists in any of a host of mediums.[5] *AmigaWorld* continued to demonstrate its commitment to the Amiga as a visual-arts platform by featuring a gallery of Amiga-produced artwork in each of its early issues, certainly an audacious (if not bizarre) practice for a practical computer magazine.

In these editorial practices, *AmigaWorld* followed clues from the Amiga design team itself, who saw the artistic potential of their creation early. In fact, members of the team considered a paint program to be a software product that was absolutely essential to the Amiga's identity, one that simply had to be available from the day the machine itself entered stores. When the work of the contracted third-party programmers of such a paint program proved underwhelming, OS (and Boing demo) programmer R. J. Mical himself devoted three precious weeks to developing the program.[6] The result, GraphiCraft, was indeed available from Commodore from day one. Although an acceptable enough initial effort, GraphiCraft would quickly be overshadowed by another program released just weeks later, this time from EA. Deluxe Paint[7] quickly became the most commonly used Amiga artistic tool of all and retained that status through the next 10 years and five major revisions. By 1989, a magazine would be able to write that "every computer has one program that exemplifies its capabilities—Lotus 1-2-3 on the IBM, PageMaker on the Mac, and Deluxe Paint on the Amiga."[8]

Electronic Arts

EA is today among the largest and most conservative of videogame pub-lishers and is often criticized for the dampening effect its predatory busi-ness practices and seemingly endless strings of licensed titles and sequels have on the artistic vitality of the industry as a whole. In the years imme-diately following its 1982 founding by former Apple marketing executive Trip Hawkins, though, EA could hardly have espoused a corporate phi-losophy more different from its (apparent) current one. EA was, as its early advertisements idealistically announced, "a new association of elec-tronic artists united by a common goal—to fulfill the enormous potential of the personal computer."[9] These EA artists placed themselves on the same level as such traditional artists as "writers, filmmakers, painters, musicians" and famously asked, "Can a computer make you cry?"[10] EA treated its artists like rock stars; its games and other software were packaged in gatefold sleeves that resembled nothing so much as album covers and always featured photos and capsule biographies of the teams behind the creations. Its progressive vision reaped rewards for EA, at least in those early years, as many of its releases won not only lavish critical praise for innovation, but also major sales success.

In another clever early move, Commodore began giving specifications, development tools, and full-blown prototype Amigas to EA well before the launch party. Its generosity garnered great rewards: Hawkins, more than any other executive in the industry, saw the Amiga's potential and made the highly respected EA the machine's earliest and most enthusiastic supporter among software publishers. EA did important foundational technical work for the Amiga during this pre-release period.

In the modern computing world, we take for granted that we can move data about from application to application and even between very disparate hardware devices, such as when we upload MP3 files from a computer to an iPod or similar player, or when we download photos from a digital camera into our desktop machine. This is made possible by the existence of stable, well-documented standards that define how various types of data should be encoded within files. Even the World Wide Web is dependent on standards for page markup (hypertext markup language [HTML]) as well as for image-storage formats and, increasingly, video and sound. Such standards were largely absent in the computing world of 1985. Not only were file formats legion and undocumented, but many software designers deliberately obfuscated their data storage under the notion that doing so would lock users into using only their products.[11] EA recognized that if the Deluxe line of creativity applications it was developing for the Amiga were to be true artistic tools rather than toys, artists needed to be able to share their work even with those who had not purchased the software used to create it. Further, they should have the option of moving data freely from application to application: importing their Deluxe Paint pictures into Deluxe Video to serve as the individual frames of an animation, for example, or moving real-world sound samples into Deluxe Music Construction Set to serve as background effects or the basis of new instruments. And if they wished to or needed to mix and match tools from competing companies to achieve their desired results, they should be able to do that as well.

EA's Jerry Morrison therefore defined, implemented, and freely shared the *Interchange File Format* (*IFF*), a sort of container file that could hold images, sounds, music, animations, and even documents, all in a standard format. Prompted perhaps by IFF's inclusion in Commodore's own standard Amiga reference manuals, other developers quickly adapted it, and it remained the standard throughout the Amiga's lifetime.[12] The flexibility that IFF brought in allowing an artist to move a project from application to application as necessary and to feel confident that other Amiga users could enjoy the project when it was complete was critical to the Amiga's success as a serious artist's computer. EA even allowed and encouraged software designers working on other platforms to use the IFF format, a harbinger of the standards-guided computing world of today where (for instance) both a Microsoft Windows machine and a Macintosh can read and edit many of the same data files.

A steady stream of EA products, both games and creativity applications, followed the first Amigas' arrivals in stores in October 1985. The most important of these applications, Deluxe Paint (hereafter referred to as "DPaint"), was the creation of an "electronic artist" named Dan Silva.

Deluxe Paint I and II

The standard for paint programs had been set in 1984 by the revolutionary and massively influential MacPaint, written by Bill Atkinson and included with all early versions of MacOS. A host of clones of varying levels of quality followed it on virtually all platforms that could reasonably support such an application as well as on some that perhaps reasonably could not, such as the graphically primitive, mouseless IBM PC. In fact, MacPaint stands as one of the most influential programs of the PC era; the Paint application included with all versions of Microsoft Windows through the release of Windows XP in 2001, for instance, is itself little more than a slavish MacPaint clone, notable only for its addition of color and, more surprisingly, its lack of some useful features from the 1984 original.

A quick glance at DPaint, with its menu of pictographic icons representing real-world painting and drawing tools to one side, might lead one to believe that it was simply the latest of this string of MacPaint clones (figure 3.1). Unlike so many of its contemporaries, however, DPaint's superficial similarity to MacPaint had more to do with a shared heritage than outright copying. MacPaint was like all of the Macintosh's bundled software in that it took its initial inspiration from a visit by Apple's Steve Jobs to Xerox PARC in late 1979.[13] Silva, meanwhile, had also worked for Xerox, on its Star project, a pioneering effort that, although marketed as a document-processing workstation rather than a traditional computer, offered a GUI, a "what you see is what you get" on-screen document display, and effortless networking with laser printers and other workstations years before Apple debuted the same innovations in the Lisa and Macintosh. Inspired by an earlier program titled "SuperPaint" by Richard

Shoup of Xerox's PARC,[14] Silva designed an in-house paint program, Doodle, for the Star, which eventually became a part of the Star's core systems software package.[15] When Silva left Xerox in 1983 to join EA, he ported Doodle to the Microsoft Disk Operating System (MS-DOS) for the in-house use of EA's development teams; this incarnation he named "Prism." DPaint started as a simple port of this in-house tool to the Amiga, but it was such a natural fit for the machine that Silva and EA decided to develop and bring it to market as a commercial product in its own right.[16] It was released as such in November 1985, becoming one of the first commercial applications available for the new machine.

Interface similarities aside, one need spend only a short period of time with MacPaint and DPaint to realize that they are very different in their capabilities and intent. MacPaint is wonderfully straightforward and easy to use, ideal for doodling or making quick sketches to be imported into MacWrite documents. Although DPaint can be approached in a similar way, it is deeper, richer, and, yes, more daunting; those who took the time to explore these qualities when it was first released were rewarded with the ability to create professional quality work by the standards of the Amiga's day. DPaint's origin as a practical tool for working artists becomes more and more evident as one spends more time with it, discovering thoughtful little touches born of hard-won experience. At the risk of stretching beyond the breaking point the real-world analogy upon which both interfaces rely, one might say that MacPaint is, in spite of its name, actually a drawing program, whereas DPaint is truly a painting application. In addition to its obvious capability to produce full-color illustrations, DPaint also offers a wealth of painterly tools for working with those colors, such as "smear," "shade," and "blend," and allows the user to mix her own

3.1 MacPaint and Deluxe Paint side by side.

colors just as a painter does in her studio. MacPaint simulates a sketcher's pencils and paper; DPaint simulates brushes, oils, and canvas.

Unfortunately, a number of glaring problems in DPaint I—such as a tendency to crash on Amigas with more than 512 KB of memory, the inability to choose a resolution mode other than through esoteric command-line switches, and a manual that essentially consists of (in the words of reviewer John Foust) "menus and a mouse, so go for it!"[17]—bear witness to a program that, for all its elegance and power, probably should have remained in development for at least another month or two. Most embarrassingly of all for a product from the company that defined the IFF standard, DPaint I makes many assumptions about the layout of IFF image files it attempts to load rather than properly parsing them, thereby rejecting or loading in corrupted form images from other applications that actually conform perfectly well to the IFF standard but merely implement it slightly differently.[18] Silva and EA fortunately followed up with Deluxe Paint II within a year, which fixed all of these problems in addition to adding a modest slate of new features. Perhaps most notable of these new features were the "stencil" and "background" effects, which allow the user to mask off parts of the image from being affected by her changes, a precursor to the layers that would revolutionize image editing with their arrival on Abode's Photoshop in the early 1990s. It was in this form that DPaint truly entrenched itself as the most commonly used Amiga creative tool as well as a computer industry standard and benchmark. Virtually everyone using the Amiga for any sort of graphical design purpose— whether in video production, game development, desktop publishing, photo processing, demo design, or just painting and sharing pictures— owned and used DPaint. Thanks to the well-understood IFF, DPaint was even used to create the artwork for many games on other platforms, whether ports of Amiga originals or games that were not released on the Amiga itself.[19]

A DPaint artist, much more so than an artist working with a modern graphical application, becomes familiar—perhaps more than she desires— with the underlying hardware running the application. She has, for example, exactly 32 colors to work with in lower resolutions (320 × 200 and 320 × 400) and 16 in higher resolutions (640 × 200 and 640 × 400), paralleling the display hardware's limitations. In order to make all possible colors available to the artist, DPaint draws the menu bar and interface gadgets in colors 0 and 1, whatever the colors happen to be. And when the user accesses the menu at the top of the screen, several colors in the palette are changed to bright, primary colors to ensure that the text there can be clearly seen, distorting any picture that uses those colors (figure 3.2).

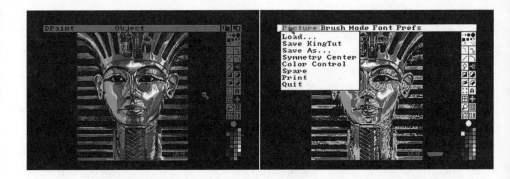

3.2 Deluxe Paint I displaying one of its most commonly used promotional pictures, of King Tutankhamen's burial mask. A comparison of the left image with figure 3.1 shows that the colors of the interface elements vary with the palette of the picture being worked on, and the right image shows the distortions that occur when a few colors of the palette are changed to facilitate easy reading of the program's menu bar.

As soon as the user ceases working with the menu, the palette of course returns to normal. Another hardware-centric feature of DPaint echoes a technique used by Luck and Mical in the Boing demo. DPaint allows the user to create some simple movement effects by cycling the RGB values stored in the color registers, exactly as Luck and Mical did to create the Boing ball's rotation. Although the technique is obviously a sharply limited one, it can be used to create the appearance of shifting shadows or rippling water—or for that matter a rotating soccer ball. This early proto-animation presaged the much more sophisticated animation features that were to come in later versions of DPaint.

In many other places, though, DPaint's use of its unique underlying hardware is elegantly abstracted from the user. Consider the screen that the user works with, containing the picture being worked on and the interface elements. It is, as expected, a single playfield stored and transmitted to the monitor exactly as described in chapter 2. Nevertheless, a logical separation between the interface and the picture must be maintained; when the user saves her work to disk, for instance, she certainly does not want to include the interface elements in the image. And there is a further problem: users expect to be able to use DPaint to create artwork that completely fills the monitor screen, yet when they are developing the artwork in DPaint, the interface obscures some of that vital screen space. To solve these problems, the image being worked on is also stored—without the obscuring interface elements—in a separate playfield elsewhere in memory. We might think of this stored image as the master copy of the image, whereas the on-screen image is the working copy. When the user makes changes to the working copy, these changes are not only reflected there but also copied into the master copy. And when the user saves her work to disk, it is the master copy that is saved, not the working copy with the interface overlaid. To work with obscured areas of the image, the user has two options. First, she can temporarily remove all of the interface elements by hitting the F10 function key. When she does so, the master copy is copied over all of the interface elements in the working area; these elements are in turn copied back into the working area when she hits F10 again. The user can also shift the picture horizontally or vertically using the arrow keys. When she does this, the master copy is copied back into the working area but shifted to reflect these manipulations. This feature became even more critical with the release of DPaint II, which permitted (for those computers with sufficient memory) pictures much larger than the physical screen, up to 1,008 × 1,024 pixels, giving the ability to make, for instance, a scrolling background for a game. (Unsurprisingly, a 1,008 × 1,024 playfield is also the largest playfield that the Amiga hardware can support under any circumstances; thus, DPaint continues to parallel the capabilities and limitations of its underlying hardware in a very direct way.) An example may help to clarify this aspect of the program.

Let us say that we are working with DPaint II in its low-resolution (320 × 200) mode. We decide to load from disk one of the lovely sample pictures that came with the program: *Seascape*, which also has a size of 320 × 200. When we do so, DPaint first loads this image into the area of memory reserved for the master copy. Next, most of this memory is copied into the playfield that Agnus and Denise use to construct the actual display we see on our monitor—the working copy. However, not all of the master copy is copied there, for DPaint's menu bar occupies the top 10 rows of the screen, and its toolbar occupies the rightmost 25 columns. Thus, the screen area left for the picture is just 295 × 190. The bottom 10 rows and the rightmost 25 columns of the master copy are not copied into the working copy (figure 3.3).

Now we decide that we wish to see the bottom and right edges of the image, so we use the arrow keys to shift the image all the way in those directions. When we have done so, other portions of the master copy—the top and the left—are no longer shown on the monitor screen, being stored in the master-copy memory area only (figure 3.4).

We can continue to shift the image as needed to view and make changes to any portion we desire. When we save our work to disk, the image stored as the master copy is of course used as the source, ensuring that its whole 320 × 200 size is stored, without the interface elements.

3.3 On the left is the Deluxe Paint screen as the user sees it; on the right is the master copy of the image being worked on, which is stored elsewhere in memory. Those parts of the master copy that are darkened are not copied into the screen that the user sees but nevertheless are still part of the image.

Silva's design is an elegant one, but also one that would have been untenable on most computers because constantly copying such large blocks of memory can be a very taxing operation. The jerkiness or hesitation that would have resulted on most computers would have been unacceptable for a serious artist's tool such as DPaint, where the user is so dependent on fluid feedback. Although MacPaint, for instance, used a similar technique, it could manage it only by working with the one-bit-plane images that were all its black-and-white display hardware was capable of. And there is another problem to deal with beyond the simple copying of blocks of data. As I discussed in chapter 2, bitplanes on the Amiga must begin on an even-numbered byte boundary; if DPaint relied on simple block copying, then its user would be restricted to shifting the image horizontally only in chunks of 16 pixels, which is far too coarse for practical use. When the user's manipulations do not line up neatly with bitplane boundaries, DPaint therefore transforms the playfield data as they are copied, shifting them left or right to make them line up with the appropriate boundaries. Again, this sort of manipulation is normally very expensive in CPU time. The Amiga, however, fortunately has a saving grace: the blitter.

Although initially designed to accomplish the fast playfield updates necessary for smooth animation, the blitter proved immensely useful to even a static paint program such as DPaint as well as to countless other applications. It is in fact a full-fledged coprocessor that lives inside Agnus,

3.4 The left screen shows Deluxe Paint's working area, and the right shows the master copy of the image being worked with. Once again, those parts of the master image that are darkened are not copied into the working area.

albeit a very limited one, able to copy blocks of memory from one location to another as well as to perform certain specialized transformations on that memory in the process. Among these transformations are exactly the sort of shifting operations that DPaint requires. At its own specialized tasks, the blitter excels, being able to copy memory at a rate of one MB per second, fully twice the speed of the 68000. Transformations performed on memory as it is being copied, such as DPaint's shifts, consume no extra time whatsoever.

The CPU passes the blitter a set of instructions and turns its attention to other things while the blitter carries out these instructions independently. Each of these "work orders" is called a "blit." When a blit is complete, the blitter notifies the CPU and awaits further orders. In DPaint, then, the 68000 effectively turns over to the blitter the expensive task of keeping the master copy and work copy in sync, for the blitter performs these tasks far faster than the 68000 ever could.

There are other uses for the working copy/master copy scheme that Silva employed with the aid of the blitter. Perhaps most significant is DPaint's implementation of the Undo button, which, as its name implies, allows the user to reverse the change she has most recently made to the image. When the user makes changes to the working copy of the image, they are not immediately copied to the master; this happens only just as the user begins *another* operation or saves the image to disk. The master copy is thus usually one step behind the working copy. Should the user click the Undo button, the two copies are swapped in memory via the blitter; the master copy becomes the working copy, and vice versa. And that is essentially all of the logic needed to implement "undo." Let us imagine that we make a change to the seascape image we have been working with. This change now exists in the working copy, but not in the master copy. If we continue working and make another change to the image, the working copy as it exists just as we begin to make that change is copied into the master; our previous change has now become, in effect, a permanent alteration. Meanwhile, the change we are now making is (again) reflected in the working copy, but not in the master. After looking at the change, we decide it does not agree with us, so we click the Undo button, and the two memory areas are swapped, erasing the change from our monitor screen. If we decide we would like to have our change after all, we can click Undo again, and the two memory areas will be swapped again. Our change—or our undoing of that change—becomes permanent only when we begin to make another change. All in all, DPaint Undo is a logically clean and elegant implementation of single-level undo, even if it does have its quirks; for instance, because both the master copy and the working copy are needed to effect the removal or replacement of the interface elements that occurs when the user presses the F10 key, pressing this key effectively commits any changes, making undo impossible. And, of course, saving an image to disk also makes the most recent change permanent because the current working copy must then be copied over the master copy to ensure that the latest version of the image is saved.

DPaint also allows its user to work with two images simultaneously, switching between them via the Swap menu. This feature is immensely useful because it allows the user to copy and paste pieces of images, to do various blending and combining actions, and to match colors and palettes. The user can also copy her current work into the spare area before making major changes, thus keeping an original readily available if those changes should go wrong beyond the single-level Undo function's ability to correct. Once again, this feature is enabled by the master copy/working copy scheme. Blocks of memory are reserved not for one master copy when DPaint begins, but for two. Only one of these copies is active at any time, however, in the sense that it is linked to the working area on the user's screen. When the user swaps images, any changes to the current image are first committed by copying them into the active master copy; then the other master copy is made the active one, and it is copied into the working area. The only major drawback to this scheme is that the user cannot implement Undo after swapping images—another quirk she simply has to get used to.

Deluxe Paint III

DPaint I arrived in late 1985 into a community of enthusiastic early adopters who expected the Amiga, so much better than anything that had come before, to remake the computing world in its image almost overnight. Not only did they expect it to revolutionize gaming and to become the first affordable computer to be a serious artistic and musical tool, but they also expected it to replace the stodgy, ugly IBM PC in offices around the world[20] and to cause even bigger problems for the vastly more expensive and vastly less capable Macintosh.[21] Big players in the world of business software such as Borland and WordPerfect had, after all, already started developing their products for the Amiga.

By the time DPaint II arrived in late 1986, the faithful believed in the machine as strongly as ever but were justifiably worried about its future. The overnight revolution they had predicted had not come. The Macintosh soldiered on and had even begun carving out a successful niche for itself as a desktop-publishing tool; the business world remained either completely ignorant of the Amiga or scornful; and many software publishers, Borland included, had already canceled their planned Amiga products due to low Amiga sales and perceived lack of interest. Even in the games market, always Commodore's forte, things had not worked out as expected for the Amiga; the cheaper Atari ST had won the first round there, with many more units sold and many more games available.[22] In fact, only about 100,000 Amigas in total were sold in that first year.[23] Most blamed Commodore's inept marketing department, which did not seem to understand the revolutionary nature of the machine it was promoting but rather traded in tired banalities that treated the Amiga as just another everyday computer—albeit one expensive for home use and incompatible with most of the software used in the office.[24] It is hard not to compare Commodore's feeble efforts with the creative and inescapable media blitz with which Apple introduced the Macintosh in early 1984, not to wonder what Apple's marketing department could have done with a machine like the Amiga. As it was, some wondered whether the Amiga had a future at all or was destined to go down as a footnote in computing history, victim of an inept and financially unstable Commodore.[25]

The fact that a Deluxe Paint III eventually appeared in early 1989 is of course proof that these worst fears were not realized. Commodore made perhaps its single smartest move ever with the Amiga in 1987 when it replaced the Amiga 1000, elegant in appearance but too expensive for most home users and too impractical and unexpandable for many professional users, with two new models, the 500 and the 2000. Even in 500 and

2000 form, the Amiga did not conquer the world, at least not in the tangible way its users in 1985 had so confidently predicted,[26] but it did carve out for itself some relatively stable and even profitable niches. These two models in fact defined an odd split personality that persisted throughout the Amiga's remaining lifetime. In its 500 form, the Amiga was the inexpensive game and home-hobbyist machine par excellence of its era, an identity driven home by its compact if hardly beautiful all-in-one case that looked like a sort of pumped-up Commodore 64. In its 2000 form, the Amiga was a serious, professional artistic tool used in a variety of fields, in particular video production. Although the 2000 also lacked the trim elegance of the 1000, its big case, similar in appearance to the IBM PC AT ("Advanced Technology") of the era, accommodated a generous array of internal expansion slots for hard drives, processors, and memory as well as more specialized tools such as generator locks (genlocks) and frame grabbers. Neither machine fundamentally improved upon the technological capabilities of the original Amiga design, but together they did resituate the machine in the market in a more satisfactory way. And at least to a reasonable extent the market responded. Although the Borlands of the world would never give the Amiga serious attention again, 1987 through 1990 were its best overall years in North America,[27] years of huge excitement and energy among the faithful and even of considerable if not breathtaking, commercial success; by early 1989, more than one million Amigas had been sold.[28]

A huge variety of creativity tools was available for the Amiga by 1989, with more appearing almost weekly. Remarkably in this fast-evolving market, the venerable DPaint II remained the standard tool for general-purpose drawing, painting, and image manipulation. Although many applications had tried, none had yet equaled its combination of power and elegant ease of use—or, at least, managed to do so and also overcome DPaint's entrenched status as the Swiss army knife of Amiga graphical tools. The belated arrival of DPaint III, written once again by Dan Silva, was therefore greeted with real excitement as a potential raising of the bar in this area. Silva did not disappoint. He had recruited a team of professional artists and animators making use of the Amiga in such fields as video postproduction and graphic design, and their input assured that the DPaint tradition of being a realistic, practical tool for working artists continued.[29] In addition to its collection of new features and conveniences, DPaint III supported two special video modes that artists had been requesting for a long time, one involving colors, the other resolution: *Extra-Half-Brite (EHB)* mode and *overscan* mode.

EHB mode was a last-minute addition to the Amiga, so last minute in fact that the first batch of Amiga 1000s produced did not support it at all; the users who purchased these machines were punished for their early adoption of the Amiga by needing to purchase the revised Denise and have it installed to gain access to the mode. Key to EHB mode is another capability given to Denise: the ability to process not just five but six bitplanes in low-resolution modes (320×200 and 320×400) only. In spite of this ability, the original Amiga's color table is always restricted to a maximum of 32 entries. In EHB mode, Denise therefore makes use of bitplane 5 somewhat differently than she does its companions. First, she processes the other bitplanes and the color table normally to derive the color for a pixel. Before sending the pixel to the screen, however, she looks at bitplane 5. If the bit she finds there is 0, she sends the pixel in the normal way. But if it is 1, she halves each of the pixel's RGB values and drops the remainders. For example, imagine that the processing of the first five bitplanes and the color table result in an RGB color of bright red: red 15, green 0, blue 0. Denise then finds that the relevant bit of bitplane 5 is set to 1. She therefore halves all three values, resulting in red 7, green 0, blue 0—a much darker, less intense shade of red. This shade, rather than the original, is then sent to the display. EHB mode thus allows 64 colors on the screen at once, with the significant detail that each of the last 32 colors corresponds to one of the first 32 at half-intensity (figure 3.5). Although this limitation obviously somewhat restricts the mode's usability in many situations, for some common scenarios, such as the creation of shadows cast behind objects or letters, it is ideal. DPaint III even makes the creation of shadows and certain other effects in EHB mode easier through a special EHB brush that partially automates the process.

As the name "overscan" suggests, this area is the part of a screen image above, below, or to one side of its normal boundaries. Its existence on computers of the Amiga's era is an artifact of television. Early televisions varied by a considerable degree in the size, shape, and proportions of the images they showed. These variances occurred even among examples of the same model and even within the very same television due to such factors as temperature, wear, and the precise voltage level of the household power. Even most *cathode-ray tube* (*CRT*) monitors are beset by similar—but far less extreme—variations, although most do offer controls to adjust them. The makers of early television broadcast standards thus stipulated an overscan area: a generous border around the screen on which nothing critical should be displayed, because some viewers may not be able to see it at all. Early computers, many of which were designed to operate with unpredictable televisions in lieu of specialized monitors,

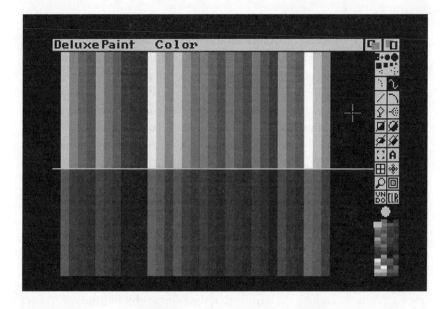

3.5 Deluxe Paint III running in EHB mode, displaying all 64 possible colors. The top half of the image consists of the 32 colors defined in the color table; the bottom half contains the "half-brite" equivalent of each. One can clearly see from this image how useful the mode can be to create shadows.

generally had a generous border around their display, not only to ensure that even the user viewing their display on the oldest television could see absolutely everything, but also for aesthetic reasons; the border created a framing effect for the display and served as a slightly sneaky way to reduce the size of the low-resolution displays typical of the time, thus making them look less coarse and unattractive. In this characteristic, the Amiga followed the lead of its contemporaries, but it is unique in also allowing the programmer to turn off the border and extend the playfield to fill the entire display, thus increasing potential maximum resolutions as far as 704 × 480, albeit with the understanding that some of the image may spill past the border of poorly adjusted or poor-quality displays. This increase is obviously useful in itself and was employed by plenty of game and application programmers as a way of squeezing more detail onto the screen, but overscan mode is even more important in the video-production realm because the large borders around most computer displays of the time were unacceptable for professional presentations. The Amiga's ability to eliminate them was thus a godsend and a key to its success in this field.[30] It is possible to create overscan-size images even in DPaint II; one simply stipulates an image size equal to the size of the desired overscan mode, then pans around the image using the arrow keys. One can later view the image in its full-screen, overscanned glory using a separate utility or import it into an animation or video-production application that supports overscan. Yet being able to view an image in full size within DPaint III rather than guess at its final appearance was quite a convenience for the many artists and media producers who worked virtually exclusively in overscan mode.

If EHB mode and overscan were much appreciated features, they were also fairly standard features for Amiga creativity software by 1989, features that DPaint II had rather conspicuously lacked. Their inclusion in DPaint III was thus somewhat to be expected. The "killer feature" in DPaint III, however—the one that surprised everyone—was its capability to do animation.

It should not be difficult to imagine how animation might be produced on the Amiga without relying on trickery such as the cycling of color registers or the viewport manipulations of the Boing demo. Because the image on the screen is a copy of the playfield stored in the Amiga's memory, repainted 60 times per second, changes introduced into that playfield will necessarily appear on the screen almost the instant they are made. It is therefore possible to produce the illusion of movement using the same principle of motion blur as does a film or a child's flip book. And, indeed, DPaint III approaches animation in exactly this way. Its artist creates a series of still frames, each an individual picture of the sort she might have created with DPaint I or II. DPaint III, however, allows her to combine these frames to create animations. The technique, often called "page-flipping animation," is the same one used for the creation of cartoons since the dawn of film.

But even a brief animated production created using such traditional methods—for example, one of the classic shorts produced by Disney in its golden age—requires the efforts of dozens of artists and weeks or months of time, for every single frame of the animation must be laboriously drawn and colored by hand. By default, a DPaint III animation runs at 30 frames per second; drawing all of those frames one by one is clearly an untenable proposition for a single user. And, of course, even computerized implementations of traditional techniques must improve upon their inspirations, or there is a little reason for their existence. DPaint III, however, provides its would-be animator with quite a number of tools to aid her in generating all of those frames. First and most obvious, the change from frame to frame in an animation is very small; the animator can therefore work by simply modifying the previous frame rather than continually starting over from scratch. More surprising are the quantity and depth of tools DPaint III provides for automating the process of animation. The artist can select a section of a picture—known (rather oddly) in DPaint terminology as "a brush"—and request that specific transformations be performed on it over a number of frames of her choosing: it can be gradually moved, flipped, rotated, accelerated or decelerated, and so on. The artist can also create and place "animbrushes," which are themselves made up of a number of cycling frames of animation. Using DPaint III's other tools, one can create, for instance, an animbrush of a bird with flapping wings and then send it flying across the sky. Each frame of an animation created using such automated techniques is always accessible as an individual picture, to be further modified by hand as necessary.

Silva faced quite a challenge in implementing such a system on the Amiga. His most obvious problem was memory. A single frame of even a low-resolution, 32-color animation occupies a little more than 39 KB; a single second of animation—30 frames—would thus seem to require more than one MB—a daunting amount at a time when the average Amiga owner probably had about one MB total in her entire machine. Granted, serious artists and animators were likely to have much more memory, perhaps as much as nine MB; but, on the other hand, such users were also much more likely to need to use the Amiga's higher-resolution modes to create work that would look acceptable when transferred to video. And even vast amounts of memory could not overcome certain facets of the Amiga's design.

Agnus is a *direct memory access* (*DMA*) device, meaning that it reads and writes directly to the Amiga's RAM without passing its requests through the CPU. Having to do so would of course defeat Agnus's key purpose of removing from the CPU the burden of having to process most graphical and sound data. This independence does, however, introduce considerable design complications, for under absolutely no circumstances can two devices access the same memory at the same time. Thus, during those times that Agnus is accessing memory—for instance, to send a play-field through Denise on its way to the monitor screen or to send sample sound data through Paula on their way to the speakers—the CPU's access to memory is blocked. Agnus in fact serves as a memory gatekeeper of sorts, allowing access by the CPU only when such access will not interfere with her own operations (figure 3.6). Because the design of the 68000 series dictates that it will access memory every other cycle at most, the performance bottleneck is normally not huge; during the 50 percent of the time that the CPU does not attempt to access memory, Agnus has adequate time to perform her functions. That does not, however, always hold true: "There are some occasions though when the custom chips steal memory cycles from the 680×0. In the higher resolution video modes, some or all of the cycles normally used for processor access are needed by the custom chips for video refresh."[31] Agnus was initially able to access—and to prevent the CPU from accessing—only the first 512 KB of memory, known as *"chip RAM."* At the time of DPaint III's release, Commodore was just beginning to distribute an upgraded version of Agnus, known as *"Fatter Agnus,"* that increased this number to 1 MB.[32] Memory beyond these limits and therefore within the CPU's exclusive domain is known as *"fast RAM."*

The chip RAM/fast RAM divide has particular ramifications for graphical applications such as DPaint III because it means that data that need to be accessible to the custom chips, such as the playfield that Denise paints onto the monitor screen, must be placed within chip RAM, no matter how much additional fast RAM is available. Although fast RAM cannot be accessed by the custom chips, it does have another advantage, from whence it gets its name: the custom chips can never block the CPU from accessing this space, even during the most audiovisually intense operations. Thus, clever programmers and even users learned to segregate their data within the Amiga's memory by their category, placing multimedia data in chip RAM and placing program code and other types of data in fast RAM, in this way keeping Agnus and the CPU from stepping on one another's toes as much as possible. (This segregation, of course, assumes the existence of fast RAM; the original Amiga 1000, for instance, sold with only 256 KB of RAM *total*, rendering such distinctions moot until the user

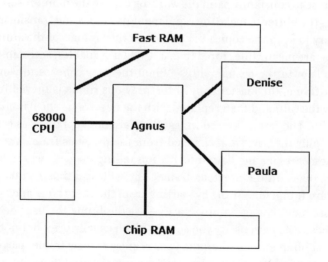

3.6 The Amiga's memory scheme and Agnus's role as "gatekeeper" to the chip RAM for the CPU

decided to invest in some expansions.) As 68020-, 68030-, and 68040-based Amiga models and accelerator boards appeared, these considerations took on even more significance: these CPUs might run at clock speeds of 40 MHz or more, but they are forced to slow down to the 7.16MHz of the Amiga's original 68000 when accessing chip RAM in deference to the still unaccelerated Agnus. When accessing fast RAM, however, they can make use of their full potential speed. Thus, on a seriously performance-oriented Amiga, the more fast RAM the better because the goal must be to keep the CPU's access to chip RAM to an absolute minimum.

But what of DPaint III, an application that, like so many on the Amiga, deals exclusively with the sort of multimedia data that would seem to require the intervention of the custom chips? Silva had to use some clever programming to take advantage of additional fast RAM while also making sure that data are available to the custom chips when they need it. Further, he had to find a way to store an animation in a more compact way than as a simple series of complete frames.

When the user works with any given frame of an animation, or, for that matter, when she simply works with a still image with no expectation of animating it, that frame is stored in DPaint III exactly as I have already described for DPaint I or II: as a working copy visible to the user and a master copy separate in memory. Further, the user still has available DPaint's swap area where a master copy of another picture or frame may be stored for her to manipulate, whether separately or conjointly with the first picture. All of these playfields are stored in chip RAM, allowing Agnus and Denise to constantly paint the working copy to the monitor screen and allowing the blitter to make the rapid memory copies and transformations necessary to keep the copies in sync. The other frames of the animation, if extant, are meanwhile stored in fast RAM (if available), accessible to the CPU but not to the custom chips. When the user chooses to work with another frame, the master copy of the previous frame is moved into fast RAM by the CPU and then replaced with the new frame she has chosen to work with. The frames stored in fast RAM are not kept there as complete images; only the parts that changed from the previous frame are stored, with the necessary ancillary information telling the CPU where to apply these changes on the previous frame. The CPU can thus reconstruct an animation frame for editing by starting from the first frame and applying the subsequent changes until it arrives at the frame the user desires to edit. These calculations are the source of the usually brief but noticeable delay that often ensues when the user requests a new frame, particularly if that frame is deep within a lengthy or complex animation—for just as an Amiga artist must sometimes make compromises in choosing between color depth and resolution, so must an Amiga programmer sometimes choose between storage space and processing speed. When the user is done working with a given frame, it is compared with the frame immediately previous, and the changes are recorded; the frame immediately following must of course also be updated. None of these abstract data manipulations requires the custom chips and thus can be conducted by the CPU in fast RAM.

Further complications arise, however, when the user wishes to view her complete animation because the frames must be generated quickly, 30 times per second. Here DPaint III uses a technique known as *double buffering*. Two separate playfields are reserved in chip RAM. The first frame of the animation is generated into one of these playfields, and Agnus and Denise begin to paint it to the screen. As they do so, the CPU generates the second frame into the second playfield. On a North American Amiga, Agnus and Denise paint the currently active playfield to the screen 60 times per second; therefore, when they have painted the first playfield twice, and the second frame is now ready in the second playfield, they are asked to begin painting this second playfield, and the CPU returns to the first playfield to generate the third frame. The user sees only smooth, fluid animation, with no jerking or tearing, and can be blissfully unaware of the work going on behind the scenes.

This process ironically illustrates some of the limits of the Amiga's custom hardware, limits that were already becoming noticeable in 1989 as faster processors and larger RAM configurations were becoming more common. When playing back an animation, DPaint III makes no use of the blitter that is so useful for so many other graphical tasks, for the frames must be copied to chip RAM from fast RAM, an area the blitter is unable to access. The CPU must do all of the copying work, just as it would on a competing machine without a blitter. And even if the CPU is a 68020, 68030, or 68040 running at 25 MHz or more, it must still slow down dramatically when actually writing data to chip RAM. An operation like this one, involving both chip RAM and fast RAM, is the worst of all scenarios, able to take full advantage of neither the blitter nor a more powerful CPU. To ensure that the frames are copied quickly enough for the animation to play smoothly, DPaint III must therefore disable any other programs that might be running and effectively take complete control of the Amiga for itself during animation playback.

A Deluxe Paint III Project

A very simple sample project illustrates how DPaint III's innovative animation features work. The same project also gives me the opportunity to show some of DPaint's static painting features. The project's basis is a tutorial written by Barry Solomon and published in the January 1990 issue of *Amazing Computing*. Solomon's goal was to provide practical instruction, but I have quite different goals. I wish, first of all, to convey some of the experience of a working artist using DPaint for a real-world application; and, second, I wish to introduce or reinforce relationships between the operation of DPaint and the design of the hardware platform on which it runs. As with the Boing demo reconstruction in chapter 2, this section is best read in company with the supporting materials on the book's Web site, which include a video of the finished product and, even more useful, a video of the construction process that I am about to describe.

The project is the creation of a very simple animated title. Postproduction titling was one of the Amiga's mainstay uses in video production; quite a number of specialized programs that performed only this function were on the market by 1989. For our simple project, though, DPaint III will more than suffice.

Just like a programmer coding a demo such as Boing, an artist working with an application such as DPaint must first of all decide what combination of resolution and bitplanes is appropriate for her work. And once again, although "as many as possible of each" may seem the appropriate answer in the abstract, increasing both the resolution and the bitplane count carries costs—in memory and, especially if we wish to do animation, in processing time. Therefore, the more appropriate real-world answer is, "As few of each as will allow me to achieve my goals." In the Boing demo, Luck and Mical used the Amiga's lowest resolution with the maximum number of easily manipulated colors; for this project, we will use its highest resolution, with just two bitplanes for a total of four colors. The Amiga's high-resolution mode is an interlaced resolution, which is of critical importance for transferring our work to video (I discuss this factor in detail in chapter 5). We will also turn on overscan for a final resolution of 704 × 480. We will use overscan because we want to create the illusion of a title flying onto the screen from below it; this effect would be spoiled by a border.

The normal DPaint working screen now opens, with the default color palette that can be seen at the bottom right of figure 3.7. We now change these colors to ones more appropriate for our project by using the palette adjustment tool, which allows us to make adjustments using either the RGB model native to the Amiga or the "hue, saturation, value" (HSV) model developed by Alvy Ray Smith as a more intuitive alternative to RGB for DPaint's distant ancestor SuperPaint at Xerox's PARC;[33] DPaint automatically converts the HSV values to RGB. We use standard RGB values,

3.7 The Deluxe Paint III working screen with the palette adjustment gadget up. Note that due to our use of overscan mode, the program uses every bit of screen area.

adjusting the four available colors respectively to red (red 15, green 0, blue 0), white (red 15, green 15, blue 15), blue (red 0, green 0, blue 15), and a tinted green (red 6, green 15, blue 3). Changing these colors that are also used to draw the interface results in a rather ugly working screen, but we have to accept it.

At this point, DPaint still assumes that we are working with just a single image. We wish, however, to create an animation. We inform DPaint of this goal now, setting the frame count for our animation to 30. DPaint then proceeds to build our animation in fast RAM. The animation uses very little space there right now because only changes from frame to frame are stored there—changes that are in this case nonexistent because the animation consists of 30 identically blank frames.

The (still blank) image that was created for us when we started the program still remains in chip RAM and in our working area on the screen, but DPaint now understands it to be the first frame of a 30-frame animation rather than an image designed to stand alone. We wish, for reasons that will become clear, to edit a different frame—the very last one, in fact. When we jump to this last frame, a number of background transformations occur, transparently to us. The image we have just been editing is recorded in fast RAM as the first frame of the animation stored there.

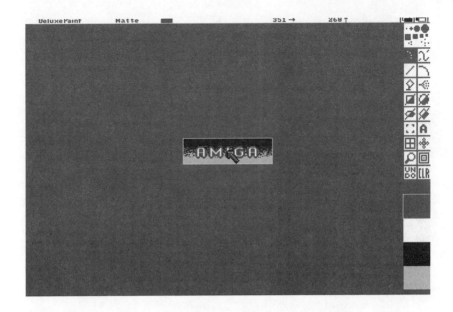

3.8 The logo we wish to animate, which we have drawn into the thirtieth frame.

Next, the contents of frame 30 are calculated by invisibly paging through the animation, applying changes frame by frame. (In this case, again, those changes are nonexistent, making this process very quick.) And frame 30 is finally copied into the areas of chip memory reserved for our working and master copies and thus displayed on the screen for us to edit just like any other DPaint image.

DPaint III provides quite a variety of tools for drawing and painting on images or animation frames, many of which would likely be immediately familiar to you if you have spent any time at all working with modern painting or image-manipulation applications. We can, for instance, insert text into images in a typeface, size, and style of our choosing; draw simple shapes such as rectangles; perform color gradient fills; cut out sections of an image to place elsewhere; and add colored outlines to sections of our image. In fact, these capabilities are exactly the ones we will use to create a simple logo centered on the frame, as shown in figure 3.8.

Our goal is to have the logo we just created appear to fly in from in front of and below the screen. We might, of course, attempt to accomplish this effect by hand, laboriously repositioning and rotating the logo on each of our 30 frames. DPaint III provides a better way, though, allowing us to perform automated transformations of sections of the screen (figure 3.9).

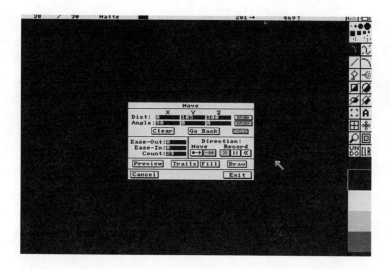

3.9 Deluxe Paint III's Move requestor

The Move function allows us to work either forward or, as in this case, backward, specifying where we want a section of our image to end up. DPaint then recalculates all of the affected frames of our animation to include the movement we have requested. Doing so is computationally intense and can thus take some time, particularly on a stock 68000-based Amiga model; the result, though, is a complete animation created with no further intervention on our part at all (figure 3.10).

Of course, the result is not breathtaking by any means. It does, however, provide a plausible foundation for a more ambitious project. Every individual frame of the animation remains always accessible as a static image. We can therefore further modify the animation at any level of granularity we desire, painting by hand in the frames or adding more automated transformations to some or all of the frames. We can also, of course, add more frames at any time to continue or precede the existing animation sequence.

If you have made use of modern two-dimensional (2D) animation applications such as the one found in Adobe Flash, much of what I have just described likely struck you as familiar. Indeed, Flash and DPaint III often operate in remarkably similar ways. If Flash offers features that DPaint III lacks, notably the options of using sound and layers, DPaint III can point in return to its rich library of painting and image-processing

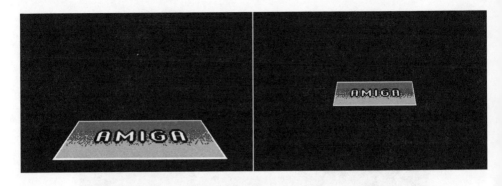

3.10 Our Deluxe Paint III animation in progress. See this book's Web site for a video of the animation in its complete form.

tools that have no direct equivalent in Flash. DPaint's ability to stand alongside Flash and other modern animation applications without embarrassment is a remarkable testimony to Silva's vision and technical finesse—as well as, of course, to the Amiga itself.

Deluxe Paint IV

By the time of Deluxe Paint IV's arrival in late 1991, the stodgy green-screened IBM PC clone had finally disappeared, replaced by a new generation of "multimedia PCs" running Microsoft Windows and featuring sound cards capable of CD-quality audio, video graphics array (VGA) and Super Video Graphics Array (SVGA) cards capable of displaying hundreds of colors on screen at once, and, increasingly, CD-ROM drives capable of storing almost inconceivable quantities of music, video, or pictures. Against such monumental improvements, Commodore offered the new Amiga 3000 and 500+ with their *Enhanced Chip Set (ECS)* architectures, which included such welcome improvements as a full two MB of chip RAM and some new, extremely high-resolution video modes. These modes, however, were limited in their utility by their restriction to just four colors, and ECS otherwise offered only the most incremental of gains over the architecture Jay Miner and team had begun designing almost a decade earlier. Amiga loyalists might point to certain qualities that still set the platform apart, such as its multitasking OS, but for the first time the Amiga was clearly behind in a whole range of critical technical areas, many of them in its traditional strongholds, graphics and sound. Amiga publications from this period reflect growing justifiable concern and dismay over Commodore's seemingly lackadaisical attitude toward research and development. With a new generation of CD-ROM-based games beginning to appear for MS-DOS and Windows machines and a new generation of game consoles such as the Sega Genesis and Super Nintendo Entertainment System to compete with, the Amiga's reputation as the ultimate game machine was fading fast, taking with it whatever general consumer cachet it had managed to garner, eating into sales of low-end machines, and sending many game developers scurrying for healthier platforms. Commodore had always ridden a financial rollercoaster, but it was now also bereft of the cushion of the virtually effortless revenue that the Commodore 64, once seemingly evergreen but now dying at last, had generated for years. Now the bad quarters and accompanying management shakeups were no longer followed by better ones, only worse.

Thanks to capabilities that do not show up so well on a comparison chart as well as a library of powerful, professionally tested hardware and software adjuncts, the higher-end Amiga models nevertheless continued to survive and even thrive in various sorts of video-production applications. In fact, one can see the focus on this one remaining profitable niche becoming even more pronounced in the North American Amiga magazines of this latter period, which at times read more like video-production journals than general-interest computer magazines. It is hard not to wax a bit wistful when contrasting Doug Barney's February 1992 *AmigaWorld* editorial, which states that the Amiga is a "specialized machine" applicable only to certain purposes,[34] with founding editor Guy Wright's 1985 premiere issue statement that the Amiga is nothing less than "a catalyst for the future of computing."[35] Still, without its specialized niche, the Amiga would likely have been dead already.

DPaint's corporate parent, EA, was also in a very different situation in late 1991. Trip Hawkins had just left the company he founded to begin another, and with him departed the last vestiges of the old EA of rock star programmers, high-minded rhetoric, and the view that "we see farther"[36]— all replaced by less visible leaders who instilled the pragmatic, conservative approach that stills marks the company today. The Amiga, the same machine to which Hawkins and EA had once committed themselves so strongly, was fading in prominence in the mainstream computer market and fast becoming little more than an occasional afterthought for EA's game-development divisions. It is therefore a sign of the Amiga's continued viability in certain artistic fields that EA developed yet another greatly expanded version of DPaint at this time just for that platform. DPaint IV offered artists yet more new painting and animating features, many of considerable power and sophistication. Once again, though, one new feature was discussed more than all the rest: its belated, oft-requested support for yet another special Amiga graphics mode, *Hold-and-Modify* (*HAM*) mode.

Like EHB mode, HAM mode relies on Denise's capability to process a sixth bitplane when drawing low-resolution screens, but it uses that sixth bitplane in a very different way. Here, only 16 base colors are defined in the color table, even though with six bitplanes we can actually store any number from 0 to 63 for each pixel. If a given pixel is less than 16, Denise simply places the appropriate base color from the color table there. If it is 16 or greater, however, she uses this value to modify the color she has just previously output; from this process comes the mode's name. If the pixel's value is between 16 and 31, Denise will modify that color's blue component; between 32 and 47, the red; between 48 and 63, the green. In the first case, Denise first subtracts 16 from the value; in the second, 32; in the third, 48. She now has a number between 0 and 15, which she substitutes in the RGB component of the previously output pixel as appropriate. Finally, this modified color is output to the screen and can be further modified by the *next* pixel if necessary. I can best illustrate how all this works in practice with an example.

The first pixel on the screen should always be a base color because the color modifications that give HAM mode its name need to start from something. (If this first pixel is *not* a base color, an error message or crash will not result, but the output *will* be unpredictable and undefined.) So, then, let us say that Denise, after combining the six bitplanes to derive the first pixel, ends up with the number 5. Seeing that this number is less than 16, she takes it as a base color and turns to the color table. There, she finds that color 5 equates to a dark shade of purple: red 7, green 0, blue 7. She therefore outputs this color to the monitor for the top left pixel. As she moves to the next pixel, the six bitplanes decode to 55. Because this number is greater than 16, Denise knows that she must *modify* the color previously output rather than use the color table. Further, she knows from the fact that the number is between 48 and 63 that she must modify the green component of that color. She therefore subtracts 48 from the number, yielding 7, and substitutes that number for the green component of the color just previously output. The end result is red 7, green 7, blue 7: a neutral gray. Denise sends this color to the screen for the second pixel and continues on. The third pixel might contain a value that further modifies the gray she has just output, or it might contain another of the base colors. It might even contain a 23, 39, or another 55, numbers that would "modify" the previously output pixel to arrive at the exact same color.

Although HAM mode has the potential to display every one of the Amiga's 4,096 colors *somewhere* on the screen, only about one-third of them are available for any given pixel due to this encoding scheme that favors—even to some extent requires—the gradual blending of shades rather than sharp transitions. This limitation can make the mode a very difficult one for artists and programmers to work with. Indeed, it is completely unsuitable for many applications. It is simply too awkward, for instance, to be of much use to game developers.

HAM was born of a long-standing fascination Jay Miner had with flight simulators. In investigating the design of the large commercial units used for pilot training, he discovered that their graphics operated on essentially the same principals I have just described. At this stage of the Amiga's development, it was still seen as primarily a game machine and thus likely to be connected to a television rather than to a monitor. Miner believed that the restrictions that accompanied HAM would not matter a great deal under this scenario because televisions lacked the ability to display sharp color transitions under any circumstance; adjacent pixels bleeding into one another was the norm there, as anyone with memories of early home-computer or game consoles can likely attest. When it became clear that the Amiga would be a higher-end computer connected to a proper monitor, Miner regarded HAM as of little practical utility and requested that it be removed. However, as Miner himself stated, "The guy who was doing the actual drawing of the chip layout itself said, 'If we take that off, it's going to leave a hole in the middle of the chip, and we don't have time to re-layout the whole chip to take advantage of that hole. So let's just leave it in, and if nobody uses it that's fine.'"[37] This is a classic example of a platform designer's failure to see the potential of his own creation as well as a very isolated instance of Miner's vision failing him, for HAM mode proved to be critical to the Amiga, being well nigh perfect for at least one very important application: the display of photographic images, which are made up of just the sort of gradual color transitions around which HAM mode is designed.

To say that DPaint was late to the HAM party would be rather an understatement. The first HAM-mode painting programs, Photon Paint by MicroIllusions and Digi-Paint by NewTek, had appeared in 1987, and HAM mode digitizers, the forerunner to modern scanners and digital cameras, were on the market before that. For years, artists had clamored for the addition of HAM mode to DPaint, but Silva, perhaps unwilling to clutter his elegant, intuitive design with HAM's fussiness, refused to accommodate them. Thus, DPaint, although always regarded as the best all-around Amiga paint program, always carried the implied asterisk, "as long as you do not need to work in HAM mode." In the end, Silva never did give in and add HAM support; its existence in DPaint IV is likely due to the fact that Silva had left EA after finishing DPaint III, putting his code into the hands of two other programmers, Lee Ozer and Dallas J. Hodgson, to be expanded.[38]

Painting in HAM mode can unquestionably be cumbersome. When HAM mode is activated, the simple palette at the bottom right of the screen becomes a complicated affair of multiple pages. Further, when painting in any but the first 16 primary colors, the artist will often find that the results are not quite what she expects. Because it can often take up to three pixels to transition completely from one color to another in HAM, she is likely to see her hard edges become a blurry mixture of tints, resulting in an appearance rather like that of an old or poorly adjusted television screen.

HAM mode is perhaps more useful for manipulating and adjusting images, in particular photographic images, than for creating them from scratch, for here DPaint IV's suite of blending, stenciling, shading, and transparency effects truly come into their own. And HAM can be surprisingly useful for solving other problems. For instance, artists working on the Amiga, like artists working on other platforms today, often wished to combine images or sections of images into one, something DPaint always encouraged and facilitated through its "Spare" picture area. Even so, the process is greatly complicated by color-palette considerations; if one wishes to combine parts of two 32-color pictures with nonidentical palettes, for instance, one must reduce the *total* number of colors used to just 32, a tedious process that involves some painful compromises. With HAM mode, though, such combinations are much easier to accomplish, even though HAM's unique restrictions also mean that the result will likely still not have complete fidelity to its originals (figure 3.11).

Even those who chose not to do their DPaint IV editing in HAM mode were in fact still using it, for Ozer and Hodgson also made use of HAM, along with certain other unique features of the Amiga's hardware, on the color-mixing gadget used by painters working in all graphics modes. Figure 3.12 shows a low-resolution, 32-color image being edited in DPaint IV. The user has brought up the color-mixing gadget at the bottom of the screen.

The horizontal line of 32 colored boxes there show the colors used in the picture and therefore necessarily also used to draw the bulk of DPaint's interface. The color mixer itself, though, is drawn in colors not found in this palette of 32—for instance, the greenish blue shades the user is currently working with within the mixer. The user can experiment with colors here as much as she likes, choosing to incorporate each one into the palette of the picture (and the rest of the interface) only when she has absolutely settled upon it. This feature for allowing experimentation is a nice improvement to the old mixer shown in figure 3.7, in which every

3.11 Eight images from earlier versions of Deluxe Paint, all originally with very different color palettes, combined into one using Deluxe Paint IV's HAM mode. The results are not perfect, but they are acceptable enough for many applications. Note also the gadget just below the color selection at the bottom right, indicating that this grid of 16 colors is just grid A of many grids available to the artist. However, because this grid represents the 16 primary HAM colors, they are the only ones guaranteed to show up with perfect fidelity when the artist uses them.

slight change was immediately reflected in the image and interface. But how is it accomplished, given the restrictions of the Amiga's hardware and given that the picture itself and the main DPaint working interface are allowed only 32 colors? The answer lies with the other custom coprocessor housed within Agnus: the copper.

The copper—short for "coprocessor"— is like the blitter in that it is a full-fledged custom coprocessor capable of carrying out tasks simultaneously with the main CPU. That said, in contrast to even the blitter's limited functionality, the copper is an extremely simple processor indeed; whereas the blitter can be programmed to perform a fair variety of memory moving and transforming tasks, the copper offers just three opcodes, or programmable instructions, to the programmer. As Commodore's own system documentation says, however, "you can do a lot with [these instructions]."[39] Only one of them actually does anything in the immediate sense: MOVE. Again as stated by Commodore's documentation: "The MOVE

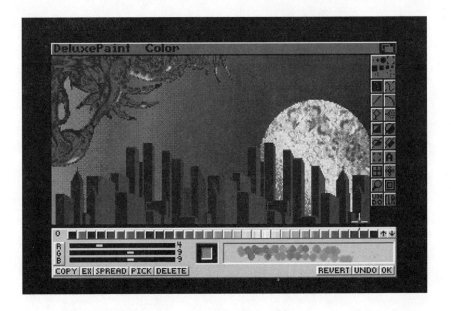

3.12 Deluxe Paint IV's color-mixing gadget

instruction transfers data from RAM to a register destination."[40] A register is a special location in memory that holds certain values critical to the Amiga's operation. I have already used the term *register* to refer to entries in the color table, which consists of 32 registers, each defining one of the current RGB color values. Other registers are involved with disk access, peripheral control, and audio. Most, though, are like the color table in containing essential information about the current display. The copper, then, can alter these critical values independently of the CPU. This independence may seem a useful convenience, but hardly earth shattering. The copper's real value and power actually stems from another of its instructions, one that does not actually *do* anything at all: WAIT. WAIT tells the copper to go to sleep until Agnus has reached a certain position—specified in horizontal or vertical coordinates or both—in her ceaseless scanning of a playfield and only then to continue to the next instruction in the program. Synchronization with the screen-painting process is in fact so critical to the copper that the program, called a "copper list," is started again at the beginning of every paint.

One of the most often cited examples of the Amiga's unusual video capabilities stems directly from the copper: the ability, still unique even today, to display multiple virtual screens of varying color depths and resolutions simultaneously on the same physical display. In my earlier discussion of the Amiga's display, for the sake of simplicity I spoke of screens as monolithic, singular entries inside the computer's memory. This description is not completely accurate. Like most modern computers, but unlike its contemporaries, the Amiga supports multiple virtual screens of varying resolutions and color depths.[41] These screens are stored in memory using the encoding already described, but only the currently active playfield is actually painted to the display—again, just like on a modern computer. Under AmigaOS, these screens can be envisioned as being stacked one behind another. By grabbing a screen's title bar with the mouse, the user can pull it down to reveal screens underneath it, even if those screens are of radically different resolutions or color depths (figure 3.13).

When Agnus reaches a boundary between virtual screens in her relentless scanning of the playfield, the copper steps in to reconfigure various registers to point her to an entirely new playfield with its own resolution, color table, and so on. Agnus then continues to scan the remainder of the screen to completion—unless, of course, yet another screen is visible farther down, in which case the copper steps in again.

3.13 An Amiga display showing two radically different virtual screens on the same physical monitor screen. The AmigaOS Workbench screen at the top is 640 × 200 resolution, with just four colors. The picture of the sports car is in overscanned 384 × 480 resolution and HAM mode.

Before Agnus and Denise begin the painting cycle anew, the copper once again adjusts the appropriate registers to return Agnus to the uppermost screen. There is a significant limitation to the manipulation of virtual screens: screens can be dragged up or down and thus appear above and below one another, but they cannot be moved left or right to appear beside one another. Because the physical screen is painted left to right and then top to bottom, two virtual screens arranged side by side this way would require thousands of copper interventions per paint, a hopelessly taxing and unworkable situation.

The DPaint IV palette mixer is actually a separate virtual screen, as wide as the monitor but just 67 pixels tall. As a separate screen, it is not bound to the color or resolution of the main application screen; in fact, it always runs in HAM mode regardless of the format of the image the user has chosen to work with, thus giving her access to all 4,096 colors to mix and match and choose between, all without altering the palette of the actual image until she is ready. A very close look at figure 3.12 reveals the telltale traces of HAM. In particular, the colored boxes representing the 32 colors currently in use are not completely solid, but rather display the fringing typical of HAM at their borders, where they come into closest contact with the very different colors used to draw the mixer interface. However, HAM mode is almost ideal for much of the work that takes place on the palette mixer—the mixing of shades together to form new, blended hues.

Deluxe Paint IV AGA and Deluxe Paint V

The moribund Amiga platform received a tremendous shot of life in late 1992, when Commodore introduced yet two more models, the 1200 and the 4000. Unlike their predecessors, these machines at long last represented a true next generation for the Amiga; two of the three custom chips were brand new, with Lisa replacing Denise and Alice replacing Agnus. These *Advanced Graphics Architecture (AGA)* Amigas offered a vastly upgraded suite of display modes, with horizontal resolutions potentially exceeding 1,200, vertical resolutions potentially exceeding 600, and a color palette numbering in the millions.[42] These modes at last, in other words, brought the Amiga back at least to rough parity with most models of the Macintosh and Windows multimedia PCs, even if they were still lacking in some very significant respects that I address later. Although most Amiga users would agree that the AGA machines ideally should have appeared at least three years earlier, their belated arrival was greeted with an almost audible sigh of release by an Amiga community that had been deeply concerned by Commodore's years of inaction.

For all of its vastly improved capabilities, AGA was actually a fairly straightforward next step for the Amiga, expanding on the original architecture rather than revolutionizing it. The planar graphics system remained, but the new Lisa chip now allowed playfields to contain up to eight bitplanes, for 256 colors on screen at once, in virtually all of the standard graphics modes; and those colors were now defined via RGB values in the range of 0 to 255 rather than just 0 to 15, for no less than 16,777,216 possible colors in lieu of the original 4,096. Of the special graphics modes, EHB was now largely unnecessary but remained in the new chip set as a legacy mode to support older software. The more significant HAM mode, however, was in much stronger evidence; AGA features the *HAM8* mode, the "8" referring to the number of bitplanes used in its creation. (The older HAM mode was thus retroactively renamed "HAM6.") Not only does HAM8 mode use eight rather than six bitplanes, with the last two modifying the color contained in the first six in a way effectively identical to that of HAM6, but it can operate in virtually any of AGA's available resolutions.

A revised AGA version of DPaint IV followed the 1200 and 4000 in fairly short order. EA's continuing support of such a decidedly minority platform was perhaps encouraged by Commodore, who in these latter years began bundling copies of DPaint with many of its Amiga models. Although offering only a handful of other new features, this version supported virtually all of the Amiga's AGA and legacy (now dubbed the Original Chip Set, or *OCS*) color and resolution combinations.

As happened so frequently in the Amiga's history, the new hope of AGA was immediately followed by the bitterest of disappointments. Commodore desperately needed the mass-market-oriented Amiga 1200 in particular to be a successful heir to the Amiga 500's legacy if the company and the platform were to remain viable. The company had for once done most of the right things, pricing the unit at an aggressive $599, which made it an attractive alternative to the pricier Windows and Macintosh machines of the era, and making sure it was ready in time for the all-important 1992 Christmas buying season. Due to parts and manufacturing snafus that were a direct result of Commodore's perpetually poor management, however, production slowed to a virtual standstill shortly after the new machine got off to a relatively promising start.[43] There were vastly fewer Amiga 1200s available than there were consumers wanting to buy them, and sales of older models, still in plentiful supply, dried up as consumers now considered them obsolete and undesirable. Commodore's sales for November 1992 were actually higher than its sales for December, a phenomenon unprecedented in consumer electronics, and sales plummeted again in

January, falling off by another 70 percent.[44] This period was, in short, a financial disaster for Commodore—the event that, more than any other single incident, sealed the company's fate. Although Commodore would survive for another year, its financial situation became so precarious that it could do little but struggle fruitlessly to keep its head above the rivers of debt it had accrued. Further Amiga research and development came effectively to a halt as the engineering staff was cut to the bone, and the 1200 and 4000, greeted with such hope and excitement as a second wind for the platform, instead became the Commodore Amiga's swansong.

It is surprising, therefore, that Ozer and Hodgson were allowed to continue to work on yet another version of DPaint even as Commodore sunk into insolvency and finally, in April 1994, declared bankruptcy, spelling the end of the Amiga as a viable, significant computing platform, at least in North America. DPaint V snuck out of EA in early 1995, the last product EA would release for the Amiga—appropriately enough, as DPaint I had been the first. DPaint V sported the usual variety of new features and thoughtful touches, most notably including support for the new 24-bit graphics boards that were becoming increasingly common among the Amiga diehards (and about which I have more to say in chapter 9). Released with no promotion or real interest by EA, DPaint V marked the end of this line of remarkable software that had been such a fixture and even symbol of the Amiga through the previous decade.

In the years that immediately followed, rights to the Amiga name and intellectual property changed hands several times, going to the German company Escom, then moving on to the American company Gateway 2000, and finally ending up in 1999 with the startup Amiga, Incorporated. Although the latter did license the Belgian software company Hyperion Entertainment to produce the first complete revision of AmigaOS since 1992, a project that Hyperion remarkably managed to complete in 2006, new Amiga hardware is available today only in expensive, semiassembled kit form, and the sense of community that used to mark the Amiga now also lives in other, noncorporate=managed platforms such as Linux. And although old Amiga games remain popular to play via emulators such as the *Ultimate Amiga Emulator* (*UAE*),[45] the number of people still using Amiga hardware for everyday computing would seem to be fairly minuscule, at least in comparison with the number of those who use other computing platforms. Rumors of accounting irregularities and an obvious lack of financial resources dog Amiga, Incorporated, which was recently involved in an ugly lawsuit with former software partner Hyperion that raises serious doubts about future support for AmigaOS. Although hope springs eternal among the Amiga faithful, the objective observer would be hard-pressed to construct an argument for the Amiga as a truly viable general-purpose computing platform either now or in the future. The best Amiga ideas have been so thoroughly woven into other, better-supported platforms that it can offer most users today little beyond the evocative, nostalgic name "Amiga."

The Legacy of DPaint

It is difficult to express how different the computing world of DPaint I was from that of DPaint V. In the former, most people still regarded computers as mysterious, esoteric machines, with little of value to offer the serious artist; in the latter, almost everyone accepted them as essential everyday design tools in a multitude of fields. DPaint, in its quiet way somewhat akin to its creator Dan Silva, forced a significant portion of that transition until, like the platform on which it ran, the snowball it had begun to form overtook it under the guidance of companies better managed, better funded, and more visionary than Commodore. Throughout its lifespan, DPaint remained intimately connected to its host, many of its strengths and weaknesses mirroring the Amiga's own, and its marketplace success and ultimate failure also symbiotically linked to the Amiga's fortunes. DPaint's evolution can be seen in the rich body of work created with it, as Rodney Chang noted in 1989: "I see my evolution as an Amiga artist going hand in hand with the improvements in the software. My work helps document the progress the software makes."[46] And just as with the Amiga, DPaint's legacy to the computing world is in evidence everywhere to those with the historical perspective to see it. Adobe Photoshop and the GNU Image Manipulation Program (GIMP), among many other applications, burst through the graphics industry doors first cracked open by DPaint. Even the term *computer art*, bandied about and debated so heatedly in the days of DPaint I, has ceased to be a useful signifier in today's world, where much or most art is computerized in one way or another. Artist David Em noted as early as 1990 that "the computer has become another accessible tool, like a pencil."[47]

Perhaps the most important artistic trend of the postmodern era has been a turning away from the ideal of the artist as a "pure" creator sitting down in front of a blank canvas to create something from nothing toward modification, recontextualization, and reclamation of existing materials. This trend is notable not only in the visual arts, but also in many other art forms as well—perhaps most notably music. Andy Warhol was at the forefront of this emerging trend in the 1960s, as illustrated by works such as his iconic series of portraits of Marilyn Monroe, painted not from scratch but rather created from rather banal publicity shots of the actress. Those images are more refined than the hurried portrait of Debbie Harry that Warhol created on that Amiga at Lincoln Center, yet the final effect is not hugely dissimilar. Now consider how the images were created. Warhol described the creation of the *Marilyn* series thus: "In August 62 I started doing silkscreens. I wanted something stronger that gave more of an assembly line effect. With silkscreening you pick a photograph, blow it up, transfer it in glue onto silk, and then roll ink across it so the ink goes through the silk but not through the glue. That way you get the same image, slightly different each time. It was all so simple quick and chancy. I was thrilled with it. When Marilyn Monroe happened to die that month, I got the idea to make screens of her beautiful face the first Marilyns."[48] Warhol may have described the process as "quick" and "simple," but how much quicker and simpler was it to create Harry's portrait, done in a matter of moments on an Amiga and with the same element of chancy unpredictability in the automated functions used to process it? It was in allowing the artist to combine and alter existing images easily, whether taken from the real world via a digitizer or from some other source, that DPaint and its many worthy competitors on the Amiga most obviously affected everyday artistic practice. Warhol scholar Donna De Salvo writes that "more than any other artist of his generation, Andy Warhol understood how the reproduced image had come to reflect and shape contemporary life."[49] What better way to "reflect" and "shape" that imagery than via a tool such as DPaint and its modern successors?

And yet, after looking at a large number of classic DPaint images in researching this chapter, I also found myself feeling a certain sense of loss about the path computerized art has largely chosen not to take. Most computer-generated imagery today is either created computationally, such as in the 3D-modeling packages that have become so ubiquitous in the games industry, or is based on the manipulation and recombination of already-existing images. The Amiga was a pioneer in both fields, as parts of this chapter and all of the next describe. Yet I also admire the work of classic Amiga artists such as Jim Sachs, who simply loaded up DPaint and created his works by hand using the painterly strokes seldom seen in computer-generated visuals today. Many of DPaint's painterly metaphors may seem quaint to the Photoshop professional of today, yet they evince a certain purity that has a charm all its own. Like so much of the best Amiga software, DPaint is simply *fun*, inspiring many who would never have their work featured in a gallery or a game or a video production to load it up at idle moments to play, to doodle, to see what they could do with this thing.

One dedicated user called it "the greatest videogame ever devised" and frankly admitted to buying an Amiga just to run it.[50] The days when the very existence of an aesthetically appealing image on a computer screen was cause for surprise, excitement, and (perhaps) concern are long gone, but this sea change merely makes some of the finest work done with DPaint—some of which can be seen on this book's accompanying Web site—easier to appreciate on its own intrinsic merits. For a computer that was so celebrated for its visuals, the Amiga was such an appealing tool for artists paradoxically because the very quality of those visuals let, in Chang's words again, "people see the art and not the computer"[51] for the first time.

Behold the robot juggling silver spheres. He stands firmly on the landscape and gleams in the light. He is only a microchip phantom, yet he casts a shadow. You see his reflection in the refined orbs he so deftly tosses. He inhabits space, in a pristine computer's dreamscape. Though he looks strangely real, he exists only in the memory of the Amiga.—Eric Graham, "Graphics Scene Simulations" (1987)

In November 1986, a time when the Boing demo was still considered an impressive demonstration of the Amiga's capabilities, Commodore began distributing a new demo to dealers, electronic *bulletin-board systems* (*BBSs*), and public-domain software collections. This demo, known simply as "the Juggler," had been written by a self-described "ex-astronomer and software developer living in the mountains of New Mexico"[1] named Eric Graham. It consisted of a single looping animation of just 24 frames and less than one second's duration that portrayed a toylike robot juggling three glass spheres while standing in a highly stylized environment consisting of a checkerboard floor and a painterly blue sky. The animation was brief indeed and in many ways very simple—but it was also the most impressive demonstration of an everyday computer's multimedia capabilities that anyone had yet seen. And not only did the Juggler *play* on an Amiga, but it had also been entirely *created* on a standard Amiga 1000 with just 512 KB of memory. Many people's first reaction to this information about the demo's creation was simple disbelief. When Graham first sent the demo to Commodore, for instance, the staff insisted he must have rendered the images on a mainframe or specialized graphical workstation and refused to believe in its veracity until he sent them the source code and tools he had used in its creation.[2]

Oddly enough in light of its stylized design, the Juggler demo impressed so much because it looked so *real* (figure 4.1). At a time when HAM mode was still imperfectly understood and of limited projected utility, the Juggler displayed its full potential for perhaps the first time. The robot stands amid the countless shades and gradients that mark a real environment as opposed to the solid blocks of uniform color that were the norm for computer graphics of the time. A light source glints off his metallic torso and casts a realistic shadow behind him, and, as the final coup de grace, each of the spheres is actually a mirror, reflecting back an appropriately distorted and ever-changing image of its surroundings as it flies through the air. The verisimilitude of the whole was astounding in its day and can still impress even today. Certainly no other PC of 1986 would have been remotely capable of displaying anything like it—thus, the Juggler's prominent place in Commodore's marketing of the Amiga.

In fact, the Juggler was easily one of the best promotional tools in the Amiga's arsenal and likely sold more Amigas than the entirety of Commodore's other confused and ineffectual promotional efforts combined. It became a fixture in the display windows of Amiga dealers around the world for years; as late as 1989, Victor Osaka first had his interest in the

4.1 Eric Graham's Juggler demo (1986)

Amiga's artistic potential piqued by a Juggler in the display window of a Software Etc. store in Los Angeles. "There was a colorful animation of a Juggler fashioned in sort of a 'Michelin Man' model," he recalled.[3] Osaka soon purchased the top-of-the-line Amiga of that year, an Amiga 2500, and became one of the most prominent members of the Amiga's community of artists. The Juggler also turned up in other, more surprising places, such as the 1987 video for the Tom Petty song "Jammin' Me," for which Graham received all of $100 and a copy of the video on tape.[4] In the Amiga community, Graham became a veritable celebrity. Curiosity about the programming techniques behind the Juggler was so intense that the glossy flagship publication *AmigaWorld*, never noted for its in-depth technical coverage, devoted a cover and a considerable number of pages to an explanation of the demo's creation and its implementation by Graham, with lengthy source-code extracts.

For all that, a discussion of how the Juggler demo actually *plays* can be dispensed with rather quickly. Unlike the Boing demo, which is generated programmatically as it plays, the Juggler consists only of a series of pre-rendered animation frames and a utility to play them back. To save disk space and memory, these frames are stored using the same technique that Deluxe Paint III would later employ for its animations, with only the changes from frame to frame being recorded. These frames are likewise played back using the same double-buffering technique used by DPaint III and later editions, as described in chapter 3. Of course, the Juggler appeared two and a half years before DPaint III, when animation techniques on the Amiga were still in their comparative infancy. Its superb implementation of page-flipping animation was therefore significant in itself and inspiring to many, quite possibly including Dan Silva.

But the truly revolutionary aspect of the Juggler demo is not how its frames are played back, but rather how those frames were generated in the first place. As Graham himself described the demo in early 1987, "This colorful automaton is not your everyday computer graphics robot. He wasn't carefully rendered with a paint program, nor was his image captured by a video frame grabber from a picture or a model. He and his surrealistic world were 'automatically' created with a C program."[5]

From 2D Painting to 3D Modeling

DPaint and programs like it are often referred to as either 2D *paint programs* or, perhaps more usefully, *raster-graphics editors*, the term *raster* meaning the grid of many pixels that make up a single image. (*Raster* and the Amiga-specific term *playfield* refer to essentially the same thing.)

DPaint has no understanding of the images its user creates beyond the color of these pixels. Although it includes many useful functions to aid the artist in drawing shapes and lines, filling areas with colors or gradients, and (particularly in later versions) even rotating sections of an image along three dimensions, its understanding of these tasks is strictly in the moment. As soon as the artist is done drawing a line using the built-in tool, for instance, that line is integrated back into the grid of colored pixels that form the image, with no independent existence. DPaint has no understanding of *line* as a concept from that point on, any more than it can distinguish Venus's eye from her hair in one of DPaint's most famous promotional pictures—or any more than it can understand the concept of Venus herself, for that matter. Venus exists to DPaint merely as colored points of light. The burden thus rests entirely with the artist to arrange those points to create a believable image of Venus, just as a conventional painter uses strokes of color on canvas for the same purpose. And like that painter, she can use the geometrical rules of perspective, well understood in the visual arts since the Italian Renaissance, to arrange those points of light in such a way as to create the illusion of three dimensions—of depth in addition to width and height—on the 2D monitor screen. Nevertheless, her creations remain to DPaint just a 2D grid of colored pixels. There is nothing else "behind" the image.

Now let us consider a very different way of creating an image on the computer, one in which the computer understands the shapes and objects that form the image as well as the environment in which they exist as distinct entities. In such a scenario, we can describe to the computer the details of these objects—their size, shape, material—along with certain other important details about the environment, such as the location, intensity, and shade of light sources and the location of the "camera" that will capture the scene. In effect, we are not creating an image, but rather a virtual reality, a universe to be simulated inside the computer. Our output consists of "photographs" of that universe that we have asked the computer to take for us to provide us with our only visual window into it and, indeed, our only tangible evidence of its existence. To create one such photograph, the computer translates the model universe into a raster of pixels, a process known as *3D rendering*.

Such an approach is inevitably much more demanding of memory and processing power than the alternative, not to mention requiring some unique technical skills of the artist who designs the universe being simulated. But in return we stand to gain a great deal. For instance, we can quickly generate new versions of any given scene by changing the light source or sources, camera location, or the locations of an object or two in our universe. Because we take into account the interactions of light with the objects in our universe, we can create scenes with a verisimilitude that would be almost impossible to re-create by hand, featuring realistic shading and shadows. If we set our objects in motion and make the camera that captures our universe a motion-picture camera rather than a single-frame camera, this sense of realism becomes even more pronounced, as is shown so well by the Juggler demo. And finally, if we add an interactive element and at least a modicum of physical simulation, we can make our simulated universe one that can be truly lived in and manipulated by the viewer; this is the basis of many modern videogames.

Three-dimensional modeling was hardly a new concept even in 1986. In fact, its origin can be traced back to the early 1960s. Sketchpad, a program developed by Ivan Sutherland at MIT at that time, is generally considered the first interactive graphics-creation program and thus the first ancestor of DPaint, MacPaint, and the many other programs like them. The way that Sketchpad stores and displays its image data is, however, fundamentally different than the system employed by these raster-graphics editors. The shapes and other geometrical constructs that make up its images are stored not merely as a raster of pixels, but rather as individual objects. If a Sketchpad user creates a line, a square, and a circle, for instance, Sketchpad understands each of these shapes as its own unique entity: its location, its size, its line thickness, its rotation angle, and so on. Such a system is known as a *vector-graphics* system. Vector graphics are ideal for a program such as Sketchpad, which was designed not to be a tool for fine art with all its subtleties and irregularities, but rather to be (as its name would imply) a sketching or drafting tool for engineers. Because the program retains an understanding of the individual components of the image, those components can be modified at any time: expanded or shrunk, stretched or squeezed, pulled from place to place, rotated along the X or Y axis. As changes are made, Sketchpad calculates and "store[s] the locations of all the spots of a drawing in a large table in memory and . . . produce[s] the drawing by displaying from this table."[6] Sketchpad is, in other words, mapping its model environment onto raster-oriented display hardware, just as Graham would later do in translating his model universe into an animation.[7] Sketchpad thus represents not so much the first painting program as the genesis of computer-aided design (CAD) tools as well the origin of 3D modeling systems such as that used to create the Juggler demo and those that are omnipresent in computer graphics work in many different fields today. That said, if Sketchpad can be said to simulate a universe, that universe must be akin to that in Edwin A. Abbott's *Flatland*, for the original program has no notion of depth. Later research, however, much of it conducted by Sutherland himself, remedied this problem soon enough. In the process, Sutherland and other researchers invented many of the technologies, theories, and algorithms that still drive 3D graphics today.

This research was of limited initial utility for designers and programmers of early PCs due to those machines' sharply limited memory, processing power, and display hardware. Although remarkable early games such as *Flight Simulator* (Bruce Artwick, 1980) and *Elite* (David Braben and Ian Bel, 1984) took advantage of some of this research to showcase simple 3D environments of their own, the first truly physically believable and aesthetically pleasing, albeit noninteractive, 3D universe to appear on a PC was that of the Juggler demo. The Juggler thus marks the point where the work of researchers such as Sutherland found a practical home on the PC. Indeed, Graham himself had been experimenting with 3D modeling for 20 years on large institutional computers by the time he purchased his Amiga and designed Juggler: "I always felt that computers were meant for more than just crunching numbers, first I thought in terms of physical simulations, then of course rendered images and virtual environments. There is always a sweet spot when affordable hardware becomes just capable of fulfilling a dream. The Amiga was that hardware and the Juggler took advantage of that moment."[8] Although the 68000 was a fairly powerful processor in 1986, other 68000-based computers were available. More important to the fulfillment of Graham's dream was another, more unique element of the Amiga's design: HAM mode, with its unprecedented 4,096 available colors that allowed the subtle blending of shades and interactions among light sources and objects that are key to rendering a realistic scene.

SSG

Graham created Juggler using a C-language program of his own devising, which he called "SSG," most likely an abbreviation for "spherical solid geometry."[9] That program received very limited distribution beyond Graham himself and appears, along with the scene data used to render Juggler, to be lost to history in its complete form. Nonetheless, enough information remains—most notably from the large chunks of source code Graham published in the in-depth *AmigaWorld* article on Juggler and from Graham's own recollections—to reconstruct its operation. SSG is strictly a command-line tool, with no user interface at all. Its user feeds it a scene file written separately in a text editor and then must wait patiently while it renders her image. At last, it outputs the results and saves them to disk.

Surprisingly in light of the Juggler's kinetic realism, SSG has no built-in animation capabilities; Graham worked out the expected motion of the spheres and the Juggler from frame to frame by hand using sine-wave functions, then inputted each instance of the revised data into SSG one by one to render each screen singly, as an image in its own right. Finally, he used a separate utility to record the changes from frame to frame and output the animation file.[10]

In *Principles of Three-Dimensional Computer Animation*, a standard modern introductory text on the field, Michael O'Rourke breaks down the complete 3D-rendering process into six components: the object geometry, the camera, the lights, the surface characteristics, the shading algorithm, and the rendering algorithm.[11] The first four of these components consist of information that the user must supply to a 3D modeler; the modeler then performs the latter two calculations using this information, resulting in the final rendered scene. Although SSG is vastly more primitive than even later 3D modelers written for the Amiga (not to speak of modern applications), it can be described in terms of each of these components.

As in a modern 3D modeler, each object in SSG's universe must be defined in terms of its geometry and its location in the scene. Unlike modern applications with their complex polygons, however, SSG supports just one shape: a perfect sphere. The geometry and position of each sphere can thus be defined simply by its radius and a set of X, Y, and Z coordinates that mark the distance of its center from an arbitrarily chosen point of origin. These spheres stand alone to form the glass baubles that the Juggler throws as well as his eyes. In addition, they can be compacted together into something that Graham calls a "sphere-tube," "a sequence of spheres along a line with slowly changing radius."[12] By overlapping spheres in a sphere-tube, SSG can form more complex, tubular shapes such as the Juggler's torso and limbs.

SSG also requires that its user position a single virtual camera to capture the scene. Like an object, the camera is positioned in the scene via a set of X, Y, and Z coordinates. In addition, the user must state in what direction the camera points, via "two numbers, one for the number of degrees it is pointing away from north, and one for how many degrees it is pointing above or below the horizon."[13] Finally, she can set the focal length of her virtual camera, which has the effect of widening or narrowing its field of view and potentially magnifying the objects it captures, just like a zoom lens on a real camera.

With only the data just described, it would be possible to construct and display monochrome wire-frame 3D scenes. To go further, though, and construct truly believable scenes rather than mere mock-ups, SSG requires more information about the virtual universe it is being asked to draw. Its user must address not just the objects in her universe, but also the qualities of the light that exists there and the ways in which the light and the objects interact.

The SSG user must therefore next define the "lamps" that light her scene. Each is another sphere positioned somewhere in the scene via X, Y, and Z coordinates. Like the other spheres, each lamp has a radius and can be seen if within the camera's field of view. The user can specify the color of each lamp, which can be any of the Amiga's 4,096 available colors, using a familiar RGB value; this chosen color will also be the color of the light that radiates outward from it equidistantly in every direction. (Each lamp, in other words, is akin to a bare light bulb rather than a spotlight.) Unlike a modern 3D modeler, SSG ties no concept of intensity to its lamps; every lamp is equally bright, meaning that the only way to increase the degree of illumination coming from a certain angle is to move the lamp closer to its target or simply add another lamp in that area. In addition to any number of lamps, SSG does allow the user to request some quantity and color of ambient lighting, "diffused light that comes from all directions" to "soften the shadows."[14] In the real world, of course, there is no such thing as true ambient lighting because every ray of light must ultimately have a source. Like most modern 3D modelers, however, SSG allows such lighting as a way of simplifying a virtual reality that is already more than demanding enough on both the human who designs it and the computer that renders it.

Finally, the SSG user must describe how her lighting will interact with the other objects in her scene; she must, in other words, describe her spheres' surface properties. Once again, her options here are very limited in contrast to later programs. She provides each sphere or sphere-tube with a single RGB value representing its color—or, stated more accurately, "the fraction of red, green, and blue light that is reflected from its surface."[15] And she defines the reflective properties of each sphere or sphere-tube as one of just three possibilities: "First, the surface can be dull, in which case light scatters in every direction; second, the surface finish can be shiny, with most of the reflected light being scattered, but a little being reflected in one specific direction; finally, the surface can be like a mirror, with no light being scattered and all reflected light going in one direction."[16] Each sphere or sphere-tube can have but a single color over all its surface, and that surface must have the same reflective properties everywhere.

With all of this information available at last, SSG can calculate the final rendered image. Broadly speaking, there are two ways to approach this task. The first way, often referred to today as the *rasterization* approach, breaks this process into two stages that correspond neatly to the fifth and sixth components of O'Rourke's outline of the 3D-modeling process. The modeler examines the relative properties of the lights and the objects in the scene and uses a shading algorithm to adjust the colors of the objects to reflect the lighting. The programmer of the 3D modeler has her choice of many, many algorithms to employ, from faceted shading, which gives every surface a single, consistent overall color, to more subtle (and computationally intense) processes such as Gourad, Lambert, or Phong shading. (Or the programmer can even skip this step entirely if she has chosen not to implement lighting in her modeler; at least one early Amiga 3D modeler, Videoscape 3D, took this approach.) The appropriately shaded objects are then rendered to the screen one by one by applying to them the well-understood geometrical rules of distance and perspective, with objects closer to the camera of course capable of obscuring objects behind them. Rasterization techniques are capable of producing very pleasing results when a suitable algorithm is paired to a suitable type of scene. In fact, they are used almost exclusively by modern 3D videogames as well as in many other applications.

But SSG uses a different approach. That approach, *ray tracing*, was first explicitly described in print by Turner Whitted in 1980,[17] although others, including Graham himself, had been experimenting with the technique for years before this publication.[18] Ray tracing combines O'Rourke's shading and rendering components into a single algorithm. It simulates the play of light within a model universe to create an image of the scene viewed through the "window" of the monitor screen, the 2D surface—or, more correct, the projection plane—upon which we will draw our 3D universe. In addition to yielding the most lifelike images of any rendering method, ray tracing, in contrast to most 3D-graphics algorithms, is also very simple conceptually. In simulating the real properties of light, it brings a certain elegance all too absent from other algorithms. Shadows, for instance, appear automatically in a ray-traced scene rather than needing to be laboriously calculated as in other shading and rendering algorithms. And hidden-surface routines—methods of determining which parts of objects are obscured by other objects, for which there is a huge body of often baroque literature in the 3D-graphics field—are completely unnecessary in a ray tracer; again, they happen automatically as a result of the core ray-tracing algorithm.

Like all ray tracers, SSG traces the path of rays of light between the viewer's eye and the scene, passing through the projection plane in the process (figure 4.2). It does this, however, in reverse: tracing the rays not from the scene to the eye, as they travel in the real world, but rather from the eye back to the objects. Imagine that the camera lens that captures a scene is covered with a fine mesh; each square on this grid represents a single pixel on the monitor screen. A virtual viewpoint—our viewing "eye"—is slightly behind this screen, its exact position being determined by the chosen camera focal length. SSG traces a line from this point, through each of the squares on the grid, and on through the scene the camera is capturing; each line represents a single ray of light. Perhaps this ray strikes one of the objects in our scene. If so, there is work to do.

If the object's surface is dull, SSG calculates the final color of the pixel in question by considering both the color of the object and the qualities of the light rays that the point receives from the various lamps in the scene: "We calculate the light by considering lines from the point to each of the lamps illuminating the scene. So long as nothing blocks a line, the illumination depends upon the brightness and color of the lamp and upon the

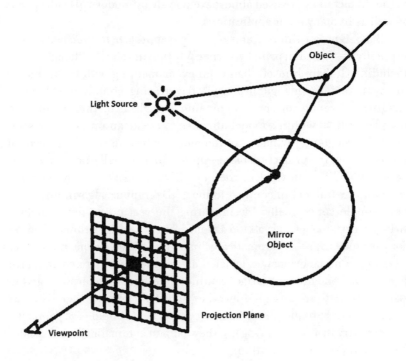

Figure 4.2 Ray tracing

distance from the lamp to the point. As the light striking an object becomes more oblique, the illumination per unit area decreases."[19] If the object's surface is shiny, there is the added possibility of a glinting effect, which will occur if the amount of light the point receives from a single lamp exceeds a certain threshold. (One can clearly see this effect on the upper part of the robot's torso in the Juggler demo.) Finally, in the most complicated case, the object may be a mirror. In this case, the pixel's angle of reflection is calculated and traced through the scene to determine its final color.

It is of course also possible that a ray may move all the way through the scene without striking any object at all. In this case, the appropriate section of either the checkerboard ground or the blue sky is placed there, depending on whether the pixel is below or above the horizon line. In the case of the ground, this (dull) pixel is shaded appropriately to reflect the light that reaches it, using the approach just described. However, the lighting is not considered in coloring a pixel to represent the sky; an arbitrary shade of blue is always chosen, the exact shade depending on the pixel's position on the virtual horizon.

SSG is constrained by the limitations of HAM mode in realizing its idealized scene on the Amiga's display hardware, for, as discussed in the previous chapter, the number of sharp color transitions that can be performed in HAM is strictly limited. SSG must therefore sometimes make compromises in the colors of certain pixels. The choice of colors in the 16 registers that define the base colors is critical to minimizing HAM's color distortions. SSG is fairly sophisticated in its handling of these registers, though, as Graham explained in 1987: "At first I don't use any of my 16 direct colors. When I first encounter a sharp transition, I assign the color value to one of the free registers. As the display progresses, when I encounter another color transition I look to see if the contents of one of the color register values is close enough; if it is, I use that value rather than use up one of the remaining registers."[20] The key question here, then, is what constitutes "close enough." This value is hard-coded into the SSG application itself, although the technically adept user can of course alter the source and recompile to better suit the demands of the scene she is creating. SSG should ideally use all 16 registers over the course of drawing the complete scene but should not use them up too early so that, for example, there are no registers still available to facilitate critical sharp transitions in the bottom half of the image.

Ironically, the conceptually simple ray-tracing algorithm is notoriously demanding of the computing hardware on which it runs. Even utilizing the Amiga's lowest-resolution mode of 320 × 200, SSG must trace the path of 64,000 individual rays of light through the scene, one for each pixel. And where those rays strike an object, it must further trace more rays—back to the lamps or back to the objects to be reflected in the case of a mirror—to determine the final color for that pixel. Each frame of the Juggler demo took about one hour to render.[21] Because of its slow speed, ray tracing has generally been considered unsuitable for interactive 3D applications from the Amiga's day to today.

SSG and the Juggler nevertheless spawned a veritable subculture of "render junkies"[22] who created and distributed among themselves images and animations of often stunning quality. Although SSG itself remained a somewhat limited tool, with distribution also limited to the approximately 1,000 disks Graham copied and mailed out by hand upon request,[23] other Amiga programmers were soon enough inspired to author more flexible and powerful ray tracers. Perhaps the most notable of these programmers is David Buck, whose DKBTrace garnered a large following of enthusiastic users. Like SSG, DKBTrace and similar programs come equipped with no user interface at all; their users must describe their scenes entirely via text using a rather esoteric markup language. A single sphere in DKBTrace might be described like this[24]:

```
OBJECT
    SPHERE < 0.0 25.0 0.0 > 40.0 END SPHERE
    COLOR Blue
    AMBIENT 0.3
    DIFFUSE 0.7
    BRILLIANCE 7.0
END_OBJECT
```

Command-line-driven ray tracers, in spite of or perhaps because of their complexity and their steep learning curves, have come to hold an established place in *hacker* culture. The process of designing a scene in this way can be immensely appealing and addictive, and viewing a newly rendered image for the first time is rife with discovery and excitement.

DKBTrace was eventually ported to other platforms and still later morphed into POV-Ray (for "Persistence of Vision Ray Tracer"), the most popular free ray tracer of today, around which an active community still persists. Textually driven ray tracers, almost always distributed as free software, were not long the only option for the Amiga artist, however; Graham's next project after SSG and the Juggler would allow users to design scenes interactively using a full GUI.

Videoscape 3D and Sculpt-Animate

At the Second Amiga Developer's Conference in November 1986, the same month that the Juggler made its debut, Allen Hastings presented two videos created entirely with an Amiga and a 3D modeling and animation program of his own devising.[25] The sequences that Hastings displayed were much lengthier than Graham's demo, running for minutes and containing many thousands of frames, but the program used to create them possessed no lighting or shading algorithms at all and did not make use of HAM mode, and the images created with it were therefore less impressive than the Juggler. Having been spliced together and recorded onto videotape rather than running "live" on an Amiga, these sequences were also more difficult to exchange. For these reasons, they did not have the same sensational impact as the Juggler, but they were sufficient to attract publishers interested in the program used to create them. Hastings soon signed a contract with Aegis to develop his software into a full-fledged commercial product.

Graham elected to use his experience developing SSG and the Juggler for the same purpose and began work on what would become Sculpt 3D on December 26, 1986.[26] His goals for the project were lofty: to build a full-fledged, flexible, 3D modeler and ray tracer to replace the limited SSG and to build upon the modeler a full GUI that would allow the user to work with her scene interactively. Graham realized these goals in remarkably short order; the first working prototype was ready by "about April" 1987.[27] There followed negotiations with a number of publishers, including EA, which "didn't understand what Sculpt was all about," and Aegis, which Graham rejected so as not to interfere with the plans of his friendly rival Hastings.[28] The choice came down to two: Byte by Byte, a small but early and prolific publisher of Amiga applications, and NewTek, another small company that I discuss more fully in the next chapter. Graham elected to go with Byte by Byte in the end because "they seemed more professional," a decision he would eventually come to regret in light of Byte by Byte's subsequent handling of his creation.[29]

Hastings's program and Graham's program were named Videoscape 3D and Sculpt 3D, respectively, and reached stores virtually simultaneously in mid-1987. The two programs thus share the honor of being the first of their kind, not only on the Amiga, but on any PC. But Graham's creation was the more sophisticated and innovative of the two. Although Videoscape offered animation, it still had no lighting or shading component whatsoever and was also saddled with a scene- and object-design process that was little more intuitive than the text files used by SSG.

Moreover, Videoscape not only did not support HAM mode but actually locked the user into a single palette of colors hard-coded into the program itself. A review gamely tried to accentuate the positives but finally had to admit that "the images [Videoscape] produces tend to be a bit flat and lifeless."[30] Sculpt 3D was free from such compromises and restrictions, even if on its initial release it was only capable of rendering static scenes, a likely concession to the need to be first in what was rapidly turning into a race involving not just Aegis and Byte by Byte, but several other publishers as well—a third 3D package, Forms in Flight from MicroMagic, appeared within days of the first two. Graham and Byte by Byte, meanwhile, released an animation add-on to Sculpt 3D well before the end of the year; the resulting hybrid was called Sculpt-Animate 3D. All this activity prompted Lou Wallace to write in *AmigaWorld* that "while 1986 was the year of paint and animation, 1987 is the year of 3-D."[31] By the time a considerably improved version of Sculpt-Animate 3D was released as Sculpt-Animate 4D—with the fourth dimension apparently (and suddenly) representing motion—at the end of 1988, quite a number of other 3D-modeling applications were available, with more in the pipeline, all heirs to the excitement generated by the Juggler.

A Sculpt-Animate Project

To illustrate Graham's approach to 3D modeling in depth, this section offers a practical demonstration of using Sculpt-Animate 4D, but most of it applies equally to Sculpt-Animate 3D—and almost as well to the other 3D modelers that borrowed many of Graham's innovations.

When one first boots Sculpt-Animate, one is greeted by the working area shown in figure 4.3. This screen always runs in the Amiga's 640 × 200 resolution mode, with three bitplanes for a total of eight on-screen colors. The final images and animations that Sculpt-Animate produces can, however, be in any of a large variety of resolution and color combinations. The abstract data that describe a scene, which the user works with using the interface shown in figure 4.3, are kept consistently separate from the final rendering process and from the display hardware used to create an image or animation from those data. This separation is so complete that Sculpt-Animate 4D can be used to render images with more colors or resolution than the Amiga on which it runs is capable of displaying; these images can then be moved to video equipment or graphics workstations for display and perhaps further manual editing.

Figure 4.3 also illustrates Graham's solution to the most fundamental problem of designing a 3D modeler: although the application must model

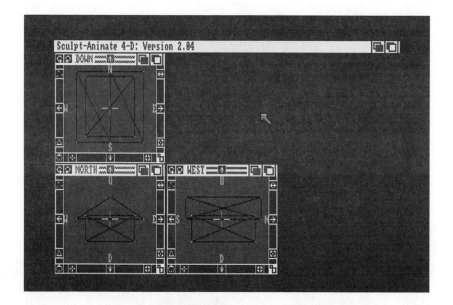

4.3 Even this very simple model of a house shows some of the confusion that the Sculpt-Animate 4D triview can bring. Only in the north view is the object recognizable for what it actually is; in the other views, it appears as a bewildering array of overlapping lines and vertices because no clipping is performed, and the viewer has no other way of determining what parts of the object lie in front of others in the projection plane.

a 3D scene, the screen on which the user works with that scene can display just two dimensions. Graham therefore employed an interface he called the "triview." Each of the three small windows provides a view into the same area of space, but from a different perspective. The top left window shows the scene viewed from above and looking down; the bottom left from the south and looking north; and the right from the east and looking west. The user can use each of these windows to manipulate two of the scene's three dimensions. Changes she makes in one window will always be immediately reflected in the other windows. The windows are always inextricably linked, not only looking into the same virtual universe but always viewing the exact same area of space in that universe. Only the perspectives from which they view that space vary.

Working with the triview is not, at least initially, a terribly intuitive process; only over time does one develop a feel for it. In addition to trying to adjust to working with the varying perspectives offered by the triview boxes, the user must also deal with the fact that objects in the triview appear not as solids, but as wire-frame outlines of the edges and vertices that form them. There is no concept of clipping; edges and vertices that should be obscured by others (and that will be in the final rendered scene) appear unobscured in the triview. Particularly when the user is working with complex objects, this absence of clipping combined with the varying perspectives can make Sculpt-Animate enormously confusing for the beginner. Nevertheless, at some point the program "clicks" with those who stick with it, as is proven by the large body of impressive work created with it.

As Graham did with SSG, he chose in Sculpt to build all of his objects from a single geometric primitive. Instead of the rather limiting sphere, though, he made that primitive the triangle. Every object in Sculpt-Animate, then, is formed from a series of triangles, each of which is further composed of three vertices or corners—each with an X, Y, and Z position in the scene—and the three edges or lines that connect them. These vertices and lines together outline the faces of the triangles, the only part visible in the final rendered image. (Conversely, these faces are invisible within the triview windows, but the vertices and lines that form them are visible.) It may seem at first blush that attempting to build a scene entirely from triangles would ultimately be as limiting as building one entirely from spheres, but in fact this is not the case at all. First, vertices and edges can be shared by more than one triangle; a complex Sculpt object has more the appearance of an interwoven mesh of vertices and lines than of a network of triangles. Sufficient numbers of triangles, even though their vertices can be only straight lines, can produce something of an impression of a curved surface if packed tightly together. And in a partial exception to the general triangle rule, the user can request that certain edges be formed into splines, or vertices connected by smooth curves rather than straight lines. In the end, then, anyone sufficiently skilled and patient working on an Amiga with sufficient memory can construct almost any imaginable object in Sculpt-Animate.

A very simple sample project demonstrates how an artist might use Sculpt-Animate. We will create a pair of simple shapes, design a scene around them, and finally use Sculpt-Animate's animation tools to set one of them in motion. Figure 4.4, showing a frame from the animation in its final form, should serve as a useful reference as we work through the process of creating it. The full animation is available for viewing on this book's Web site, as are the Sculpt-Animate 4D data files used to build it and a small sampling of other work done in Sculpt-Animate during the program's years as one of the premiere Amiga 3D-modeling packages.

Our first step must be to build the two objects in the scene. One approach would be the manual one: to lay down each vertex for each object and then connect them together with lines. Building objects of any complexity in this way, however, can be both difficult and tedious. Luckily for

4.4 This chapter's Sculpt-Animate 4D sample project in its final form

the user, Sculpt-Animate provides her with a collection of preformed geo-metric primitives that she can use either on their own or as the building blocks of more complex objects. As an early 3D modeler, Sculpt-Animate's options here are somewhat limited even in comparison to later Amiga modelers, but they are nevertheless hugely useful, for they allow us to insert spheres, hemispheres, cubes, prisms, disks, circles, cylinders, tubes, or cones automatically into our scene. We can in fact build the pyramid simply by choosing the cone shape from a menu. Upon doing so, Sculpt-Animate asks us how many points should be used to form the base. We choose just four, resulting in a very credible pyramid (figure 4.5).

Because our other shape—the orbiter—does not conform to any of Sculpt-Animate's built-in primitives, its construction will be slightly more involved. We begin, surprisingly, by requesting a circle. By specify-ing that the circle should consist of just five points around its circumfer-ence, we end up with something that is not terribly circular at all—a pentagon, just what we need to begin to build our orbiter (figure 4.6).

Because we built the pentagon with the downward-facing window of the triview active, it floats horizontally in our scene, like a hula hoop on its side. It has as of yet no true physical existence in our scene because the vertices and lines that form it do not form triangles or, in turn, solid faces. Were we to render our scene at this point, the pentagon would therefore not appear at all. We decide, however, to use this pentagon as the basis of

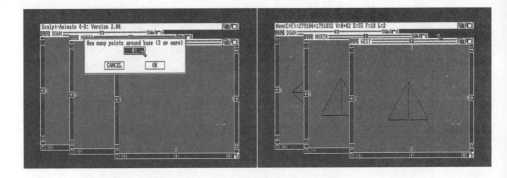

4.5 Building the pyramid in Sculpt-Animate 4D

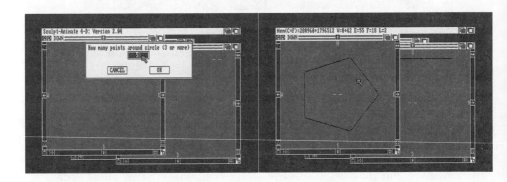

4.6 Building the pentagonal base of our orbiter in Sculpt-Animate 4D using the "Circle" function

our orbiter. We carefully place two more vertices equidistantly above and below the pentagon using the west-viewing triview window (although the north-viewing window would work equally well) and then use Sculpt-Animate's drawing tools to connect these vertices with those of the pentagon, forming triangles in the process. The result is a true solid object with ten individual faces that will show up in the final rendered image (figure 4.7).

Once we position the objects appropriately in relation to one another, the first and most complex stage of creating a 3D scene—designing and positioning the objects themselves—is complete. Even this simple example should demonstrate how a Sculpt-Animate artist must constantly switch from triview window to triview window in building her scene; becoming

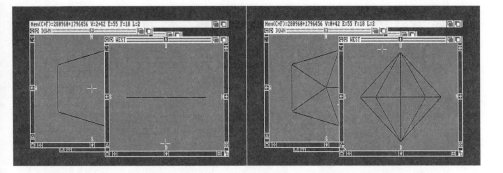

4.7 Building the second object for our Sculpt-Animate 4D sample project

a Sculpt-Animate expert thus largely involves practicing with the program enough to make the nonintuitive triview interface intuitive. And our use of the "circle" primitive to build a pentagon illustrates another facet of 3D modeling, particularly in this early era, that is important for the would-be 3D artist to grasp: many program functions can be used in surprising ways. The artist working with Sculpt-Animate or a similar application collects a veritable treasury of such tricks as she gains experience.

Having built and positioned our objects, we must now place our camera. Thanks to Sculpt-Animate's GUI, this procedure is considerably simpler than it was in SSG, for we can place the camera anywhere we wish in our scene by using the mouse. Rather than having to specify the horizontal and vertical orientation of its lens using numbers, we place a second point, a target for the camera, within our scene with the mouse; this, then, is the point the camera will be aimed toward (figure 4.8).

In addition to allowing the user simply to position the camera, Sculpt-Animate also allows her to change other settings relating to it. As in SSG, she can set a focal length; Sculpt-Animate, however, makes the photography metaphor even more explicit in allowing her to choose to use either a normal, wide-angle, or telephoto lens or a custom setting that roughly corresponds to the focal length setting of a 35-millimeter camera. She can even manually set an exposure time for her camera and tilt it left or right in the hands of her (imaginary) photographer. For our project, we decide to use a wide-angle lens so as to capture the entirety of our scene. As amateur virtual photographers, we let Sculpt-Animate choose the best exposure time for our scene rather than try to set it manually, nor do we introduce any tilt to the camera.

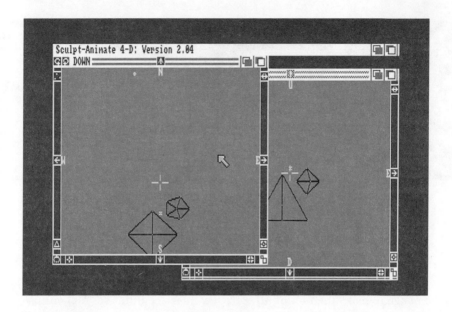

4.8 The camera positioned within our Sculpt-Animate 4D scene. In the active downward-looking triview window, the camera itself is represented by the small circle almost at the window's northern boundary. The camera's target is the small X located between the two objects that make up the entirety of the scene itself.

Next we must place our lamps. Again, Sculpt-Animate simplifies this process even as it expands our available options. Using the mouse and the triview, we place two lamps in our scene (figure 4.9).

One lamp illuminates the scene as a whole, and the other is positioned lower and closer to the eventual path of the smaller, orbiting shape, which creates a glinting effect as well as shadows that will be particularly noticeable when we animate the scene. Like SSG, Sculpt-Animate allows us to produce colored rather than bright white light from our lamps if we wish. Unlike SSG, it also allows us to set the intensity of each lamp; we can adjust the standard setting of 100 upward or downward for more or less intensity. In this sample project, however, we leave those settings alone, contenting ourselves with white lamps of the standard intensity. In an interesting twist, lamps in Sculpt-Animate have no physical existence in the scene outside of the light they produce, in marked contrast to SSG, where lamps are physical spheres that just happen to glow with light rather than merely reflect or absorb it.

Next we need to set the surface properties of our objects' faces, which we can change by selecting the faces in the triview using the mouse and calling up the appropriate menu item (figure 4.10).

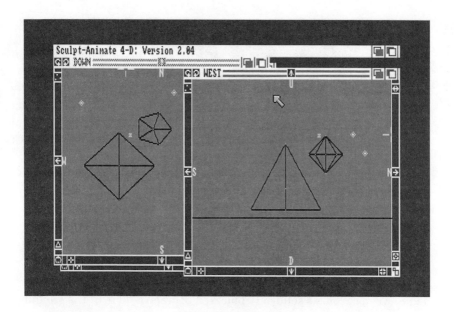

4.9 Lamps added to our Sculpt-Animate 4D scene are represented by the two small white diamonds visible in both the westward- and downward-facing triview windows

The most obvious of these properties, of course, is color, which we can set to any of the Amiga's available 4,096 colors using either the standard RGB system or the alternative HSV system described in the previous chapter. We choose a bright red for our pyramid: red 15, green 0, blue 0. For our orbiter, we choose a golden hue: red 15, green 11, blue 4. We can also choose a surface texture for each face, which dictates to a great degree how each face interacts with our light sources. Our available options here have been expanded from the three in SSG to six: dull, shiny, mirror, luminous, glass, or metal. We decide to make both objects shiny. Finally, we can choose to turn smoothing on for each object. Doing so causes Sculpt-Animate to use a special technique known as "Phong shading" on that object during the rendering process, which tends to smooth out edges and impart a more rounded appearance;[32] it is, in other words, one more way for Sculpt-Animate to overcome the limitations of its triangular building blocks to render curved, natural-seeming shapes. In our case, however, natural realism is not a goal; we like our sharp edges just fine, and so we leave smoothing off.

Before rendering our scene, we must manipulate two more elements to achieve the appearance we wish. First, we add the ground, which Sculpt-Animate models as a single horizontal face stretching into infinity. This

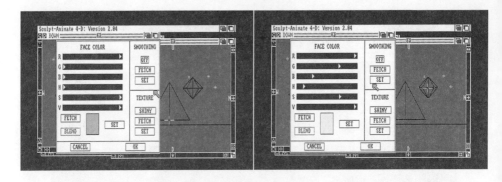

4.10 Setting the properties for each of our objects' faces in Sculpt-Animate 4D. In the left image, we modify the central pyramid; in the right, the orbiting shape.

face can be either solid or a checkerboard pattern like that of the Juggler demo. We make ours a solid dark blue: red 0, green 0, blue 9. The ground shows up in the triview as a horizontal line (figure 4.11).

Finally, we adjust the ambient illumination of our scene. Sculpt-Animate allows this lighting to be of any color and intensity we wish, defaulting to red 2, green 2, blue 2. We bump up this intensity to red 6, green 6, blue 6, producing a neutral gray background illumination to augment somewhat the effects of our two lamps and to prevent the contrast between the light and dark areas of our final image from being too extreme.

And so we are ready at last to render our scene. Like SSG, Sculpt-Animate is capable of rendering using a ray-tracing algorithm ; indeed, doing so yields the best overall images. There are, however, good reasons why an artist might choose not to use ray tracing. Most obviously, ray tracing is, as discussed earlier, a very slow rendering technique, particularly on a computer of the Amiga's era. Even our scene consisting of just two simple objects and two lamps takes 40 minutes to render using ray tracing on a stock 68000-based Amiga; more complex scenes can take dramatically longer, stretching into hours or, in the case of complex animations, days or even weeks. Serious artists generally upgraded their Amigas to the more powerful members of the 68000 family that were developed later, but ray tracing nevertheless remains a slow process. One must also consider that developing a Sculpt-Animate scene is not really the straightforward process I have just described, but rather one that is fraught with trial and error even for the experienced artist—the general pattern being to add or modify elements and then perform a render to see how they appear, repeating these actions again and again and again.

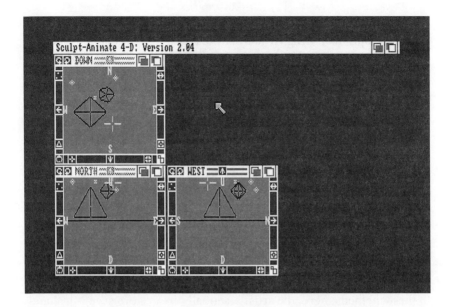

4.11 Our Sculpt-Animate 4D scene with the ground added. The ground is represented by the horizontal line visible in the northern- and western-facing triview windows.

Therefore, most artists took advantage of one of Sculpt-Animate's other options while developing their project: using ray tracing only for the final image.

And, indeed, the Sculpt-Animate artist can choose to render her images in quite a variety of ways, balancing image quality against rendering time. The simplest and fastest rendering method is wire-frame mode, in which objects are drawn in just two colors, as vertices and the lines that connect them. There is no notion of lighting in this mode or of solid faces or clipping; lines and vertices that should be hidden by the solid faces of an object show through. This mode is essentially the same as the view shown in the triview windows themselves, albeit rendered in proper 3D perspective. The other modes render objects as solids but differ in the sophistication of their clipping routines and the realism of their modeling of the properties of light. Even some of the modes that do not use ray tracing are nevertheless often capable of producing very pleasing and realistic-looking images. Sculpt-Animate's "scanline snapshot" rendering mode, for instance, uses a technique that is commonly found in the 3D engines used in games and other interactive virtual environments of today, where ray tracing remains unsuitable due to its slow performance.

In addition to choosing a rendering method, Sculpt-Animate also allows the option of using virtually any of the Amiga's available resolution and bitplane-count combinations, including overscan modes. Of course, when rendering to a high-resolution screen, the artist loses the option of using HAM mode, thus making Sculpt-Animate's ray-tracing ability effectively useless; the available 16 colors simply are not enough to represent through ray tracing even a simple scene like the one we have created. Nevertheless, there are situations where an artist is willing to sacrifice ray tracing and HAM mode for a sharper, crisper, high-resolution image. For our project, we choose the 320 × 400 resolution, the highest nonoverscan resolution that allows us to use all 4,096 colors of HAM mode.

But there is still one more element to add to our project: animation. Sculpt-Animate is surprisingly flexible here, giving the user two completely different methods to choose from or—as is more likely for a real-world professional—the option to mix and match according to the demands of an individual project. Key frame animation is the conceptually simpler of these methods; here, the artist essentially creates two scenes by hand, using the methods already described, and then asks Sculpt-Animate to generate automatically an arbitrary number of in-between frames that transition the scene from the first to the second state. Animators often refer to this process as "tweening." The tweening process can be repeated as many times as necessary to create the final animation. For instance, we can create another scene by moving our orbiter one-fourth of the way around the pyramid using the triview, then ask Sculpt-Animate to extrapolate from these starting and ending points a seven-frame animation sequence. We can then repeat the process three more times, moving our orbiter farther and farther along its path until it eventually arrives back at its starting point on frame 28. We must create the animation in these four stages to ensure that Sculpt-Animate fully understands how to move the orbiter. If we create only the frame with the orbiter at the halfway point of its rotation, for example, Sculpt-Animate would choose the most direct path, running it straight *through* the pyramid. The key frame animation method is a perfectly valid approach to creating our animation. We, however, choose Sculpt-Animate's other animation method: global animation.

In global animation, we define the path our object will follow in the animation within the triview. We begin by adding a circle, this time a proper one built from 28 vertices and line segments. We place it so that it surrounds the central pyramid. Rather than serving as the basis for an eventual solid object, this circle defines the path that the orbiter will follow. We logically tie the circle to the orbiter, telling Sculpt-Animate that it should serve as the plan for a 28-frame animation—one frame for each vertex along its circumference. Finally, we render the whole as an IFF animation, with only the changes from one frame to the next recorded. The rendering is of course not a trivial process, consuming many hours of computing time on a 68000-based Amiga even for our rather trivial project. We must be thankful that Sculpt-Animate provides the option of previewing an animation relatively quickly using wire-frame graphics before we have to commit to the full rendering process.

We can set various options for the animation as a whole (figure 4.12). Most critical of these options for us is the duration for which each frame should be displayed. Duration is set in "jiffies," each of which corresponds on a North American Amiga to one-sixtieth of a second. Sculpt-Animate defaults to 2 jiffies, or 30 frames per second. We prefer a slower, more stately appearance for our orbit, however, so we set this value to 7 frames per second, which has the effect of slowing down the orbiter, albeit at the cost of some fluidity to its motion. We can, of course, achieve the same effect without losing fluidity by leaving the duration variable alone and instead adding many more frames to mark the path of our orbiter, but that animation would require roughly three and a half times as long to render. Amiga artists had to make such difficult trade-offs constantly.

Of course, we can do much, much more to make our simple animation more impressive and effective. We might, for instance, define a "tumble" for our orbiter using the triview to make it rotate in its orbit. But what we have done already should suffice to give a basic understanding of how an artist would interact with Sculpt-Animate to create works of vastly greater

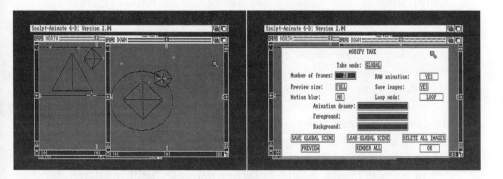

4.12 Adding animation to our Sculpt-Animate 4D project. The left screen shot shows the triview with the path for our orbiter to follow added. The right shows one of the "Modify Take" requestors that let us set many options for our animation, preview it, and, finally, render it to an IFF file.

scope, depth, and aesthetic appeal. It should also be remembered that Sculpt-Animate was by no means the only tool in the arsenal of most artists who used it, thanks largely to the portable IFF. For instance, an image or animation could and frequently was loaded into a raster-based paint and animation program such as DPaint for further additions and manipulations. Other tools could likewise be used to embed sound and music or even textual titling into a finished Sculpt-Animate animation. A typical creative project of any depth done on an Amiga would utilize many different tools of many different types.

There was a certain sense of adventure about 3D modeling, ray tracing, and animating on the Amiga, whether one chose to use a free command-line-driven program such as DKBTrace or a pricey commercial product such as Sculpt-Animate and its many successors. Having only rather limited preview functions, one never quite knew how one would be rewarded for one's work in putting together a scene and often could invest days or even weeks of computer time to a lengthy render that was ultimately unacceptable. An extreme level of dedication and Zen-like level of patience were required to create an animation that might last no more than a few seconds. When the results are viewed in this light, the quality and quantity of 3D images and animations created on the Amiga rather astonish.

Sculpt-Animate's Successors

The ultimate fate of the Sculpt-Animate line on the Amiga was anticlimactic for such a pioneering application. By 1989, color-graphics boards were available for the Macintosh that gave it display capabilities to rival the Amiga, albeit at vastly higher prices. The Macintosh software market was also less sensitive to price than that of the Amiga, which meant that Byte by Byte could sell its products for the former platform for much more money. Eager to enter what it perceived to be greener (and perhaps less competitive) pastures, the company therefore ported the program to the Macintosh, a process doubtlessly simplified by Graham's decision to keep the modeling interface and data scrupulously separate from the hardware used to display the finished product. Further development of Sculpt-Animate for Amiga was soon abandoned, although active development for the Macintosh continued under Graham's guidance until 1995.[33]

In a sense, though, Sculpt-Animate's defection hardly mattered, for by 1989 a large number of other 3D modelers and ray tracers had pushed through the door Graham had cracked open. And they just kept on coming for years in a bewildering blur of evocative names: Turbo Silver, Caligari,

Imagine, just to begin a list of the more usable and popular titles. Together they refined and expanded on the Sculpt-Animate template at a blistering pace, managing to make that program look almost quaint just a few years after its release. Hastings continued to build on the foundation he had laid with Videoscape 3D, sticking with the Amiga for many years after the Amiga version of Sculpt-Animate had been left an orphan. After a change in publishers from Aegis to NewTek, Videoscape begat LightWave 3D, perhaps the definitive Amiga 3D modeler and an application that remains (in its modern Windows and Macintosh incarnations) a beloved staple of the animation industry to this day.

All of these programs proved useful in a host of fields: video production and postproduction, multimedia presentations, game development, product prototyping, educational applications. And plenty of amateur artists used Amiga modelers just for fun, distributing their creations for free via the BBS network and perhaps, if their creations were really good, competing in something like the annual Badge Killer Demo contest that prompted some of the most impressive Amiga multimedia creations. As Steven Blaize noted in *AmigaWorld* in 1992, 3D was "everywhere" by the early 1990s,[34] and for a number of years the Amiga was the best overall platform on which to create it short of high-end, expensive workstations. Not only was Amiga 3D software often more mature than on other platforms due to the Amiga's head start in the field, but the Amiga had other, more subtle advantages. For instance, as discussed in detail in chapter 5, its unique video output made transferring creations to videotape almost effortless. And in light of the computational demands of the 3D-modeling process, the Amiga's multitasking capability was another boon; artists—in particular amateur artists without access to another computer—could let their creations render away in the background while they used the machine for other work or play.

Other platforms, however, eventually took the Amiga's leadership role away in this area as in others by steady, dogged improvement of their hardware and software. Autodesk's 3D Studio, for instance, as first published for MS-DOS-based machines in 1990, was a rather primitive, awkward program that seemed cause for little concern from the Amiga developers. By the time 3D Studio Max appeared in 1996, however, the program had improved immensely and was well on its way to becoming the game industry—dominating juggernaut it remains today. And yet for all its power, 3D Studio Max retains a surprising similarity to Sculpt-Animate, as is revealed by even a quick glance at the GUI of its latest incarnation; the familiar triview remains at its heart.

Of course, 3D is *still* everywhere today, even more so than in 1992. Most animated movies and television shows, including high-profile releases such as those from Pixar Studios, are modeled and animated completely in 3D, and even many nonanimated films, such as the *Lord of the Rings* trilogy, make extensive use of 3D graphics to augment their real-world footage. Interactive 3D environments have come to dominate many forms of computer gaming and are key to the creation of persistent online worlds such as *World of Warcraft* and *Second Life*. Indeed, most modern computers now come equipped with specialized display hardware designed just for rendering 3D graphics. Interactive 3D applications have historically used rasterization techniques rather than ray tracing for reasons of performance, but even that practice may be changing soon; as of this writing (2011), ever more powerful computers are at last bringing interactive ray tracing within the realm of practical possibility, and ray-traced games and virtual worlds may very well begin to appear soon.[35] To say that this 3D revolution would not have happened without the Amiga and Eric Graham would be overstating the case, but certainly both the platform's and the individual's contributions were immense in bringing 3D from the expensive, dedicated workstation to the practical, affordable, everyday PC.

With the arrival of the Amiga, many people saw an opportunity to pursue an individual vision that had heretofore eluded them due to technological constraints. Trip Hawkins of EA, for instance, realized that he could employ the machine to advance his company's artistic vision, to create at last aesthetically satisfying videogames worthy of refined appreciation, and Eric Graham realized that he now had access to technology that would let him tinker with 3D modeling and ray tracing in a practical rather than purely conceptual way. The principal figures behind NewTek, a company that would remain associated with the Amiga for some fifteen years and that would end up being the most important of all to the platform over the long term, have a similar story. The company's eventual vice president, Paul Montgomery, had been toying for years with video production prior to the Amiga's arrival but had been consistently dissatisfied with the tools available to those without access to a full-blown professional production studio.[1] He wanted to create video productions on a budget, perhaps even in the home, that did not *look* like amateur creations. Yet he remained stymied in his quest—until the arrival of the Amiga.[2] NewTek's founder and president Tim Jenison had also dabbled in film and video production for years and even at the height of the company's success would still consider himself something of a "frustrated filmmaker."[3] At the time of the Amiga's debut, Jenison was working for a company called "ColorWare," where he filled the roles of both hardware and software engineer in developing a variety of innovative products for the eight-bit Tandy TRS-80 Color Computer. Perhaps the most notable (and forward-looking) of these products was a very impressive MacPaint-like paint program called "CocoMax."

With the arrival of the Amiga, however, Jenison left ColorWare and the Color Computer behind quickly to begin NewTek as a one-man garage startup from his home in Topeka, Kansas.

PCs and the nascent music CD aside, the 1980s was still largely a decade of analog consumer electronics—in fact, the last such decade—marked by analog television and radio broadcasts, analog video and audio cassette tapes, and analog film-based cameras. To interface with such devices, a computer needs to be able not only to convert the analog into the digital for import into its memory, but also to convert the digital into the analog for export back into the wider world. And it also needs to be able to display (or, in the case of music, play) the digitized data it has collected from the analog world with sufficient fidelity to the originals to have been worth the effort of digitizing it in the first place.

For all the impressive statistics quoted in those early previews and reviews of the Amiga 1000, the two features that most excited Jenison and Montgomery were therefore not the ones that generally made the headlines. One of these features, HAM mode, has already found a prominent place in previous chapters and does so again in this one. The other—the machine's ability to output *interlaced* video suitable for use with standard video-production and broadcast equipment—is new to this chapter. Together, HAM and interlace were the keys to perhaps the most revolutionary of all the changes wrought by the Amiga. The visual world of the PC was suddenly not a limited, primitive, isolated one, but one that had access to the rich visuals found not only in real life, but also in other technological means of expression, such as photographs, film, and video.

Interlace

Two of the original Amiga's four standard resolution modes—those with a vertical count of 400 rather than 200 pixels—are interlaced modes. This design choice is one of the most significant on the Amiga, with both a negative and a tremendously positive impact on its history. As Oran J. Sands III wrote in a contemporary article on the subject, these modes were at the same time "one of the worst features ever offered on a computer" and "the best thing to happen to [the] computing world."[4] To understand these interlaced modes and all of their ramifications, we first must understand more about how a screen image gets from memory to the monitor.

Both conventional televisions and the CRT computer monitors that were universal during the Amiga's heyday operate on the same principles. The glass just behind the screen is coated with phosphors that can hold an electric charge for a very brief period, during which the phosphors glow, their brightness depending on the strength of the charge. An electron gun is mounted in the base of the television; this device sweeps across the screen from left to right and top to bottom many times per second, firing charged electrons at the phosphors to cause them to glow in a pattern dictated by the television or monitor's signal source, which might be a broadcast station, a computer, or something else. In a color display, the phosphors are actually of three different types, glowing either red, green, or blue, with each type responding to its own precisely aimed electron beam. These types are grouped closely together, so that when individually struck by electrons they seem to blend together to form single colors that vary with the relative charge of each phosphor.

The number of scan lines the electron gun draws in each of these cycles is a very important figure because it equates to the screen's vertical resolution. From the standpoint of picture quality, a higher vertical resolution is obviously better because it allows a sharper and more detailed image. Equally important is a screen's *refresh rate*, a measure of the number of complete screen cycles the electron gun makes in a single second. Each of these cycles is a single hertz (Hz); thus, a 60 Hz display is refreshed 60 times per second. Individual phosphors maintain their glow only very briefly before starting to fade, which can be perceived on a screen with a low refresh rate as a visible flicker. (However, this property of the phosphors is critical to the display of motion; if they held their charge too long, the result would be a visible streaking effect.) On a computer screen, with its requirement to display finely detailed, often textual images, a refresh rate of 60 Hz is generally considered an absolute minimum, and even this rate can introduce eye strain with prolonged viewing, particularly at higher resolutions; 75 Hz or even 85 Hz is more ideal.[5] Even at the time of the Amiga's introduction, computer monitors were often quite flexible in being able to lock onto quite a variety of vertical resolutions and refresh rates and operate correctly. Televisions and video equipment, however, were not so flexible, being bound tightly to the *National Television System Committee* (*NTSC*) format in North America and the *Phase Alternate Line* (*PAL*) format in Europe. I focus my discussion here on NTSC, but it should be noted that the PAL standard operates on the same fundamental principals; only the details of its implementation are different, although sufficiently so as to allow PAL in most situations to yield a somewhat better-quality image.[6]

The NTSC standard dates from the very dawn of television broadcasting, having been defined in 1941 by the US government and then revised in 1953 to accommodate color signals while remaining backward compatible with the original standard. Its designers wished to specify a

484-scan-line screen but soon encountered a problem in doing so. Early televisions needed an easy and inexpensive way to time their painting cycle and employed for this purpose the frequency of the alternating current that was their power source: 60 Hz. The primitive broadcasting and receiving equipment of the era, however, lacked the bandwidth to refresh fully a 425-line screen 60 times per second. The NTSC designers therefore chose to interlace the screen. Rather than painting the complete screen on each cycle, a technique known as *progressive scanning*, an NTSC television paints only every other line each time through. This alternate scanning allows a refresh rate of 60 Hz, albeit one that paints each line only 30 times per second, which during the early television era brought it within the available bandwidth of the available equipment. A certain amount of flicker inevitably results, but for television applications this does not present as much of an issue as it does for computer applications, for a number of reasons. First, viewers tend to sit much farther back from a television than from a computer monitor, and they do not focus so much on the details of the image there as the broader strokes; and no one reads large quantities of closely printed text from a television screen, as they often do from a computer monitor. And television screens almost constantly display images in motion, which tends to mask flicker, whereas computer monitors frequently contain relatively static displays. Finally, televisions mostly display photographic images made up of many, many colors, which blend into one another somewhat gradually. Computer screens, especially in the Amiga's era, display vastly fewer colors, with sharp contrasts between them; consider the contrast between the black characters and white background on a typical word-processing screen in comparison to the smooth blending of shades in a photograph or film frame. The computer screen's sharp contrasts tend to emphasize flicker, whereas the television screen's transitions smooth it away. For these reasons, computer designers have generally chosen to depart from the NTSC standard, outputting progressive-scan video rather than interlaced video at refresh rates of 60 Hz or greater for *every* line, with vertical resolutions that vary according to machine and screen mode. The Amiga's designers, though, were an exception.

As I researched this book, I often found myself asking questions regarding intentionality in relation to the Amiga's design: To what extent were Miner and his team aware of the uses to which users would put this or that unique attribute of their creation? These questions become especially important to ask in light of the habit that many Amiga fans have of almost deifying the design team, gifting them with nearly superhuman wisdom and vision. Visionary as they undoubtedly were, in reality their vision sometimes failed them. HAM mode, for instance, was, as described in chapter 3, almost a happy accident, an interesting hack that Miner inserted into the display hardware without having a firm justification in his mind for doing so and, indeed, that he later tried to remove. In the released machine, of course, HAM mode proved itself ideal for the display of digitized photographs as well as for the program-generated photorealism of ray-traced pictures, uses that never occurred to Miner. The situation with the Amiga's support of interlaced video is even more complicated.

In the Amiga's early design phase, when the platform was still envisioned primarily as a game console rather than as a full-fledged PC, Miner's team was faced with a dilemma. If the Amiga was to be a game console only, it absolutely had to be possible to connect it directly to a standard television rather than requiring an expensive, specialized monitor. Other computers that were designed to connect to a television, such as the Commodore 64, had a vertical resolution of about 200 lines. Miner and team wanted to allow Amiga programmers the possibility of doubling that figure—perhaps, in the minds of at least some of the designers, to make the Amiga more useful for applications beyond the playing of games. For better or for worse, the only way to create 400 lines of vertical resolution on a standard NTSC television with its limited bandwidth was to interlace the screen.[7]

That said, there was also more than practical expediency behind the decision. As Miner and team labored on the Lorraine throughout 1983, a new game was causing a sensation in the otherwise moribund world of the stand-up arcade machine: *Dragon's Lair*. Essentially a (minimally) interactive cartoon, *Dragon's Lair* operates entirely from a laser videodisc (the forerunner to the modern DVD), splicing together short animated sequences in response to the player's inputs. As a ludic experience, it is problematic at best: the player must memorize and execute a series of precisely timed inputs to advance through the linear plot, with failure at any point leading to one of many admittedly amusing death sequences; no other possibilities are allowed beyond this total-success or total-failure dichotomy. The game did, however, get the Amiga team thinking about the possibilities for mixing conventional computer-generated imagery with video. Although they were still thinking largely in terms of videogames and certainly never anticipated how far NewTek and others would eventually take the merger, they were on the right track.[8]

Indeed, the NTSC format became bound up with the most fundamental design choices made by Miner and team. Most notably, the custom chips' standard clock speed of 7.16 MHz is exactly twice the NTSC color-subcarrier frequency of 3.58 MHz;[9] this correspondence facilitated keeping Agnus and Denise synchronized with the demands of refreshing the screen on a timely basis. As the Amiga's design evolved and it was resituated as a PC rather than a game console, the ability to use a television in place of a monitor as the primary display device lessoned in importance. Nevertheless, the basic format of the video signal, if not the ports and cables that carried it, remained uniquely compatible with the NTSC standard and thus uniquely sympathetic among computers of the era to interfacing with televisions, VCRs, video cameras, and other everyday video hardware.

But this sympathy does not extend equally to all of the available resolutions. Two of the four standard modes, 320 × 200 and 640 × 200, are not interlaced; these modes operate on the progressive-scanning principle with a refresh rate of 60 Hz. In other words, only half as many scan lines are present as in a conventional television display, but each is refreshed 60 times per second; the result is a solid, flicker-free display suitable for text. (Although even a 60 Hz refresh rate is less than ideal for more recent, higher-resolution displays, it was acceptable for the relatively small monitors and low resolutions of the Amiga's time.) The interlaced resolutions of 320 × 400 and 640 × 400, meanwhile, conform perfectly to the NTSC standard, with NTSC's extra 84 vertical lines being used to form the border around the display.[10] The interlaced modes can show much more vertical detail—thus allowing, for instance, twice as many lines of text on screen in a word-processing application—but each line is refreshed only 30 times per second, as in a television display. These modes therefore share with television the same flicker problem, exasperated hundredfold by the Amiga's need to display detailed, high-contrast, static, textual images.

That flicker was certainly a constant bane to many Amiga users and probably eventually caused a fair number of purchasers or potential purchasers to look elsewhere. One solution to the problem—albeit a pricey one—was to purchase a high-persistence monitor whose pixels held their electrical charge and maintained their glow for a much longer time than a standard monitor of the time would, thus eliminating flicker. Although this solution was acceptable for applications involving relatively static displays, such as word processing, it was problematic in the extreme for animation, games, or anything else involving rapid screen updates, for the very high persistence that eliminated flicker led to ugly streaking and tearing effects in these situations. Another, better solution was to buy a "flicker fixer," a device that would intercept the video signal in transit to the monitor and convert it into a 60-Hz progressive-scan format before sending it on its way. Again, though, this solution required the purchase of the flicker fixer itself as well as a potentially more expensive monitor able to accept the altered video that the fixer put out.

Another less immediately visible but no less taxing annoyance also stemmed from the compromises the Amiga's designers had to make to support interlace: the machine's pixels are not square. Although one might expect a rectangle of, say, 10 pixels wide by 10 pixels high to appear as a square on the Amiga's monitor, this is not in fact the case. Further, the shape it *will* assume varies in conjunction with the exact resolution mode currently active: individual pixels are extremely horizontally elongated in 620 × 200 mode, mildly horizontally elongated in 320 × 200 and 640 × 400 modes, and vertically elongated in 320 × 400 mode.[11] The counterintuitive nature of this variation was a constant headache for Amiga artists and programmers alike.

But even without a high-persistence monitor, users willing to experiment with color and monitor settings could do a great deal to minimize the annoyance of flicker even in textual applications. The 320 × 400 mode is particularly useful for HAM because the smooth blending of colors required in this mode also hides the presence of flicker almost completely. Its extra 200 lines of vertical resolution being too tempting to pass up, this mode became by far the most popular for working with photographic images. The benefits and importance of interlace to the Amiga are enormous, for interlaced video was key to its dominance in the field of video production, a dominance that continued for a time even after Commodore's demise left the machine effectively an orphan. This dominance was enabled largely by an additional piece of hardware with which the Amiga is wonderfully suited to operate: the generator lock, or *genlock*.

Commodore introduced the first Amiga genlock in early 1987. This unassuming beige box *could* be used as a simple converter to interface between the Amiga's RGB display connection and the component video connections of most television and video equipment of the time. One could then simply use the television in place of a monitor, perhaps for playing games; the image quality for serious productivity or creativity applications was mediocre at best, though.[12] More interestingly, one could run the output through a VCR to record pictures, animations, or presentations created on the Amiga. Although this ability is certainly useful, the genlock got its name from yet other abilities. A *second* video source—whether it be a video camera, a VCR, a laser-disc player, or something else—can also be fed into the genlock. The two images are then synchronized—or locked—together and output as one to the receiving television or VCR, with the Amiga's screen image overlaid on the other input source. This combination is possible only because both the Amiga and the other video source share the interlaced NTSC format. (The genlock functions correctly only in the Amiga's interlaced resolution modes.) When the genlock is used in this way, the first color in the Amiga's current palette—color 0, generally used for the screen background as a whole—becomes transparent, revealing whatever lies beneath from the other video source. This capability opens up boundless possibilities for video production. One can now—to take a simple, common, and obvious example—create custom titling text using one of the many software packages available for this purpose and overlay it on one's personal video footage to surprisingly professional effect. It is even possible to mix the Amiga's sound as well as video with that of the other source. Because the custom chips run at exactly twice the NTSC color subcarrier frequency, when genlock is used, they can actually synchronize themselves to the external video timings provided by the genlock rather than relying on the Amiga's own internal clock, ensuring absolutely precise synchronization with the external video source.

In addition to making it relatively easy to output Amiga video to any standard NTSC device and to combine that video with input from another NTSC source, the Amiga's interlace support and its ability to synchronize itself to an external source also made it ideal, at least by the technological standards of its time, for importing, storing, editing, and displaying images captured from the real world by an NTSC video camera. This process was known as "digitizing," and it was here that NewTek first established its reputation.

Digi-View

A scant few months after the Amiga first appeared in stores in 1985, a handful of exciting images began to circulate in the platform's public-domain software-distribution channels. Like the Juggler, these images were not only stunning in their time, but also the first harbinger of a revolution to come, for they were full-color photographs reproduced on the Amiga's screen with a clarity easily the equal of many television broadcasts (figure 5.1).

Although the Juggler still remains impressive enough in its way even today, it is rather more difficult to convey adequately just how remarkable these images were in their time, a time when the idea of displaying photographs on a computer screen seemed almost the stuff of science fiction. Suffice to say, then, that what looks to us today like an innocuous gathering of random everyday images rather obviously culled from the pages of glossy mainstream magazines was a staggering sight at the time. They owed their existence to the Amiga's HAM mode as well as to a piece of

5.1 Sample images distributed by Tim Jenison to promote NewTek and its upcoming video digitizer. Created very early in 1986, these images represent the first quality color photographic reproductions ever seen on an everyday PC screen.

hardware invented by the creator of these images, Tim Jenison. This invention was not only the Amiga's first color digitizer, but also the first such device capable of importing color images from the outside world into an everyday PC of any stripe with truly satisfying results. When it arrived as a commercial product in late 1986, NewTek branded it "Digi-View."

I do not, of course, mean to imply that the very concept of the digitizer originated with NewTek. In 1957, a team of engineers led by Russell A. Kirsch at the National Bureau of Standards developed the first image digitizer, which consisted of "a rotating drum and a photomultiplier to sense reflections from a small image mounted on the drum."[13] From this device, the image data were sent to the Standards Electronic Automatic Computer (SEAC) to be stored in memory and displayed on an oscilloscope screen. The resulting image was hardly a perfect reproduction of its original containing as it did only one bitplane and thus reducing all colors to either black or white, but it was sufficient to produce recognizable analogs of at least some carefully chosen real-world images. From this beginning sprang a whole field of image-capture and image-processing research conducted on large computers at many institutions.

Like similar research into 3D graphics, this body of research found its way onto early PCs, but only slowly, constrained as those machines were by their limited memory, processing power, and display capabilities. By 1985, though, various consumer-grade digitizers were available for machines such as the Apple II and Commodore 64. These devices were remarkable for existing at all and could create black-and-white images that were recognizable and even attractive when their sources were carefully chosen and captured. The systems were, however, ultimately almost as limited as the system employed on the SEAC mainframe so many years earlier.[14] Although other digitizers capable of producing more pleasing results were available for machines such as the IBM PC, they "cheated" by replacing their hosts' primitive display hardware with their own self-contained display systems. This configuration made them not only very expensive, but, again, of very limited utility because their output could not be incorporated into or manipulated with other software on their hosts. Perhaps the most practical digitizer of the pre-Digi-View era was Koala's MacVision, which was both reasonably priced and took advantage of the Macintosh's relatively advanced display capabilities to produce images of quite acceptable quality. But it, like its host, was limited to black and white only.

Digi-View was not even the first digitizer for the Amiga. In the months before the Amiga's launch, Commodore worked closely with another small startup that called itself "A-Squared Systems" to develop the Live! digitizer,[15] which marked a major step forward for the contemporary state of the art in being able to digitize in color and, remarkably, in being able to capture real-time images "live" from a video camera or other video source. By contrast, even a relatively advanced digitizer such as MacVision required, depending on the quality mode selected, 6 to 22 seconds to complete an image scan,[16] meaning that it could be used only to capture still frames from video, existing pictures, or live images that contained absolutely no movement. It was an early prototype of Live! that Andy Warhol used to capture Debbie Harry's portrait at the Lincoln Center launch party described in chapter 3. In spite of A-Squared's huge head start on NewTek, however, Live! did not come to the market until much later. The original plan had been for Commodore itself to sell Live! but the product was trapped in a limbo stemming from the rollercoaster ride that was Commodore's month-to-month financial situation, endless management shakeups, and the accompanying changes in direction.[17] By the time A-Squared had disentangled itself from Commodore, launched the customary lawsuit for breach of contract,[18] and made other plans to distribute Live! the launch party was two years in the past, and Live! was no longer such a unique device in the burgeoning Amiga graphics market.

Business matters aside, Digi-View was quite different from Live! in its design and intent. Unlike digitizers such as Live! which were often called "frame grabbers" to reflect their emphasis on real-time video capture,

Digi-View was a slow-scan digitizer. Capturing images with Digi-View was a slow and somewhat laborious process more reminiscent of early daguerreotype photography than of the point-and-shoot capabilities of Digi-View's descendent, the modern digital camera.[19] In addition to an Amiga, the Digi-View hardware and software, and a black-and-white NTSC video camera (even for color digitizing, as I explain soon) , the serious Digi-View user also required a carefully designed studio space for her work, with properly positioned lighting. The Digi-View device itself would be almost unnoticeable in such a studio, being an unobtrusive box about the size of a pack of playing cards that hung from a port on the Amiga. Into this box was fed the signal from the video camera.

A video camera contains a lens that focuses light onto a grid of tiny diodes known as "photosites." Each photosite is struck by a unique portion of the light arriving through the lens, the brightness of which it translates into an internal electrical voltage, with more light resulting in a higher voltage. Another portion of the camera's circuitry incessantly scans the grid of photosites, left to right and top to bottom, outputting the results as series of voltage modulations to be captured and utilized by another NTSC-compatible device, such as a television screen, a VCR, or, in this case, a Digi-View. The signal is an analog signal, and NTSC is an analog standard in that it does not consist of a series of discrete points of data, each potentially representing a single pixel in the manner of an Amiga playfield, but rather of a continuous, undelineated stream of gradual variations. As just described, a single NTSC frame consists of 484 of these individual streams of analog data, sent interlaced at the rate of 242 streams per cycle over the course of two painting cycles. The lines are separated by a synchronization pulse that lets the receiver know where one ends and another begins. When the camera has completed a single frame, it starts again at the top to paint the next frame, working at a rate of 30 frames per second.

The Digi-View's job, then, is to translate this analog stream into a digital grid of pixels that the Amiga can process and display. It accomplishes this translation by sampling from this fire hose at a series of discrete points, piping the voltage captured at that instant through an ADC that operates in the same way as those described in chapter 2 in connection with sound sampling. Each of the sampled voltages represents a brightness level in one tiny area of the image source and thus becomes a number between 0 and 15, with 16 being the number of tonally neutral shades the Amiga is capable of displaying—0 being pure black, 15 being pure white, and the numbers in between being a series of graduated shades of gray. (In other words, if one insists that the red, green, and blue components of a given shade in the Amiga's RGB color system remain exactly equal, one is left with a choice of 16 shades.) These numbers are fed to the Amiga itself, where the Digi-View software combines them into a grid of pixels in memory—a playfield, ready to be output to the monitor or saved to disk. Through its ADC, Digi-View has thus translated the analog world into a digital form suitable for a digital computer such as the Amiga, although some of the richness of the analog original is inevitably lost due to the Amiga's limited screen resolution and color palette.

Digi-View has other sharp limitations, the most notable of which is its lack of speed. The video camera follows the NTSC standard in painting a complete representation of its source for Digi-View 30 times per second, but this rate is far, far faster than Amiga can process enough samples of those data to create an acceptable digital version. The Amiga thus must sip very judiciously indeed from the analog fire hose, taking in and converting only a very small portion of each successive paint. Specifically, it attempts to digitize just one column of each frame. Digi-View was most often used to digitize images for display in the Amiga's lower-resolution modes, which have a horizontal resolution of 320 pixels. Each line from the video camera must therefore be sampled 320 times, at exactly equidistant intervals, to form a single complete image. On the first frame received after the digitization process is begun, the Amiga samples only the first of these points for every line; on the second frame, it samples the second point, and so on, until a complete image of the whole has been captured after the 320th repetition. Because frames are sent to Digi-View at 30 per second, this entire process requires 10.67 seconds (320 total frames / 30 frames per second). Any movement at all by the source completely spoils the results because the Digi-View will then be capturing not a single scene, but portions of a multitude of slightly different scenes. The Digi-View photographer, like the daguerreotypist, is therefore limited in his choice of subject matter to already extant static images (such as those magazine clippings whose images created such an initial stir in 1986), inanimate objects, or living subjects who are able and willing to hold absolutely still throughout the process.

If the Digi-View user wishes to scan in color and thereby take advantage of HAM mode for true photorealism, as the vast majority did when Digi-View was introduced, the process becomes even more time consuming. The same black-and-white camera is used in a process as ingenious as it is low tech. Digi-View comes with a set of colored filters, one each for red, green, and blue. Using these filters, the user captures each section of the color spectrum separately. First, she places the red filter over the lens of her camera, which allows only red light to reach the photosites, creating an image containing only that part of the light spectrum. She digitizes this image in the normal manner, then repeats the process using the green and blue filters, leaving her with three grayscale images, each of which actually represents just a certain portion of the entire spectrum. Once these three images are safely stored in the Amiga's memory, the Digi-View software combines them into one full-color HAM display, using the first image as the source of the red component of each pixel, the second for the green component, and the third for the blue component. Of course, as in the HAM-mode applications described in previous chapters, occasional compromises must be made due to the very limited number of sharp color transitions allowed in HAM. However, because such transitions are actually quite uncommon in the real world of analog color, these compromises become an issue less often when working with photorealistic digitized images than they do when working with many other kinds of graphics. Perhaps more significantly, digitizing in color requires more than half a minute just for the digitizing process itself, plus the time used in swapping color filters. And again, the slightest movement in the scene or a significant change in the light falling on that scene or, for that matter, even a slight movement of the camera itself spells disaster for the resulting image.

Many of Digi-View's restrictions are the result of its being a "dumb" device, consisting of little more than the ADC itself. All of the computationally intense work of digitizing must be done by the Amiga. Later Amiga digitizers such as the Live! system that were capable of operating in real time or near real time were "smart" devices, capable of capturing an entire frame of data at once, storing it in their own internal memory, and then sending it to the Amiga at a manageable pace. These frame grabbers also had the significant advantage of being able, as their name would imply, to capture single full-color frames from a variety of video sources beyond a video camera, most notably from videotape. (Digi-View could actually capture from such devices as well, but only from a paused source and only in gray scale, the color filters obviously being unusable in such a scenario which provided no camera lens to cover.) Although often invaluable for the professional, such devices were also, of course, vastly more expensive than the simplistic little Digi-View. And in having to rush through the job of digitizing, they also often yielded results that were actually worse than the typical Digi-View image.

Digi-View, then, remained somewhat unique as an inexpensive digitizer for the everyday Amiga user. It retained its low price and focus on the everyday user, and the rewards it reaped were significant. Selling at a street price of less than $200, Digi-View remained the digitizer for the Amiga masses even as more advanced and expensive devices soon surpassed most of its capabilities. More than 100,000 units were eventually sold, a remarkable number considering the relatively modest sales totals of the Amiga platform itself and enough that in May 1994 NewTek could claim Digi-View to be "the best-selling image capture device, on any platform, in the history of computing."[20] Digi-View was inexpensive enough that many could afford to buy it simply to experiment with and to use casually just for fun. Amiga BBSs were soon inundated with digitized images as users shared their favorite creations, a forerunner of modern services such as Flickr. And in another harbinger of the future, many of these images were sexually explicit and, indeed, constituted perhaps the first widely distributed high-quality digital pornography.[21]

The first NewTek product to follow Digi-View was similarly affordably priced and made an ideal companion. At a time when a version of Deluxe Paint with support for HAM mode was still years away, NewTek's Digi-Paint allowed one to touch up and manipulate one's newly digitized HAM images without first converting them to fewer colors. Again, many of the resulting images were harbingers of today's world of Photoshopped visual mash-ups, a future when low-cost image-processing technology can make almost any photographic evidence suspect.

Desktop Video

HAM mode and interlace combined with digitizers and genlocks laid the groundwork for an Amiga-abetted revolution in video production. As discussed in chapter 3, the Amiga's support for overscan modes was another boon of almost equal importance, for overscan allowed the user to do away with the chunky border around the display and work with the entirety of the screen. Like many revolutions, however, this one took some time to get off the ground; it was 1987 before practical digitizers and genlocks were widely available and before Amiga users as well as the computer industry press at large began to understand the true potential of this combination of technology. When they did, though, they gave the technology a buzzword all its own: *desktop video*, a phrase deliberately evocative of the desktop-publishing phenomenon that had become the claim to fame of the Amiga's 68000-based rival, the Apple Macintosh. This term describes the use of a PC to aid in serious, potentially professional-quality video production and postproduction. Just as the Macintosh and laser printer could replace the traditional typesetter and printing press at a vastly reduced cost, so could the Amiga, accompanied by a genlock, possibly a digitizer, and some modest consumer-grade video equipment, replace professional video-production equipment costing tens or hundreds of thousands of dollars.

One could of course do visual arts on the Amiga with the intention of sharing one's work only within the Amiga hobbyist community, perhaps distributing it as demos or simple still images over the BBS network or via disk collections of public-domain software. If one was more ambitious as well as sufficiently skilled, one could also sell one's work to entertainment-software publishers to be incorporated into the games that thrived for several years on the Amiga in North America and for considerably longer in Europe. If one wished to reach beyond the relatively small community of Amiga users, though, one had to face the harsh realities of being a digital artist trapped in a still-analog world. One could attempt to capture one's work in print, but one would, as Paula Hible was quoted as saying in chapter 3, be left with a "thin sheet of shitty paper with a printout on it,"[22] a work of art deprived of the brilliant colors it possessed in its natural environment, the monitor screen, and deprived of even the potential for motion and sound, both as vital as still imagery to the Amiga's identity as the first multimedia computer. The only medium that might satisfactorily capture one's work from the monitor screen and enable others who had perhaps never even heard of the Amiga to appreciate it was video. Thus, a huge portion of Amiga-based creative work, including that done with paint and animation applications such as DPaint and 3D-modeling applications such as Sculpt-Animate, was ultimately widely distributed thanks to the technology described in this chapter. Having devoted considerable space in each of the previous two chapters to describing the experience of using the applications that were their main subjects in the abstract, I think it more appropriate here to focus on specific users who took advantage not only of the technology described in this chapter but also of pioneering applications such as DPaint and Sculpt-Animate to begin forging those connections between the computer and everyday life that have become so commonplace today.[23]

The simplest possible Amiga desktop video setup consisted of little more than an everyday Amiga system and some typical consumer electronics that virtually all Amiga users already had in their homes (figure 5.2). The Amiga 1000 came equipped with a built-in port that output a color-composite video signal of the sort used by most consumer video equipment of the era, although the quality of this signal was not considered ideal. The composite video port of later Amigas output only grayscale video, albeit in much better quality. If one was dissatisfied with these options, however, one could purchase a composite video encoder for less than $100. This simple device accepted a signal from the Amiga's standard

RGB-monitor output port and translated it to a composite video signal while also passing it on unmodified to the standard Amiga monitor. The composite signal is then fed into an everyday VCR for recording images and animations being played on the Amiga. This setup, which includes neither a genlock nor a digitizer, is quite limited; one cannot mix the Amiga's video output with other video, nor can one capture and make use of external imagery. And there is also no facility for adding sound to the video. Nevertheless, for many applications of the era discussed in this book it could be very useful even with all its limitations.

Daniel J. Barrett used a setup similar to figure 5.2 to teach introductory programming and computer science concepts to students at Johns Hopkins University in 1991.[24] Frustrated with the limited utility of the blackboard as a visual aid for demonstrating dynamic, evolving systems, Barrett took to creating simple animations on his Amiga, using general-purpose graphics packages such as DPaint and Aegis Animator as well as simple demonstration programs he coded himself and recording the results on videotape. He could then play back these snippets of video at appropriate points in his lectures, adding live explanatory narration as they played. The limitations of his approach were of course significant, but Barrett was already dreaming of the next step: "[A] problem is that video projectors are not interactive; I currently need to plan the entire video in advance, and narrate it as it is displayed. Instead, I would like to bring an Amiga directly into the classroom and connect it to a projection unit, giving me greater flexibility during the presentation."[25] Although Barrett's dream of bringing an Amiga into the classroom would have to go

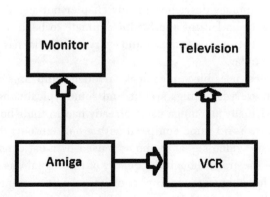

5.2 An extremely simple desktop video setup such as might have been used by Daniel J. Barrett for his classroom demonstration videos

unrealized (not least because a laptop version of the machine was never produced), connecting a computer to a projector for just this purpose is not only possible but commonplace today. Barrett's innovations thus presaged the ubiquitous multimedia PowerPoint presentations now found in so many classrooms and boardrooms.

Figure 5.3 illustrates a setup that is much more flexible and capable than Barrett's, if also considerably more expensive and complex. We now have a video camera with which we can shoot original footage in the real world. We can play this footage back on one of our two VCR's, routing it through a genlock that allows us to superimpose on it postproduction titling or other effects we have created on our Amiga; we record the resulting combined video on our second VCR. We can also use the genlock to add music or sound effects, for, just like video, audio from the Amiga can be routed through the genlock, which combines it with the audio from our real-world footage and sends it on to be recorded by the second VCR. And we now have a digitizer at our disposal, which allows us to capture imagery from the real world to be altered or manipulated on the Amiga, then sent on to videotape just like imagery that originated within the computer. Although a setup like this, particularly if one invested in truly professional-quality equipment, would not have been a trivial investment for most people, it would have cost but a tiny fraction of the cost of similar capabilities before the arrival of the Amiga. In fact, many started video-production businesses built around their Amigas, executing small-scale contracts for small businesses and civic organizations who could not possibly have afforded a traditional production. Amiga magazines of the day were filled with stories about and advice for beginning just such an endeavor.

One of those stories was Jane Baracskay's.[26] Having owned an IBM PC-centric independent computer-consulting business for several years, Baracskay hit upon the idea of producing a training video to help her clients with routine tasks and problems and ease her own telephone support burden. After receiving startlingly expensive price quotes from several traditional production companies, Baracskay began exploring the option of doing it herself using an Amiga. From this experience was born a new company, Kona-Kini Productions, which produced six complete videos in just its first year. Using a setup much like the one shown in figure 5.3., Kona-Kini specialized in promotional and instructional videos, mostly for small businesses located close to Baracskay's Brunswick Hills, Ohio, home: a fund solicitation tape for a private school, several instructional videos for a local builder, a motivational video for employees at the Akron/Canton branch of Merrill Lynch, and so on. Presaging the more

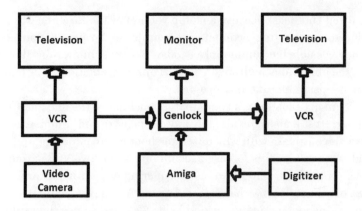

5.3 An intermediate-level desktop video setup such as might have been used by an ambitious amateur or a professional doing small-scale contract work

personal video culture of today, Kona-Kini also produced short video résumés for individuals. Such a production might begin with a short video interview of the subject, over which titling could be superimposed via the genlock, stating the individual's name, qualifications, and important points from the interview. (By the time Kona-Kini was formed in late 1988, titling had become such a common use for the Amiga that several specialized software packages competed with one another to perform that task alone, and many more would soon follow.) The interview might then fade into a scrolling list of the subject's accomplishments, with an attractive image representing the subject or her field as a background. This image might have been drawn from scratch using a program such as DPaint or digitized via Digi-View and perhaps modified via Digi-Paint or another image-manipulation program to suit the production. Kona-Kini still exists today and still does largely the same kind of low-cost productions for the same kind of clients, although the arrival of the digital age and the DVD of course means that the equipment it uses now is quite different.

Baracskay's story was inspiring but not hugely unusual. By 1989, Amigas were to be found everywhere in the field of low- and midrange video production. They labored anonymously, behind the scenes, but for those with knowledge of the platform, the Amigas' telltale technical fingerprints were in plain evidence almost everywhere, not least on television. Derek Grime described one late night's channel surfing: "I saw a furniture store's prices scroll by in twenty point diamond script. A realtor's houses for sale appeared to have been scanned in with Digi-View. A used car dealer's logo flipped around the screen, an effect that could only have come from Deluxe Paint III. The Amiga was everywhere."[27] Amiga-created animations were even shown on the Jumbotron during Super Bowl XXIII in Miami in January 1989.[28]

For all of the success of Kona-Kini and so many other small Amiga-based video-production companies, they still had to operate under constraints that kept the most ambitious of video productions, such as series produced for network television, inaccessible to them. Such productions in the late 1980s still required the services of specialized and expensive hardware as well as specialized and expensive technicians to operate it. And yet Amigas frequently found a home even in these environments. Here they were not the centerpiece of the production studio but rather served as a useful, inexpensive source of graphics and effects to be incorporated with other elements in the completed production (figure 5.4). Already in 1986 Amigas were used to create graphical effects on the television serial *Amazing Stories*,[29] but they found their most publicized early home the following year, on a show built around a short-lived but intense pop-culture phenomenon known as "Max Headroom" (figure 5.5).[30]

An odd, lumpy mixture informed equally by cyberpunk science fiction such as William Gibson's as by the vacuous Hollywood cult of celebrity, Max Headroom was a disembodied artificial intelligence from "20 minutes into the future" who lived in computer networks and communicated through a video screen. He first appeared as star of a one-off British television drama in early 1985. Stints as the host of music-video and celebrity talk shows followed, first in Great Britain and then in the United States, as did his most prominent exposure as an advertising spokesman for New Coke. In 1987, Max was given his own weekly primetime television series in the United States, which followed from the original British drama to

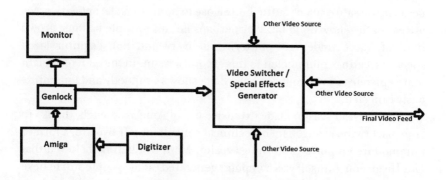

5.4 An Amiga integrated into a studio capable of doing professional television or film production

5.5 Max Headroom. The shifting lines behind him were quite likely generated by an Amiga.

chronicle the adventures of a team of investigative reporters living in a dystopian future. The show was a far cry from what one might have expected in light of the gimmicky character that provided its name, often presenting a surprisingly sophisticated and even brave satire of mass media while introducing for the first time to the mainstream television audience many ideas from the cyberpunk genre that had taken the world of written science fiction by storm with the publication of William Gibson's landmark *Neuromancer* just a few years earlier. A brief trial season of just six episodes in the spring of 1987 pulled ratings that were good enough to convince ABC to bring the show back as a regular in its fall lineup. However, perhaps because the American public was not prepared for such ideas, or perhaps because the satire struck sufficiently close to home to make network executives set the show up to fail,[31] or perhaps because people had just grown tired of Max's trademark stuttering delivery and non-sequitur-laced speeches, ratings plummeted in this second season. In the end, only eight more episodes were produced before the show was quietly and ignominiously canceled.

That second season made extensive use of Amigas, though, thanks in large part to the evangelism of technical consultant Jeff Bruette, a former Commodore employee and Amiga zealot. Many at the time believed that Max Headroom himself was computer generated (some people still believe it), but this was certainly not the case. Such sophisticated, realistic character animation was far beyond the capabilities of any computer of the mid-1980s, including the Amiga. Rather, Max was portrayed by actor Matt Frewer, wearing an elaborate, form-fitting latex mask sculpted and applied anew for each appearance by John Humphreys and a suit made from stiff, shiny fiberglass to convey the desired artificial look.[32] Yet it is very likely that the patterns of colored lines that always waved "behind" Max on the screen were generated on Amigas during that second season as a replacement for earlier non-computer-generated, hand-drawn animations.[33] This effect would have been accomplished using a common production trick known as *chroma-key compositing*, used then and still today to facilitate television news weather forecasts among many other functions. Frewer, dressed as Max, was filmed in front of a screen made from a single solid color, likely green in this case. This video feed was sent to a device known as a "video switcher" or "special-effects generator" (SEG), which was programmed to replace all green areas with video from another feed. (This means, of course, that Frewer himself could not have any green on his own person.) The alternate feed came from an Amiga and provided the shifting background pattern. The SEG also added other effects to the video and the audio, on occasion momentarily freezing the video or dropping a few frames to give Frewer's motions a jerking, artificial appearance and looping and distorting brief snippets of the audio while skipping over others to create Max's trademark stuttering speech patterns. Finally, the combined manipulated video and audio feed was sent on its ways to be recorded by a professional videotape recorder for later television broadcast.

The Amiga's close association with Max Headroom even today is perhaps somewhat undeserved because the Amiga was never more than an ancillary (if useful) tool for his creators. Amigas were in fact most usefully employed in other aspects of the show that bore Max's name, most of which centered on the living person whose memories and personalities provide the raw material for the Max construct, reporter Edison Carter. In keeping with the show's cyberpunk setting, much of the action takes place on in-world video and computer screens; Carter, for instance, always carries an elaborate "camera" with him on his investigative missions, which provide to his "controller" back at his television station's headquarters not only a constant video feed, but also current information on his health, his exact location, and environmental conditions around him, overlaid on and framing the actual video. And many plotlines revolve around hacking into networks or keeping hackers out. These sequences are accompanied by fancifully animated computer displays and equally fanciful, if meaningless, technobabble from the characters involved. It is well documented that virtually all of these graphics, a very significant portion of the show, were created on Amigas during that second season, using everyday software and genlocks. Producer Brian Frankish summed up the Amiga's contribution to his show: "They [Amigas] are a necessary function in communicating the concepts of our show. We are dealing with information, where it comes from, its sources and where it's going. That's what these graphics are about. With a computer, we don't need a keying video switcher because the computer has a built-in keying ability. The kid [Bruette] types in the stuff, the fellows hit the right keys, it goes together in the video trailer, it plays back on the stage, whoosh: it's that simple."[34]

In the wake of its prominent if short-lived usage on *Max Headroom*, the Amiga found a role in generating similar in-world computer graphics on quite a number of productions, including even substantial feature films such as *Robocop 2*.[35] Yet its capabilities, remarkable as they were, remained too limited for it to challenge dedicated professional SEGs and graphical workstations for a role at the heart of such productions. In 1990, however, another revolutionary product from NewTek changed that.

The Video Toaster

As Tim Jenison was creating and shipping the first copies of Digi-View from Topeka, Paul Montgomery, living in the heart of Silicon Valley, had already given up a real-estate business to devote himself entirely to his new passion, the Amiga.[36] Montgomery founded the first, largest, and most influential Amiga users group, the aptly named First Amiga Users Group, and got a job with EA working as a sort of liaison between that company and the Amiga creative community that used its Deluxe line of products. This role soon put him into contact with Jenison. Excited by Jenison's vision of NewTek and the Amiga's possible future and frustrated by EA's already waning commitment to the platform, Montgomery left EA to join with Jenison in 1987.[37] Together the two men formed a strong partnership not dissimilar to that of Steve Wozniak and Steve Jobs during the early years of Apple Computer. Jenison, like Wozniak, was a hardware hacker in the classic mode, turning out elegant, visionary designs, but he was also a quiet man, preferring to stay in his workshop and well away from the press and the trade-show circuit. Montgomery, meanwhile, was like Jobs, something of a born promoter, glib and articulate and never happier than when demonstrating an interesting new gadget for the technology press. Nor was he above using sex appeal to promote NewTek's products. Soon after his arrival, NewTek premiered a demo that featured "Maxine Headroom," in reality the company's attractive sales manager Laura Longfellow in costume, complete with Max's trademark stutter.[38]

Montgomery later hired a model, Kiki Stockhammer, to star in promotional videos and demonstrate NewTek's products at trade shows; she became a well-known celebrity and sex symbol among Amiga users.

With Jenison's technical acumen and Montgomery's business and promotional instincts, NewTek was poised to realize these men's dreams of changing the world of video production by bringing to the masses technologies that had previously been accessible only to those working on major productions. Montgomery, never short of enthusiasm or hyperbole, spoke of this project in revolutionary, utopian terms. The agent of that revolution would be a gadget that Montgomery first began whispering about almost immediately after his arrival at NewTek: the Video Toaster.

But revolutions, especially technology revolutions, take time. Thus, the Toaster failed to appear in 1987, 1988, or even 1989. Would-be users had to content themselves with a series of eager previews in the trade press, each of which seemed to describe a more ambitious product than the last and most of which ended by saying that the Toaster was at last just a few months from release.[39] The Video Toaster seemed a classic victim of feature creep and overoptimistic time scheduling, problems that small, engineering-driven companies such as NewTek are particularly prone to fall victim to. In the end, though, the Video Toaster story had a happier ending than many similar examples of "vaporware," for in December 1990 the Toaster shipped at last and promptly created a wave of excitement not just within the Amiga community, but also within the technology press— an excitement that had not been prompted by the Amiga since the platform's launch more than five years earlier. Even magazines dedicated to competing platforms that were not accustomed to giving coverage to the Amiga, such as *MacWorld* and *PC World*, could not ignore *this* development, and celebrities such as the comedy magic duo Penn and Teller as well as musician and video producer Todd Rundgren were soon singing the Toaster's praises in very public ways. And more mainstream media outlets also took serious notice; the *Washington Post*, *Business Week*, *USA Today*, *Time*, the *Los Angeles Times*, and *Rolling Stone*, among many others, gave the Toaster generous coverage. NewTek and the Toaster were the subject of a three-minute story on NBC's *Nightly News* on June 10, 1992. The piece played like a preview of the many stories that would start appearing on this and similar programs in droves a few years later with the beginning of the Internet bubble, focusing on the "work hard/play hard" corporate culture espoused by Jenison and Montgomery and opening with the vaguely bemused, vaguely condescending title "Revenge of the Nerds." Near its end, Jenison plainly stated NewTek's vision for the Toaster: "What we are trying to do is to make it possible for ordinary Americans to make network-quality television." Indeed, most of NewTek's promotional efforts of this period had exactly this ring of idealistic, populist evangelism, a tone that sometimes clashed with the *other* side of NewTek's corporate personality—the diehard, dog-eat-dog capitalist with a fondness for Ayn Rand's objectivist philosophy.[40]

The Video Toaster was equal to the hype; it very nearly was a complete video-production studio on a card, just as NewTek claimed in that *Nightly News* segment. It was such a complex, ambitious device that it can be difficult to describe quickly or succinctly when one moves away from such abstracts. When it was introduced, there was an undercurrent of confusion to much of the coverage both inside and outside the Amiga-focused press, a certain note of "yes, OK, it's revolutionary—but what exactly is it?" First and most fundamentally, the Toaster was a replacement display board that bypasses the Amiga's normal display hardware in favor of the hardware built into the Toaster itself, allowing true 24-bit color, meaning up to 16.8 million colors on screen at once. Because it replaced a stock Amiga's display hardware so completely, the Video Toaster could not utilize the rich library of graphics applications the Amiga had accrued by 1990. NewTek's solution to this dilemma was simply to write its own applications and to include them with the Toaster. Most notable of these applications was Toaster Paint, the next logical evolution of Digi-Paint supporting full 24-bit pictures, and LightWave 3D, a very impressive 3D-modeling and animation package designed by Allen Hastings, author of the earlier Videoscape 3D. Although NewTek never promoted the Toaster for such purposes, a user could use this hardware and software combination as a standalone graphics workstation. However, the Toaster's real purpose becomes clear when we consider how a user could mix these computer-generated graphics with video from the real world. The Toaster could in fact accept as many as four incoming video feeds, to be manipulated and combined with one another or with computer graphics live, in real time. In the process, the Toaster user could apply a wealth of effects to them—some striking, but many others quite subtle—that had previously been unavailable to low-cost video producers. The presence or absence of such effects had previously marked the boundary between the low-cost video-production work that the Amiga had commonly been used for previously and the work of better-funded and equipped professionals working out of "proper" studios. With the arrival of the Toaster, that gap was erased.

For instance, consider transitions, or cuts, from one scene or feed to another. Professional productions such as those typically seen on television generally accomplish such cuts through a variety of wipes and fades that make them less jarring. Desktop video productions, meanwhile, had previously been marked by "hard" cuts that (perhaps subconsciously) marked them out in the viewer's mind as low-cost or even amateur productions. For the first time with the Toaster, desktop video producers had access to the same transition effects produced by a full professional-quality switcher found in a network news or sports studio. Some of these effects were quite striking; a scene might "shatter" to reveal the new scene behind it or shrink, spin, and finally fly off the screen. Many such effects were impressive enough to be included in video not as a transition aid, but as a special effect in their own right. The Toaster's "Chroma F/X" module likewise allowed the user to manipulate the colors in a scene, giving it a blue or red cast to suit the mood of the production. Owing to such possibilities, the Video Toaster lent itself particularly well to a certain type of slick, high-technology promotional video that NewTek, under Montgomery's guidance, was unsurprisingly very adept at making in order to market the Toaster. Various feeds could also be combined together in various ways, with graphics created in LightWave or Toaster Paint and titles created with the Toaster's bundled titling software superimposed over the whole. The advance that the Toaster represented over previous Amiga desktop video software and hardware was remarkable indeed; Max Headroom, impossible to realize without the aid of a specialized SEG a few years earlier, would have been fairly trivial to re-create with a Toaster-equipped Amiga and its suite of effects.[41]

NewTek's own populist rhetoric aside, Toasters probably ended up more often in already extant professional production environments than they did in the hands of hobbyists. For all the cost saving and newfound convenience the Toaster represented, making full use of it did require some fairly expensive equipment that was not commonly found even in small production businesses such as Kona-Kini. For example, keeping in synchronization multiple video sources to send to the Toaster required the use of external *time-base correctors* (*TBCs*) that could cost more than the Toaster itself. The Toaster's effect on bigger-budget productions was, however, much more dramatic as Toaster-equipped Amigas quickly began to appear in roles that the Amiga alone had previously been unable to crack. Unsurprisingly in light of NewTek's claim that it represented a television studio on a card, many Toaster-equipped Amigas found homes in the television broadcast studios of network affiliates and cable providers across the country. They were a particular godsend to less-prosperous stations serving smaller markets, which could use them to produce slick effects that their limited budgets had not previously allowed. But television stations were only one segment of Toaster users; the device had an impact in many more areas. For example, Toasters found a niche driving the large video displays found in professional sports stadiums such as Joe Robbie Stadium, home of the Florida Marlins baseball team;[42] here their ability to manipulate video on the fly and generate effects in real time made them ideal for tracking scores and keeping the crowd engaged over the course of an unpredictable ballgame. And as NewTek refined the Toaster's hardware and software to address complaints and add frequently requested features, the Toaster gradually went Hollywood, taking a place at the vanguard of another revolution, this one in the way special effects were produced.

The pilot episode of *Babylon 5*, a science-fiction television series soon to become very familiar to Amiga and Toaster enthusiasts, premiered on February 22, 1993. The show took place mostly aboard a huge space station, the eponymous Babylon 5, and thus demanded many special-effects shots of the station's exterior as well as of other spacecraft traveling, docking, or occasionally doing battle with either the station or one another. Such scenes had traditionally been created by filming meticulously crafted and painted model miniatures, adding in postproduction only relatively simple effects to simulate laser bursts, explosions, or the glow of spacecraft engines. The producers of *Babylon 5* parted with tradition in hiring the small company Foundation Imaging to create the show's space-borne sequences using a suite of Toaster-equipped Amigas. Such a use of *computer graphics imaging (CGI)* in film was not precisely new; major Hollywood productions such as *Tron* and *The Last Starfighter* had previously made use of such techniques. As Foundation's visual effects director Ron Thornton pointed out, though, *The Last Starfighter*'s CGI effects had required a $15 million Cray X-MP supercomputer. Foundation, less than a decade later, was able to produce equally impressive effects using a rendering farm of twelve Toaster-equipped Amigas running LightWave 3D.[43] The entire visual effects budget for *Babylon 5*'s pilot episode was $250,000; Thornton estimated that figure to be about one-fourth the cost of an episode of *Star Trek: The Next Generation*, another space-based show of the same era produced using traditional models.[44] The savings in time and added flexibility to make changes on little notice were equally impressive. Small wonder that the American Amiga community, by this time with little good news to read, talk, or write about outside the realm of video production, greeted *Babylon 5* with such excitement. Those beautifully animated 3D sequences represented not only a vindication of NewTek's years of labor on the Toaster, but also the fruition of the platform's multimedia potential and especially of its 3D-rendering history, the culmination of a journey that had begun some seven years earlier, when Eric Graham began experimenting with the technique on his unexpanded Amiga 1000 in what already in 1993 seemed like a more primitive world (figure 5.6). For Hastings, who had been at the forefront of developments in Amiga-based 3D graphics almost from the moment he bought his Amiga 1000 in November 1985,[45] the moment must have been particularly sweet.

And *Babylon 5* was certainly not the only prominent production to make use of Amigas in this era. Another science-fiction show that premiered that year, *seaQuest DSV*, follows the exploits of a submarine in a dystopian future where environmental devastation has forced humankind to move almost entirely underworld; the show plays like "a combination of *Star Trek* and *The Hunt for Red October*."[46] The *seaQuest* itself, the submarine at the heart of the show, was created and rendered entirely with Light-Wave 3D, as was much of the rest of the underwater environment. Yet another show of the era, *Quantum Leap*, used the Toaster's suite of effects to create two magical characters who continually morph "from old to young, and male to female" right before the viewer's eyes.[47] Nor were Amigas restricted to television productions; for instance, the admittedly B-grade horror fantasy *Warlock: The Armageddon* used Amigas for many of its special effects.[48] More impressively, at least a few effects sequences in the 1993 summer blockbuster *Jurassic Park* were rendered with LightWave 3D.[49] It was a spectacular year for NewTek, a year of widespread acceptance of the Toaster throughout the Hollywood ecosystem, of more fawning

5.6 An in-space scene from the pilot episode of *Babylon 5*, generated entirely in LightWave 3D running on Video Toaster–equipped Amigas

mainstream media profiles, and even of an Emmy Award in the engineering category for "developing computer technology that has brought many editing tools out of high-priced editing suites, and made them available on desktops of the television creative community."[50] That same year, Foundation Imaging received its own Emmy for its visual-effects work on the *Babylon 5* pilot. This was exactly the sort of mainstream coverage and acceptance the Amiga community had thought would come back in 1985 and had continued to dream of in the years since.

How unfortunate, then, that neither the Amiga nor Commodore were often mentioned in discussions of the Toaster outside of the core Amiga community. Although some might consider it ungrateful, NewTek seems to have made a conscious effort after 1990 to distance itself from the platform that formed both its own heritage and the Toaster's host. From the beginning of the Toaster era, NewTek's promotional materials never mentioned the Amiga or showed the logos on the host machines, preferring to cast the Toaster as a standalone turnkey solution not tied to any existing computing platform. NewTek even encouraged its dealers to sell the Toaster and its host as a single package under the NewTek banner, making no mention of the Amiga's history and capabilities as a standalone PC. In support of this decision, NewTek might argue with some justification that a Toaster-equipped Amiga really owed much more to NewTek than it did to Commodore. Although NewTek did continue to take advantage of some unique aspects of the host platform, such as its internal timings that made it so easy to synchronize to NTSC video, the Toaster largely bypassed both the host's unique custom-chip-driven display architecture and AmigaOS, the twin pillars that really defined the Amiga as a platform. In fact, the Toaster was every bit as complicated a piece of hardware—and a much more modern one—as the Amiga itself. Jenison and his small team at NewTek actually spent more time developing the Toaster and bringing it to market than Jay Miner and his team did in realizing the original Amiga, and NewTek certainly did a better job supporting and updating the Toaster than Commodore ever did with the Amiga. The Toaster arguably owed a greater debt to the vibrant Amiga community from which it sprang, with its new ways of thinking about the potential of multimedia computing, than to the now aging hardware that still formed its host.

The vision and spirit of possibility that always surrounded the Amiga even in its declining years were, however, by no means inconsequential to NewTek's own corporate history. Montgomery said in 1994, "The best way to describe the Amiga market is that things you're just hearing about on the PC and saw a year or so ago on the Macintosh, we were talking about in 1986. Being from the Amiga market is like being from the future. We've gone through it all. We read *MacWeek* or *PC Computing* and say 'Ha, ha, ha aren't those companies cute. Look, they're thinking what we thought. Boy, they're in for a surprise.'"[51] The Video Toaster was the very embodiment of the Amiga approach to computing in the abstract, but it had increasingly little to do with Jay Miner's specific implementation of that approach. One can also speculate that NewTek, a creative, savvy, healthy company, wanted to tie its future as little as possible to Commodore, a company that was none of these things. Certainly by 1993, the NewTek–Commodore connection was an ironic one indeed, with the former experiencing its breakout year just as the latter plunged into its death spiral. As a further illustration of the two companies' relative positions by this stage, there was some brief speculation that NewTek, for all its success still a relatively small company serving a fairly specialized market, might actually purchase the Amiga rights and intellectual property from Commodore, once one of the largest general-purpose PC manufacturers in the world, strictly to ensure that the Toaster would continue to have a viable host platform.[52]

NewTek did not buy Commodore, but it did manage to survive and flourish after the end of the Commodore era. Already in 1993 it introduced its first non-Amiga-based product: the Screamer, which allowed one to offload 3D rendering from the Amiga's aging CPU to a Windows NT–based machine equipped with a much more powerful Intel 486 or Pentium processor. The writing was clearly on the wall—and, indeed, NewTek gradually weaned itself from the increasingly aged and scarce Amiga hardware in the following years, porting its products to the PC and finally dropping the last vestiges of Amiga support starting in the new millennium. Amigas, some equipped with Toasters and some not, continued to be commonly used in television and video-production studios until then and well beyond. I am aware of at least one Video Toaster–equipped Amiga in active, daily use as a broadcast-title generator in a cable television studio in 2006, some 13 years after its initial acquisition by the station,[53] and it is very possible that some remain in use even today in similar legacy roles.

Be that as it may, Amigas are certainly no longer in the front lines of Hollywood productions, as they suddenly, amazingly were for at least a short time. Foundation Imaging, for instance, in need of more computing horsepower than their aging and now unsupported Amigas could provide, made the decision to switch its *Babylon 5* work to Windows-based machines in the summer of 1995, when NewTek introduced a version of LightWave 3D for that platform.[54] Many other providers of such high-end effects work were making similar decisions around the same time.

From today's perspective, we can place the productions of that land-mark year 1993 in their proper historical context as being at the vanguard of nothing less than a revolution in the way special effects are created. Within a few years, the handcrafted models that had been used to create the special effects in such beloved and acclaimed films as *2001: A Space Odyssey*, *Star Wars*, and *Blade Runner* became hopelessly passé. Today even the most casual filmgoer knows the abbreviation CGI, and some entire films, such as *Sky Captain and the World of Tomorrow* and *Sin City*, make virtually no use of traditional sets of any sort, instead placing their actors in elaborate digital environments that have no existence outside of a com-puter's memory. Many of these productions continue to rely on LightWave 3D, now running on modern Windows and Macintosh machines. This popular program, which of course has its roots in Videoscape 3D, one of the first two proper 3D-modeling systems ever to appear on a PC, remains one of the most obvious modern legacies of the Amiga and its innovations.

In early 1994, just a year after their most dramatic success, Paul Mont-gomery and several senior engineers suddenly left NewTek. The split was apparently due to a dispute with Jenison over corporate direction,[55] although to my knowledge no further details have ever surfaced. Mont-gomery took with him a certain amount of NewTek's shiny, revolutionary aura, but the company has remained a healthy concern to today. It is now a stable, mature company serving an existing market; the capabilities it offers that were once so revolutionary are now considered normal. Although it remains under Jenison's careful guidance, its populist rhetoric has also been dampened somewhat, perhaps inevitably for a company whose products have been so embraced by the very big production com-panies it once urged its customers to challenge. Nevertheless, NewTek, now an established quantity inside and outside of Hollywood, with a rack of Emmy and Oscar awards, is the greatest survivor of an Amiga market that did not produce very many such financial happy endings to go along with its innovations.

Whither Desktop Video?

Like a similar buzzword of the Amiga era, *desktop publishing*, the term *desktop video* has largely ceased to be a useful signifier today—not because either faded away, but because the technology they described has become so commonplace. The term *desktop publishing* described document-cre-ation capabilities worthy of a professional publication, including the ability to mix many types, styles, and sizes of fonts, the ability to include images, and the ability to flow text around said images or form it into columns. It further implied that all of these features should be presented to the user through an easy-to-understand, "what you see is what you get" interface, meaning that the representation of the document on her computer screen should correspond as closely as possible with that document in its final printed form. All were radically advanced, revolutionary features when they appeared on the Macintosh in the mid-1980s; today, of course, they are commonplace and are included (along with many even more sophisticated tools) in every serious word processor. The divide between the desktop-publishing application and the word-processing application has effectively disappeared. PCs today are likewise involved in every phase of the production process of not only low-budget video productions, but also the most elaborate of Hollywood films. This combination of the computer and film and video has become so commonplace, so much the accepted way of doing so many aspects of production and postproduction, that it no longer requires a unique signifier to set it apart from the noncomputerized methods that are now hopelessly obsolete.

Because the Amiga, like all PCs of its era, lacked the memory and disk capacity to store large amounts of video and the processing power to play it back with adequate fidelity and speed, its unique suitability for video hinged only partially on its exceptional graphics capabilities for its era. Even more important was its unique ability to interface with the established world of analog video production through devices such as digitizers, genlocks, and (eventually) the Video Toaster. Today, the world of video production itself has gone digital, rendering such abilities—and even NewTek's dream of a Video Toaster in every would-be filmmaker's living room—moot. An amateur video producer of today likely records her footage on a digital video camera with its own internal hard drive measuring in the tens or hundreds of gigabytes, then transfers her footage to her computer for editing and postproduction using a nonlinear editing software package such as Final Cut Pro. For someone who is used to working with such a clean, powerful system, the Rube Goldbergesque desktop video setups diagrammed earlier in this chapter must look painful indeed. Even the interlaced NTSC standard to which the Amiga had to conform is now largely a thing of the past, having been phased out of television transmission in the United States in favor of digital signals in 2009. The electronic world of today is an almost completely digital one.

The Amiga provided a bridge from there to here, though—from an era when video production was accessible only to the professional or the wealthy to our age of podcasts and YouTube, an age when a group of sufficiently dedicated amateurs can make a credible movie. The Amiga did so not only by interfacing so easily with the video equipment of its time, but also by providing a home for software such as DPaint, Sculpt-Animate, and so many others that gave artists the ability to create something worthwhile to put down on tape. This democratization of the means of cultural production is perhaps the most inspiring aspect of the technological developments of the past quarter-century and is certainly, at least in my opinion, the Amiga's most exciting and lasting legacy.

Up to this point, I have focused my attention on the Amiga's unique hard-ware design, in particular its revolutionary graphical capabilities. But a user's experience of a platform is dictated not only by that platform's hard-ware design, but also by its most fundamental enabling software: its OS. In fact, in the years since the Amiga's introduction, a computer's OS has steadily grown in importance in relation to its hardware design. For all the attention given to Apple's stylish external designs, the real appeal of the modern Macintosh for most users lies with its attractive and intuitive OS X; likewise, both Microsoft's corporate, proprietary OSs and open-source, community-developed OSs such as Linux run on the same commodity hardware in spite of their radically different design philosophies, distri-bution models, and user experiences. This general trend holds true also for the Amiga. Years after the machine's once remarkable multimedia capabilities were surpassed and its unique, tightly coupled hardware design became more a burden than an advantage, users clung to the Amiga for its elegant OS.[1] AmigaOS is certainly the main remaining appeal of the Amiga for those stalwarts who continue to do their everyday computing with the platform. The latest major revision, version 4.0 released in 2004 by Hyperion Entertainment, contains no support at all for the classic Amiga chip set and is instead designed to run on modern PowerPC-based hardware. And at least two other, newer OSs, known as AROS (for "Amiga Research Operating System") and MorphOS, are essentially clones of the original AmigaOS design that run on modern hardware. Even at the time of its launch in 1985, the Amiga's OS assumed unusual importance in comparison to most machines of its day. The Amiga 1000's ability to multitask, perhaps its most widely trumpeted feature aside from its graphical capabilities, is a direct result not of the machine's hardware, but of its OS design.

I have already occasionally tried in these pages to offer a more sober corrective to a certain idealized narrative of the Amiga's development that has become the dominant one in many circles. An incredible collection of talent congregated at Amiga, Incorporated, and there was an unusual amount of camaraderie and dedication that swirled around them. That said, it is also worth remembering that Amiga, Incorporated was in the end a business enterprise that aimed to deliver the next big game machine or home computer or both and, it was hoped, to profit greatly from the enterprise; it was not a project for a utopian tomorrow. Nor was the Amiga creators' vision of the final product quite as unified and complete as is often portrayed. Jay Miner, still spoken of in worshipful terms by Amiga zealots, was indeed a magnificent, creative engineer, but he did not provide the sort of holistic vision that one might expect from someone called the "father of the Amiga" or that, say, Steve Jobs did for the team that developed the original Macintosh. Miner was very much a hardware engineer; when asked to discuss the software side of the platform in later years, he sounded somewhat out of his depth and made a telling habit of referring to the "software guys" from time to time when discussing AmigaOS or the early demos, as if to people engaged in another field of endeavor entirely. In the words of Miner's close colleague Joe Decuir, who worked with him not only on the Amiga, but on the Atari VCS, 400, and 800: "We learned with the [Atari] 2600 that we could not foresee the creativity of the rest of the community. We deliberately designed the hardware as a platform for other smart people."[2] It should be noted that Miner never sought the adulation that was showered upon him—indeed, he always seemed to find it rather bemusing—and was always quick to grant others credit for their contributions to the Amiga. The vision behind AmigaOS's multitasking capability, for instance, he attributed entirely to some of those "smart people" for whom he had designed the hardware, in particular software team head Bob Pariseau.[3] (Most other accounts make multitasking the vision of Carl Sassenrath; Miner was perhaps not involved enough with the software team to know this.)

Although the Amiga's hardware design was very much the creation of Miner, Decuir, and a third engineer, Ron Nicholson, the history of the creation of the software presents a more complex picture. There is no "father of AmigaOS" in the sense that Miner can be considered the father of the hardware design, for what emerged from the freedom that Miner granted to his charges was not so much a unified team working on a single grand vision as several brilliant individuals pursuing their own most cherished computing dreams. The spirit of individuality that marked AmigaOS's development comes through in R. J. Mical's descriptions of those times: "We were trying to find people that had fire, that had spirit, that had a dream they were trying to accomplish. Carl Sassenrath, the guy who did the Exec for the machine . . . it was his lifelong dream to do a multitasking operating system that would be a work of art, that would be a thing of beauty. Dale Luck, the guy who did the graphics [library] . . . this was his undying dream since he was in college, to do this incredible graphics stuff."[4] Some frustration with this team of individualists and dreamers, so empowered and perhaps also sometimes infected with the arrogance of youth, does creep through from time to time in other perspectives of the period. Tim King, in charge of an outside development house who provided one component of AmigaOS, said of Mical that he "was/is a larger-than-life character who did Intuition 'his way' and it didn't follow the 'official' Amiga guidelines; for example intuiton.h was huge, and the guidelines said to keep header files small and to the point."[5] Some of the ideas that went into AmigaOS do tend to pull against one another somewhat or to pull against Miner's hardware design. Although not necessarily offering a repeatable model for development, the team nevertheless did create a remarkable OS, indeed, the first to run on an everyday PC that the more sophisticated world of institutional computing would have considered worthy of the name. That this gestalt incorporated so many voices so successfully is a tribute to Miner's low-key trust in his young colleagues and, of course, to the excellence of these colleagues themselves.

As of this writing (2011), AmigaOS has gone through three major rewrites and many smaller revisions and continues to be updated at least semiregularly. However, its general structure has remained consistent through the years. We can therefore often talk about AmigaOS in broad strokes in a non-version-specific way. Where I must deal in specifics, I bias my discussion toward the more historically important (if less capable) earlier versions of AmigaOS.

AmigaOS in Context

Computer scientist Brian L. Stuart uses what he calls the "Triangle of Ones" to describe the earliest computer systems: one user running one program at a time on one machine. In this early era, all programming was what programmers today refer to as *bare-metal programming*, meaning that programs operated by directly manipulating the hardware of the computer itself, with no intervening layer of software—in other words, with no OS.

The earliest true computer to go into operation in the United States, the Electronic Numeric Integrator and Computer (ENIAC, 1945) could originally be programmed only by physically rewiring the machine's circuitry, although later revisions made it possible to enter programs by means of a simple switch panel. In either case, these early programs were noninteractive, meaning they could be entered into memory and set to work on a given batch of data, but they could not be controlled by the programmer after that point; she could only wait until they completed and examine the resulting output.

But both then and now many programs must carry out very similar tasks in the course of their operation, and recoding these tasks again and again for every problem to be solved was both tedious and inefficient. Early computer scientists therefore soon began developing shared *libraries* of code to perform these tasks, which could be stored and called by programs when needed. For instance, if many programs needed to produce printed output, the series of steps required to do so could be encapsulated within a library, allowing a whole sequence of characters to be sent there with just a single call to the library in question. These libraries were the first step toward OSs as we know them today.

It can be argued that the first true OSs arrived in the mid-1950s with the advent of *batch-processing* systems. Because computers in this era were still rare and expensive, it was important to use them as efficiently as possible. Batch-processing systems allowed programmers to punch their programs onto cards using a separate, less expensive piece of equipment rather than having to waste time programming the computer directly. These programs could then be queued onto card readers attached to the computer itself, whose simple OS was programmed to run them quickly, one right after another, in sequence, thus maximizing the computer's precious operating time and allowing many more programmers to share it. Batch processing did not really break the Triangle of Ones, however, because the computer continued to run just one program at a time and to do so noninteractively. Computing in this era was a very different experience from today, more akin to operating a mechanical than a digital device.

The widespread arrival of *terminals* consisting of CRT screens and keyboards in the early 1960s finally made computing an interactive experience. At last, programs could be written that could respond to user commands as they were running. And yet the problem of scarce computing resources still remained. In response, a new generation of more sophisticated OSs were written that allowed more than one user to share a computer through separate terminals attached to the same machine. This greater sophistication also demanded that the computer be capable of running more than one program at the same time because each connecting user would presumably be working on his or her own project. Thus, this new generation of *time-sharing*, multitasking OSs shattered two legs of the Triangle of Ones simultaneously: multiple users were now running multiple programs on one machine and doing so interactively. The modern computing paradigm was born. Over the ensuing years, research institutions such as MIT as well as business interests developed many time-sharing OSs of increasing sophistication. By far the most historically and technically significant of these OSs was Unix, developed at AT&T's Bell Labs in the late 1960s. The team behind Unix incorporated many of the best ideas from the OSs that had proceeded Unix to create a flexible and expandable OS that was adopted by an entire generation of hackers.[6] Unix still runs on countless institutional computers today, and Linux, an open-source clone of sorts developed for PCs, runs on many servers, desktop computers, and electronic appliances in use today. Linux, though, dates back even in its earliest, most underdeveloped form only to 1991. At the time that Jay Miner and team were developing the Amiga in the early 1980s, nothing approaching the sophistication of Unix was available for a PC.

OSs are complex subjects worthy of years or a lifetime of study. We might, however, collapse their complexities down to a few fundamental functions: to provide an interface for the user to work with the computer and manage her programs and files; to manage the various tasks running on the computer and allocate resources among them; and to act as a buffer or interface between *application software* and the underlying hardware of the computer. Just before the Amiga's 1985 launch, PC OSs were simplistic in the extreme, for these functions were either trivial or nonexistent. With the notable exception of Apple's Macintosh, OS user interfaces consisted of little more than a blinking command prompt. And the PC world still functioned firmly within the Triangle of Ones that the institutional computing world had shattered many years ago. In such an environment, the second and third functions of an OS were largely moot: with only one program allowed to run at a time, resource-management concerns were nonexistent, and, without the need to concern oneself with crashing or otherwise interfering with other programs, bare-metal programming was not only acceptable but expected. *MS-DOS*, for example, already the established standard in the business world by 1985, provided just 27 function calls to programmers, the vast majority of them dealing only with disk and file management.[7] Everything else the application programmer had to provide for herself, either by programming the hardware directly or through third-party software libraries. And MS-DOS, though it was little more than a shared library of interrupts that might arguably not even have been blessed with the designation "OS" had it existed in the more sophisticated institutional computing world, was quite advanced by PC standards, sufficiently so to become a mainstay of the "serious" world of the business PC. Even Apple's new MacOS, by far the most sophisticated OS on the market in 1985, offered no multitasking capabilities and would not for many more years.[8]

When AmigaOS appeared, it marked a new standard of sophistication for PC OSs in offering not only a rich, full-featured (for the time) mouse-driven GUI, but also a rich suite of accessible functions and libraries for the programmer as well as—most remarkably of all—true *preemptive multitasking* that allows the user to run as many programs at the same time as she has memory and CPU power for. The latter capability shattered one leg of the Triangle of Ones—the others would fall in later eras of the PC—and was nearly unprecedented.[9] Although taken for granted today by everyone who listens to an MP3 file while browsing the Internet, the addition of multitasking to an OS complicated the designers' job exponentially. AmigaOS could not allow to every program unfettered access to the computer on which it ran; it had to manage and allocate resources—notably CPU time, memory, and hardware devices—to each. The designers of AmigaOS thus had to take their engineering inspiration more from OSs running on large institutional computers—most notably Unix—than from the primitive PC OSs of 1985.

The Exec

The heart of an OS, the part of it that is always running and always in memory, is known as the *kernel*. Most OSs have historically been built around *monolithic kernels*, meaning that virtually all of the OS's functionality—from process and memory management to disk and file management to networking and much more—resides within the kernel. As OSs and our expectations of them grew increasingly elaborate, many designers began to opt for *microkernel* designs instead, which move as much of this functionality as possible out of the kernel and into other processes that can be updated or otherwise altered separately from the kernel at the core of the system and that can even be unloaded from memory entirely when not needed. The end result is an arguably more flexible and efficient design that is easier to modify and update and that does not consume resources for OS elements that are not in use.[10]

In addition to its many other innovations, AmigaOS represents one of the earliest implementations of a microkernel OS design on a PC. The microkernel—responsible for only the most basic, essential tasks of resource, memory, and process management—is known as the *Executive* (*Exec*). The Exec is of course always running. It was created by a software engineer still in his midtwenties, Carl Sassenrath, who was lured to join Amiga Corporation by the promise, "If you come here, you can design whatever operating system you want."[11]

Depending on the circumstance, each program running under AmigaOS might be referred to as a "task," a "thread," or simply a "program." Instead, though, I use the term *process*.[12] A process, then, is "a single instance of a running program,"[13] a series of linear instructions to be executed. A theoretically infinite number of these processes—although obviously and inevitably bound by the machine's memory and other resources—can be running on the Amiga at the same time from the user's standpoint. When we view the Exec from the standpoint of a systems programmer, we quickly realize that this multitasking is in a sense an illusion—albeit a very effective and practical illusion. The Amiga's CPU, like virtually all microprocessors developed prior to about 2000, is capable of executing only one instruction at a time. Nothing AmigaOS does can change this fundamental fact, even though the Amiga's hardware architecture of course allows it to delegate certain subsidiary tasks to the custom chips. It therefore multitasks by prioritizing the running processes and switching among them very quickly, thus creating the impression that all run simultaneously. More recent OSs also operate on the same principle.[14]

It is the task of the Exec, which is running as the root process of everything else, to allocate CPU time among all these other processes. Although it might seem most democratic simply to allow each process an equal slice of the CPU pie, in practice this solution is hardly desirable. Applications started by the user are not the only processes running on the machine; others are spawned by the Exec itself to help it to manage the machine's resources. These processes, by their very nature, often need to be given priority over applications. Each disk drive installed on an Amiga, for example, has its own accompanying process to handle all input and output requests to that device. These processes should run at a relatively high priority, higher certainly than an application program, for such a program is dependent on them, for example, to open and read in a file containing the user's document in a timely fashion. (As this example implies, processes can and frequently must communicate with one another; our word processor would send a message to our disk-drive process requesting that it load a certain file.) Most processes actually have nothing at all to do the vast majority of the time; they spend most of their time waiting for a signal to be passed to them from AmigaOS—a signal that originates from the user, from some piece of hardware, or from another process. Our hypothetical Amiga word processor, for instance, assuming it is properly programmed, simply goes to sleep between key presses or other user activity, allowing its CPU time to go to other processes.

Each process is accompanied by a changeable *priority* between -127 and 128, with a higher number equating to greater relative priority. Only a relatively small subset of this range, however, is commonly used. Critical OS processes often run at a priority of 10, 15, or 20; user processes such as our word processor run at a priority of 0 unless the user or the program explicitly requests otherwise. The Exec makes use of these numbers in quite a straightforward way. Any processes that are sleeping—waiting on a keystroke or a disk drive or something else—are discounted entirely. The CPU is then given over to the remaining process with the highest priority. Should another process with a higher priority enter into a running state, the previous process is supplanted by the new. If two or more processes with equal priority are at the top of the chain, the Exec simply allocates CPU time equally among them; and, of course, when a running process completes or goes into a waiting state, it immediately drops out of competition for the CPU, ceding it to other running processes of lower priority (if present). This scheme may seem surprisingly and perhaps even dangerously simplistic, but in practice it works quite well in most circumstances. Because in practice the vast majority of processes spend the vast majority of their time waiting, the Exec is normally constantly switching among processes rather than simply running the process with the highest priority. Assuming all processes are properly coded and given a reasonable priority—an assumption that admittedly does not always hold true, as we shall see—there should be few or no instances of a single process coming to dominate the machine as a whole. For example, the Amiga's internal electronics are so much faster than its disk drives that the processes associated with these drives, even during intensive file input/output, still spend a considerable amount of time sleeping, waiting for the drives to do their work, thus allowing other processes access to the CPU. Running these disk processes at high priority assures that the Amiga takes maximum advantage of its drives' transfer capacities, whatever they may be.

Clever users can make good use of the Exec's scheduling system. A ray-tracing program, notorious for its intense, time-consuming calculations, might be set to run at a priority of -5; it will then happily work away in the background, using only computing power that would otherwise have gone to waste, not affecting the user's foreground work at all (assuming she has sufficient memory to contain everything).

Of course, each running process also consumes other machine resources beyond its CPU cycles. Most obviously, each process requires some amount of RAM to run. We can place the memory consumed by a process into two categories: the memory consumed by the actual instructions to be executed (*code space*) and the memory the process uses to store user data and information about its current state (*data space*). Our word processor, for instance, will have its code residing in its code space throughout its execution. In addition, that code will need to allocate memory through the Exec to contain the letter that we attempt to load after opening the word processor itself; this memory is the word processor's data space. Only one address in the Amiga's memory is always assigned the same information;[15] everything else is allocated to AmigaOS and its running applications as needed by the Exec, which maintains a map of all this space and what lies where within it. As applications begin and end, memory to contain them is allocated and freed. Similarly, when we close our letter within our word processor, the memory that contained the letter is freed and returned to the general system pool; when we open another document or start an entirely new one, our word processor must again request the necessary memory from the Exec. When the Exec grants this request, it passes back to our word processor a pointer containing the address in the Amiga's memory now reserved for our word processor's use. It is now up to our word processor to make use of this block of memory—and only this block of memory—as it sees fit and of course to communicate once again with the Exec to free that block when we close our new document or close the word processor itself.

AmigaOS's Libraries

The other elements of AmigaOS are built atop the Exec in layers that can be loaded and unloaded from memory as needed. These layers and some functions of the Exec itself are available to application programmers through a system of shared libraries; using these libraries, programs can make requests of AmigaOS. The system just described, by which applications can request memory of the Exec for the storage of their internal data, is one example of this application–OS communication, but AmigaOS provides many more functions, often built on one another in layers. Dale Luck's "graphics.library," which provides a suite of powerful if fairly low-level functions for doing graphics and animation, for instance, sits below R. J. Mical's *Intuition* library for building GUIs to applications. And built on both of these libraries is the *Workbench*, the Amiga's standard GUI desktop from which the user can run programs, set her various system preferences, and so on. (Workbench is essentially the equivalent of the Macintosh's Finder or Windows' desktop.) Although Intuition and Workbench were inevitably compared upon the Amiga's release to the only mass-market GUI-based OS available during its development, MacOS, Mical claims that MacOS did not have as much influence on Intuition as one might expect; he points rather to the sophisticated Unix-based Sun workstations that were used in developing the Amiga as a stronger influence.[16] The fact that the Intuition interface is quite different from and arguably more usable than the early Macintosh's—employing, for example, a two-button rather than a single-button mouse—would seem to bear this out, as does the fact that the notoriously litigation-prone Apple never found cause to sue Commodore over the design.[17]

In addition to basic building blocks like those just described, AmigaOS also includes some surprisingly esoteric features for such an early PC OS, such as the "translation.library," which translates written text into synthesized speech suitable for output through the Amiga's audio channels, as well as a suite of sophisticated high-precision math functions. Such features were made possible by AmigaOS's microkernel design, which meant that they did not have to consume precious computing resources when they were not in actual use. In fact, this applies even to AmigaOS's seemingly more core elements: a game that demands every bit of the Amiga's resources and is not concerned about disallowing multitasking can dump higher-level, resource-hogging libraries such as Intuition and the Workbench to work with AmigaOS only at a lower level—a level that is admittedly more demanding on the programmers, but that can also be programmed more efficiently. Even everyday Amiga users could make similar choices; many experienced users, for instance, chose to work with the Amiga only through its alternate, less resource-hungry *command-line interface* (*CLI*) rather than the Workbench.

Easily the most unfortunate of these layered elements of AmigaOS, the one jarring aesthetic flaw in its design, is the *AmigaDOS* layer that is responsible for disk management and input and output. The Amiga team had originally conceived of a disk-management layer called "Commodore Amiga Operating System" (CAOS), the development of which they contracted out to another company whose name has never surfaced to my knowledge. That project unfortunately collapsed under some combination of design and business disputes,[18] leaving Commodore and Amiga desperate to find an alternative they could incorporate quickly. They found it in the Trivial Portable Operating System (TRIPOS), owned by the British company MetaComCo, which already ran on other 68000-based hardware. Much of TRIPOS was hacked into AmigaOS as AmigaDOS in relatively short order,[19] but it was an ugly fit; unlike the rest of AmigaOS, which was written in C, TRIPOS was written in a more primitive predecessor to that language, Basic Combined Programming Language (BCPL), which has very different ways of structuring its data. Most serious Amiga applications were also written in C, and thus communicating with the TRIPOS-derived portion of AmigaOS's identity became a constant headache for system and application programmers alike. Perhaps in part due to the inefficiencies inherent in its BCPL-based design, AmigaDOS is also the only element of AmigaOS that tends to feel sluggish and clunky to work with, not only to programmers but also to users. Commodore rewrote certain elements of AmigaDOS in C for later revisions of AmigaOS, but much had to remain so as to avoid breaking compatibility with earlier programs.

The Guru Meditation Error

AmigaOS is imbued with the personalities of the tiny team that created it—to an extent that is not possible with most OSs, which are usually the product of large, conservative corporations or huge, dispersed teams of programmers or both. Its creators' personalities are reflected not only in the sparely elegant designs of the core AmigaOS components themselves, but also in other, more obvious ways. When early versions of AmigaOS crash, for instance, they display a flashing red screen stating, *"Guru Meditation Error"* (figure 6.1).

There is some discrepancy in the details of various accounts of the Guru's origin, but the broad strokes remain the same. Mical and Luck, who along with Carl Sassenrath were the software engineers most important in AmigaOS's development, were something of an inseparable pair at Amiga Corporation, working insanely long hours there together, to the extent that they effectively lived in the office at times. During the five to fifteen minutes it took the company's Sun workstations to rebuild a new version of AmigaOS for testing, they would assume a lotus position and shut their eyes in hopes of catching a few minutes of sleep. Their colleagues began jokingly referring to them as "gurus," and eventually their "guru meditations" made their way into AmigaOS.[20] Another version of the story, told on occasion by Mical, involves the Joyboard, an early controller produced by Amiga, Incorporated for the Atari 2600 game console to help fund development of the Amiga itself. An interesting forerunner of the Nintendo Wii's naturalistic controllers, the Joyboard is a broad, flat unit that the user stands on and controls by shifting her weight from side to side and back and forth. Although ideal for a limited subset of games, such as

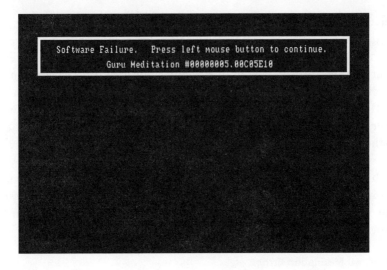

6.1 The Guru Meditation Error screen, AmigaOS 1.x's equivalent of the infamous Microsoft Windows "Blue Screen of Death"

the ski racing game that Amiga packaged with it, the Joyboard was too expensive, too fragile, and too limited in its application to catch on. One game involving the Joyboard, however, was never released commercially but nevertheless became quite popular at Amiga's offices: *Zen Meditation*, in which the player must sit perfectly still for as long as possible. The Guru Meditation Error thus suggests that the user play this game, meditating to find a solution to whatever problem has caused her Amiga to crash.[21]

In addition to these inspirations, Sassenrath was motivated to create the Guru at least in part by the example of MacOS, which displayed a picture of a bomb when the machine crashed rather than simply freezing on a blank screen, as did most computers of the time. As Sassenrath said, "You're going to want to have a sense of humor. If your machine fails like this, and you've lost two hours worth of editing, you're going to want to laugh about it somehow."[22]

A Hybrid OS

Before an OS can do anything, it must of course be placed into its host machine's memory. Most computers today, as did a fair number even in 1985, come from the factory with only a minimal amount of code stored in ROM. This code, known as the "bootstrap," performs some very basic hardware initialization and then looks to disk—hard disk today, more commonly floppy disk in 1985—for a proper OS to boot and turn over further control to. This approach has considerable advantages. Most notably, it allows the user to upgrade freely and even to choose among rival OSs that run on the same hardware, thus permitting, for instance, the same architecture to run either Microsoft Windows or the open-source Linux OS. It also carries certain disadvantages: an OS loaded from disk takes up precious space in both a computer's RAM and disk storage, and the process of loading and initializing an OS from disk takes time, meaning the user cannot make instant use of the machine after turning it on. In this era of fast, cavernous hard disks and microprocessors capable of addressing almost infinite quantities of cheap RAM, these concerns do not carry as much weight as they did in 1985. Yet they weighed heavily enough with many computer manufacturers of that era—in particular manufacturers of less expensive, more limited machines—that they chose to place their entire OSs, such as they were, into their machines' ROM memories. There, the OS was instantly available on power-on without the need to access the often slow floppy-disk-based or even cassette-based permanent storage typical of the era, and its code need take up none of the machine's precious RAM. In fact, many home computers, such as the Commodore 64, sold with no permanent storage at all, making a ROM-based OS the only possible solution for making them even ostensibly useful to those who did not choose to buy additional peripherals.

Every Amiga ever sold included at least a single floppy drive, but the machine's designers nevertheless chose something of a hybrid of the two OS-storage approaches just described. The core of AmigaOS, consisting of the Exec as well as essential libraries such as "graphics.library," Intuition, and much of AmigaDOS, resides in permanent internal storage on a single ROM chip, 256 KB in size in the machine's early years and growing to 512 KB with the release of AmigaOS version 2.0 (1990) and beyond. Commodore referred to this part of AmigaOS as "*Kickstart*."[23] The suitability of this approach to an OS of AmigaOS's complexity is debatable, for although it carried with it the advantages named earlier, AmigaOS had enough intricate pieces that it could not be placed into ROM and forgotten—like, say, the Commodore 64's simplistic OS. It instead had to be upgraded occasionally to correct bugs and add new features necessary for keeping up with the times. AmigaOS 1.3 (1988), for instance, added such necessities as the ability to boot from one of the hard disks that were growing increasingly common as well as support for automatically recognizing and configuring the multimegabyte memory expansions that creative professionals were finding increasingly invaluable. Upgrading AmigaOS was a hairy proposition indeed in comparison to the same procedure for other computers because it required the user to open her Amiga physically and swap the motherboard-mounted Kickstart ROM chip. The difficulties involved likely kept AmigaOS upgrades from appearing as quickly as they otherwise might have.

One might even say that the Amiga's approach had the disadvantages of both the ROM- and RAM-based OS-storage approach without many of the advantages of either. Even though its OS is largely ROM based, the Amiga remains, like virtually all PCs more complex than eight-bit machines such as the 64, heavily reliant on disk storage. It must in fact be "booted" from either a floppy or hard disk, which Commodore referred to as a "Workbench Disk," an odd choice of names considering that even Amiga users who chose to ignore the Workbench and work exclusively with the CLI had to make use of it still. On this disk are other, less commonly used libraries, such as the "translator.library" and the high-precision math routines, which AmigaOS loads into memory only when they are actually made use of.[24] Also on this disk are disk- and file-management programs and other utilities that, like in MS-DOS and Unix, reside outside the OS proper as individual executable programs. Various custom routines can be inserted into one of these boot disks to change the behavior of AmigaOS or even to bypass it entirely either to program the hardware directly (as many games do) or to load a completely different OS (for instance, Commodore's own short-lived Amiga Unix or one of the many Unix and Linux distributions that followed).

In hindsight, building so much of AmigaOS into ROM was arguably not the wisest choice. It is perhaps best explained by the platform's heritage. In its original incarnation as a game console, the OS (what there was of it) would of course be expected to live on a ROM chip, as the OSs of more modern game consoles still do today; OS upgrades are not such a concern for these more limited devices. Also, placing the OS in ROM was simply the way it had always been done, both for Jay Miner with his history of designing game consoles and inexpensive home computers and for Commodore with its own history of simple eight-bit machines such as the PET, the VIC-20, and of course the 64.

Implications of AmigaOS's Design

The Amiga ROM Kernel Reference Manual: Libraries, one of Commodore's series of official technical Amiga bibles, includes the following prominent plea or disclaimer in its introduction:

The Amiga operating system handles most of the housekeeping needed for multitasking, but this does not mean that applications don't have to worry about multitasking at all. The current generation of Amiga systems do not have hardware memory protection, so there is nothing to stop a task from using memory it has not legally acquired. An errant task can easily corrupt some other task by accidentally over-writing its instructions or data. Amiga programmers need to be extra careful with memory; one bad memory pointer can cause the machine to crash (debugging utilities such as MungWall and Enforcer will prevent this).

In fact, Amiga programmers need to be careful with every system resource, not just memory. All system resources from audio channels to the floppy disk drives are shared among tasks. Before using a resource, you must ask the system for access to the resource. This may fail if the resource is already being used by another task.

Once you have control of a resource, no other task can use it, so give it up as soon as you are finished. When your program exits, you must give everything back whether it's memory, access to a file, or an I/O port. You are responsible for this, the system will not do it for you automatically.[25]

In part due to the limitations of AmigaOS's (by modern standards) rather primitive original hardware, in part due to its pioneering nature as a sophisticated multitasking PC OS at a time when that very concept was a new one, and also perhaps even in part due to a certain philosophical approach, a notion that everything on the computer should be accessible and elegantly tunable by the user, AmigaOS lacks a number of safeguards and features that have come to be considered indispensable on modern computers. The Amiga user is forced to depend on the programmers of the applications she uses to do things the right way and to follow the advice given in the manual—and much more—to the letter. When she fails to do so, or when bugs sneak in, in spite of her best efforts, the result is far too often a visit by the Guru.

To understand why running serious applications—in particular multiple serious applications—on AmigaOS can so often feel like building a house of cards, we need to return for a time to the Exec's scheduling and memory-management functions. For the Exec to do its job properly, it requires certain behaviors from its programmers—behaviors that programmers in 1985 in particular were little used to abiding by because they were more accustomed to programming on much simpler, single-tasking OSs. Further, AmigaOS, unlike its successors, does nothing to enforce those behaviors; its designers only plea for them, as in the quotation from the manual.

I have already noted that most programs running on a PC spend most of their time waiting. This fact holds true not only on the Amiga, but also on both its predecessors and its contemporaries. *How* a waiting program waits is of little importance on those other, single-tasking machines, but uniquely critical on the Amiga. Let us consider the common scenario of a program waiting on the user to press a key in response to an on-screen menu or simply to clear a message from the screen and continue the program's operation. The *Commodore 64 Programmer's Reference Guide* recommends the following simple construction in that earlier machine's dialect of the Beginner's All-Purpose Symbolic Instruction Code (BASIC) programming language[26]:

```
10 GET A$: IF A$ ="" THEN 10
```

The GET command places the contents of the keyboard buffer into the variable A$; if the buffer is empty, indicating that the user has not yet pressed a key, A$ is also left empty. This code, then, simply loops again and again, constantly GETing A$ from the buffer and checking to see if something has been stored in that variable, indicating that the user has pressed a key at last. The entire CPU is devoted to this task of reading the keyboard buffer again and again, spinning its wheels with the same urgency it would use for complex, critical calculations. This approach is known as a *busy wait* and was not only quite common on early PCs but, as the reference to it in the advice section of Commodore's own official reference documentation indicates, officially sanctioned. The Commodore 64's limited OS and hardware actually supported no other approach. In the Amiga's multitasking environment, however, busy waits are deadly to the performance of the system as a whole, for while a process spins its wheels in this manner, it is pointlessly consuming CPU cycles that might be needed by other processes to perform real work. If these processes are running at a lower priority, they will even be blocked from the CPU entirely—by a program doing nothing more than waiting for input from the user.

A properly written program on the Amiga does not busy wait, but rather requests that the OS notify it when certain events occur—the pressing of a key, the selection of a menu with the mouse, and so on—and then simply goes to sleep, consuming no CPU cycles at all while it waits to be notified of some event worthy of its attention. When such an event occurs, it wakes up to perform the appropriate processing and then quite likely goes back to sleep to await the *next* event. This approach is known as "event-driven programming," as contrasted with the older *procedural programming* illustrated earlier and used by most programmers working on PCs in 1985. The Amiga employs it not only due to its multitasking capabilities, but also due to its rich GUI, which creates the possibility for many active on-screen menus, buttons, text-entry fields, and other widgets at once. Trying to keep track of all these input possibilities through constant active polling is not practical for a single application; that task is better left to the OS as a whole. Indeed, the event-driven paradigm was pioneered on the PC not by the Amiga, but by the slightly earlier Apple Lisa and Macintosh, machines that did not initially support multitasking but did feature similarly rich GUIs. Not coincidentally, these machines as well as the Amiga were built around the 68000-series processors, whose extensive set of interrupts make them a natural choice for the event-driven approach.

But habits are not always easy to break, and teaching programmers coming from other machines to embrace this new approach was often difficult. In fact, although AmigaOS's "native tongue," C, and many other advanced languages deployed on the machine support event-driven programming quite well, *AmigaBASIC*, which shipped with every Amiga during the machine's most commercially prominent years, offered only half-hearted support for event-driven programming. AmigaBASIC program listings found in magazine articles and books make use of "busy waits" with disconcerting regularity in exactly the manner just illustrated and in violation of Commodore's explicit advice. In many situations, AmigaBASIC offered no other choice. Like AmigaDOS, AmigaBASIC was a poor, rushed fit for the Amiga, one that indoctrinated programmers with bad habits that they likely took with them when graduating to C or another language. Small wonder then that few Amiga users mourned AmigaBASIC's passing when Commodore chose to discontinue distributing it with AmigaOS 2.0 and beyond.

Modern OSs are of course not bereft of poor programmers who continue to employ busy waits. The event-driven paradigm is, however, much better understood and familiar to programmers today than it was during the Amiga's time, thus making mistakes of this sort much less common. And to deal with programs that insist on employing busy waits, modern OSs sport more sophisticated process scheduling that does not give absolute, unfettered CPU access to the running process with the highest priority. Although a busy-waiting process will still waste countless CPU cycles, it will at least not *completely* block all other processes from accessing the CPU, and the system as a whole will thus not grind to a complete halt—

although performance of all other processes will of course be greatly degraded.

Memory management is another area where AmigaOS made new and somewhat unprecedented demands on its programmers. As already noted, an application program is expected to request from the Exec the memory that it requires for its operation. The Exec then returns a pointer to a block of memory of the requested size, and AmigaOS trusts the application not to write to memory outside of those bounds. However—and this is key— nothing beyond the application programmer's skill and good nature absolutely prevents such unauthorized memory access from happening. Every application on the Amiga *can* write to any address in the machine's memory, whether that address be properly allocated to it or not. Screen memory, unallocated memory, another program's data, even another program's code or for that matter its own—all are fair game to the errant program. The end result is usually a Guru or an even more spectacular crash.[27] A nonmalicious programmer who wishes her program to be a good AmigaOS citizen would of course never intentionally write to memory she has not properly requested, but bugs of exactly this nature are notoriously easy to create and notoriously hard to track down, and on the Amiga a single instance of one can bring down not only the offending application, but the entire OS.[28]

Modern OSs avoid these problems through the use of *virtual-memory* addressing; when a program requests memory, it is returned not a true address within system memory as a whole, but rather a virtual address that is translated into a true address as an intermediary step each time the program accesses its data.[29] Each program is thus effectively sandboxed from everything else, allowed to read and write only to its own data space; only the OS itself has access to the whole. All modern PC microprocessors feature a *memory-management unit* (*MMU*) that can automatically and quickly translate from virtual to real memory addresses and vice versa, making this constant process fast and fairly transparent even to the OS. Although MMUs are available for some models of the 68000 line as add-on accessories or (beginning with the 68030) even built in, AmigaOS, needing as it does to run on the full Amiga line, was never designed to take advantage of them. And although implementing virtual memory in software is certainly not theoretically impossible, it is not terribly practical on limited hardware such as the original Amiga—hardware that the machine's designers had already stretched to its limits. Thus, the Amiga user doing serious work, particularly if she makes extensive use of multitasking, must limit herself as much as possible to software she has tested extensively and believes she can trust and must leave the rest to fate—and learn to save her work regularly, of course.

Virtual memory has another potential benefit that might have served AmigaOS well. In this discussion of the Exec's memory management so far, the naive assumption has been made that any amount of memory requested by an application is always available. This, however, is obviously not the case, particularly when it comes to the Amiga's precious chip RAM, which alone can contain certain types of multimedia data. If the Exec is unable to carve out a suitable contiguous block of memory to satisfy an application's request, it must refuse that request, informing the requesting application of this refusal by returning what is known as a null pointer, a zero (0), in place of a valid memory address. Many programs written by sloppy or inexperienced programmers fail to confirm that their memory request was in fact granted. They rather try to write to the (invalid) returned pointer, which results in a Guru or similar disastrous failure.

Even if we discount concerns about sloppy programming, it would be nice if the Exec were able to allow the user to stretch the machine by not automatically refusing such requests. Modern OSs take advantage of their virtual-memory design to do exactly this: when an allocation request is made that exceeds the limits of the machine's physical memory, a certain portion of that memory that the OS has judged to be infrequently accessed is copied into what is known as a "swap file" in the hard disk. The physical memory space these data occupied can then be cleared and allocated to the other application. When swapped memory needs to be accessed again, it is copied back into physical memory, potentially (thanks to virtual-memory addressing) at an entirely new location and potentially displacing some other block of seldom-accessed memory that is copied to hard disk in its stead. There is obviously a point of diminishing returns to such a scheme, when the amount of hard-disk access required bogs the entire system down to the point of unusability, and the observant user realizes it is time to close an application or two. Yet in many cases the user is willing to sacrifice some speed in return for being able to run all of the programs she wishes to at once, and in all cases it is certainly preferable to a crash caused by a sloppily programmed application. But even had the early Amiga models for which AmigaOS was first designed been able to implement some form of virtual memory, they would not have been able to use such a scheme because most were not equipped with hard disks. Thus, simple refusal became the Exec's only option.

And AmigaOS places still further memory-management burdens on its programmers, burdens that are not quite such a concern for programmers working on other OSs. Once an AmigaOS application *has* been allocated some memory, it is responsible for freeing that same memory when the memory is no longer needed or before the application itself terminates. If it fails to do so due to design carelessness, bugs, or abnormal termination, the memory it requested remains still in use in the Exec's view. Because the only application that can free that block of memory is no longer running, this memory is lost entirely to AmigaOS and all other applications running—or that might begin running. It can be reclaimed only by rebooting the machine entirely. *Memory leaks* of this nature are unfortunately very common on the Amiga; users may literally see their free memory disappear over the course of several hours and various applications, until they are left with a machine incapable of running even a single relatively complex program and are forced to reset. Less technically informed users, of course, may never even understand how or why this is happening, much less be able to identify the specific guilty application(s). Although it is always good programming practice to free any memory previously requested, programmers coding on modern OSs do not have to be quite so concerned about doing so because these OSs come equipped with automatic "garbage-collection" routines to clean up after a sloppy application and recover its allocated memory upon the application's termination, whether it has crashed or just neglected to clean up after itself.

The Hardware/OS Divide

The Amiga's hardware and OS designs were pioneering but were perhaps not always the most perfect of matches. As already noted, one of the most important functions of a multitasking OS is to control access to the computer's various hardware resources. These resources include not only CPU cycles and memory, but also all of its other hardware, from its video hardware to its disk drives to its sound device to its printer. Once again, AmigaOS does a somewhat imperfect job, at least by modern standards. Commodore's *Amiga Hardware Reference Manual* states that "for maximum upward compatibility, it is strongly suggested that programmers deal with the hardware through the commands and functions provided by the Amiga operating system."[30] Bare metal programming, then, is strongly discouraged but not absolutely prohibited by AmigaOS, as a later sentence makes clear: "If you find it necessary to program the hardware directly, then it is your responsibility to write code which will work properly on various models and configurations."[31] AmigaOS has all the hooks necessary for a polite, proper application to share the multitasking environment with others, but it does not absolutely enforce this behavior. Just as the Amiga's full memory map is ultimately accessible to all and sundry, its hardware is laid bare for each and every program to access at any time. It is certainly safe to say that many Amiga game programmers in particular paid no attention at all to the *Hardware Reference Manual*'s advice; their creations often took over every aspect of the machine in ways that would horrify a "proper" systems programmer. The results were something of a mixed blessing. On the one hand, and as chapters 7 and 8 in particular demonstrate, these bare-metal programming techniques allowed Amiga programmers to get performance and effects out of the Amiga that would have been impossible strictly through the added abstraction and inefficiency of AmigaOS; on the other, though, their creations often break when run on hardware that varies only slightly from that for which they were designed.

Although game programmers were by far the worst offenders, many application programmers, tempted by the siren call of the directly accessible hardware and the lure of improved efficiency, could not resist the temptation to take shortcuts around the "official" way of programming the Amiga. The result is a whole collection of applications that run properly only under certain AmigaOS revisions or that run only on certain Amiga models or configurations or that run properly as long as they are lucky and do not attempt to access a certain piece of hardware that another application is already using in the correct, AmigaOS-approved way. And yet, just as with games, many of these applications achieve effects that might have been impossible through AmigaOS channels.

Modern OSs simply do not allow these sorts of shenanigans; just as they sequester each application within its own virtual-memory sandbox, they also allow hardware access only through library calls. Of course, cheap and powerful modern hardware makes such calls an easy luxury for modern programmers—a luxury that many Amiga programmers working on that machine's limited hardware felt was too expensive by far.

A Hacker's OS

Having documented AmigaOS's limitations at considerable length, I now feel behooved to reiterate what a remarkable, forward-looking OS it truly was when viewed in its proper historical context. The designers of AmigaOS were working virtually without precedent in implanting a multitasking OS truly worthy of the name into a small, relatively inexpensive, consumer-level computer. Far more remarkable than the things AmigaOS omits are the things it does do and does correctly. In fact, its very pared-down nature gives AmigaOS an appealing elegance in this day when OSs feel the need to include everything from Web browsers to digital-rights management in their core code. To help ourselves understand what makes AmigaOS so unique and so beloved by a certain type of user even today, it may be useful to compare it with the *next* most sophisticated PC OS available in the mid-1980s, MacOS.

Although AmigaOS perhaps shares a certain sense of whimsy with early versions of MacOS, the overall characters of the two OSs are markedly different. The Macintosh "bomb" dialog displays little or no information about what caused the error that was prompted or how it might be prevented in the future, presumably in line with the Macintosh's design philosophy of being a "computer for the rest of us," free of any technical jargon that might confuse the everyday user. The Guru Meditation screen, in contrast, "cute" as it may be, provides precious information about what caused the crash and how. The Guru screen shown in figure 6.1 includes two long numbers in *hexadecimal*, the base-16 numbering system frequently used in programming: 00000005 and 00C05E10. The first number tells the user that a task has attempted to divide a number by 0, which is of course mathematically impossible; the second provides the address in memory of the task in question. Thus, the skilled programmer or even user can determine from this message what program caused the problem and what the nature of that problem was. Similarly, although the Amiga provides a mouse-driven Workbench similar to the Macintosh's Finder that is very suitable for many everyday tasks, it also provides the more flexible and powerful CLI that MacOS lacked until the advent of OS X in 2001. Whereas the Macintosh tries not to bother its user with any technical details, expecting that user to go to Apple or to the publishers of her application software with any problems, AmigaOS, for all its friendliness and whimsy, does not hesitate to expose its inner workings to its user where it judges it to be appropriate. This feature made the Amiga a favorite of many hackers who held the Macintosh in contempt for Apple's perceived condescension toward its users; Commodore engineer Dave Haynie spoke for many hackers when he called the Macintosh "the dumb blonde of the computing world."[32] But the other side of that coin, it must be said, is that many users genuinely prefer the Macintosh's approach. They do not want to involve themselves in the technical details of the machine sitting on their desk, and they think of the computer as a simple tool rather than as an end in itself. For these users, AmigaOS perhaps exposes too much of its inner workings at times, such as when it asks its user to come to grips with the esoteric difference between chip and fast RAM or asks her to choose how much stack space to allocate to each program she starts. This "problem," if indeed one considers it to be one, was perhaps one of the several that seemed to keep the Amiga perpetually on the edges of both the home- and business-computing mainstream.

As touched on in chapter 2 in the context of the "logo wars," Commodore itself had difficulty accepting the personality of the platform it had purchased, leading to repeated conflicts with Miner's team. From the beginning, the team had been in the habit of embedding secret messages—known as "easter eggs" in hacker parlance—into AmigaOS. These messages were generally harmless enough, whether listing the programming and engineering credits that Commodore was never eager to include in their official documentation or declaring the Amiga "still a champion." By the time that the second minor revision (version 1.2) of AmigaOS shipped in 1986, however, the relationship between Commodore and the Amiga team had deteriorated enough that someone on the team saw fit to include a bitter message hardly in keeping with AmigaOS's usual friendly demeanor: "We made Amiga, They f— it up." Although there is every reason to consider this message a symptom of the worsening relationship between the team and Commodore rather than the cause of a final rupture, the fact remains that Commodore let go the last remnants of Miner's original team in Los Gatos, California, soon after the message appeared; all further Amiga software and hardware engineering was done either in Commodore's West Chester, Pennsylvania, complex or in a West German affiliate. Some members of the West Chester team, notably the outspoken and articulate Dave Haynie, had a strong and quirky hacker ethic of their own, but Commodore did win some battles to give AmigaOS a more staid, buttoned-down character. The Guru, who had by that time become a beloved symbol of the Amiga in his own right, was one of the victims in these battles; he finally disappeared with the release of AmigaOS 2.0 in 1990, replaced by the vanilla "system failure" message Commodore had wanted all along.

ARexx: The Ultimate Hacker's Tool

As such an eminently "hackable" OS, AmigaOS hosted a lineup of inspired programs, many available for free via organs such as the Fred Fish disk catalog of public-domain software, that could take advantage of its flexibility in surprising and innovative ways. Near the top of any list of important Amiga software and a fine exemplar of the "Amiga way" is William Hawes's ARexx programming environment.

ARexx is based on the programming language REstructured eXtended eXecutor (REXX), first created by an IBM researcher named Mike Cowlishaw around 1980. REXX comes from a computing world very different from the PC world and from the world from which so much of AmigaOS took its inspiration—that of smaller institutional systems commonly found in universities and research institutes running OSs such as

Unix and the Incompatible Timesharing System (ITS). It is rather a product of the third and generally least discussed world of computing: the mainframe. These machines, by far the largest, most powerful, and most expensive in general production, are commonly found only at large companies and government installations. The mainframe world of the 1950s through the 1970s, dominated by the conservative IBM, was made up of huge, building floor–spanning machines administered by a "priesthood" of lab-coated technicians trained and, one might even say, indoctrinated by that company.[33] By the 1980s, the priesthood model had begun to break down, but the culture around the mainframe was still very different from the somewhat scruffy, free-spirited hacker culture of Unix. The focus of the mainframe, then and now, was not on interactivity, but on batch processing, on churning through huge amounts of data—payroll, tax records, census data, bank transactions—as quickly as possible. Mainframes in 1980, like mainframes today, most commonly ran one of two powerful but arcane batch-oriented OSs developed by IBM: the Multiple Virtual Storage (MVS) OS or the Virtual Machine (VM) OS.[34]

Although Cowlishaw was himself an IBM employee, his purpose in creating REXX was to transfer some creative potential from the priesthood to users who were perhaps not professionally trained as programmers. For many purposes, REXX could serve as a replacement for IBM's notoriously cryptic and fiddly Job Control Language (JCL) for automating the flow of work—often called the "batch cycle"—through a mainframe. REXX's straightforward, English-like syntax, not to mention its dropping of the requirement that every character line up to a certain column (a legacy of the punched cards that were once used to store JCL scripts), made REXX simplicity itself in comparison to the alternatives. It was, in Cowlishaw's words, "tuned for what people wanted to do and the way they wanted to write programs,"[35] as opposed to using a syntax that was biased toward the way a computer manipulates data and instructions. After several years of in-house development, REXX began shipping with VM as an official IBM product in 1983.[36] The language was appealing and flexible enough that ports to various PCs soon began to appear. However, Hawes's ARexx, which he began selling independently in 1987, stood out from this pack, taking advantage of AmigaOS's unique capabilities to exceed even the original mainframe version in flexibility and power.

ARexx and other variants of REXX are examples of what is often called a "scripting language" or a "glue language." ARexx programs, often called "scripts," are not compiled into the binary code that the Amiga's CPU can natively understand but rather are interpreted at runtime in the manner of MS-DOS batch (.BAT) files or Unix shell scripts. Like those languages,

ARexx is not designed to create large, complex applications such as those that were the subject of this book's earlier chapters, but rather to aid the user in automating quicker, simpler operations. ARexx's unique capability, which sets it apart from all other versions of REXX and even from powerful scripting languages in use today such as Perl, Python, and Tcl, is its ability to talk to any of those more complex applications that provides an ARexx port, asking it to carry out tasks just as if the user had made the same request using the GUI. In effect, it lets the Amiga user program her system at the metalevel, taking automated control of an entire suite of installed applications.

I can demonstrate this control through a practical example that integrates three disparate applications from three separate developers, all of which include ARexx support, but which were not explicitly designed to work together: Nag Plus, an appointment manager and personal-time scheduler from Gramma Software; ProWrite, a word processor from New Horizons Software; and Superbase Professional, a relational database from Precision Software.[37] We will play the role of a person who must make a number of scheduled calls to clients or contacts during her working day; perhaps we are a salesperson or a project manager.

The heart of Nag Plus is its calendar, wherein we record the names of people we intend to call and the dates and times we intend to call them (figure 6.2).

Even when we are not actively inspecting or updating the calendar, Nag Plus continues to run, minimized quietly in the background. Like most processes, it spends the vast majority of its time sleeping when in this minimized state, thus freeing the CPU to focus on other tasks. It does, however, ask AmigaOS to wake it once every minute. When this happens, it checks if any "nags" are scheduled for that minute. If not, it simply goes back to sleep; if so, it announces the nag by popping up a textual alert on our screen and optionally playing a sampled sound or speaking the text of the alert in a synthesized voice using AmigaOS's unique "translate.library" or both. At 3:00 PM, we receive a nag that it is time to call someone named Thomas West. We have configured Nag Plus to fire a custom ARexx script of our own devising when we right-click over a calendar entry like this one. Nag Plus passes to this script the text of the entry in question, whereupon the script looks in a certain directory on our hard drive—the one where we keep the notes we make during calls—to see if a file named after the client in question exists. If so, the script starts our word processor, ProWrite, loads the file, places the cursor at the bottom of it—ready for us to make further notes during our call—and returns control of the computer to us.

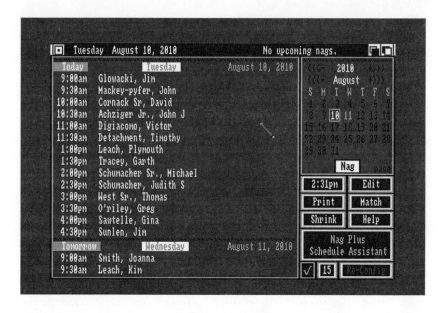

6.2 Nag Plus's calendar

If the notes file does not exist, however, our script's job becomes somewhat more complicated. It instead starts Superbase (if that application is not running already) and searches our company's mailing-list database for a client with the name in question. If the name is found, the client's relevant information—title, company, address, the all-important phone number, and so on—is extracted, and ProWrite, if not running already, is started. Our script creates a new document in ProWrite to serve as our notes file, inserting into it as a header the client's information (figure 6.3).

We can now make notes as needed during our call, saving the whole under the automatically generated file name when the call is complete. Should we need to call Dr. West again, our script will load this same file for the next call rather than generating a new one, thus allowing us to pick up right where we left off.

As with my previous case studies, this one is of course a somewhat simplistic example of ARexx automation; it does not account for many special cases and error conditions. That said, it should serve to convey some of ARexx's potential. Certainly much more might be done here. We might, for example, use one of a number of ARexx-compatible applications and a modem to automatically dial the client in question, or we might

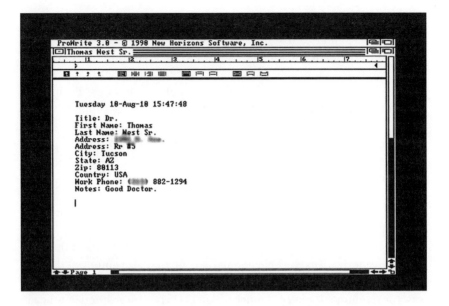

6.3 A call notes file prepared in ProWrite by an ARexx script, with the client's information automatically inserted and the cursor placed for us to make further notes over the course of the call

use another ARexx script, this one triggered from ProWrite, to insert our notes about a client back into the company's database when our call is complete.

Automation like this, which leverages major GUI-based commercial applications against one another, is very difficult to accomplish on most modern OSs, even though those systems support a plethora of scripting languages; there is no equivalent to the ARexx port on Windows, MacOS, or even, for the most part, Linux. I can see two major reasons why the "ARexx way" never migrated to those systems: first, allowing scripts such thorough-going control of applications and even the OS as a whole inevitably engenders serious security concerns; and second, it is very difficult to get a standard like the ARexx port accepted across the thousands of applications that modern OSs support. Although, as chapter 7 shows, the Amiga was certainly not without its share of viruses, I know of no seriously malicious uses of ARexx, even though the potential certainly existed; perhaps the segment of the Amiga community that commonly used ARexx was simply too different from that which spawned viruses and trojans. Acceptance of the ARexx standard, meanwhile, was indeed a problem in early years but was helped along immensely when Commodore chose to make ARexx a standard part of AmigaOS beginning with AmigaOS 2.0 in 1990. From soon after that date, an ARexx port was simply considered a basic requirement of any serious application, and those application developers who failed to include one could expect to hear about that failing in no uncertain terms from reviewers and potential customers. Even independent-minded NewTek felt behooved to build ARexx support into its Video Toaster software suite. This kind of near-universal acceptance of a standard is of course difficult to create in the world of commercial software and would be much more difficult to foster in the exponentially larger software market of today.

Thus, ARexx looks likely to remain a unique creation. Like AmigaOS itself, it requires an informed, careful user to take it to its full potential, but that potential is remarkable indeed. Neither AmigaOS nor ARexx suffers fools gladly, but in a way that, among modern OSs, only Linux and other Unix derivatives can bear comparison to, they also empower the user to do with the machine what and how she will. And seen from within, the way a programmer looks at it, much of AmigaOS is even aesthetically beautiful, a collection of interlocking parts that do exactly what is necessary quickly and efficiently and nothing that is not. There is a feel of naive technical idealism about AmigaOS that places it within a certain strand of computing tradition and that perhaps explains some of its appeal to a community of hackers that still speak of it reverently even today. One is reminded of another pioneering OS: ITS, developed by the MIT Artificial Intelligence Laboratory in the institutional-computing era of the late 1960s. Like AmigaOS and ARexx, ITS offered major innovations—the ability for a single user to run multiple programs simultaneously and the computing world's first full-screen text editor among them—along with a trusting, empowering attitude toward its users that is perhaps problematic in the "real world." ITS had no support for passwords at all and exposed every user's files to every other user, all in service of the hacker ideals of sharing, openness, and transparency.[38] Viewed in the light of this tradition, AmigaOS's dogged assumption that its users and programmers know what they are doing and its refusal to waste precious memory and CPU cycles in policing them do not seem so striking. If modern OSs give their users a complete home to live and work from, AmigaOS provides its users with just the basic foundations and the necessary tools to construct whatever sort of edifice they desire. ARexx is but one of the more remarkable among such structures, all enabled by the creative and technical talents of their designers and by the friendly, empowering OS which served as their host.

In late 1987, a member of the staff of *Info*, a major Commodore 64 and Amiga magazine of the era, attempted to boot WordPerfect on one of the magazine's Amigas. On this occasion, however, he was greeted not with the expected word processor, but with the strange, vaguely sinister message shown in figure 7.1.[1] In full, it read, "Something wonderful has happened. Your AMIGA is alive!!! And, even better . . . some of your disks are infected by a VIRUS!!!"

A computer virus was not a new concept even in 1987; the idea had been speculated on, although apparently without a concrete implementation, among hackers and computer scientists even prior to the birth of the PC.[2] In 1982, a 15-year-old American high school student named Rich Skrenta used an Apple II to create what was quite possibly the first virus to be implemented: the oddly named Elk Cloner, which spread from floppy disk to floppy disk, displaying a mocking limerick on every fiftieth infection.[3] Intended only as a practical joke among friends, Elk Cloner did not spread widely. By 1984, however, the abstract idea of the computer virus was threatening enough to be the subject of a major presentation at the Department of Defense/National Bureau of Standards Computer Security Conference of that year.[4] The author of that presentation and the accompanying paper, Fred Cohen, was prescient, for in 1987 viruses suddenly began to appear in the wild in numbers, not only on the Amiga, but on MS-DOS machines, on the Macintosh, and even on large, critical institutional computers. The situation was serious enough—or at least novel enough—to draw the attention of the *New York Times*, which announced in a rather fear-mongering article published on January 31, 1988, that

7.1 The SCA virus announces its presence

computer systems in many places and of many types were "under siege."[5] Meanwhile, the Amiga community struggled to understand its own virus problem, and as fear and rumors spread through the community, Commodore soon felt the need to assign an employee, Bill Koester, to research the virus and try to determine how to stop it.[6]

An Examination of the SCA Virus

A virus must solve three essential problems: how to infect a system in the first place; how to preserve itself even through reboots; and how to spread itself to other disks and systems.

As described in the previous chapter, although much of AmigaOS is stored on a ROM chip inside the machine, at power-on an Amiga looks for a disk to boot that contains more OS components as well as the details of the user's personal configuration. At the time that what became known as the "SCA virus"—from the last line of the message and standing for the puzzling "Swiss Cracking Association"—began to spread in 1987, this boot disk generally had to be in the first floppy-disk drive, the one that came with every Amiga sold, mounted into the case itself.[7] After performing some self-checks and initializations, AmigaOS checks this drive for a disk containing what is known as a *boot sector*, a special area at the disk's very beginning present only on bootable disks. If it does not find such a thing, or if no disk at all is in the drive, it requests, via a graphic that has become

7.2 AmigaOS 1.2 requests that a boot disk be inserted

one of the Amiga's iconic images (figure 7.2), that the user insert a "Workbench disk" and waits for her to satisfy this request.

When the user inserts the disk, AmigaOS executes a very small bit of code that is found on the boot sector itself, which performs a tiny but important step needed to initialize AmigaDOS. AmigaOS then continues on to execute the user's startup script that sets up her preferred computing environment and finally gives the user control of her now completely booted machine.

It is, however, possible to replace this boot-sector code with something else, and doing so was not at all uncommon. Many game makers in particular used the boot sector to completely change the Amiga's normal behavior, booting into a custom environment that largely bypassed AmigaOS in the interest of maximum efficiency—and, of equal importance, that made copying and sharing their games much more difficult. The SCA virus insinuated itself into an Amiga using the boot sector. There is room for about 1,000 bytes of code in the boot sector, of which the normal boot code uses only a handful. When an Amiga booted from an infected disk that contained the SCA virus in its boot sector, the virus code executed first, copying itself from disk into a fairly out-of-the-way location in the machine's memory. It then executed the normal boot-block initialization code and returned control to AmigaOS. Thus, the user simply saw her machine boot in the normal way and was completely unaware that the virus now lived in her machine's memory. And so the SCA virus solved the first of its three problems.

But the greater challenges were still ahead. Like most computers, an Amiga can be reset at any time, whereupon AmigaOS reinitializes itself and attempts to boot off the first floppy drive once again, as if the user had turned the machine off and back on. This process of *"warm starting"* does not deliver quite as clean a slate as does a *"cold start."* Although the tables that AmigaOS uses to know what processes certain areas of memory are allocated to are cleared, the memory itself remains unaltered until it is overwritten by other processes. Thus, the SCA virus's code remained where it copied itself in memory even after a warm start. But how to convince the CPU to execute that code again?

For this, the virus relied on a feature of AmigaOS known as the *"Cool-Capture"* vector. A program can place a directive into this special part of memory to notify AmigaOS that it would like it to execute certain code during AmigaOS's initialization phase, before AmigaOS even looks for a disk to boot from. The CoolCapture vector is of course lost when the Amiga is shut down completely because all memory is necessarily cleared at that time; it thus provides a way for a program or at least some piece of a program to survive warm—but not cold—starts. The CoolCapture vector has some very good, very useful applications, which explains why AmigaOS's designers chose to provide it. Many users of the 1980s and 1990s, for instance, made use of RAM disks, virtual disk drives that exist only in the Amiga's memory, but that can be read from or written to just like real disks. Particularly for users with large memory expansions but no hard drives, working with RAM disks was often vastly preferable to having to deal with frequent accesses to the comparatively slow and balky floppy drives. Some RAM-disk implementations used the CoolCapture vector to reallocate the memory that contained them after a warm start, thus preserving their contents even through crashes and resets. A user could now copy her frequently used programs and data into a RAM disk once at the beginning of her day and have lightning-fast access to them from then on—as long she did not power down her machine or experience a power failure, of course.

Like so many useful computing features, though, the CoolCapture vector is also vulnerable to misuse by the likes of viruses. The SCA virus used the CoolCapture vector to ask AmigaOS to execute at every reboot the code that the virus had tucked away in memory when the machine was booted from the first infected disk—thus solving the second of its three problems, that of surviving through reboots. Now, it needed only a mechanism to spread itself to other disks.

When the virus executed, it modified one of the most fundamental functions of AmigaOS, known as "DoIO" ("Do Input/Output"), which reads or writes raw data on the surface of a disk. The modified version analyzed each request sent to DoIO, of which there were likely hundreds or thousands over the course of a computing session, to see whether it met the very specific criterion of being an attempt to read a disk's boot sector during system startup. If this was not the case, as it was not the vast majority of the time, DoIO functioned normally. If it was the case, however, the virus checked to see whether the disk in question was already infected. If not, it wrote a new copy of itself to the boot sector, with only one modification: one byte, a counter, was incremented by one. If this counter was now evenly divisible by 15, the virus displayed its boasting message; the effective result of this process was that the message appeared with every fifteenth disk that was newly infected. Whether the message was shown or not, control was soon returned to AmigaOS, which booted normally.

Amiga users of the late 1980s tended to reboot their machines much more frequently than do most computers users of today, whether because of system crashes or simply because they were switching from one game to another. Also, in this era telecommunication was quite slow in most circumstances, leading Amiga users to frequently pass around software and data on physical disks rather than through electronic networks. Finally, both pirate BBSs and more legitimate ones had various means of compressing an entire disk into a single file for storage and transfer, to be unpacked again onto a physical disk by the recipient. This method of compression had the side effect of also preserving any viruses that might have been contained in the disk's boot sector. These cultural factors helped the SCA virus to solve its third and final problem, spreading not only through the disks of an individual user's collection, but also onto other systems and disk collections.

The SCA virus was only a proof of concept, designed to do nothing more malicious than attempt to survive and spread itself. It was born in July 1987, the product of a bet between two young European hackers: "The question was whether a virus would fit into the 1,024 bytes of the boot block of an Amiga floppy disk (well actually 1,024 minus some boot code which had to be present)," explained the virus's creator recently. "He [the other hacker] said he doubted it, so I had to prove him wrong to save my honor.:) Once I found out the really simple concept of reproduction I used, there was plenty of room left. That's why I put in the fancy graphics with the bar and all the text. Just to show that these 1,024 bytes are more than enough."[8] The "something wonderful has happened" tagline was inspired by the film *Short Circuit*, a science-fiction comedy about a sentient robot that had been in theaters a year earlier.[9] The virus's author traded pirated commercial software regularly by post with the friend with whom he had made the bet. He therefore decided to announce his success by sending the virus to the friend on one of these disks. This friend unfortunately had many more trading partners and thus unleashed the virus into the wild before realizing he had been infected. It spread through the underground software piracy network, reaching the other side of the world, Australia, within a couple of months.[10] After reaching North America from Europe, by one report on a pirated copy of a German game called *Mouse Trap*,[11] the SCA virus spread wildly there for some months, accompanied by fear and rumors out of all keeping with the reality of the virus's operation. It even infiltrated at least one commercial-software house, which sold disks infected with the virus to customers.[12]

The SCA virus's author had never heard of Elk Cloner and for that matter had no specific knowledge of any already extant virus. He was inspired only by more general articles on the *idea* of a virus.[13] The SCA virus was, therefore, in its way quite an original piece of conceptual engineering. It was an adolescent prank and an irresistibly interesting hacking idea rather than a truly malicious creation. That said, it did present a grave danger if one of the disks to which it spread was not a normal AmigaOS boot disk but rather contained a custom boot sector of its own that the virus proceeded to overwrite. In this way, the virus could potentially render useless an entire library of commercial entertainment software as it spread through a user's disks. And because the virus, whether out of the programmer's desire for it to stay hidden or simply bad programming practices, did not properly allocate the memory it used, AmigaOS could give this memory to other processes for the storage of their code or data; the likely result was an ugly, unexplained crash.

Nevertheless, at least by the standard of later Amiga viruses, the SCA virus was easy to detect—after a certain point it literally announced its presence—and easy to eradicate; one needed only to cold-start the machine with a disk one was certain was not infected and then to use AmigaDOS's "Install" command to rewrite the boot sectors on all infected disks. The virus's programmer was as shocked as anyone at the progress of his creation. He attempted to rehabilitate SCA's reputation somewhat by releasing a "virus killer" that could examine disks and memory and eradicate the virus, if found, from both places and that would even immunize disks against reinfection.[14] In an accompanying text file, he also took pains to explain that, contrary to some of the more fanciful rumors, the virus could not destroy program files not located in the boot block or destroy source code or other text files.

The SCA virus has attained some measure of infamy not so much for the destruction it caused as for being the first of a whole host of viruses to come, many of them much more insidious and much more destructive. Soon after the initial hysteria had begun to die down in the face of solid information from people such as Koester and even the SCA hackers themselves, the inevitable happened: a second virus appeared, created by someone who called himself the "Byte Bandit." This virus did not helpfully announce its presence after a certain period of time but did periodically blank the screen during a computing session and ignored the user's inputs unless she entered a secret code on the keyboard.[15] It spread itself to any disk that was inserted into a floppy drive, not just to disks that the machine attempted to boot from. And from then on, the viruses just kept coming. Some—perhaps even most—were, like the original SCA virus, essentially elaborate and often crude practical jokes, such as the Revenge virus that turned the mouse pointer into a phallus.[16] Others, however, were deeply and intentionally destructive. The Lamer Exterminator, for example, occasionally overwrote random disk sectors with the word *Lamer!* repeated again and again, corrupting whatever files happened to be using those blocks, and to guard against detection and eradication it intercepted any attempts to examine the boot sector on which it resided, returning to the caller an image of a clean, uncorrupted boot sector instead.[17] Some later viruses abandoned the boot sector to attach themselves to individual files instead, which allowed them to spread through even hard-disk-based systems that were never booted from floppies.

So many viruses were soon at large that some hackers began to create viruses that would detect the presence of others and compete against them in various ways. SystemZ, for example, was an apparently well-intentioned if misguided effort that checked for other viruses on the boot sector of every disk inserted, politely notifying the user of infections and asking her if she would like to have it infected with SystemZ instead.[18] More useful was the blizzard of more legitimate antivirus software—freeware, shareware, and commercial—that quickly appeared. In yet another harbinger of the computing world of today, *AmigaWorld* eventually began advising its readers that a "current virus checker should be installed on every Amiga system,"[19] and enterprising software publishers made tidy profits with their elaborate inventions that promised to keep users safe from the latest scourges.

Technical details and solutions aside, many users who were forced to interrupt painting, ray tracing, video production, or programming to deal with these nuisances were still left asking just why they existed at all and where they came from. Who were the "Swiss Cracking Association" and the "Byte Bandit?" Who, for that matter, were the "lamers" that needed to be "exterminated"? These questions marked a collision between two very different Amiga cultures that, viruses aside, mixed to remarkably little degree.

A Split Personality

Previous chapters of this book have described an Amiga personality that was known by many North American artists, both amateur and professional, as well as by many programmers and engineers who came to the platform with a grounding in traditional computer science. The typical Amiga of this milieu was the Amiga 2000, professional in appearance and intentionality. With its cavernous case containing numerous slots for expansion and its detached keyboard, the 2000 looked little different from the businesslike IBM clones of its day—or, indeed, from a Dell or Hewlett-Packard system of today. The typical 2000 might have been owned by a video producer or software developer and by the end of the 1980s was likely to be considerably expanded beyond the machine that Miner and team had first designed: perhaps with a newer and faster CPU, a large hard drive, several megabytes of additional fast RAM, and perhaps a networking card, a genlock, and (by a year or two later) a Video Toaster. This market, centered on if not exclusive to North America, was served by glossy, stylish "lifestyle" magazines such as *AmigaWorld* as well as by more nitty-gritty, scruffier technical journals such as *Amazing Computing*.

The Amiga's alternate personality, meanwhile, was centered in Europe and was characterized by the simple, all-in-one-case design of the Amiga 500, expanded, if the owner was lucky, with no more than a second floppy drive and perhaps an extra half-megabyte of RAM. The typical 500 was housed in a living room or a bedroom and was used most frequently, if not exclusively, to play games. This market was served by garish, excitable magazines such as the British *Amiga Power* and the German *Amiga Joker*, which focused entirely or almost entirely on the latest hot games. In this context, the Amiga was not a professional artist's tool or a serious software-development platform, but rather an inexpensive home computer and game machine, the logical evolution of the popular Commodore 64. As such, it sold in vastly greater numbers in Europe, racking up sales that, particularly in the last few troubled years of Commodore's existence, the North American division of the company could only dream of. That a single core design could become so beloved by two such different constituencies is a strong tribute to its strength and flexibility.

The version of the Amiga that debuted in Europe just a few months after its North American counterpart was in fact a subtly different machine, designed to be compatible with the European PAL video standard rather than the North American NTSC standard.[20] Its CPU was therefore clocked slightly slower, to 7.09 MHz rather than 7.16 MHz, to allow the machine to synchronize itself easily to the slightly different PAL video timings. A more exciting difference, though, was that its standard vertical screen resolutions were increased by a considerable amount, from 200 to 256 lines in noninterlaced modes and from 400 to 512 lines with interlace. Welcome as the additional resolution was, these differences would prove a real headache for software developers who wished to distribute games and graphical applications on both sides of the Atlantic. PAL-designed software running on an NTSC machine would generally not crash, but the bottom one-fifth of the display would be cut off, hidden below the border of the NTSC screen. Likewise, running NTSC-designed software on a PAL machine would result in a display compressed into the upper four-fifths of the screen, with an ugly blank area below. And the slightly different clock speeds could play havoc with some types of programs, such as the fast-action game that depended on millisecond-precise timing.

The Amiga 1000's sales in Europe were at least as disappointing as those in North America and for similar reasons: it was a relatively expensive machine sold by a company best known for its inexpensive home computers and was poorly promoted. These problems were in fact even more pronounced in Europe, where the markets were more sensitive to price than markets in North America and indeed were often content with systems that would have been considered hopelessly obsolete on the other side of the Atlantic. (For instance, slow and unreliable cassette tapes remained the standard mode of permanent storage in Europe on the Commodore 64 long after North America had adopted the floppy disk.) Beginning with the release of the Amiga 500 in 1987, however, the Amiga began to gain real traction in Europe. By 1990—ironically, just as North American Amiga sales were passing their peak and entering a long, slow decline—the Amiga 500 was hugely popular there and considered the next step up for many children, adolescents, and adults who had begun computing with the Commodore 64. In the last quarter of that year, Europe accounted for a staggering 85 percent of Commodore's total sales,[21] and it is safe to say that the relative ratios did not improve in North America's favor after that point. Thanks to production cost cutting that made the Amiga ever cheaper, a dazzling library of games, and the relative expense of the new generation of Microsoft Windows–based "multimedia PCs" that was coming to dominate North America, the Amiga flourished as a game machine in Europe right up through the 1994 Commodore bankruptcy and continued as a significant player there for several years after that. Even the AGA Amiga 1200, little more than a poorly distributed afterthought in North America, sold in significant enough numbers in Europe to attract considerable support from game publishers.

I would not for a moment claim that Amigas were not used for "serious" purposes in Europe or that suburban North American bedrooms during the Amiga's best years there did not contain a significant number of battered Amiga 500 game machines. I do believe, however, that the general trends are tangible enough. As I was writing this book, I naturally had the opportunity to describe the project to a fair number of friends and colleagues in both North America and Europe. I learned quickly enough from these conversations that most North Americans have never heard of the Amiga; only the occasional serious hacker or artist knows the platform and its significance. In Europe, though, most people of a certain age are well aware of the Amiga and often have fond memories of playing games on their own or a friend's machine. The Amiga's history in Europe is thus very different and in many ways more successful and more satisfying than its history in North America. Bound up with that history is an underground computing culture—amoral, chaotic, and often crude, but also vibrantly creative, exciting, and in its own way technically masterful. It was largely from this culture that the viruses came, but it was also this culture that spawned some of the most impressive technical and artistic creations that ran on the platform.

The "Scene" in Europe

The underground culture that came to be known as the "demoscene" predates the Amiga 500 and even the 1000, having been born on earlier platforms, most notably the Commodore 64. Its roots lie in the "cracking" and illegal trading of commercial software.

Software piracy is as old as the commercial-software market itself. A very young Bill Gates famously wrote an open letter to the nascent computer hobbyist community in early 1976, berating its members for stealing what was both Microsoft's first product and perhaps the first piece of commercial software ever sold for a PC, a version of the BASIC programming language distributed on paper tape. As more practical and polished PCs reached the market in the years that followed, piracy only increased. Although piracy was (and remains) widespread among all types of software, it was a particular problem for entertainment-software publishers, perhaps because games had such appeal to young people with limited income to purchase them. In response, software publishers began to employ a variety of countermeasures to protect their investment. Most of the time, such measures took the form of altered disk formats that could not be read by ordinary disk-copying software, but elaborate password-lookup schemes that required the game's manual or a physical code wheel packaged with it also became increasingly common as time went on. Some truly concerned (or paranoid) companies even employed both methods for the same game. Individuals, mostly teenagers, took it upon themselves to "crack" these measures and distribute the results. In response, software publishers implemented new and more complicated protection schemes, which were inevitably broken in time by these *crackers* in an ever-escalating cycle of challenge and response.

By the early 1980s, individuals and groups in North America and in particular Europe had begun to promote their skills and their ability to inject cracked versions of the hottest new software into pirate-distribution channels within days or hours of their release. They took fanciful, self-aggrandizing nicknames, or "handles," and pooled their resources into collectives with names such as "Apple Mafia," "Dirty Dozen," "Warelords," and "German Cracking Service." Fueled by angst and a nihilistic worldview inspired by heavy metal and punk rock as well as by an adolescent need for acceptance and validation, a crude social Darwinism ruled the scene, with the most skilled and connected crackers almost worshipped and lesser lights cruelly excluded and dismissed as "lamers." Indeed, like so many subcultures, the cracking scene developed its own distinct vocabulary of odd phrasings, distorted spellings, and portmanteau words that are still used in some segments of Internet culture today. They allegedly replaced the word *software* with *warez*, *hacker* with *haxxor*, and *elite* with *eleet* to circumvent electronic law enforcement filters that might be tracking their activities,[22] but one senses that such constructions were in reality more important to these "sceners" as markers of inclusion and exclusion.

In Europe, games and other software were usually traded on disk via post rather than through the network of BBSs that sprang up in North America because even local calls in Europe were generally billed by the minute, which made impractical the large amounts of time online that the slow modems of the era required to upload and download large programs. In fact, the most prominent organs of communication within the scene soon became "diskmags," electronic newsletters created and distributed on disk by one or more groups. Inside a diskmag, one could find all of the latest scene news: where the next "copyparties" would be held, who was cool and who was lame (that is, according to the group that put out the diskmag), who were now allied and who were now enemies (both of which could change with dizzying speed), and debates over such burning controversies as whether girls should be allowed to participate in the scene. Later diskmags grew surprisingly sophisticated, booting into elegant interfaces to enable the reading of their content and featuring music and pictures in addition to text. Some were almost as technically impressive as the cracks and demos they covered.

Much about this underground culture, made up as it was almost entirely of adolescent males, is distasteful, even shocking to adult sensibilities of both its time and our own, but to characterize its inhabitants as merely "boys acting out" does a real disservice to the technical genius of the best crackers, who managed again and again to break ever more sophisticated copy-protection systems, generally within hours, and all while working with no formal computer training and the most limited equipment. For this elite group, cracking soon transcended the desire to play games for free. The time they had to invest into cracking and the time that went into cultivating trading partners and maintaining their social position within the scene, combined with the day-to-day pressures of ordinary teenage life, in fact left most with little time for *playing* games. The addictive joy rather lay in the challenge of the crack itself, of pitting their own skills against the best schemes that publishers could devise—and, of course, in bragging at length about their accomplishments after the fact. Although crackers loved to play up a sort of gangster persona for themselves in the process, their outlaw status was at least theoretically genuine and sometimes had serious real-world consequences. Police in West Germany, France, and Scandinavia in particular were prone to swoop down on the dwellings of the largest traders, armed with search warrants and the full force of the law.[23]

Although one can safely say that software piracy has been common in every time and place with access to PCs, at the time of the Amiga 1000's introduction the cracking scene was particularly vibrant in Europe, where it centered particularly on the Commodore 64, a hugely popular game machine for which a constant flood of new games provided ample grist for the crackers' mill. Some crackers started to ply their trade on the Amiga in relatively short order; the first Amiga crack to appear was apparently of the game *Tetris* and was released by the Austrian collective Megaforce in February 1986.[24] Only somewhat later, however, after the introduction of the less expensive Amiga 500 in 1987, did crackers begin to migrate to the platform in large numbers, in most cases moving to it from the Commodore 64.

In the brutal meritocracy that was the cracking scene, it was of course important that crackers leave their marks somehow on the games they distributed so as to receive fair credit for their work. Such marks often initially consisted of no more than an individual or group's initials entered into a game's high-score leaderboard or perhaps a bit of altered in-game text,[25] but crackers soon took to placing custom-programmed graphical introduction sequences on the disks that housed the cracked games. These sequences advertised the group and its prowess, sent out "greets" to the group's friends, and perhaps dispatched some "flames" to those with which it was at war. Over time, these "crack intros," or *cracktros* in the scene's language, grew increasingly elaborate and impressive, soon becoming an art form and a field of competition in themselves. Many groups eventually began to "hire" members not to crack games, but rather to program the most impressive cracktros possible. Many groups were soon devoting more time and energy to their cracktros than to the cracking itself, and the results often audiovisually outshone the games to which they were attached. The next step was perhaps inevitable: groups began to release *demos*—noninteractive, computer-based multimedia pieces—to stand on their own merits as artistic and technical creations, a development that began as early as 1988 and reached a sort of critical mass by 1990 or 1991.[26]

This "demoscene" that evolved to supplement and eventually largely to replace the cracking scene carried much of the same underground feel as its predecessor, but it became in time a friendlier place, focusing as it did on creation rather than theft. Although crackers from a fairly early date had been in the habit of hosting occasional informal "copyparties" to exchange software and socialize, "demoparties" reached new heights of organization and participation. In 1991, the first instance of "The Party," an annual event in Denmark that eventually ran for more than a decade, attracted more than 1,000 visitors,[27] a record for a demoparty, and the numbers continued to increase from there. By 1994, the best-attended demoparties were attracting several thousand visitors. By this point, the swapping of pirated software, if it took place at all, was very much ancillary to these gatherings' real purpose: for groups and individuals to display their latest demos and participate in contests judged by the other attendees. A win or even just a high placing at a major demoparty could make one's reputation in the scene. Indeed, by the early 1990s many collectives, some of them formerly crackers, limited their activities exclusively to creating ever more impressive demos. In an odd but satisfying turnaround, software piracy now became the afterthought of a vibrant and creative, if still very much underground, association of digital artists. The astonishing aesthetic and technical evolution of this form of multimedia art can be demonstrated through an examination of two demos: one from 1989, when the stand-alone demo was just beginning to separate itself from the cracktro; and one from 1992, when the demoscene was fully established and already producing some dazzling work with an aesthetic vision to match its technical virtuosity.

Both of the demos, which I discuss in detail in the next two sections, as well as quite a number of other standout demoscene creations are available for viewing on this book's accompanying Web site. As always, you will likely find the discussion of much greater value if you view the demos before or as you read on.

Red Sector's *Megademo*

Red Sector Incorporated, a West German cracking group, produced their *Megademo* for the Tristar Party, which took place on September 9, 1989, in Venlo, a town in the Netherlands. Upon its release, *Megademo* was notably mainly for its sheer ambition and size, filling two floppy disks, more than the vast majority of commercial games of the era. As with most demos of this period, one views *Megademo* by booting an Amiga directly from the first of its disks, whereupon it uses some custom boot-sector code to take complete control of the machine, bypassing entirely the OS and all of its trappings. It is bare-metal programming in its purest form, a fact that Red Sector advertises with pride in *Megademo* itself: "no DOS, no libraries." Rather than use the standard AmigaDOS disk format and system of files and directories, the demo writes all data in raw form to specific tracks and sectors, which allows the data to be read back in with maximum efficiency, and it does so not by using the normal AmigaDOS libraries, but rather by directly controlling the drive's read head. This technique also makes *Megademo*'s code and multimedia assets difficult to modify or even examine. The disks are completely unreadable by the usual AmigaDOS tools and copyable only by a "deep" copier that exactly mirrors the actual tracks and sectors of a disk rather than simply copying the files that its AmigaDOS file system claims it to contain. *Megademo*, like virtually all Amiga demos, is coded in pure assembly language, with no intervening compiler to introduce inefficiencies. Such techniques allow it to meet one of the key requirements of a respectable demo: to start doing something interesting as soon as possible after the user inserts the disk and to provide constant visual and auditory action from that point on. Thus, even as *Megademo* loads each of its eight distinct main parts from disk, it plays a catchy tune and displays some simple graphics to keep the user's attention. The ability to do this type of "multitasking" was abetted by the Amiga's custom chips. Paula, for example, in addition to handling sound, can also perform disk operations largely autonomously.

This continuous action set the Amiga's demos apart from those created for other machines and was thus a great source of pride to groups such as Red Sector. For all of the scorn that groups within the scene were apt to heap upon one another, they reserved their ultimate contempt for those too "lame" to recognize the Amiga's superiority. Diskmags and other scene productions were littered with jabs at other platforms, with the Atari ST and IBM PC clones singled out for particular attention. The best demos, meanwhile, were revered within the scene not only as tributes to the groups that created them, but as proof of the Amiga's status as the greatest computer ever made. This platform nationalism could get extreme indeed, prompting lengthy online flame wars with supporters of other platforms that could bring together groups who otherwise detested one another in the defense of their beloved Amiga. In embracing the Amiga so fervently and in so closing their minds to the possible virtues of other platforms, the members of the scene were perhaps not unlike other adolescents who identify equally strongly with their favorite music groups.

In addition to using Paula to load data from disk as animations and music play, *Megademo* displays the unique strengths of the Amiga's hardware in many other ways (figure 7.3). Its bracing hard-rock- and techno-inspired soundtrack, for instance, could have been matched by few other machines of the era and is also played by Paula autonomously as the screen is filled with animated visuals. And virtually the whole demo is presented in full overscan mode; being able to fill the whole screen in this way was quite a novelty among computers of 1989. The colored bands of color that strobe through much of the text and other visual elements are perhaps the most prototypical of all Amiga demoscene effects and, again, are a direct result of the hardware on which *Megademo* was created to run. To produce these "rasterbars," the copper is programmed to change certain color registers at the end of every scan line. The result is not only visually striking, but trivially cheap in computing resources and quite easy for even a novice programmer to implement—thus, its popularity with the early demoscene, to the point of becoming something of a derided cliché even within the scene in later years. *Megademo* as a whole represents a superb encapsulation of the early demoscene look and attitude, which Anders Carlsson has aptly described as an "aesthetical maximalism": "more graphical elements, more mathematical effects, and more sounds made a *better* demo."[28]

But some unusual elements are to be found here as well. Two sequences make use of what the scene called "vectorgraphics," a form of simple 3D modeling (see chapter 4). One, a sequence called "Vectorballs," represents an example of the aboveground Amiga creative culture bleeding into this European underground because it shows strong evidence of having been inspired by Eric Graham's groundbreaking 1987 *AmigaWorld* article on the Juggler and 3D modeling. Not only does its overall look correspond with images produced by Graham's early modeler SSG, but it even features some of the SSG-generated balloon animals that were shown in that article. The unusually moody music and smooth animation of this section, which also features many Boing balls grouping themselves into various figures, makes it the most aesthetically impressive sequence in *Megademo*.

Another surprising aspect of *Megademo* is the amount of control it gives to the viewer, allowing *her* to decide when she has seen enough of each sequence and even to control some aspects of the sequences using a joystick. *Megademo* concludes with a multiple-choice quiz that asks an odd mix of questions about the tempest-in-a-teacup social world of the scene ("Why did Red Sector and Defjam join together?"), the technical design of the Amiga ("In which chip is the blitter implemented?"), and even general computer history ("Who developed the first computer?"—a notoriously thorny question to which Red Sector unsurprisingly provides the

7.3 Some scenes from Red Sector's *Megademo* (1989). *Clockwise from top left*: the animated (and musical) loading display that appears between sections, featuring Iron Maiden's mascot Eddie; a sequence featuring twin dancing and singing Arnold Schwarzeneggers; the unusual closing sequence, an interactive quiz; and Red Sector's version of Eric Graham's famous Juggler. Notice how the sequences take advantage of overscan mode to fill the screen to its physical borders.

following answer: the German Konrad Zuse). A user who answered a sufficient number of questions correctly was rewarded by having his name and information recorded onto the disk itself, immortalized there for whomever else that copy of *Megademo* was traded to. Interesting as this interactive element was, it appeared in few later demos, virtually all of which were designed to play nonstop, with no user intervention. The modern demoscene's FAQ file even makes this absence of interactivity an explicit requirement, stating that demos "run linear from start to finish and are non-interactive."[29]

Megademo is rather less impressive formally than it is technically. From its opening seconds, when a throaty cartoon villain's voice announces without a hint of irony the demo's title, we are confronted with a very adolescent aesthetic. One can argue that *Megademo* is little more than a compilation of impressive but not always terribly innovative cracktros. A shamble of pop-culture artifacts of the sort typical of the scene's teenage male demographic piles up over its course without much rhyme or reason, including Eddie, the cyborg mascot of heavy-metal band Iron Maiden, and Arnold Schwarzenegger in *Terminator* garb. Also present is some typical Amiga symbolism, such as the aforementioned Boing balls, the Juggler, and Max Headroom. As in the loading screen, many sections are accompanied by "scrolltexts," yet another cracktro staple, in which Red Sector members make the grandiose pronouncement that "we disassociate ourselves from the swapping of 'Evil'"—"Evil" being an individual who apparently failed to make good on some obligation; denounce another group, Curity, calling them "lamers," the ever-popular staple insult of the scene; and expound on their drinking exploits and favorite beverages. There is also a bit of scatological humor, such as a brief sequence featuring a farting worm and the belches that accompany a wrong answer in the quiz that concludes *Megademo*. Most disturbing, the demo also includes a number of racist jabs. Most of the text is written in English, ironically the lingua franca of a scene that had relatively little participation from groups based in primarily English-speaking countries, but there are occasional lapses into the group's native German.

State of the Art

To see how far the Amiga demo came in a short time, one can look to *State of the Art*, released by the Norwegian group Spaceballs at the second edition of The Party, held in Aars, Denmark, December 27–29, 1992. *Art* is an astonishing achievement, displaying a mature aesthetic perspective in full flower. Unlike *Megademo*, whose effect on the viewer depends on an appreciation of the limited hardware on which it runs, even to some extent on a technical knowledge of said hardware and thus the difficulty of the specific techniques Red Sector employs, *State of the Art* gives an exciting show that is inspiring even to those with no knowledge of its technical underpinnings. Of course, when one learns that the demo runs and was created on a stock 1987-vintage Amiga 500 with one MB of memory, one can only be more impressed.

Like *Megademo*, *State of the Art* comes on a bootable disk—just one this time—and dispenses entirely with such niceties as AmigaDOS and OS calls. In fact, in its original form it would not even run on anything other than an Amiga 500 with exactly one MB of memory because it uses hard-coded memory addresses rather than properly allocating memory from the OS. Should those specific addresses not exist, should they not be chip RAM, or should they contain other needed information, as is likely on any Amiga configuration not identical to the one used to develop the demo, the result is a visit from the Guru.

Unlike *Megademo*, there is no interactive element to *State of the Art*; the viewer simply boots from the disk, sits back, and enjoys the show (figure 7.4). That show is simple enough to describe: a stylized dancer's silhouette gyrates through a series of varying backgrounds and effects as an increasingly manic dance number plays. The demo takes obvious inspiration from the house music that was tremendously popular throughout Europe at the time, where huge numbers of young people gathered together, often illegally, for dance parties known as "raves." In fact, there are interesting parallels between the demoscene and raves, both being underground, tremendously creative subcultures created and inhabited almost entirely by people under the age of 25, and both being of essentially the same vintage. Not only would the music not sound out of place at a rave or house club, but many of the demo's effects evoke the atmosphere of the dance floor. There is, for instance, a sequence where the image blinks on and off from frame to frame, the background going from white to black, evoking the strobe lights that are a dance club staple. The dancer is occasionally replaced by a series of evocative words and phrases in a stylish art deco script that flash on the screen so quickly that they make more of a subconscious than an intellectual impression. These parts of the demo remind me of many modern electronic literature works, such as Yong-Hae Chang's multimedia poem "Dakota." As the approximately five-minute demo nears its end, the music speeds up to a tempo that is beyond the capability of any human musician (or dancer), finally exploding orgasmically into silence and a final credits screen: "Phew! Spaceballs: Simply State of the Art." This light touch makes a marked contrast to *Megademo*'s heavy-handed self-aggrandizing. *State of the Art* as a whole is a refreshing experience when played after earlier demos, replacing strident nihilism and "dark" bona fides with the joy of being young and alive. It is *sexy* and as stylish a piece of multimedia art as one can wish for. It succeeds so well today, when the technology used to create it is so absurdly dated, precisely because it is *not* about blitter or copper effects, not about self-referencing its programming techniques.

Even so, the techniques behind *State of the Art* do make an interesting study indeed. That the dancer's silhouette moves with such verisimilitude is less surprising when one learns that it has its origin in a *real* dancer, a young former disco-contest champion who also happened to be the girlfriend of one Lone Starr, the chief coder and creator behind the demo.[30]

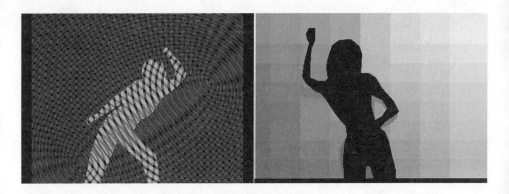

7.4 Scenes from Spaceballs' *State of the Art* (1992)

Lone Starr developed essentially unaided a program to convert the outline of the videotaped dancer into the vector-graphic data used to construct *State of the Art*'s dancer: "Major Asshole [another member of Spaceballs] had some ideas of how to save animations from videotape as 2d-vector figures, and soon I began to write a program where I could make such animations. This program had many possibilities. I could morph, zoom and move objects, and it was able to do animations up to four planes. It took 5 months before the final version of this tool was finished."[31] It is amazing that Lone Starr was able and willing to develop such a program, equivalent in intent and, if we are to judge by the results, also in capability to some of the most sophisticated professional tools on the Amiga software market. He did so essentially alone and from scratch and all for the purpose of creating a free piece of multimedia art likely to be seen only within a small subculture. I do not know of a better demonstration of the demoscene's skill, ambition, and odd artistic idealism.

Although *State of the Art* won The Party's demo competition in 1992 and is considered one of the demoscene's all-time classics today, it was not greeted with universal adoration at the time. The technology used to capture the dancer was, as just noted, remarkable indeed, but a vocal part of the demoscene demanded that all effects must be created in real time computationally rather than played back from captured data. Members of another group in the scene, Skid Row, took it upon themselves to correct the memory-allocation problems that made *State of the Art* impossible to run on so many Amigas and in the process inserted a sour message into the final title placard: "How could this demo win????? Lame programming and useless trackloader."[32] Other commentators had similar sentiments, which they often delivered in the fractured diction still common to the scene: "Why does he do demos? He should get himself a videocamera and make music videos NOTHING is realtime in this prod";[33] "Is this a demo? We are still not sure";[34] "Mr. Lonestarrrrrrr, you cannot convince me that a bunch of jumpin' zombies make a winnerdemo";[35] "the filled vectorcube is nice, although it is precalculated."[36] Such commentators saw demos as essentially demonstrations of technical skill and thus were dissatisfied with the relative lack of flashy effects in *State of the Art*. Lone Starr replied that "we won because this demo had a new different style, and it was a demo all kinds of Amiga-owners would enjoy, not only the coders."[37]

Retrospectively, of course, *State of the Art* was and is exactly that, and one of a cluster of demos released in 1991 and 1992 that ushered in an era of new aesthetic maturity. Creators were soon making use of ray tracers, 3D modelers, and digitized images to supplement pure code. The AGA-generation Amigas in particular gave them the power to create demos that work as short narratives or avant-garde films, and thus by 1995 the Amiga 1200 had largely replaced the 500 as the standard demoscene machine. Some demos blurred the boundaries between demos and the video productions I examined in chapter 5 in being produced on videotape, using the Amiga's desktop video capabilities to combine computer-generated effects with real-world video. One example of this approach, *Global Trash II* by Swedish group The Silents, was even reportedly played on MTV Europe.[38] For those who still hewed to the old, code-centric style, meanwhile, a subclass of demos, the "coder demo," was born. Particularly popular with pure coders were the intro demo competitions many demoparties began to hold, which were open only to creations that occupied no more than 40 KB on disk, including code and data.

Trackers

Whatever their subcategory, virtually all demos created in the scene prominently featured musical soundtracks, in most cases relying on their music just as much as their visuals to convey their message. Good demoscene musicians could win for themselves as much fame and respect as coders or artists and often released songs to stand on their own, unattached to a demo. The diskmags published charts of the most popular current hits, and demoparties generally hosted musical competitions to go along with their demo competitions. Even today the work of the best Amiga demoscene musicians is remembered and venerated on the Internet via such organs as the Amiga Music Preservation Web site.[39] Like all of the works of the demoscene, these musical creations are all the more remarkable in light of the constraints under which they were produced.

Even computers of the generation immediately before the Amiga that were possessed of exceptional sound capabilities, such as the Commodore 64 with its three-voice Sound Interface Device (SID) chip, lacked the power to store and reproduce real-world sound. They instead could generate only quite simple, regular waveforms using software synthesis.[40] Although Paula could be and often was programmed using similar techniques, the Amiga, along with its contemporaries the Atari ST and the first-generation Apple Macintosh, was among the first PCs capable of making any practical use of sampled sound. To understand the scale of the technical challenge in that usage, though, we might consider the amount of memory required to store one second of sampled CD-quality sound: (44,100 samples per second * 2 bytes per sample * 2 channels), or 176,400 bytes, approximately 172 KB. A typical demoscene Amiga 500 with one MB of RAM that dedicated its memory to nothing but audio storage would thus be able to store less than six seconds of CD-quality sound, but a single Amiga floppy disk cannot even hold that much. Granted, modern music-storage formats such as MP3 reduce required storage space dramatically (at varying loss of quality) using compression techniques, but the Amiga 500 *also* lacks the processing power to decompress these data and send them to Paula fast enough for them to be of use. Actually, even the shortest chunks of uncompressed CD-quality sound are a nonstarter on the Amiga, for Paula can handle a maximum sample rate of only 28,867 samples per second and supports only eight-bit sound resolution. Therefore, the Amiga musician had to content herself with lower fidelity playback, although the sound quality is by no means atrocious even to the modern ear. More significant, the modern solution to storing a song on a computer, which consists of recording it in its entirety as one long string of samples that, even when compressed, can span many megabytes, was not a possibility on the Amiga. The question, then, was how to make use of Paula's ability to process sampled sounds, but at the same time keep the size of those samples within the limits of the Amiga's small disk and memory capacities. The answer was the *modular music file*—the *MOD*.

A MOD song consists of two components: first, a collection of very brief samples representing the song's various instruments and sound effects; and second, a score or timeline of when and how those samples should be played. Imagine a rock song played by a classic four-piece band consisting of an electric guitar, a bass guitar, an organ, and drums. To create a MOD of the song, each of the first three of these instruments can be sampled playing a single note around the middle of its tonal range. A song can then be constructed using only these samples. To represent a higher note than the original, a sample is sent through one of the Amiga's DACs at a faster frequency than the original, thus increasing its pitch while retaining its waveform and therefore its fundamental character; for a lower note, the opposite is done. (This principle is in fact the same as that which the Boing demo uses to play two very different noises from the same sample.) The drum set might be a special case, possibly requiring different samples for a bass drum, a snare, and a cymbal, although the pitch of those samples might of course be varied to represent a complex drum set with different types of each. There are significant limitations to this approach to computer music making. It works better for instruments such as pianos that produce discrete, individual notes than it does for instruments such as violins that slide fluidly up and down the tonal scale. And on the Amiga the composer is limited to a maximum of four samples playing at any one time because the hardware itself has just four sound channels. For certain types of music, though, including the hard-rock, techno, and house compositions the demoscene favored, this approach can produce impressive results indeed.

Given the Amiga's sound capabilities and limitations, this basic approach to music making on the platform is a fairly obvious one. Indeed, it was the one chosen by the two earliest serious commercial music tools to reach the Amiga market, EA's Deluxe Music Construction Set and Aegis's Sonix. And yet both of these programs, although powerful enough in their way, were hampered by somewhat unwieldy interfaces modeled too slavishly on traditional musical notation. Both programs also stored their scores and the often copyrighted samples used to play them in separate files, making it tricky to share creations or the samples used to make them with others who did not own the program. And both programs were oriented toward the professional or serious amateur musician wishing to create music for recording onto other media, whether to stand alone or to accompany live performance or, via a connection with a musical synthesizer having a Musical Instrument Digital Interface (MIDI), to be played without using the Amiga's internal sound hardware at all. Yet many Amiga users wanted efficient tools and music-file formats that could be easily played on many Amigas and shared with others and that would be easier to incorporate into other programs. Game developers, who always needed catchy music for their creations, were one group that found programs such as Deluxe Music and Sonix particularly inadequate. The beginning of a solution to their needs arrived in December 1987 in the form of Ultimate Soundtracker.

Ultimate Soundtracker was the creation of West German programmer and musician Karsten Obarski. Having already experimented for years with music on the Commodore 64 and other early home computers, Obarski was asked, soon after acquiring an Amiga, to write the music for a *Breakout*-style action game, *Amegas*.[41] At the time, music in Amiga games often consisted of a single long sample of perhaps 15 or 20 seconds, looped endlessly and monotonously. Obarski wished instead to be able to write proper, extended compositions and developed Ultimate Soundtracker to help him do that.[42] Realizing the program's potential as a tool for others, Obarski released it through the German publisher EAS Computer Technik. That first version had many limitations and idiosyncrasies and did not do well on the market.[43] In March 1988, however, a Dutch cracker and demo programmer named "The Exterminator" disassembled and extensively improved Ultimate Soundtracker, releasing the new version into the scene as Ultimate Soundtracker 2.0. This act, illegal and immoral as it may have been, ushered in the era of demoscene MOD music;[44] countless groups were soon modifying or writing *trackers* of their own and making them available for free. All these trackers shared the MOD format originated by Obarski, and tracker music became omnipresent in the scene—in cracktros and demos and as stand-alone creations. What many regard as the definitive Amiga tracker, ProTracker, was released by the Norwegian group Amiga Freelancers in late 1990. Its source code was eventually made available, and it was steadily expanded and improved for years thereafter, first by the Amiga Freelancers and then by others. The evolution of sound tracking thus parallels the evolution of the scene itself, from being primarily about trading and enjoying the creations of others to being a creative force in its own right. By the era of *State of the Art*, demosceners were making use of only a few standout commercial products such as Deluxe Paint and a handful of assembly-language authoring tools for their creations; for the most part, their own tools were simply better for their purposes.

ProTracker

Comparing figure 7.5 and figure 7.6 illustrates the contrast between a typical Amiga commercial music application such as Deluxe Music and the tracker. DMusic is written for a traditional analog musician and composer, preferably one used to sitting in classic Gershwin pose before a piano on which are perched reams of blank staff paper. This composer can use DMusic to tap experimentally on the provided keyboard, dragging notes onto the staff as she finds sequences that please her. DMusic is easy to use for those with a traditional musical education but perhaps little knowledge of computers because it hews relentlessly to its chosen real-world meta-phor and never exposes its computational inner workings. Unfortunately, this metaphor has little to do with the program's underlying technology, and the intervening layers of abstraction between the fiction of the inter-face and the reality of the Amiga's sound hardware can make the program feel sluggish and clunky at times. DMusic is most useful for the transcrip-tion of traditional pieces, such as the Bach fugue shown in figure 7.5, which can result in reasonable enough, if slightly stilted-sounding results.

ProTracker, in contrast, approaches music making as essentially a programming task. Typical of demoscene productions, ProTracker's interface ignores not only DMusic's composition metaphor, but also all of the rules of "proper" Amiga user-interface design in general to forge its own path, which consists of dozens of tiny, cryptically labeled buttons and many on-screen numbers, often presented in hexadecimal. This tool is a complex one that can require months of effort to truly master. Once it is mastered, however, its no-nonsense approach makes it a joy to work with in contrast to the labored user-friendliness of a DMusic. The difference between the two programs' personalities is exemplified by the words they use to refer to their compositions: the DMusic composer creates "scores," reflecting that program's "high-brow," traditional approach to music making, whereas the ProTracker musician creates "songs." ProTracker

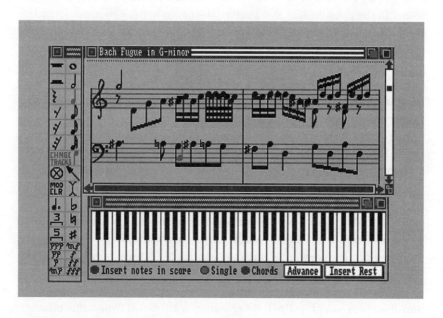

7.5 EA's Deluxe Music Construction Set (1986)

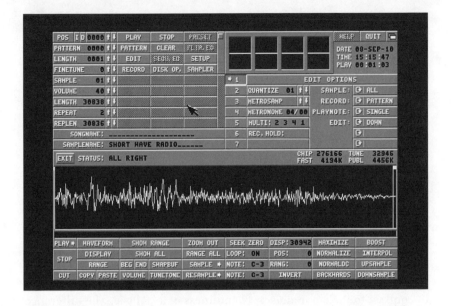

7.6 Examining a sample in ProTracker

excels at creating works of techno, house, and trance, genres that did not exist before the advent of computerized music and that, indeed, owe their sound to the possibilities and limitations of computerized music-making machinery. The best songs created with ProTracker have an artistic vitality that DMusic's staid transcriptions cannot match. To provide a window into the tools with which a tracker musician worked, I construct here a very simple sequence using a mature version of ProTracker from 1993.[45] The resulting fragment of audio is available on this book's Web site, as is a video clip of its construction.

We begin by loading a sound sample of an oscillating shortwave radio signal from a file. Examining this sample in ProTracker (figure 7.6) tells us a great deal about it: we see its waveform and learn (among much else) that it is set to loop automatically again and again after first introduced to a sound channel. And we learn that it consumes 30,942 bytes of our precious chip RAM. Composers working on ambitious songs with many samples must watch this figure carefully, particularly if they want to incorporate their work into a demo or game that will make its own demands on chip RAM.

With our sample loaded, we can now set about adding it to a composition of sorts. A complete ProTracker song is constructed from some number of patterns, fragments that can be combined in any order and repeated as often as needed. This attribute is one among others that make it so ideal for constructing pop songs and especially dance songs because these forms are commonly built on repetition. In the case of a pop song, a number of sections are arranged into a verse–chorus–bridge structure, with the former two likely repeated several times, and the structure of a typical rave or techno number is even simpler, made of constant repetition and juxtaposition of a few short sequences, perhaps with minor variations.

We can now build the first of our patterns using ProTracker's pattern editor (figure 7.7). Each pattern consists of a series of discrete sound commands applying to each of the Amiga's four channels. Channels 1 and 4 play from the left speaker, channels 2 and 3 from the right. At the start of our pattern, we have requested that our shortwave sample begin to play on channel 1; this command is represented by the alphanumeric sequence (B-2010000) shown in that position in figure 7.7. One of the first challenges for the would-be ProTracker composer is learning to decode these cryptic sequences. In this case, the sequence means that we will play at a frequency appropriate for the note B in the second octave ("B-2") the first (and so far only) sample we have included in our song ("01"). The remaining digits ("0000") can represent the various special effects we might apply to the sample. We are not currently making use of any of these effects—thus the zeros. Because our shortwave radio is a looping sample, it will continue to play again and again for the duration of the pattern unless we issue a command to channel 1 to stop it or to begin to play a different sample. Patterns can vary in length, but we have chosen to remain with the default of 64 command slots. The tempo for our song, meanwhile, is set to 125, using the standard dance-tempo measurement of beats per minute, with each beat consisting of about four command slots; this parameter can also, of course, be varied to suit the composition. With our current settings, our shortwave radio sample takes 16 slots to play through completely. Thus, it loops four times in the course of this pattern, coming only out of the left speaker. Notice that the other three channels are filled completely with zeros because they remain unused in this pattern.

For our second sample, we load a brief drum sequence that uses just 7,932 bytes of chip RAM. We copy the pattern we just created into a second pattern of the same length, then add the drum sample to channel 2. Because this sample is not a looping sample, we must manually trigger it to be played again every four slots. The result is a classic dance four-on-the-floor drumbeat that repeats 16 times over the course of the pattern,

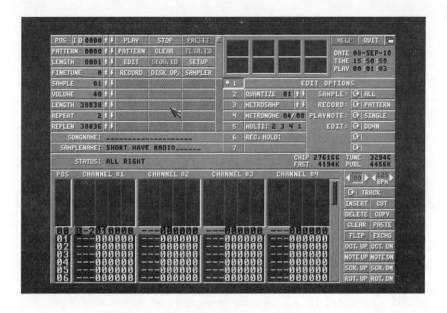

7.7 The heart of ProTracker, the pattern editor

or 125 times per minute. While the drum pounds away from the right speaker, our shortwave radio continues to cycle from the left.

We build our third and final pattern by first copying the second pattern. We then add our drumbeat to channel 4; now the drums pound out of both speakers while the radio drones away from the left speaker. We can now combine our three patterns into a composition that begins with the shortwave radio noise alone, adds a drumbeat, and then adds additional drums. And so we have the bracing beginning of a techno or rave number of the kind that was so common in the demoscene. We may wish now to introduce a melody played through the third channel, and we will of course likely introduce many variations to the patterns already laid down over the course of developing this simplistic backing beat into a full-fledged composition.

As this example illustrates, a ProTracker user must be as much a programmer as a musician, for she does not work in a conventionally musical way at all but rather produces a song by finely controlling sampled snippets. She has a large toolbox of effects that she can apply to these samples on the fly. The most basic of these effects is her ability to vary the playback frequency of a sample, which in turns varies the pitch of the sample and allows her to construct whole songs from a single sample of a given instrument. Many effects beyond that are also possible, however: she can add tone portamentos that slide smoothly from one pitch to another, add vibrato and oscillation, change the volume of the sample, even adjust the tempo of the composition at any point. ProTracker and many of its siblings are easily the most sophisticated musical tools ever made for the Amiga's internal sound system.[46]

Post-Commodore Europe

The year that marked the end of the line for most North American Amiga users and software publishers, 1994, was ironically the year in which the Amiga demoscene peaked—at least in many sceners' opinion—with a quantity and sophistication of demos not found in any previous year.[47] Meanwhile, the Amiga itself in 1994 still enjoyed a prominent place in European home computing, with relatively healthy sales of low-end machines such as the 500 and now the 1200, a large installed user base, and, particularly in the realm of games, commercial-software support to rival machines running Microsoft OSs or, for that matter, the new generation of 16-bit game consoles led by the Sega Genesis and Super Nintendo Entertainment System. Its success is a tribute not only to the design itself, but also to the business savvy of Commodore's European subsidiaries, in particular those serving Great Britain and Germany, which were almost always more innovative and competent in selling and supporting Amigas than their ostensible master in the United States. Following Commodore's bankruptcy, its British subsidiary even put together a serious proposition to acquire its failed parent's intellectual property and continue to manufacture Amigas as an independent entity.[48] In the end, though, this scheme fell prey to a better bid from German computer manufacturer Escom, which finally acquired the rights fully one year after the bankruptcy. Escom manufactured and sold new Amiga 1200s and 4000s in Europe for a brief period, only to fall victim itself to overexpansion and to declare bankruptcy in mid-1996, thus putting a final end to the Amiga's presence in everyday computer shops in Europe. Although various pieces of new Amiga hardware, including even some complete systems, have been manufactured at various times by various entities right up to this writing in 2011, they have been sold as niche products only through specialized, generally mail-order shops.

The European Amiga software market inevitably went into decline in the face of these realities. That decline was, however, a remarkably slow one. Buoyed by a large installed base of machines that still stood up quite well even to many newer computers as well as by persistent rumors that Amiga production would soon be restarted and the technology improved under this or that licensing scheme, European Amiga users enjoyed a fairly steady stream of new games until the new millennium. The last glossy newsstand magazine serving the Amiga stronghold in Britain did not fold until November 2001, more than five years after any Amiga hardware had last been seen in High Street shops. By contrast, the Amiga's newsstand presence in North America effectively ended with the folding of flagship publication *AmigaWorld* in April 1995.

Although many sceners either retired from the scene (a decision likely brought on as much by age and its attendant responsibilities as by technological change) or moved to Intel-based hardware, many others clung to their Amigas with even more fervor than gamers. In fact, many of the best Amiga-based demos postdate the Commodore bankruptcy by years. And although their quantity is not what it was in the halcyon days of the early to mid-1990s, a steady trickle of new Amiga demos continues to appear to this day, many running on elaborately, lovingly expanded boutique Amiga systems sporting PowerPC processor cards and new graphics cards. The scene itself has shrunk somewhat and changed. Gone almost entirely is its old underground and adolescent social character, unsurprisingly in light of the fact that it is still inhabited largely by the people who were present in the scene's heyday, now much older and with careers and families of their own. This demographic change was under way even in 1995, when diskmag *R.A.W.* reported that the average age of sceners was 22 years,[49] hardly "old" but likely considerably older than the average age just a few years earlier. The demoscene is thus a subculture of people who grew up together and remained together while it received only modest influxes of new members. It has gradually become identified with the retrocomputing culture, and many within it continue to code exclusively for the Amiga or for the even more ancient Commodore 64.

The Scene in Context

Particularly in the 1980s, when the scene was largely about software piracy, it was regarded with disdain by the more mainstream elements of Amiga culture, especially in North America. This fact is hardly surprising in light of the persistent and frequently deadly viruses with which it plagued the Amiga for years. In addition, the software piracy that it facilitated was a major problem for Amiga commercial-software publishers. If piracy was hardly unique to the Amiga, it was perhaps unusually damaging to the machine's always small, fragile toehold in North American mainstream computing; certainly a fair number of publishers that abandoned the Amiga cited widespread piracy as one of the reasons for doing so. Ironically, though, it is thanks to the efforts of the crackers of yore that much Amiga software, stored as it was on the notoriously unreliable medium of the floppy disk, still exists for the study of digital historians like myself. By making it possible to copy software that was designed to be uncopyable, the cracking scene preserved, albeit largely inadvertently, countless precious digital artifacts for posterity. Even in their time sceners doubtlessly gave many people a reason to buy Amigas by making freely available the most audiovisually impressive library of games of its era, thus helping Commodore if not the platform's software publishers.

And in reality, the physical and moral separation between the outlaws of the scene and the publishers was not always so great as either tended to imply. The demo coders' skill sets—ultrafast graphics routines, music composition, a general maximizing of hardware capabilities without regard for "correct," university-sanctioned approaches to programming— were exactly those skills that publishers sought for creating games, the Amiga's bread and butter in Europe. Thus, game publishers and the scene had a real, if often strained symbiotic relationship with one another. Sceners from a fairly early date circulated through game developers' offices, helping to create the very titles that other sceners promptly cracked. Developers in Scandinavia, always a scene hotbed, were particularly willing to employ sceners; the large Norwegian developer Funcom not only hired many sceners but went so far as to advertise for their services in the demoscene diskmag *R.A.W.*[50] Swedish demogroup The Silents inspired many sceners in the early 1990s when they went rejected the idea of merely working for developers and instead took control of their destiny to design and code under the name Digital Illusions a series of graphically spectacular pinball simulations that were very successful and that were even bundled with some editions of the Amiga 1200. Digital Illusions (and by extension The Silents) survive today as an EA subsidiary responsible for such recent games as the *Battlefield* series of military-themed first-person shooters. Similarly, the core members of Finnish developer Remedy Entertainment, responsible for the *Max Payne* series, were once the prominent demo group Future Crew. Such examples are only a few among many; the list of prominent sceners who worked or work in the videogame industry is long indeed.

This blurring of the lines did cause a certain amount of angst and even ethical debate within the scene, as when the group Fairlight cracked and widely distributed Digital Illusion's first game, *Pinball Dreams*. Animal of Digital Illusions (née The Silents) stated, "I will never know how much more money we would have made if it would have been left uncracked, but considering the amount of people that played this game on copy parties, I guess I could have been retired by now!"[51] (Other developers whose works the scene had been copying and distributing for years might of course be forgiven for experiencing a certain schadenfreude at Digital Illusions' sudden concern for intellectual-property rights.) By 1994, the diskmag *R.O.M.* was even complaining that the games industry was "destroying" the scene by snapping up its most talented members and keeping them too busy to work on new demos.[52]

Demoscene historian and blogger Anders Carlsson makes the heady but sustainable claim that the demoscene represents the "first digital global subculture," which makes it of immense historical importance.[53] Beyond this, though, the scene tends to resist pithy summary and categorization. Blogger Ville-Matias Heikkilä has cogently outlined three boxes within which the relatively few academics and digital historians who have seriously examined the scene have tried to place it, each of which has some merits and some failings.[54]

"The 'digital underground box,' along with the mainstream hacker culture, the open-source movement, political pirates, and many Internet-based communities." It is tempting indeed to make the demoscene a precursor of the open-source movement that changed personal computing in the late 1990s. However, the scene's social mores were quite different from those of traditional hacker culture, sufficiently so to make the drawing of overly direct connections between the two milieus feel strained at best. As Eric S. Raymond writes in his analysis of open-source culture, "Homesteading the Noosphere," hackers have an aversion to the sort of blatant self-promotion that was the norm in the scene.[55] Nor was there any real overlap, the occasional individual aside, between the people of the scene and the hacker communities that developed complicated systems such as Linux. Indeed, I feel that the aboveground Amiga public-domain software community, which created and shared—often with source code—countless useful tools, has more of the personality of the modern open-source community than does the scene. The links between those first two communities, in the form of people who came to the Amiga from institutional computing's hacker culture and went from the Amiga to Linux or other open-source OSs, are certainly much more tangible.

Although sceners were by no means unwilling to share their tools with others, as the history of ProTracker and many other applications attests, there was, especially in the early years when the scene was mostly about software piracy, a definite social hierarchy in place. One's access to software was determined by how "elite" or "lame" one was in the view of potential trading partners. We can safely attribute some of this attitude to typical teenage social politics. It is also worth noting, though, that the crackers had limited financial means in a world of scarce computing resources: unreliable physical disks shuffled around the world via post, expensive and slow telecommunications, and single-line BBSs. And theirs was of course an illegal culture, one that could not afford to be too trusting of all and sundry.[56] In this light, the politics of exclusion and secrecy is somewhat more justifiable. Raymond claims in "Homesteading the Noosphere" that crackers "hoard secrets rather than sharing them; one is much more likely to find cracker groups distributing sourceless executables that crack software than tips that give away how they did it."[57] This statement is not only unfair but factually incorrect; cracking manuals, distributed as text files sometimes running into the hundreds of kilobytes, abounded in the scene. And although most demo makers were not eager to expose their work to modification by others by distributing source code, for certain other types of projects sceners did prove quite willing to share their source, as is shown once again by the example of ProTracker.

The scene even in later years was hardly an ethically pure culture. Leaving aside the storm of viruses it unleashed and the frustration and data loss they caused to countless Amiga users, it was after all built on the theft of many hardworking developers' intellectual property. Yet its ethics were more complex than the pure hoarder's mentality that Raymond wishes to assign to it. Bruce Sterling's description of the attitudes of members of the "digital underground" of North America rings true of their European counterpart as well: "[They] perceive themselves as the elite pioneers of a new electronic world. Attempts to make them obey the democratically established laws of contemporary American society are seen as repression and persecution. After all, they argue, if Alexander Graham Bell had gone along with the rules of the Western Union telegraph company, there would have been no telephones. If Jobs and Wozniak had believed that IBM was the be-all and end-all, there would have been no personal computers. If Benjamin Franklin and Thomas Jefferson had tried to 'work within the system' there would have been no United States."[58] Some of these attitudes are not foreign to aboveground hacker culture, but the scene was more inclined simply to ignore legal niceties than to attempt to change them or to construct a better alternative system (as the open-source movement has done).

"The 'artistic movements box,' in the same corner as experimental film and video art." If the demoscene represents an artistic movement, it was unusual in its lack of self-awareness. Few sceners described their work in terms typical of artists, and most cracktros and demos, with their monotonous parade of technical tricks and their concern with of-the-moment community politics, are of more historical than aesthetic interest today.

Even well into the 1990s much about the demoscene remained crude and adolescent, and many or most creators were clearly more interested in showing off their coding skills and impressing their peers than in affecting hearts and minds. I believe, though, that *State of the Art* and a number of other demos transcend the scene's insularity to attain the status of art. In fact, much of the new-media art that has found increasing acceptance within traditional art gallery culture in recent years shows a marked demoscene aesthetic. I was particularly struck by this similarity when in early 2010 I visited Decode: Digital Design Sensations, an exhibition held at London's Victoria and Albert Museum that featured a number of real-time computational displays that would not have looked out of place at a demoparty. The sceners, scruffy adolescents as they were, were in front of trends just now coming to the fore in mainstream art. If they were perhaps unusual in their lack of self-awareness and introspection in contextualizing their work, this quality can make a nice contrast to a fine-arts world that has grown so fond of conceptual art that many artists seem to spend as much time explaining and justifying their work as they do in creating it. That said, the debates that swirled within the demoscene community over the increasing use of pre-rendered imagery in the 1990s and the legitimacy of non-real-time video productions such as those by The Silents reflect serious thought about what the demo was or should be as an art form, about where the boundaries of the form should lie, and about what restrictions should apply to creators.

The scene does not exist in isolation from other creative movements of recent times. The MOD format is particularly distinguished by its openness; anyone can load an extant MOD song into ProTracker and tinker with it to her heart's content, swapping out instruments, rewriting sections, or simply taking the samples for use in her own compositions. The sampling, remixing, and recontextualization that so distinguishes modern pop music is very much present here. And like most modern creative cultures, but unlike hacker culture, the demoscene promoted and celebrated the idea of the Creator who signs his name to his work, even if said Creator works with materials (sound samples, texts, images, and so on) that originated with others.

"The 'youth subcultures box,' just between the punks, the graffiti painters, and the LAN [local area network] gamers." Certainly there are strong similarities between the demoscene and the punk-rock ethos of do-it-yourself music making and promotion, and in the 1990s Europe's rave culture in particular permeated the scene. The demoscene was thus one more area where the Amiga integrated computing with the real world. To dismiss the

scene as only a form of youthful rebellion, however, is to trivialize its very real cultural significance and aesthetic achievements.

In the end, the scene is a unique entity, fully understandable only on its own terms. In the context of the Amiga's history, it stands as perhaps the purest of all artistic communities to make use of this artist's computer. Demos were created not for any professional goals, but for personal satisfaction and that often un-admitted goal of most artists, the admiration of one's peers, the recognition that one has done good work. Sceners often expressed disdain for people who used their computers merely as passive devices for the consumption of games and other entertainment, who never learned to make the machine sing for themselves. In so taking to heart the spirit of cheerful empowerment that seemed woven into the Amiga's very design, the scene forms an important part of the Amiga's cultural legacy. The very first Amiga program to attract significant attention was after all itself a demo. *State of the Art*, like *Megademo*, even harkens back to that granddaddy of all Amiga demos: although infinitely more complex and impressive, its dancing silhouette is often projected over a static background using the same sort of bitplane manipulations that created the bouncing Boing ball and its realistic shadow.

If there was an obvious application for the Amiga upon its release, it was playing games; the machine, after all, had been initially conceived as a game console rather than a full-fledged PC. The Amiga's combination of available on-screen colors and resolution, its unprecedented blitter-driven animation capabilities, its digital stereo-sound capabilities, and its custom-chip-abetted processing power put it on another plane entirely from the other computers and game consoles of 1985. An EA press release conveys the excitement felt by some in the games industry, who saw in the Amiga a machine with the potential to change the nature of interactive entertainment, making of it a cultural force to supplant or at least rival television:

> Today, from your living room you can watch [through television] a championship basketball game, see Christopher Columbus sail to the New World, or watch a futuristic spaceship battle.
>
> The computer promises to let you do so much more. Because it is interactive you get to participate. For example, you can play in that basketball game instead of just watching. You can actually be Christopher Columbus and feel firsthand what he felt when he sighted the New World. And you can step inside the cockpit of your own spaceship.
>
> But so far, the computer's promise has been hard to see. Software has been severely limited by the abstract, blocky shapes and rinky-dink sound reproduction of most home computers. Only a handful of pioneers have been able to appreciate the possibilities. But then, popular opinion once held that television was only useful for civil defense communications.[1]

In heralding the arrival of the first multimedia computer, EA and others relished the opportunity to unfold interactive experiences that could be immersive, aesthetically pleasing, and, most of all, *real* in a way that early videogames such as *Space Invaders* and *Pac-Man* could not. Here was yet another way for the Amiga to be a computer *of* the world.

Like so many aspects of the Amiga's history, however, its trajectory as a game machine did not quite go as its early supporters expected. Games were given nary a mention at the Lincoln Center launch party and appeared, if at all, only as afterthoughts at the bottom of early advertisements touting the Amiga's potential as a tool for business, creativity, and education. This reluctance to capitalize on an obvious strength is perhaps somewhat emblematic of Commodore's consistently ineffectual marketing department as a whole, which, in the words of a common Amiga community joke, used "Ready! Fire! Aim!" as its motto,[2] but it is also reflective of the realities of the computing market and culture of the 1980s. IBM PCs and PC clones, the standard business computers of this era, made a virtue of their lack of audiovisual capabilities and general aesthetic ugliness, promoting these failings as signs of seriousness of purpose. Even Apple clearly was not concerned about games when a year before the Amiga came out it released its Macintosh with no color-display option and virtually nonexistent animation potential. These machines, so primitive in some ways compared even to the inexpensive Commodore 64, nevertheless cost several times the 64,—as did the Amiga 1000, which had an initial list price of $1,295, not including a monitor, second floppy-disk drive, or memory expansion, all of which were essential to a truly usable system. Granted, the Amiga was a bargain in comparison to the much less technically impressive Macintosh, but advertising a computer with such a relatively rarefied price tag for its ability to entertain risked, at least in the conventional wisdom, rejection from the professionals looking for a "serious" machine. Meanwhile, the Amiga was judged to be far too expensive to attract buyers looking *just* to play games.[3]

In the end, Commodore's efforts to avoid the game-machine stigma were of no avail, for this trap was exactly the one that the Amiga 1000 fell into, tarred anyway by Commodore's reputation as a "toy" computer manufacturer, its historically poor record of support, and its poor dealer network. Most established business-software publishers shied away from the platform for these reasons, and game publishers were discouraged by its disappointing early sales. A fair number of games did reach the shelves in the Amiga's first year, but most—including those from EA, which, like all businesses, had to temper artistic idealism with sound business decisions—were ports from other popular entertainment platforms of the era, and even those that were not ports were often modest in their multimedia ambitions. It was not until the Amiga was fully one year old that a game appeared that truly showed the machine's potential and, by extension, the future aesthetic possibilities for the videogame as an artistic medium. That game was *Defender of the Crown*, and the company that developed it was Cinemaware.

Defender of the Crown

We might usefully divide a game into two components: its mechanics and its fictional context.

A game's mechanics are the network of rules and possibilities that define its play, a network that the player explores and often attempts to exploit in order to "win," to bring the system to some desirable end state. Every game, whether played on a computer, a tabletop, or a sports field, has mechanics. These mechanics may be extremely simple, as in tic-tac-toe, or enormously complex, as in a combat flight simulation that models all of the vagaries of air pressure, weather, and flight dynamics for dozens of aircraft. Whether simple or complex, however, they must be present, for this is what separates a structured, constrained game from free-form play. The quality of these mechanics, meaning both the scope of interesting interactions they allow and the elegance of their implementation, does much to determine whether a given game is a good one. Tic-tac-toe, for instance, is generally not considered a very good game because its rules, although certainly simple enough, allow no scope for interesting interactions; when played with even a modicum of intelligence, it will always end in a draw. Our flight simulation, meanwhile, may play elegantly on a computer, but if we attempted to reimplement it as a board game, it would be a nightmare, requiring literally hours of manual calculation for every second of action.

The fictional context of a game provides a setting and a motivation for its abstract mechanics. Some games do not have a context, existing purely as abstract systems. Most sports fall into this category, as do poker and many other card and board games. Even some computer games deal purely in abstracts, such as *Tetris*, called by Markku Eskelinen "probably the most successful abstract computer game ever."[4] Nevertheless, many tabletop games and most computer games do provide a context for their mechanics, giving the player a reason to play them beyond the pleasures of exploring their mechanics alone. This reason generally comes in the form of a narrative to enact or at least a fictional game world to explore. Context is sometimes done clumsily, apparently more as a belated addition to an existing abstract design than as an integral part of the design process; "Eurogames," a popular modern genre of strategic board games originating, as their name implies, mostly from Europe in general and Germany in particular, are often criticized for their "painted-on" themes, even as they include in their ranks such popular, mechanically elegant titles as *The Settlers of Catan* and *Carcassonne*. In other cases, though, context is much more integral to a game's design and to a player's experience of it, as, for instance, in a tabletop war game whose mechanics are designed to simulate as accurately as possible the circumstances of the historical battle that provides its context. Computer games are particularly unique in the emphasis they place on context, usually advertising themselves to potential players not on the basis of their mechanics, but as fictional experiences. This was as true in 1986 as it is today. Glancing through EA's advertisements of the period, we see *Dr. J and Larry Bird Go One-on-One*, which allows the player to "shoot as accurately as Larry Bird, dunk like the Doctor, while you're cheered on by the victory chants of the Boston Garden crowd"; *Skyfox*, which lets the player "get in the spaceship and fly"; and *Return to Atlantis*, which lets her "play Indiana Cousteau, oceanic hero." Although the PCs of the early 1980s were up to modeling even quite complex mechanics, their tiny color palettes, limited screen resolutions, and primitive sound capabilities sharply restricted the contextual possibilities for computer games. Aside from interactive fictions such as those from Infocom, which presented their context using rich textual descriptions rather than graphics and sounds, computer game designers were forced to ask their players to take a great deal on faith, to fill in the audiovisual gaps and substitute blocky on-screen abstracts with images from the imagination, and often to find most of the context for their play in elaborate manuals packaged with the games that contained all the story that developers were not able to squeeze into the computer's memory. These demands meant that computer games, at least beyond the immediately accessible arcade favorites, necessarily appealed only to the pioneering and the patient who were willing to find—or imagine—the mechanical and contextual beauty underneath so much surface ugliness. With the arrival of the Amiga and *Defender of the Crown*, all of that changed, as the experiential possibilities for computer games were suddenly blown wide open.

In terms of mechanics, *Defender of the Crown* is hardly a masterpiece of design. It is exactly what Cinemaware founder Bob Jacob originally conceived it as: a simplified version of the classic strategy board game *Risk* in which the player's cerebral strategizing is occasionally interrupted by a handful of action-oriented minigames that occur sometimes by player choice and sometimes by chance.[5] Neither side of its gameplay is terribly compelling in itself, with the strategic game marred by a dearth of real options, an opponent artificial intelligence that seems more random than considered, and minigames that are extremely simple and already unchallenging after just the first few attempts. Indeed, *Defender of the Crown* is an almost absurdly easy game, to the extent that once the player is conversant with the basic rules of play, she will be hard pressed to lose. The computer game in general was still in its relative youth in 1986, but suffice to say that designers had already managed to produce many much more compelling mechanical designs than this. To further exasperate the problem, *Defender* contains a serious bug that makes it even easier: if the player goes off in search of conquest and leaves her home castle entirely undefended, she is magically gifted with a retinue of soldiers equal in number to her current army abroad. If they succeed in defending the castle, these soldiers remain available for the player's further use, effectively rewarding her irresponsibility with an army twice its original size.

What rescues *Defender of the Crown* and makes of it an at least briefly compelling experience even today is the context that overlays its muddled mechanics. The game's setting is the romanticized English past of the Robin Hood legend, and from the moment the game boots, when a medieval harpsichord tune begins to play over the opening credits, it never lets the player forget that. Every lushly hand-drawn screen and burst of music are evocative of its milieu (figure 8.1). The action minigames, in which the player competes in a horse-borne jousting tournament, lobs boulders at castle walls using a siege catapult, and fences with enemies in a daring night raid on a castle, may be mechanically trivial on their own merits, but they so perfectly reinforce the context that they are somehow entertaining in spite of themselves. The simplistic strategic game similarly gains immeasurable interest from the atmosphere with which the visuals and audio imbue it. *Defender of the Crown* is not so much a game in the sense of a ludic struggle as it is a rich multimedia *experience*, a quality that many of its mechanical failings ironically serve to reinforce.

Defender's most famous sequence begins when the player is informed that "the Normans have kidnapped a Saxon lady!" If he chooses to attempt a rescue, there follows an instance of the fencing minigame. Once he successfully completes this minigame, the rescue has been effected. Afterward, "she accompanies you to your castle and during the weeks that follow, gratitude turns to love. Then, late one night . . . "

There follows a mildly risqué and beautifully drawn seduction scene in front of a flickering fire, the maiden dressed only in a see-through nightgown (figure 8.2). Although earlier computer games had certainly traded in sexuality, *Defender of the Crown* marks the first attempt to present

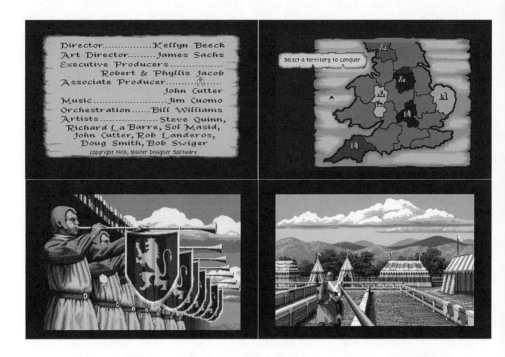

8.1 A *Defender of the Crown* gallery. At top left, the movie-style opening credits; at top right, the *Risk*-like strategic layer; at bottom left, one of the many hand-painted pictures created in Deluxe Paint for the game; at bottom right, the jousting minigame in progress.

a nuanced, romantic (as opposed to cartoonishly pornographic) vision of sexuality. Tellingly, this sequence is absolutely superfluous to completing the game and becoming king of England; it exists only to support the game's context, to add to the fictional experience.

That said, *Defender of the Crown* is in no way a narrative masterpiece. Its obvious inspiration is Sir Walter Scott's famous medieval romance *Ivanhoe*. It begins several years after the conclusion of that novel, as Richard I's death has thrown his English kingdom once more into turmoil, with open warfare about to begin again among the various Anglo and Saxon aspirants to the throne. *Defender*'s sympathies, like Scott's, clearly rest with the Saxons rather than the Normans; although the player can choose to control the fortunes of one of four lords, all these lords are Saxon. Included in the game are a number of characters from Scott's novel: Cedric of Rotherwood, Brian de Bois-Guilbert, Reginald Front-de-Boeuf, Rebecca of York, and of course Wilfred of Ivanhoe himself. Even Robin of Locksley can be visited in his haunt of Sherwood Forest. Even so, *Defender* is more a pastiche of *Ivanhoe* than a coherent sequel, at least if we are to

8.2 Rescuing and seducing a Saxon lady in *Defender of the Crown*

assume that the Templar knight Front-de-Boeuf has not arisen from his death at the end of the novel to assume the role of a Norman feudal lord and that his erstwhile lover, the Jewess Rowena, has not returned from her exile to become a noble princess in need of rescuing. And the game concerns itself with historical fact even less than did Scott; King John, the historical successor to Richard I, is nowhere to be found in this historical romance that ideally ends with the very nonhistorical outcome of a Saxon restored to the throne. *Defender* rather borrows from *Ivanhoe* only the broader strokes: the contrast between the stolid Germanic Saxons and the effete French Normans; the pomp and pageantry of the tournaments at Ashby; damsels in distress; and assaults on castles. This is *Ivanhoe* filtered through the game's more direct inspiration of many decades of Hollywood swashbucklers that both expanded on and distorted Scott's original tale.

The Cinemaware approach to computer gaming, of which *Defender of the Crown* is the first and most famous example, was conceived by the company's founder, Bob Jacob. Jacob was already a veteran of the games industry, having worked on a number of Commodore 64 titles, when he was given one of the pre-release Amigas that Commodore offered to selected industry insiders.[6] Realizing that (in his own words) "this is going to revolutionize everything," Jacob promptly started pulling together resources to found Cinemaware.[7] Jacob saw in the Amiga an opportunity to create games with what he called a "mass market sensibility," games that could appeal to everyday people as casual entertainment. This meant not only that the games would take advantage of the Amiga's multimedia capabilities to be aesthetically pleasing, but also that they should be easy to pick up and play: "no typing, get you right into the game, no manual."[8] The Amiga's capabilities were as key to the latter design goal as to the former: its mouse made simple "point and click" interfaces possible, and its relatively spacious RAM allowed Cinemaware to move all of the fictional context for their works out of the manuals and into the games themselves. The action sequences likewise would "require some timing and quick thinking" but would not be difficult to the point of frustration.[9] Cinemaware was, in Jacob's words, "my emotional reaction to the computer games of the era."[10] Looking for a structure around which to wrap this gentler approach to gaming, Jacob hit upon the movie metaphor: "I also decided that movies would be a great and creative motif for doing games—people like movies, right? It gave us virtually an inexhaustible supply of ideas. I was smart enough and cynical enough to realize that all we had to do was reach the level of copycat, and we'd be considered a breakthrough."[11] The metaphor would extend beyond the style of presentation used by the games; it would also be possible to play the games through in the time one might devote to a movie rather than asking players for the large chunk of time normal to strategy and adventure games of the day. The short duration of a single play-through would do a great service for Cinemaware games in letting the company give players a steady stream of fresh activities and multimedia content in that shorter period. Due to the limited disk-storage capacity of even an advanced platform of the era such as the Amiga, most games from other developers were very repetitive by comparison with Cinemaware's titles.

Jacob was fortunate enough to recruit a stellar team to create *Defender of the Crown*, including game designers John Cutter and Kellyn Beeck, composer Jim Cuomo, and Intuition (and Boing demo) mastermind R. J. Mical. The man who left the most memorable mark on the game, however, was art director Jim Sachs, who supervised a team of artists who created the many gorgeous pictures that are so essential to the experience. For these pictures, Cinemaware could thank not only Sachs but also Dan Silva, creator of Deluxe Paint, the program on which this project, like so many others on the Amiga, absolutely depended.[12]

Visually impressive as the final product is, it was hurried to market to be available for the Christmas buying rush, and the rush shows in the sometimes unsatisfying gameplay and bugs such as the magically doubling army described earlier. Sachs, who claimed to have worked "seven months at twenty hours a day average" under Jacob's constant pressure and to have had a nervous breakdown as a result,[13] was in the end left with many extraneous graphical sequences that there was not time to shoehorn into the final game.[14] Both Sachs and Mical were left, rightly or wrongly, with a very sour impression of Cinemaware. Neither ever worked for the company again, and Mical went so far as to request that his name be scrubbed from the in-game credits.[15] When *Defender of the Crown* was ported to other platforms, though, many of the team's discarded original plans were implemented, ironically resulting in ports that looked uglier but played better than the Amiga original.

Whatever its shortcomings, *Defender* on the Amiga was a stunning success, selling 20,000 copies in its first six weeks to a total installed user base of just 150,000 machines.[16] At a time when software that truly took advantage of the Amiga was thin on the ground indeed, *Defender* was, along with the Juggler demo, perhaps the best demonstration available of the machine's capabilities, and many copies were likely sold on that basis more so than from the consumer's desire to play the game. Gamer or not, every Amiga user simply had to have *Defender* in her or his library, and the game's high sales combined with rampant piracy ensured that most did. *Defender* was the first hit game for the Amiga and ushered in an era lasting almost four years in North America and considerably longer in Europe in which the Amiga was simply *the* premiere gaming platform. Although the game's gorgeously rendered atmosphere makes it worthy of an hour's attention even today, it is thus most significant as a signpost to the rich multimedia future of computer gaming. In fact, *Defender of the Crown* is an early example of a change that the Amiga's capabilities wrought in the very nature of the data that make up a computer game.

Just as we can at an abstract level divide a game into its mechanics and its fictional context, we can also divide the actual 0s and 1s that make up a computer game as it lives on disk or in a computer's memory into two categories: (1) actual program code, or processes, that are executed by the hosting computer and (2) the data that those processes operate upon.[17] (There is an obvious correspondence here with the programming concepts of code space and data space introduced in chapter 6.) The data can be further divided. First, there are the tables of data that describe and define a game's world; in *Defender*, for example, this data category would include the capabilities and playing styles of the other computer-managed lords with whom the player competes. And, second, there are what has come to be termed "multimedia assets" within the game industry: title screens, cut scenes, music scores, and digitized sound effects and speech. Prior to the Amiga's arrival, processes and the first category of data made up the majority of virtually all games.

An excellent case study here is *Elite*, a classic 1984 game of space trading and combat by David Braben and Ian Bell. Its universe consists of eight galaxies, each of which houses 256 star systems. Each star system has its own name, economy, even system of government. Factoring in the immensity of this universe as well as the variety of possible spaceship upgrades and enemies to fight, *Elite*, if produced by a modern games company, would likely contain gigabytes of multimedia assets. Bell and Braben's version, however, contains essentially no assets, nor does it even contain much in the way of data tables defining the game's world. It is virtually all process, with its universe—including all the details of economics, culture, and even names—procedurally generated during play from a series of mathematical Fibonacci sequences and its visuals drawn as wire frames by 3D visualization routines that procedurally create the visuals as the player sees them.[18] The entirety of the original *Elite* game fits into the 32 KB of RAM of the BBC Micro for which it was developed. *Defender of the Crown*, by contrast, filled two of the Amiga's 880 KB floppy disks when released barely two years later. It is unlikely that *Defender*'s process component is substantially larger than *Elite*'s; *Defender* is in many ways a vastly less complex and ambitious game. The difference, of course, lies in the multimedia assets that enable *Defender*'s fictional component to be so rich in comparison to the mathematically generated universe of *Elite* and that define the experience of the game for its players.

Games after *Defender of the Crown* grew dramatically in size from year to year, filling CDs, multiple CDs, and eventually DVDs. Today, they sometimes consist of tens of gigabytes of data, easily 99 percent of which consist of multimedia assets. This trend has paralleled and facilitated another trend, in which a game's fictional context has become increasingly important to the player's experience and even to the game's reception within gaming culture. *Bioshock*, for instance, perhaps the most critically acclaimed and influential title of 2007, owes its status to the gloriously devastated environments the player explores and the implicit critique it offers of Ayn Rand's philosophy of objectivism rather than to its standard first-person-shooter mechanics of play. A certain strand of gamer culture criticizes this trend, not entirely without justification, as a dumbing down of what is perceived as the purer "gamer's games" of old. Nevertheless, as the best Cinemaware works and, indeed, *Bioshock* show, the emphasis on context also raises the potential for a dramatic and cultural richness that cannot be found in *Elite*'s Fibonacci sequences.

Later Cinemaware Games

Having established Cinemaware so dramatically with their first title, Jacob and his growing company set about building on the success of *Defender of the Crown* with a series of similar "interactive movies." Their next game, *S.D.I.*, was a near-future science-fiction effort, with the player using a working version of Ronald Reagan's Star Wars missile defense plan to protect the West from attack by rogue elements in the Soviet military. After that came *King of Chicago*, a classic gangster movie homage, with the player trying first to assume control of his Chicago gang by bumping off the current leader and then trying to take over of the entire city. *Sinbad and the Throne of the Falcon*, based on the Arabian Nights legends, is the most lengthy and ambitious of these early efforts and also the one that plays most like a traditional adventure game of the era, with the player guiding Sinbad about a large map and through a variety of adventures while also managing a war at the strategic level. All of these games follow the *Defender of the Crown* template in mixing light strategy with simple action sequences, and all feature the trademark Cinemaware dollop of romantic sex appeal. All are audiovisually rich and relatively simple to play, but none have quite the charm of their antecedent; although their graphics are impressive enough, they are not quite so striking or evocative as Sachs's *Defender* creations. Perhaps stung by criticisms of *Defender*'s easiness, Cinemaware opted to increase the difficulty of these titles markedly, thus at least partially abandoning Jacob's original gaming vision. All can be very frustrating to play seriously, and the player can be exasperated by Cinemaware's refusal to add a save game feature to let her preserve her precious progress. *Sinbad* is a particular offender here; not only is the game lengthy enough to be difficult to finish in one session for the adults with limited free time who were Cinemaware's alleged target customers, but it concludes with an action sequence that is all but impossible and that costs the player all of her hard-won progress should she fail at it. *Sinbad*, in other words, frustrates its player in exactly the way that Jacob claimed to want to avoid in Cinemaware games.

Cinemaware's interactive movies from 1988 on are uniformly better designed and, although still not without challenge, much more pleasing to play while hewing to the same basic template. *The Three Stooges*, Cinemaware's only licensed title, is a genuinely funny comedy caper that makes good use of sound samples from the original films. It opens with one of Cinemaware's best sequences: the game boots to the familiar title screen and music from *Defender of the Crown*, which, just as the player is wondering if she got the wrong disks, is interrupted by Larry, Moe, and Curly marching on screen and declaring, "This looks like a kid's game!" The music for this brief faux-*Defender* actually sounds much better than the original, a telling demonstration of Cinemaware's increasing technical skill with the Amiga. Other games from this later period include *Rocket Ranger*, an old-time movie serial homage that takes place in an alternate World War II where rocket flight is a reality and Nazi Germany has a base on the moon; *Lords of the Rising Sun*, an unusually serious and strategic effort set in feudal Japan; and *It Came from the Desert*, a B-movie science-fiction send-up in which the player must protect her town from an attack by giant radioactive ants.

The year 1988 also brought the first of a new series of games from Cinemaware whose influence would, like so many other Amiga creations, far exceed their sales. *TV Sports: Football* was the first football simulation to mimic the sport's television presentation (figure 8.3). Each match opens with a pregame show from a television studio highlighting the teams' respective strengths and weaknesses before the action shifts to the field, where significant plays are succeeded by sound clips of various commentator clichés. At half-time, an on-field commentator ("John Badden") sums up the action thus far, and during games there are occasional cut-scene close-ups of the players, the coaches, and of course the inevitable buxom cheerleaders. At times, the game, with its caricature of John Madden's gung-ho persona and the advertisements of ridiculous fictional products it occasionally flashes, almost seems a satire of sports broadcasting; certainly the impression it makes, probably due as much to the technical limitations of the Amiga platform as to the game designers' intent, is much more cartoonlike than the earnest approach EA would later take with its hugely successful *Madden* series of football games. Nevertheless, *TV Sports: Football* plays quite well even today, offering a strategic depth that its cartoon surface perhaps belies as well as foreshadowing the approach EA would take to sports gaming beginning in earnest in the mid-1990s. *TV Sports: Football* was followed by three more sports titles that brought the same approach to their sports—*TV Sports: Baseball*, *TV Sports: Basketball*, and *TV Sports: Boxing*.

Cinemaware's richest and deepest game was the last of its interactive movies. *Wings*, released in 1990, grafts Cinemaware's story-heavy approach onto a World War I flight simulator, placing the player in the role of a young British pilot just out of flight school and newly assigned to the western front in March 1916, a time when the air war was just beginning in earnest following the invention of synchronizers that allowed pilots to

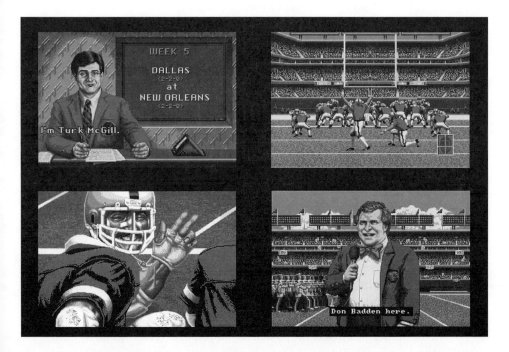

8.3 Cinemaware's *TV Sports: Football*. At top left, the pregame show; at top right, the player completes a successful field goal; at bottom left, the kicker waves to the "camera" to celebrate his achievement; at bottom right, "Don Badden" delivers a half-time report.

fire on one another without blowing off their airplanes' propellers. It then follows him through the remaining 30 months of the war and through some 250 missions that can take many hours to complete. As the months go by, airplanes, technologies, tactics, and of course aces come and go, giving the player an essentially accurate if somewhat romanticized education on World War I in the air. As one might expect in a Cinemaware game, *Wings* is more interested in providing an entertaining than a scrupulously accurate experience of flight; Jacob said that it was created as a sort of reaction to *Falcon*, the premiere flight simulator of the time, which shipped with a 365-page manual.[19] What makes *Wings* unique even among other simulators that have offered similarly lengthy campaigns is the attempt it makes not just to simulate a conflict or even a pilot's career, but to tell the story of what the war was really like for a single young pilot.

Although *Wings* never explicitly acknowledges this, one obvious inspiration for it is the 1927 silent-film classic that bears the same name. *Wings* the game even pays homage to *Wings* the film in telling some of its story through stylized silent-film intertitles. The pilot's story is, however, told mostly through a long series of diary entries that are interspersed with the actual missions, describing conditions and events around the squadron's base, the protagonist's relations with his mates, and, in sometimes harrowing detail, the crushing burden of fear and stress at a time when the average pilot's life expectancy was often numbered in days from his arrival on the front. The inspiration for this diary was that of the real-life Edward "Mick" Mannock, the greatest British ace of the war, who recorded the exhilaration and terror of a World War I fighter pilot, along with his guilt at the killing he did, in great detail before his own death in combat in July 1918. The game manual's introduction states: "There was much more to being a pilot in the Great War than surmounting the moments of battle. There were friendships, personal struggles, bouts with loneliness and longing for home. There were bars, brothels, and brawls. And most of all, there were the trying hours of being extremely young and having to grow up in a complex world that would never be the same." *Wings* is like so many other games in being about violence and war, but unlike most it attempts to bring home to its player the cost of its subject matter. Its designer, John Cutter, was responsible for many other Cinemaware games, but this one, more than the others, feels like a product of personal passion, a desire to *say* something. The phrase "interactive storytelling" tellingly appears in several places in the manual, at a time when that phrase was not so in vogue as it is today. If the game's message is sometimes undermined by the limited technical tools at its disposal, *Wings* still deserves credit as a noble, noteworthy effort to give its player a window onto lived historical experience.

Wings was unfortunately Cinemaware's swansong. Damaged by an ill-advised business relationship with a Japanese partner and ill equipped to capitalize on the increasing dominance of the Intel-based PC as a gaming platform in North America,[20] the company closed its doors in 1991, leaving behind a rich if somewhat mixed legacy. On the one hand, Cinemaware's term *interactive movie* has come to be regarded with a certain level of scorn today, courtesy of a generation of games from the 1990s that grew so obsessed with their audiovisual spectacle that they neglected to provide their players with interesting possibilities for interaction and agency. Indeed, even many of Cinemaware's efforts cannot be entirely exempted from the latter charge. On the other hand, though, Cinemaware's works showed the possibilities that the Amiga offered for creating games with a level of aesthetic nuance and storytelling depth that was virtually unprecedented in earlier years. And Jacob's original design philosophy, even if sometimes imperfectly maintained, was visionary in imagining a video-game culture inhabited not just by the stereotypical young males with patience and time on their hands, but by a broad swath of the general public. Here Jacob anticipated perhaps the most significant postmillennial development in gaming: the rise of the casual game and its community of players who are demographically very different from the stereotypical hardcore gamers.

In his 2010 book *A Casual Revolution*, videogame scholar Jesper Juul identifies five important qualities of casual games: they have bright, accessible, often humorous fictions in place of the dark, violent fictions of most hardcore games; they have interfaces that are simple and easy to understand without a manual or extensive training; they are easily interruptible, playable in bursts of just a few minutes on a coffee break or while dinner is cooking; they can be challenging but are never cruel in the frustration they provoke; and they are "juicy," meaning they reward the player with constant interesting multimedia feedback.[21] Cinemaware's most accessible titles do surprisingly well against these very modern criteria, falling down completely only on the third. (The slow disk drives of the late 1980s and the demands such titles placed on even the multitasking Amiga's resources meant that games were not terribly easy to get in and out of.) Cinemaware's games remain today unusually playable among those of their generation, due both to their simple mouse-driven interfaces and an audiovisual presentation that, if hardly as breathtaking as it was in the Amiga's heyday, remains more than acceptable enough.

Psygnosis

Cinemaware's works are wonderful examples of a certain type of high-concept gaming that flourished on the Amiga, especially during the late 1980s and especially from North American developers. They are ambitious works, created by professional teams of established programmers and artists, and they are programmed in a methodologically sound way, using the easily maintainable C programming language and manipulating the Amiga's sound and video hardware only through proper OS calls. R. J. Mical in fact did not so much program the game *Defender of the Crown* as create a game-playing engine that later programmers could employ across the entire line of Cinemaware games;[22] this approach reflects the typical (and understandable) bias of the professional programmer toward creating robust, reusable systems and tools rather than trying to create every project afresh on an ad hoc basis. Such an approach means, however, that Cinemaware's titles, for all their beautiful art and music, rarely used the Amiga to maximum efficiency, for the abstractions introduced by high-level programming languages, OS calls, and reusable game engines enacted an inevitable toll in performance.

The works published by the British company Psygnosis, meanwhile, reflect a very different approach to software development, one strongly reminiscent of the demoscene ideal of ignoring "proper" programming practices in favor of squeezing every last drop of performance out of the hardware. Jez San, programmer of the early British Amiga hit *Starglider*, summed up this culture's attitude toward the programming practices of a company such as Cinemaware: "We don't believe you can write performance software in C. You can for little sprite games—like *Marble Madness*, where you just have to move the ball around and scroll the screen—but, for 3-D with hidden line movement, it just can't be written in C. Actually, we could, but it would run 4 times slower. . . . I don't really understand why people write in C."[23] As this breed of programmers continued to learn from one another and from their own experimentation, they pushed the Amiga to audiovisual heights that made Cinemaware's animations and action sequences pale in comparison, while also (and perhaps more regrettably) largely eschewing Cinemaware's interest in storytelling, texture, and nontechnical innovation in favor of simple action-game templates. Psygnosis's predilection for stylish, technically impressive visuals also shows the influence of the European cracktros and the later demoscene. Unsurprisingly, many of the creators behind Psygnosis's games were drawn from that scene, as were some of their tools, most notably the indispensible trackers that created the thumping soundtracks that became almost as much a Psygnosis trademark as the striking visual effects.

Psygnosis rose from the failure of earlier game publisher Imagine Software. Imagine had been founded in 1982 by a team of programmers and had several big hits and a brief period of prosperity in the budding British videogame market before succumbing just two years later to a general lack of business acumen, fractious infighting, and a single hugely ambitious project, the "mega-game" *Bandersnatch*, which was to ship with additional hardware to make the popular eight-bit Sinclair ZX Spectrum computer on which it ran capable of realizing the designers' vision.[24] In a story reminiscent of more recent instances of videogame industry excess and mismanagement such as the collapse of John Romero's Ion Storm and its ill-fated *Daikatana* project, Imagine went bankrupt in 1984 without ever completing *Bandersnatch*. However, Imagine alumni Ian Hetherington and Dave Lawson managed under somewhat questionable circumstances to gather what existed of the game together before the company was shut down by the British legal system for nonpayment of debts.[25] They then founded Psygnosis to port the work-in-progress to the new generation of 68000-based machines that were much better suited to host it: the Sinclair QL, the Atari ST, and, by early 1986, the Commodore Amiga. Renamed *Brataccas* to dodge the company-destroying reputation that dogged its original title as well as perhaps to dodge the financial trustees of the failed Imagine, this game was in fact one of the first available for the Amiga.

Brataccas does little to showcase the multimedia capabilities that made the Amiga so special, but it is nevertheless a fascinating, if flawed, effort. It is essentially an animated adventure game in which the player moves one Kyne about the titular mining asteroid using an interface reminiscent of later platform games such as the *Prince of Persia* franchise. She must collect items, fight, and of course solve puzzles. Within the world of the game are many other characters who move about autonomously and who can often be conversed with via comiclike bubbles. In the process, the player can make friends and enemies of them, resulting in a surprising amount of narrative variance from one play to another. It is, all told, a remarkably sophisticated simulated universe as well as a genuinely fresh approach to the adventure-game genre. As happens so often with pioneering efforts, though, *Brataccas* is more satisfying conceptually than it is to actively play because it is plagued with an unwieldy control system that makes every action the player takes more difficult than it ought to be. Psygnosis's second game, *Deep Space*, was a space-exploration and combat game with a similarly ambitious concept and similar implementation problems to accompany it.

Psygnosis's next game and the soon-to-be standard Psygnosis approach to game design that it pioneered were quite different from these early efforts. *Barbarian*, released in mid-1987, was another platform-style action-adventure game in which the player must guide a sword-wielding barbarian through screen after screen of monsters and traps. It is a very simple game in comparison to the superficially similar *Brataccas*, but also a punishingly difficult one. Its real appeal lies in its graphical look, its smooth animation, and its fast response to the player's every action. Released almost simultaneously with the Amiga 500, which brought Amigas for the first time within the financial reach of many of the young people who were the main videogame demographic of the era, *Barbarian* became Psygnosis's first big hit, one of the games that every new Amiga 500 owner needed to have to show off his new machine, whether he acquired the game legitimately or via the piracy channels that also began to heat up in the wake of the 500. One is tempted to say that Psygnosis learned a lesson from *Barbarian*'s success, for the next six years brought from the company a blizzard of similar games, which expanded on the *Barbarian* template not so much in their gameplay as in their audiovisual effects. Indeed, within a couple of years, *Barbarian*, once a real stunner, would look downright quaint in the light of Psygnosis's later efforts. For every release such as *Chrono Quest*, an adventure game with a complex time-travel plot and relatively sophisticated gameplay, there were half a dozen stylish action games with stylishly generic single-word titles: *Ballistix, Obliterator, Menace, Agony, Awesome, Terrorpods, Leander*. The basics of most of these games were designed and programmed by tiny outside groups of young coders working on a contract basis, after which Psygnosis's in-house team of artists used Deluxe Paint and other creativity applications to add graphics and animations and give them that distinctive Psygnosis visual flair. As the company frankly admitted in a magazine feature, "Graphics are all important in Psygnosis games," the foundation of its reputation and sales.[26]

Psygnosis's distinct visual style extended beyond its simulated game worlds to its box art. While still at Imagine, Hetherington and Lawson had entered discussions with artist Roger Dean, most famous for the striking album covers he painted for progressive-rock groups such as Yes, to create box art for them, and carried that relationship along with the *Bandersnatch* design to Psygnosis.[27] Although the only piece of in-game art Dean was responsible for was the memorable Psygnosis "owl" logo, he painted virtually all of the company's box art throughout its history. Dean's distinct approach featured fantastic creatures and lurid landscapes with a bright, airbrushed sheen. He normally received his commissions long before the games they were to grace were complete and thus had to paint from imagination rather than from example.[28] The boxes thus sometimes had little connection to the games they advertised. At times, this discordance could be jarring almost to the point of hilarity, as when one compares the elaborate box art of *Brataccas* to the rather workmanlike visuals found in the actual game (figure 8.4).

Menace

It seems appropriate to analyze a Psygnosis creation from the standpoint of the company's position as a publisher known primarily for the technical excellence of its games rather than to focus on, as with Cinemaware's works, the game's more abstract qualities. The most important aspects of *Menace*—a nicely polished early Psygnosis effort designed and implemented by just two people, programmer Dave Jones and artist Tony Smith, who together called themselves "DMA Design"—demonstrate this technical emphasis. *Menace* is an example of a space "shoot 'em up" (or, in demoscene language, a "schmup"), a genre that was immensely popular on the

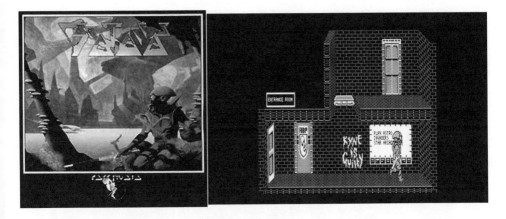

8.4 To the left, the *Brataccas* box art painted by Roger Dean, with the Psygnosis "owl" logo (also designed by Dean) at the bottom; to the right, the *Brataccas* in-game graphics

Amiga and other game platforms of its era and that was, along with platform-style action adventures such as *Barbarian*, Psygnosis's main staple. In *Menace*, the player controls a spaceship that she views from the side as she guides it through a series of horizontally scrolling levels, collecting power-ups, dodging obstacles, and of course destroying as many of the organic and mechanical enemies that infest the levels as possible while not letting them kill her (figure 8.5). Should she make it to the end of a level, a final powerful "boss" awaits, whom she must destroy before proceeding to the next level. *Menace* is perhaps most notable, at least in North America, for having been demonstrated at considerable length by *Amiga-World* magazine editor Lou Wallace and Commodore district manager Tom Stearns on an episode of the television program *Computer Chronicles* devoted to the Amiga that aired in mid-1989 and that provided the platform with one of its painfully few flashes of mainstream computer industry exposure in the years between the launch and the arrival of the Video Toaster.[29]

Upon first viewing the introduction screens, one is struck by their aesthetic similarities to the demoscene of the time; even DMA Design's name and logo are reminiscent of a cracking or demo group. Jones, about 21 years old when *Menace* was released in November 1988, could hardly have been unaware of the scene. Indeed, the European games industry at this time was almost as youth dominated as the demoscene; Jez San said in reference to the major game publisher for which he worked, Rainbird, that the average age was probably no more than 22 and that he knew of no

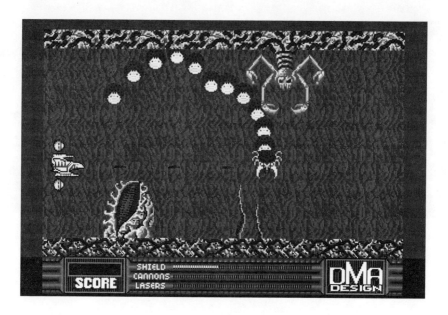

8.5 The complete *Menace* in action

one involved with the company in any capacity who was older than 30.[30] Like his less legitimate scene counterparts, Jones worked purely in the 68000 processor's native assembly language and bypassed AmigaOS entirely in favor of coding directly to the hardware, all in the interest of maximizing performance.

The analysis that follows is built up like the analysis of the Boing demo in chapter 2, in layers leading to the relatively complete first level of *Menace*. It makes an ideal capstone to the technical analyses that have preceded it throughout this book because it brings together in a single place much of what we have already learned about the Amiga's design and how it can be exploited. For this analysis, I am hugely indebted to a series of articles that Jones wrote for the British magazine *Amiga Format* in 1990, in which he explained many of the game's technical workings and provided much of its assembly-language source code, complete with invaluable comments. Both a full play-through of the game and a number of shorter clips showing each layer as it is added are available on this book's Web site, as are Jones's original assembly source and my own more readable C adaptation.[31] Although the code will likely be of interest only to programmers and those exploring the Amiga's design in considerable depth, I encourage all readers to use the video clips to enhance their understanding of the material that follows. We will now step into Jones's shoes circa 1988, discovering how he used the Amiga's unique hardware as we reconstruct the first of *Menace*'s six levels, an underwater area called the "Sea of Karnaugh."

Stage 1: The Scrolling Background

Like most Amiga games of the platform's most popular period, *Menace* uses the lowest-resolution mode because this mode both allows the most color possibilities and limits the amount of playfield data that must be shifted about in memory at high speed. Also like many Amiga games, particularly during this period when many still hoped the Amiga could conquer the North American game market as it had Europe, *Menace* is—in spite of its European origin—essentially designed for an NTSC-based North American Amiga; it does not utilize the improved vertical resolution of the PAL-based machines, with the result that when it is played on a PAL machine, a black border fills the bottom quarter of the screen. The alternative of designing for PAL would have made the game unplayable on an NTSC Amiga because part of the onscreen graphics would be cut off completely, extending as they would below the bottom edge of the monitor, and the *other* (and obviously best) alternative of maintaining separate versions for each market was at odds with the fundamentally ad hoc nature of high-performance game programming in this era. Designing for NTSC also has another big advantage: like the choice of low-resolution mode, it limits the amount of memory that must be manipulated to generate the display. *Menace* does take advantage of the Amiga's overscan capabilities for a final resolution of 352 × 224 and a display that, at least on a North American Amiga, nicely fills the monitor right to its edges.

If you closely observe the completed *Menace*, you will notice that it contains two levels of scenery graphics, a background and a foreground, each of which scrolls at a different speed. We will begin our reconstruction by implementing the slower-scrolling background layer. Readers who have attended closely to earlier technical discussions might already have an idea of how we can do this. You may recall from my discussion of the Boing demo that the "camera lens" that is the viewport can be shifted to focus on different locations in memory. It is therefore theoretically possible to set up the entirety of a *Menace* level in memory as a single horizontally elongated playfield that will always fill the screen from left to right and that uses the first 192 lines of the display (leaving the bottom 32 lines for the status panel). Because the first level is as wide as approximately 10 physical monitor screens, this playfield would need to have a resolution of (10 screens × 352 pixels per screen-line) or 3,520 × 192. This figure unfortunately presents a problem for us, though. Storing our entire background in memory will consume (352 pixels per screen-line / 8 pixels per byte × 192 lines × 10 screens × 2 bitplanes) or 168,960 bytes of our precious chip RAM. Considering that we are targeting a generation of Amigas that possess only 512 KB of chip RAM in total and that we still have so much else to implement to arrive at a completed game, this consumption is untenable. But luckily for us, it is not necessary with a modicum of programming cleverness.

We will instead define a playfield of just 800 × 192, which consumes just (800 pixels per line / 8 pixels per byte × 192 lines × 2 bitplanes) or 38,400 bytes. Using Deluxe Paint, we create a two-bitplane image to display in this playfield, consisting of a roughly serrated pattern of gray, green, and black to underscore this level's underwater environment. The image we create is 400 × 192. We insert it twice into our playfield, the two images sitting horizontally side by side. As the level begins, we see the extreme left edge of the playfield at the left edge of the screen. We then begin to scroll the background slowly to the left by panning the viewport slowly to the right, moving one pixel for every second painting of the screen, for a speed of 30 pixels per second on an NTSC Amiga (or 25 pixels per second on a PAL Amiga). Consider what happens when the left edge of the physical screen rests at the exact middle of our playfield (figure 8.6): because the two halves are exact duplicates of one another, we see on screen the same image that we began with. We therefore can move the viewport all the way back to its original starting point, and as long as this is done between screen paints, the viewer will notice nothing amiss. By cycling through the playfield in this way again and again, we can create the illusion of a lengthy background from a playfield that is in reality barely wider than two physical screens. This technique is often called a *wrap scroll*. When implemented this way on the Amiga, the wrap scroll is facilitated almost entirely by the copper, which autonomously reformulates the parameters of the display before each screen paint; the blitter need move no memory at all, and the 68000 need issue only occasional oversight instructions to the copper. Thus, we have a smooth scrolling background for very nearly free in terms of overall system load.

Before moving on, we make two modifications to the scrolling background with an eye toward the future. First, we add a third bitplane to the background playfield, leaving it for now filled entirely with 0s. Second, we implement double buffering on the background. As introduced in chapter 3, "double buffering" means that we employ not just one playfield for the background, but two, switching between them after every painting of the

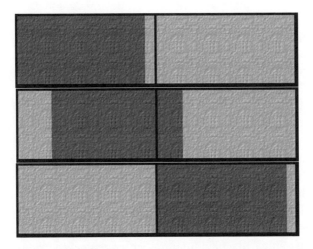

8.6 The *Menace* background wrap scroll. The complete playfield is made of two identical images placed side by side. The top illustration shows the playfield as it exists at the beginning of the level, with the part actually visible on screen shaded more darkly. The middle illustration shows the scroll in action, and the bottom shows us ready to reposition the viewport back to the extreme left without the viewer's perceiving it. Note that there is a small strip at the extreme right of the playfield that never appears on screen at all.

screen so that only one is active at a time. For now, both playfields contain the exact same pattern, making this switching as invisible to the user as it is currently unnecessary to us. Indeed, adding a bitplane and an entire extra playfield costs us a fair amount of precious memory for no apparent benefit, but both will facilitate additions we will make later, in Stage 5.

Stage 2: The Scrolling Foreground

If you just glance casually at *Menace* without thinking about its technical implementation, you will likely not even notice that its two layers of scenery (not including the player's own ship and the animated enemies she fights) scroll at different speeds—simply because the scrolling feels so natural. It feels that way because it simulates a property of the everyday world of motion: parallax. Imagine that you are standing at the edge of a busy highway on a flat plain, with a second highway also in view beyond this one, perhaps half a kilometer or so in the distance. Cars on the highway immediately before you whiz by very quickly, almost too quickly to track with the eyes. Those on the distant highway, however, appear to move through your field of view relatively slowly, even though they are traveling at roughly the same absolute speed as those closer to you. This difference is the parallax effect. Although its presence in *Menace* is noticeable only to the observant or technically thoughtful, its absence would most assuredly be noticed by everyone because movement through the levels would feel "off," neither natural nor believable. The universe of the game would lack the illusion of depth, appearing instead like exactly what it is in reality, a flat strip of images being unrolled behind the screen "window."

To simulate parallax in *Menace*, we make use of yet another of the Amiga's special graphics modes, one that is designed with games in mind and that I have occasion to introduce here for the first time: *dual-playfield mode*. In this mode, the Amiga automatically overlays two separate playfields upon one another, with up to three of the available six bitplanes allocated to each. The two playfields interact with one another similarly to the way that a single playfield interacts with a genlocked video display: the foreground playfield, meaning the one that rests on top, completely obscures the background—except where its pixels are set to color 0, which signals that these areas of the foreground are transparent and should allow the background to show through. The two playfields can even be swapped at will to make the foreground the background and the background the foreground. Dual-playfield mode does carry with it at least one serious limitation: because only three bitplanes can be allocated to each playfield, and one color register in the foreground playfield is reserved to signal transparency, the programmer is limited to just 7 colors in the foreground and 8 colors in the background, or a maximum of 15 on the entire screen. The *Amiga Hardware Reference Manual* presents dual-playfield mode's rationale thus: "A computer game display might have some action going on in one playfield in the background, while the other playfield is showing a control panel in the foreground. You can then change either the foreground or the background without having to redesign the entire display. You can also move the two playfields independently."[32] The last sentence is the key to our use of dual-playfield mode in *Menace*.

We can manipulate our two playfields independently of one another and can do anything to either of them that we can do to a playfield running in the normal single-playfield mode, including scrolling either or both playfields. Our background playfield is already scrolling at a rate of 25 or 30 pixels per second; our foreground playfield we scroll one pixel for every screen paint, or 50 and 60 pixels per second on a PAL and NTSC machine, respectively. The foreground playfield contains scenery, painted in its seven available colors. This scenery is concentrated largely along the playfield's top and bottom edges, with occasional vegetation jutting out well into its middle. Where scenery does not appear, the foreground playfield is filled with the os that indicate transparency, which allows the four-color background pattern to show through. Because the two playfields will scroll smoothly at different speeds, we will get a nice impression of realistic motion. This technique is often referred to as a *parallax scroll* and is one that the Amiga's dual-playfield capability makes it particularly suited for.

However, we still have a serious implementation problem to address. It is just as impractical to store our foreground playfield in memory as a single strip as it is to store the background that way; in fact, it is even more so because the foreground's faster rate of scroll means that we need no less than 20 monitor screens for the complete level. Nor will the simple wrap-scroll technique we used for the background suffice here; our game depends on a constant parade of new foreground scenery configurations for its visual and ludic appeal.

We begin to solve our problem by building the foreground from a series of scenery tiles, each 16 × 16 pixels in size, which we draw in Deluxe Paint. We can combine the 255 tiles we create there in various patterns to construct a wide variety of scenery; think of a tile-laying board game such as *Carcassonne* or even a jigsaw puzzle. By constructing our scenery from these larger patterns, we are able to avoid the necessity of storing every single pixel of it in memory and on disk. Instead, we combine our tile collection with a "map" of the foreground, which details which tile should be placed in each of the 16 × 16 pixel spaces that, stacked 12 high in a series of columns, make up our level. We can now reuse many tiles again and again in the course of constructing the full level. The most commonly used tile of all is filled completely with os, representing a space that shows only the background wall stored in the other playfield. *Tile-based graphics* is in fact a classic videogame technique, used by a wide variety of games in a wide variety of genres and platforms both before and after *Menace*.

Our foreground playfield is just slightly smaller than our background, 736 × 192, and like the background possesses the maximum three bit-planes of depth. As we scroll from its left to its right edge, we use the blitter to constantly copy new rows of tiles into the area of the playfield just to the right of the current physical screen. When the playfield scrolls a bit farther, those tiles become visible to the player, just as if they had been there all along. Yet when we reach the extreme right edge, we must reset our view all the way back to its original starting point. Because this reset creates an unacceptable jump in the player's view of the scenery, we therefore *also* copy the same columns just to the *left* of the physical screen. When we now reset the view back to its starting point, the player sees an exact duplicate of the scenery that exists on the other side of the playfield and notices nothing amiss at all. The result is an impression of continuous forward motion using a foreground playfield that, like the background, is actually only slightly more than two physical screens wide. The foreground scroll is obviously somewhat more taxing on computing power than the background, but we are able to use the blitter and its lightning-fast memory-copying ability along with the copper's ability to facilitate the scroll to relieve the 68000 once again of most of the burden. And because we modify only parts of the playfield that are currently out of the player's view, we do not need to double-buffer this part of the display, thus saving precious chip RAM.

Stage 3: The Status Panel

Our display currently has a blank area at its bottom because we are using only the first 192 lines of our 224-line screen for the scrolling environment. We wish to use this area for a status panel of sorts, which will eventually display the player's score along with her shields and armaments status and the all-important DMA Design logo. At first blush, implementing this panel seems a thorny proposition; unlike the rest of the screen, we do not want it to scroll, and we would like to be able to draw it using more and different colors than the 15 that are available between our two scrolling playfields. In fact, however, putting in the panel is relatively trivial, thanks once again to the copper.

You may recall from my introduction of the copper in chapter 3 that it can be programmed to adjust many parameters of the display not only between full screen paints, as we do to implement our scrolling playfields, but also at any arbitrary point *during* a paint. In this way, we can change the color palette, point Agnus and Denise to entirely new playfields, change resolution modes, turn dual-playfield mode on or off, and much more on the fly, thus effectively combining various logical displays onto one physical screen. In this case, we use the copper after line 192 to initiate what amounts to an entirely new display setup, this one a single-playfield configuration that looks to the place in memory where we have loaded the four-bitplane, 352 × 32 image of our status panel. When the screen is finished painting, the copper once again reconfigures the display hardware to return to our dual-playfield scrolling environment before beginning the next paint. In AmigaOS terms, we have combined two virtual screens onto a single physical screen; see chapter 3 and in particular the discussion of figure 3.13 for a refresher on this process.

Thus, we have our status panel, which we need only think about again when we need to update it occasionally to reflect changes in the player's fortunes.

Stage 4: The Player's Ship

The next step is to add the spaceship that the player will control in the game. We will implement this ship using one more new piece of the Amiga's graphical technology, *sprites*, whose introduction will complete the picture of the Amiga's major components that I have been sketching throughout this book.

The Amiga is hardly unique among computers in offering sprites; the original Atari Video Computer System has them, as do other eight-bit computers and game consoles from Atari, Commodore, and many others. But the Amiga's sprite system is unusually flexible and powerful. It supports up to eight sprites, each of which represents a moving object or character, such as the spaceship we wish to implement here—or for that matter the mouse pointer, which AmigaOS also implements as a sprite. Sprites are defined, positioned, and drawn separately from the rest of the screen. Each can be only up to 16 pixels wide—or 64 pixels on machines equipped with the AGA chip set—but as tall as desired and can normally be made up of up to three colors, along with transparent areas that allow the playfield(s) behind them to show through. The exact colors available for each of the sprites are drawn from the latter part of the screen color table: colors stored in registers 17, 18, and 19 can be used for the first and second sprites; in registers 21, 22, and 23 for the third and fourth; and so on, counting upward and always skipping one color register between sprite pairs. Because we make no use of these upper registers in our playfields, we are free to choose colors for our sprites from these registers without concerning ourselves about how those choices will affect the rest of our graphics. If we were using all 32 color registers for our playfields, we would obviously not have this freedom.

Critical to understanding the nature of sprites is knowing that they are not drawn into the playfield itself but are stored in memory separately, to be superimposed onto the real, physical screen only at the time when Denise outputs them to the display. In fact, sprites are so independent of the playfields that form the rest of the Amiga's display that they do not even concern themselves with the resolution mode currently employed; sprite positions are always specified in low resolution (320 × 200 if overscan is not employed). Sprites are likewise the only part of the display that can freely cross playfield boundaries, an attribute that forces us to include in our *Menace* code special checks to prevent our sprites from moving down into the panel at the bottom of the screen.

A small, two-bitplane playfield encodes the size, shape, and colors of each sprite, with color 0 representing transparence and colors 1 through

3 being drawn from the appropriate parts of the regular color table. Each sprite's current on-screen position is contained in attached X and Y coordinate values. The use of sprites not only yields dramatic performance improvements but also eases the programmer's burden immensely; with them, it is no longer necessary to modify the playfield constantly to reflect changes to the most dynamic parts of the display, and the programmer no longer needs to worry about drawing back in the background just vacated by her actors. To move a sprite, she merely changes either or both of two numbers in memory, those representing the X and Y coordinates, and lets Denise do the rest.[33] The playfield that stores each sprite's color and shape can be similarly adjusted as needed. We actually use three images of our spaceship right from the start, two showing it banking upward or downward and one showing it flying level. We swap these images in and out to reflect the ship's current motion prompted by the player's positioning of the joystick. In the completed game, the player will be able to collect power-ups that not only improve her weapons and armor but also change the appearance of her ship. We have more images on hand to reflect these changes, all drawn in the graphical workhorse Deluxe Paint.

When we begin to consider the details of implementing our spaceship via a sprite, however, we run into two significant problems. One is the fact that we would like to make our spaceship sprite fully 25 pixels wide, 9 more than the normal maximum of 16 pixels; in addition, we would like to be able to draw it using more than three colors. Luckily for us, both problems are quite easily overcome, using in the former case a bit of programming sleight of hand and in the latter some of the more advanced capabilities of the Amiga's sprite hardware. Nothing prevents two (or more) sprites from standing directly next to each other, close enough that they appear to be one. By using two sprites and moving them in lockstep, we can create the illusion of a single sprite up to 32 pixels wide. Further, the Amiga allows us to join two normal 3-color sprites into a single 15-color sprite; we need only place them directly on top of one another and turn on a register to inform Denise of our desire. The sprites' four bitplanes are then combined by Denise into a single image of 15 possible colors (plus transparency). By placing two of these 15-color "supersprites" next to one another, we can draw a large, colorful, and relatively detailed spaceship for the player to control. And just as we can decide which playfield in dual-playfield mode appears atop the other, we can also decide where our sprites rest in this display hierarchy. We take advantage of this ability to place our spaceship "between" the two playfields so that it obscures the background playfield but is obscured by the foreground (figure 8.7).

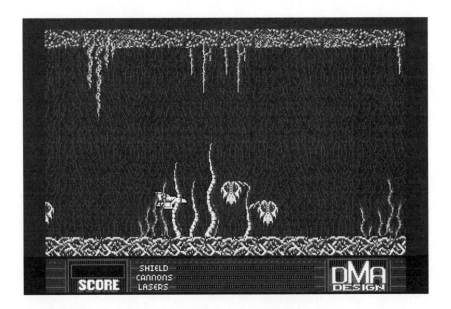

8.7 Stage 4 of the *Menace* reconstruction in action. Note that the player's spaceship passes behind nontransparent areas of the foreground playfield but remains in front of the background.

Implementing our spaceship in this way does carry the obvious drawback of consuming fully half of our available sprites, leaving precious few for the alien enemies we must still implement. That does not concern us, though, because we will create those enemies using other techniques and will in fact make no further use of sprites at all in *Menace*. It is worth noting, however, that the Amiga's modest total of eight sprites, like so much else about the machine, can be (and often were) stretched in surprising ways. Most significant, one can use the copper to manipulate the eight sprite channels on the fly during the screen-painting process, reconfiguring any or all of them to point to different sprite definitions in memory at the end of any given line. Thus, the programmer can actually place many more than eight sprites on the screen as long as no more than eight ever come to occupy the same line at once. The sprite system might therefore be better described as supporting eight sprites per *line* rather than eight per screen. AmigaOS actually provides a great deal of support for maximizing the available sprite channels in the form of *virtual* sprites that are automatically assigned to hardware sprite channels as needed during screen painting, albeit at some inevitable loss of speed when compared to the hardware-banging approach we are using for *Menace*.

Stage 5: Enemies

The next stage is by far the most daunting: we must implement the various enemy aliens that the player must kill or avoid to complete a level. Much—perhaps most—of this stage's complexity involves instilling in the aliens some simple artificial intelligence to make them fly about the screen in various patterns and hunt the player's ship. Although this topic is fascinating in itself, I do not discuss the logic in depth here because it is both daunting and abstracted from the unique details of the Amiga's architecture that are my primary concern. Suffice to say that over the course of the level on which a player is playing, enemies come at the player in a series of waves, each wave consisting of up to 12 aliens. Each alien's behavior is controlled by a unique script, defining its movements and behavior from the moment it is spawned until it flies out of view or is killed. When one wave is completely finished, the next (along with its associated individual scripts) automatically begins. It is also worth noting that by freeing the 68000 from many more mundane chores of display and system management, the blitter, the copper, and the custom chips allow more cycles to be devoted to the aliens' artificial intelligence, thus potentially making them more challenging and more believable. Thus, the Amiga's unique architecture, far from being useful only for more and better eye candy, actually creates the potential to make *better* as well as prettier games.

Turning from artificial intelligence to the details of hardware implementation, the obvious way to render the aliens at first blush is via sprites. The sheer quantity of aliens, however, makes that a difficult proposition, indeed. Although we might attempt to shift the sprite channels about via the copper during screen painting, doing so would be a nightmare of complexity, as would devising algorithms to assure that no more than eight sprites ever come to occupy the same line. And although we might use AmigaOS's libraries to do some of this sprite-manipulating work for us, this approach is simply too slow for a complex action-game showcase such as *Menace*. We therefore decide to take another approach, using *blitter object blocks* (*BOBs*) for our aliens.

Unlike sprites, there is nothing conceptually new about BOBs; they are simply small areas that the blitter blits into and out of our playfields. We begin by drawing our various aliens in Deluxe Paint, producing a series of images, each within a rectangular frame 32 × 24 pixels in size. Each image uses three bitplanes for a maximum of eight colors. Of those eight colors, the first three must be the three that we are already using to paint the green, gray, and black backing texture, but the next five may be any that we choose for that particular wave. Before a wave begins, we adjust the background palette to match the colors desired and then use the blitter to draw these images into the background playfield again and again, moving them through their trajectories until they finally disappear, whether through death or simple departure. It was to facilitate the aliens that we made the background playfield three bitplanes deep; that third bitplane, unused until now, gives us the extra colors we need to draw our aliens. When we begin implement this scheme, though, we find we have some problems.

You may recall from earlier sections of this book that the 68000 and many other Amiga components are only designed to access memory blocks that begin with even-numbered addresses and that they vastly prefer to deal with memory in chunks of two bytes (16 bits, often called a "word") at a time. The blitter is no exception here; in fact, it can deal *only* with full words of memory. As our aliens move about the screen, though, they must occupy positions in the playfields that do not line up neatly to word or even byte boundaries. We move them into these positions by using a special shift register on the blitter, which allows us to skew the source data to the right or left as we copy, filling in the boundaries that are thereby exposed with 0s (figure 8.8).

The data shown in this figure might of course be one of our aliens being copied into a playfield—or, for that matter, a Deluxe Paint image

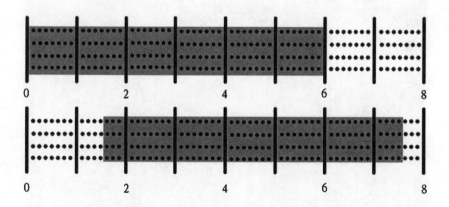

8.8 A blitter shifting operation. The upper illustration shows the source blit, which consists of three words (six bytes) that begin at an even-numbered address in memory. The bottom illustration shows the destination blit, in which four words are written, with the data skewed 13 bits (or pixels) to the right. The areas at the left and right in the bottom illustration that do not contain the source data are still part of the blit but are filled with 0s during the shifting operation.

being copied from the master-copy playfield into the working-copy playfield, as described in chapter 3. The blitter's shifting capabilities illustrate once again how, far from being "merely" a high-speed, general-purpose memory shuffler, it was designed from the start with the special requirements of graphics and animation in mind.

Alas, when we begin to draw our blitter-shifted aliens into the playfields, we see the results shown in figure 8.9.

The trails of aliens streaked across the screen stems from the fact that we are drawing our BOBs *into* our playfields but never taking them *out* again. To eliminate these streaks, we need to implement a three-step process that takes advantage of our forethought in Stage 1 of this project in making the background playfield double buffered and thus actually two playfields. When a given playfield is no longer the active one, we first take a snapshot of the background areas into which we are about to draw our BOBs, copying them into another area of memory for safekeeping, using the blitter. We then blit the BOBs themselves into the playfield, as we did before; this playfield is now ready to be painted onto the screen. When this playfield is once again the inactive one, we copy the stored backgrounds back into place before repeating the whole cycle again. Double buffering is essential to this process because it gives us time to make these

8.9 *Menace* in action without a background-clipping algorithm for the on-screen BOBs

alterations to the screen without the user seeing the bits and pieces being cut out and pasted in. Although there is a short period between successive paints of even a single-buffered screen, known as the "vertical blanking interval," it is not sufficient for the quantity of operations we need to perform here, for the process just described is quite a taxing one. Twelve active aliens require no less than ((12 playfield background to holding area copies + 12 alien to playfield copies + 12 holding area to playfield background copies) × 3 bitplanes per copy), or 108 copy operations, for every round of movement, and the Amiga must of course also manage the foreground and background scrolls, the player's ship, and all of the artificial intelligence and game logic in a timely manner. All this is made possible only by the blitter's ability to copy blocks of memory about fully twice as quickly as the 68000 itself.

Our aliens now look much better, but there is still another problem to be solved.

As illustrated in figure 8.10, our aliens appear as solid rectangular blocks that are obviously separate from the surrounding background. This appearance stems of course from the fact that solid rectangular blocks—and not irregular alien shapes—are exactly what we are using the blitter to copy. Unfortunately, the blitter can only be programmed to deal with

8.10 *Menace* with a background-clipping algorithm for the aliens in place, but without background masking implemented

regular rectangular shapes. What we need, then, is a way of introducing transparency to our aliens. This task is somewhat trickier than it was with our ship sprite because now we are working with objects that are *part of* the playfield that we wish to show through as background, not with a separate element of the display. The blitter, however, gives us a way.

Up to now we have used the blitter only to copy a single source block of memory to a single destination, possibly shifting left or right along the way. The blitter, though, is actually capable of accessing *three* sources and of merging and manipulating those sources in many ways beyond the shifts with which we are already familiar. We will use these possibilities to create the transparency effect we desire, in effect stenciling our aliens into the background playfields rather than simply copying them. We begin by making a fourth bitplane of sorts for each of our aliens. Each bit of this extra bitplane is set to 1 if that same bit in *any* of the other three bitplanes is set to 1; otherwise, it is set to 0. This setting provides us with a mask of the alien's shape, showing where any color other than color 0, which we want to define as transparency, exists. Next, we program the blitter to access three sources in the course of each alien copy operation: the mask bitplane, defined as source A; the actual alien bitplane to be copied, defined as source B; and the data that already exist in that part of the destination playfield, defined as source C. (Source C and the destination are, in other words, the same.) And we ask the blitter to perform some simple logic on these three sources to determine what is actually copied into the playfield. If a given bit is set to 1 in source A, that bit is copied from source B. If, however, a given bit is set to 0 in source A, that bit is copied from source C; in other words, it stays the same. Thus, we can have our irregularly shaped aliens and even unusual creatures such as bubbles that are transparent in the middle (figure 8.11).

A remarkable advantage is that the blitter can access multiple sources and perform logical transformations like those described here in the course of a copy without using a single cycle more than would a straight source-to-destination copy. Although the aliens themselves are inevitably taxing on system resources, the calculations that enable their transparency are effectively made free by the blitter's design.

Stage 6: Collision Detection

In order to turn *Menace* into a proper game, we still need to be able to detect when the player's ship comes in contact with its deadly alien adversaries. Such contact should gradually drain the ship's protective shields and, when the shields are exhausted, destroy the ship entirely. We need, then, what game programmers call a *collision-detection routine*.

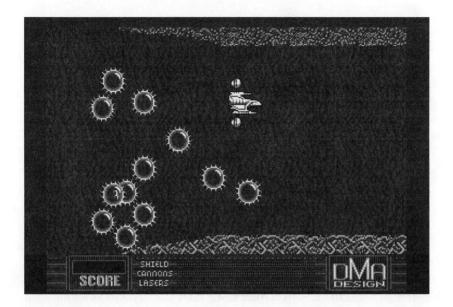

8.11 The *Menace* aliens with bitplane masking used to achieve transparency

On most platforms of the Amiga's era, the programming of such a routine would be a complex endeavor, indeed. The Amiga's design, however, makes it almost trivial, for we can simply ask the Amiga to tell us when any sprites we choose come into contact with any other given elements of the display. In this case, we ask to be informed when one or more of the sprites that compose the player's ship comes into contact with the third bitplane of the background playfield only; in other words, when the ship passes over an area of the third bitplane that is not filled with os. Because that bitplane is reserved for the alien BOBs only and has no part in the rest of the background, the Amiga will thus signal a collision only when the ship is in contact with an alien. Denise sets a flag in a special memory location after every paint in which the collision requirements we have specified are met. We only need write some relatively trivial routines to check that flag and if necessary respond to it by draining the ship's shield energy and eventually destroying the ship and ending or restarting the level. Because Denise automatically handles collision detection as a preexisting part of her normal screen painting, collision detection is yet again effectively a free gift of the Amiga, one that adds no significant processing drain to our game. Hardware-based collision detection is in fact one of the most often overlooked advantages of the Amiga because it reduces tasks that are thorny and processing intensive on other platforms to little more than a footnote on this one.

Stage 7: Weapons

Having made it possible for the aliens to destroy the player's ship, fairness demands that we also give the player some weapons to respond in kind. Although the weapons can conceivably be implemented as sprites, we choose to make the bolts from the ship's lasers by using BOBs. In a significant wrinkle, we draw these BOBs not into the background playfield that houses the aliens, but rather into planes 0 and 1 of the foreground playfield. (We need no more than four colors to represent these simple bolts of energy.) As with the alien BOBs, we use an extra bitplane of mask data to stencil the bolts into place, allowing the background to show through, and use the blitter's shifting capability to let us draw them into any arbitrary location on the screen. We must of course also erase the bolts before drawing them anew farther along their journey, just as we did with the aliens, by storing the old playfield backgrounds in a buffer in another part of memory until we draw them back in. Yet because we allow no more than three bolts on screen at any time, and because they are quite tiny—only two bitplanes of 16 × 2 pixels in size—they do not dramatically tax the already very busy blitter. We therefore do not bother with double buffering the foreground playfield. Because these BOBs are so tiny, we have reason to hope that the laser bolt–drawing process can complete during the vertical blanking interval, and even if it does not, the player is likely to construe a certain amount of bleeding or tearing as intrinsic to the nature of these bolts of energy—a visual effect rather than a defect, as it were.

Finally, we need to know when a laser bolt strikes an alien. This knowledge is somewhat more problematic than determining when an alien strikes the player's ship, for the Amiga's hardware collision detection checks only for collisions involving sprites. We will therefore press the blitter into service one more time in a somewhat surprising fashion.

As already discussed, the blitter is capable of combining data from any or all of three source channels in the process of writing to the destination. Just as we can choose to enable or disable these sources, we can also choose to disable the destination. This ability, combined with a special flag—the "BZERO" flag—that the blitter sets at a certain memory location, allows us to use the blitter as a tool for making logical determinations. We set one source channel to one plane of the BOB that represents the laser bolt that we have already drawn into the foreground playfield and set another to the area of plane 2 of the background playfield that the bolt is passing over; the third source channel and the destination channel go unused. We then ask the blitter to perform what is known in computer science parlance as a logical "AND" on the two sources during the course of the copy, which means that we copy to the destination *only* those bits (or pixels) that are set in *both* of the sources—in other words, only those pixels that are occupied by both the laser bolt and an alien. Because we have disabled the destination channel, this "copy" operation does not actually perform a copy at all. However, as a normal part of its operation, the blitter automatically sets the BZERO flag any time that the result of its last operation was nothing but 0s. Therefore, we can check this flag immediately after our "copy" and, if it is not set, know that our laser bolt has indeed struck an alien. We must still proceed at this point to determine which alien was struck by comparing the on-screen position of each alien with the position of the laser bolt. By giving us a fast way to determine if a laser has struck anything at all, the blitter lets us avoid having to make these time-consuming calculations—which mostly yield no results—with every single frame; we make them only when we know there has indeed been a collision.

Menace: A Summing Up

I have heretofore in this book avoided discussing or including actual program code, but it seems worthwhile to make one exception here. What follows is the main loop of the original *Menace*, as written in 68000 assembly language by Dave Jones, which gives an overview of how all of the parts I have just described interlock to form a finished, playable game.

```
vloop bsr     waitline223        interrupt set at vertical
      not.b   vcount(a5)         position 223 (panel start)
      beq     twoblanks          alternate every frame
      lea     copperlist(pc),a1  set up registers for routine
      move.w  pf2scroll(a5),d0   checkpf2
      move.w  pf1scroll(a5),d1
      bsr     checkpf2           and branch to it
      bsr     moveship
      bsr     check.collision
      bsr     erase.missiles
      bsr     levels.code
      bsr     update.missiles
      bsr     drawfgnds
*     bsr     print.score
*     bsr     check.keys
      bsr     check.path
```

```
          bra     vloop
twoblanks
          bsr     checkpf1       the following routines are
          bsr     flipbgnd       only executed every second frame
          bsr     moveship
          bsr     restorebgnds   restore backgrounds behind
                  aliens
          bsr     process.aliens
          bsr     save.aliens    save the backgrounds behind
                  aliens
          bsr     draw.aliens    and then draw the aliens

          tst.b   kill.game(a5)
          beq     vloop
          bra     alldone
```

This main loop, like most action games on the Amiga, is built around Agnus and Denise's ceaseless screen painting. Its first step is to wait for the beam to reach screen-paint line 223, which corresponds with pixel line 192, the end of the main action area and beginning of the status panel. The program thus avoids updating the main action area as much as possible while the beam is still painting it yet also grants the Amiga some extra time to perform updates beyond the vertical blanking period alone by beginning to process the next frame of action even while the beam continues to paint the static status panel. The loop performs one of two sequences that are alternated with every successive paint. Here I describe only the most significant and essential of the routines that make up these sequences.

One sequence scrolls only the foreground playfield by one step via "checkpf2"; checks the joystick controls and updates the player's ship's position and appearance accordingly via the "moveship" routine; checks for collisions between aliens and the ship via the "check.collision" routine; erases missiles drawn on the previous go-round by painting the stored background back into their positions via the "erase.missiles" routine; moves and paints the missiles in anew, checking for collisions between them and the aliens via the "update.missiles" routine; and, finally, via "check.path" checks to see if all currently active aliens are dead or have moved off screen, in which case more aliens are introduced. The other sequence scrolls both the background and foreground playfields by one step via "checkpf1"; swaps the active background playfield to facilitate double buffering there via "flipbgnd"; updates the player's ship via "moveship"; restores the stored backgrounds to positions just vacated by aliens via "restorebgnds"; uses the game's simple artificial intelligence logic to determine the next move for each active alien via "process.aliens"; saves the backgrounds where aliens are about to be drawn into a buffer via "save.aliens"; and, finally, draws the alien BOBs into their new positions via "draw.aliens." Note that only the movements of the player's ship and the scroll of the foreground playfield are updated with every single paint; most elements are updated only every *other* paint, for an effective frame rate of 25 per second on a PAL machine or 30 per second on an NTSC machine. This rate is fast enough for the game's purposes, and dividing the processing into two sequences like this allows it precious extra time to get everything done.

There is, of course, much more to the complete *Menace* than what I have described here. When killed, some aliens leave behind "power-ups" that the player can grab to improve her weapons or armor, and the player should receive points and occasional extra lives for killing aliens and making progress. Each level should end with an attack by a fearsome "boss" monster, and there should be six levels in all, each with different scenery and different alien challengers. And, of course, there should be sound effects and the omnipresent thumping tracker-composed soundtrack that was such a Psygnosis trademark. All of these elements are built on the foundation I have laid down here, though.

The Legacy of Psygnosis

Much as Commodore and even many Amiga users might have tried to downplay the Amiga's original conception as a pure game console, those origins show through in the hardware in countless ways. A comparison to the Amiga's most obvious 68000-based rivals, the Atari ST and the first-generation Apple Macintosh, only underscores the point; neither of those platforms supports sprites or a dual-playfield mode, and, of course, neither has anything like the Amiga's copper and blitter. The Amiga in its heyday hosted games that would literally have been impossible on any other platform. And remarkable as the Amiga's core capabilities were even upon a cursory inspection, the teams of developers that worked for Psygnosis kept finding ways to stretch them. Just one year after the release of *Menace* in 1988, Psygnosis published Reflections Interactive's *Shadow of the Beast*, an action-adventure stunner that featured 12 music tracks to *Menace*'s one, 12 levels of parallax scrolling to *Menace*'s two, and many dozens of colors on screen at once thanks to some clever copper programming. *Shadow of the Beast* was the most audiovisually impressive videogame one could play in one's home at the time of its release and made *Menace* look painfully sparse. Packaged elaborately in a huge box with the usual striking Roger Dean artwork outside and a T-shirt inside, *Shadow* was a watershed for Psygnosis and Amiga gaming and spawned two sequels, the first in 1990 and the second in 1992, that raised the bar of multimedia excellence even farther. The three games also represented another, less fortunate Psygnosis trend, however: they seemed to hate their players, being almost inconceivably difficult to win fairly. "Trainers" and cheat codes circulated quickly enough through the Amiga's gaming and cracking communities, though, thus allowing players at least to see everything the games had to offer and show off these elements to others.

Having perhaps seen the writing on the Amiga wall, Psygnosis allowed itself to be acquired by Sony Corporation in 1993, an event that marked the end of its time as an Amiga-focused games publisher; its last trickle of Amiga games that had already been in the pipeline at the time of acquisition appeared in 1994. Sony transitioned the company into a console-focused developer, with a particular emphasis on its Sony Playstation console, under development at the time en route to its 1995 premiere. With several titles available at launch, Psygnosis became a significant developer for the Playstation, with such popular titles as the *Wipeout* series of racing games to its credit, until its brand name was rather unceremoniously eliminated in 1999 following a round of corporate reorganizations.

Some of the development teams that used Psygnosis as a publisher also transitioned successfully to the new generation of console platforms. Reflections, best known for the *Shadow of the Beast* series on the Amiga, came to specialize in racing games on the consoles, producing the *Destruction Derby* and *Driver* series; it released the fifth game of the latter in 2007. And DMA Design, the tiny team responsible for *Menace* and a number of other Psygnosis titles, eventually morphed into Rockstar North, the studio responsible for the innovative, massively popular, and massively controversial *Grand Theft Auto* series. Dave Jones himself left shortly before the watershed game of that series, *Grand Theft Auto III*, but remains active in the videogame industry.

While DMA Design was still an Amiga developer, Jones was responsible for designing and programming another long-lived franchise: *Lemmings*. It is the most atypical of Psygnosis games and the last thing one might have expected from Jones and DMA Design when one considers their earlier games such as *Menace*. Each of the 120 levels in *Lemmings* places the player in charge of a tribe of the titular rodents in some sort of hazardous environment. True to the popular myths if not the reality of their real-life inspiration, these cute but stupid creatures will walk off of cliffs or into pools of acid with suicidal cheer. The player must guide as many as possible to the level's exit, which she does by bestowing special abilities upon individual members of the tribe, turning them into diggers that tunnel through the earth, builders of bridges that can span cliffs or water, or simply blockers that prevent their mindless comrades from marching past them to their doom. *Lemmings* starts out easy but gets difficult soon enough. With dozens of lemmings marching among and into countless hazards, the pace of the higher levels becomes frenetic indeed, a challenge for the reflexes as well as the mind. Despite the challenge *Lemmings* can present, however, it never fails to feel welcoming and friendly, perhaps in part due to the charming little creatures themselves, who exclaim "Let's go!" at the start of a level and let loose a forlorn "Oh, no!" when something goes wrong. Like a classic cartoon, *Lemmings* also includes a bit of dark humor to balance the cuteness; some levels require the player to sacrifice a few lemmings for the greater good by turning them into walking bombs, and the player always has the option to "nuke" a level and all of its inhabitants when the frustration gets too extreme. *Lemmings* is like a game from a later era in its kindness to its player; once a level is completed, the player receives a code that lets her start again at the next whenever she chooses, meaning that she is never forced to replay a difficult or frustrating level after she has finally conquered it. The levels themselves not only provide a variety of challenges but are often built around an amusing theme. One of my personal favorites is "A Beast of a Level," which plays on a caricaturized version of the first level of *Shadow of the Beast*, including comically ominous background music. The sight of these ridiculous cartoon creatures bobbling through this dark science-fiction world is hilarious. A similar absurdist sense of humor is in evidence everywhere; even the on-screen pause button is marked not with text, but with a set of tiny paws for a horrid pun.

Lemmings is easily Psygnosis's best all-around game. In a pleasing example of quality receiving its just commercial reward, it also became a huge hit. It obsessed the Amiga community for months after its release, with many European magazines devoting pages in issue after issue to solving its more difficult levels. DMA and Psygnosis, recognizing that they had a good thing, were quick to follow up on *Lemmings*, first with an expansion pack and then with a full-fledged sequel, and Psygnosis also funded ports to virtually every other gaming platform of the era. *Lemmings* has remained continuously available in one form or another since its original 1991 release, a rarity indeed in the fast-moving world of the videogame. The respected eldest member of an entire genre of quirky and challenging yet accessible puzzle games, it remains available today for the Playstation 3 console as well as for the handheld Playstation Portable. Its original 1991 version, meanwhile, stands as yet another Amiga-based harbinger of gaming's future in the way it jettisons the "dark" nerd bona fides of science fiction and high fantasy, challenges but never punishes, and remains indefatigably "juicy."

One can certainly question whether the Amiga fully realized the almost utopian dream of its potential as expressed by Trip Hawkins and others in its heady early days, but its gaming legacy, in both titles themselves and developers to whom it gave a start, is a rich one. The popularity of Amiga games played through emulators is certainly still considerable today, perhaps because the Amiga is the earliest gaming platform whose visuals and audio, at least in the more aesthetically pleasing titles, are good enough not to appear absurd to players of today, and because in the more complex titles its mouse-driven interface is vastly more intuitive than the keyboard-driven alphabet soup of other platforms from the era. In fact, some of the Amiga's best titles look more contemporary today than they did 10 years ago. Casual-game developers and independent developers, working in small teams much like those that developed for Psygnosis, have revived many old genres that were popular on the Amiga, having realized that enormous big-budget productions with their high system requirements and the major demands they make on their players' time and expertise are not the only experience that players desire; indeed, such games are exactly what many casual gamers do *not* desire. The result has been a welcome return of games that reflect the individuality of the small teams who created them, games that are as easy to pick up and play for a bit as they are to explore in depth, games that reward commitment but do not demand it. In other words, games like *Lemmings*.

In spite of achieving real success in certain niche markets in North America and in many living rooms and bedrooms in Europe, the Amiga did not quite conquer the world in the way that many believed it would in those heady days of 1984 and 1985. Having devoted a book to explaining why I believe the Amiga to be both a revolutionary piece of technology and the most important link between the pioneering early years of personal computing and the ubiquitous digital culture of today, I feel behooved to ask here at book's end why the Amiga is no longer a vital force in modern computing. To begin to answer that question, I would like to continue for a time with the subject of the previous chapter: games, the Amiga's most sustained niche in Europe in the same way that video production was for the platform in North America.

Myst and *Doom*

Two pivotal if very different games appeared on competing machines in 1993 that marked the beginning of the end of the Amiga's time as a premiere gaming platform: *Myst* by Cyan Studios and *Doom* by id Software. Both were huge hits, the sort of titles that sell not only themselves, but the hardware on which they run, and both were—for very different reasons—well beyond the capabilities of the vast majority of Amigas.

The Amiga's basic storage format, a 3.5-inch floppy disk capable of holding up to 880 KB of data, was considered quite expansive at the time of the machine's release in 1985. This judgment was, however, made in the absence of any previous experience with multimedia computing. As soon as game developers and others began to pack their offerings with the graphics and sound data that were the platform's calling card, the Amiga's floppy disks began to feel restrictive indeed. Within a year, ambitious games such as *Defender of the Crown* were already requiring two disks. Yet simply shipping games on more and more disks was not an entirely viable solution. Although many Amiga users equipped their machines with two floppy drives for convenience, few had more than that; thus, playing games that spanned three, four, or more disks could turn into a nightmare of disk swapping. The obvious solution to that dilemma was to copy all of the floppy-disk content to a hard disk for actual play, but although hard disks did become increasingly common as the years went by, there unfortunately remained plenty of floppy-only Amigas. In fact, these unexpanded systems were almost always the ones used primarily or exclusively for playing games.

Cinemaware found constant pausing to request that the user insert another disk incompatible with its aesthetic of constant, immersive activity and thus limited most of its titles to a maximum of two disks. This limitation necessarily restricted the amount and quality of visuals and audio Cinemaware could include in each game even as the company invested considerable effort into developing compression technology to maximize each disk's potential. *Rocket Ranger*, for instance, could include only a few choice bits of the digitized speech that Bob Jacob would have preferred to have throughout, having to rely instead mostly on text to communicate its story to the player.[1] Although not so thematically ambitious as Cinemaware, Psygnosis also ultimately found the 3.5-inch disk format restrictive; in contrast to early single-disk efforts such as *Menace* and *Barbarian*, 1992's *Agony* spanned three, with all of the requisite annoying swapping. Indeed, many Amigas in Europe sported just a single floppy drive for storage, further exasperating the problem.

The Amiga was positively crying out for a new storage technology that was just starting to engender discussion within the computer industry at the time of the platform's debut: the CD-ROM drive, which had a coming-out party of sorts in March 1986, when Microsoft hosted a conference on the emerging technology that came to be called the "Woodstock of the computer industry" in the technology press.[2] With its potential to store more than 500 MB on a single inexpensive and portable plastic platter, the CD-ROM seemed to many like the ideal distribution medium for multimedia-intensive Amiga games; among those with this view was Jacob, whose Cinemaware invested considerable funds into developing the format.[3] CD-ROM drives, however, remained very expensive for their first few years on the market and in the absence of any apparent interest or leadership from Commodore were painfully slow in making their way to the Amiga at all because manufacturers tended to focus on the larger installed base of IBM PCs and PC clones, even though those machines lacked the audiovisual capabilities to take full advantage of a format that seemed tailor made for a multimedia computer such as the Amiga. After all, the Amiga's very design, as recounted in chapter 5, had been partially inspired by the first videogame to take advantage of emerging optical-storage technologies, *Dragon's Lair*. Nevertheless, Commodore did not mate a CD-ROM drive to an Amiga until 1991 and even then did so only in the form of a product called *CDTV* (for *"Commodore Dynamic Total Vision"*), a multimedia appliance that housed Amiga hardware internally but was packaged externally as a television component similar in appearance to a VCR or laser-disc player. In a bizarre decision, Commodore studiously avoided using the Amiga name in connection with CDTV, promoting the latter instead as an entirely new product line. Although visionary in some ways, CDTV, like its close competitor the Philips CD-i, ultimately failed to take off in the face of the Microsoft Windows–based multimedia computing boom. CDTV's successor *CD32* was marketed more as a pure game console than as a general-purpose multimedia appliance, and with its 14 MHz 68020 processor and AGA chip set would have seemed, at least technologically, to be poised to offer stiff competition to the first CD-ROM-based consoles to arrive from Nintendo, Sega, and 3DO. Unfortunately, it was released in late 1993, by which time Commodore was in full freefall, and, despite encouraging early sales in Europe and especially Great Britain, was far from sufficient to save the company. In another incredible decision, considering that by the early 1990s CD-ROM-equipped multimedia PCs running Windows were flying from the shelves, Commodore never offered an official Amiga model with a CD-ROM drive as standard equipment. As Commodore resolutely filed the Amiga serial numbers off of CDTV and CD32, actual Amiga users were forced to content themselves with a variety of cobbled-together and expensive CD-ROM solutions from small venders or even Macintosh products that used the same *Small Computer Systems Interface (SCSI)* for disk drives that was common on the Amiga. The only exception was Amiga 500 users, who could purchase a balky and expensive CDTV add-on kit from Commodore.

As a new generation of CD-ROM titles expanded the possibilities for gaming on Windows and Macintosh machines in exactly the ways that Jacob had dreamed of when starting Cinemaware, the Amiga thus remained largely tied to its miniscule floppy disks. This disparity was made painfully evident with the release of *Myst*, an immersive if admittedly slow-paced adventure game that lets it player explore a beautifully rendered, almost photorealistic landscape of sight and sound. Key to *Myst* was its use of a first-person point of view; rather than view and manipulate an avatar on the screen, the player finds herself *inside* the environment, viewing it through the eyes of her alter ego. *Myst*'s graphics and sound were not beyond the capability of an AGA Amiga, but it used the CD-ROM format to store an unprecedented quantity of both. The ideal companion to show off a new multimedia PC, *Myst* undoubtedly sold many nontechnophiles on the potential of CD-ROM and also sold plenty of the Macintosh and Windows machines on which it ran en route to becoming the top-selling PC game of its generation.[4] A belated port of *Myst* finally came to Amiga owners who had equipped their machines with CD-ROM drives in 1997, but by that time the game, like the Amiga platform itself, was already looking dated.

Doom, meanwhile, had a long-term impact on the world of gaming far exceeding even that of *Myst*. The latest of a series of experiments with interactive 3D graphics by id programmer John Carmack, *Doom* shares with *Myst* only its immersive first-person point of view; in all other respects, this fast-paced, ultraviolent shooter is the polar opposite of the cerebral *Myst*. Whereas the world of *Myst* is presented as a collection of static nodes that the player can move among, each represented by a relatively static picture of its own, the world of *Doom* is contiguous. As the player roams about, *Doom* must continually recalculate in real time the view of the world that it presents to her on the screen, in effect drawing for her a completely new picture with every frame using a vastly simplified version of the 3D-rendering techniques that Eric Graham began experimenting with on the Amiga back in 1986. First-person viewpoints had certainly existed in games previously, but mostly in the context of flight simulators, of puzzle-oriented adventures such as *Myst*, or of space-combat games such as *Elite*. *Doom* has a special quality that those earlier efforts lack in that the player embodies her avatar as she moves through 3D space in a way that feels shockingly, almost physically *real*. She does not view the world through a windscreen, is not separated from it by an adventure game's point-and-click mechanics and static artificiality. *Doom* marks a revolutionary change in action gaming, the most significant to come about between the videogame's inception and the present. If the player *directs* the action in a game such as *Menace*, *Doom* makes her feel as if she is *in* the action, *in* the game's world.

Given the Amiga platform's importance as a tool for noninteractive 3D rendering, it is ironic that the Amiga is uniquely unsuited to *Doom* and the many iterations and clones of it that would follow. Most of the Amiga attributes that we employed in the *Menace* reconstruction—its scrolling playfields, its copper, its sprites—are of no use to a 3D-engine programmer. Indeed, the Intel-based machines on which Carmack created *Doom* possess none of these features. Even the Amiga's bitplane-based play-fields, the source of so many useful graphical tricks and hacks when programming a 2D game such as *Menace*, are an impediment and annoyance in a game such as *Doom*. Much preferable are the Intel-based machines' straightforward chunky playfields because these layouts are much easier to work with when every frame of video must be drawn afresh from scratch. What is required most of all for a game such as *Doom* is sufficient raw processing power to perform the necessary thousands of calculations needed to render each frame quickly enough to support the frenetic action for which the game is known. By 1993, the plebian Intel-based computer, so long derided by Amiga owners for its inefficiencies and lack of design imagination, at last possessed this raw power. The Amiga simply had no answer to the Intel 80486s and Pentiums that powered this new, revolutionary genre of first-person shooters.

Throughout its history, the Amiga had always to some extent replaced brute power with finesse and efficiency. Even the original machine's 68000 was, after all, clocked almost one full megahertz below that of the Atari ST and Apple Macintosh. The requirements of games such as *Doom*, however, were a problem the Amiga could not dance around, and as *Doom* exploded in popularity, these games became increasingly the only games many gamers wanted to play. The Intel platform was soon being tailored to them via special 3D-graphics cards that removed some of the mathematical burden of 3D rendering from the CPU, just as, in an earlier era, Miner and team had designed the blitter and copper to help out with the 2D games that were popular then. Versions of *Doom* did make their way to the Amiga after id released the source code to the engine in 1997, but even this relatively primitive 3D engine runs acceptably only on Amigas that have been dramatically expanded beyond their original capabilities. In a supreme irony, one might say that the 3D revolution that began on the Amiga ultimately killed its parent, for although the Amiga was the most suitable platform in existence for that purpose in 1986, it lacked the tools to make the great leap to interactive 3D. Without the mainstream exposure that cutting-edge games could offer and with only niche markets such as desktop video to continue to sustain it otherwise, the Amiga was in a tough spot indeed after *Myst* and *Doom* appeared, not only in North America but soon enough in Europe as well.

The Blame Game

But why was the Amiga not improved fast enough—if not to maintain the huge lead it had over other platforms in 1985, then at least to keep up with them?

The standard response to such a question among current and former Amiga users is to place the blame squarely at the feet of the Commodore management team, whose neglect and incompetence finally led to the end not only of the Amiga, but of Commodore itself. And certainly there is a great deal of truth to this argument. At no point from the time Commodore acquired the Amiga in 1984 until its bankruptcy and liquidation in 1994 was it anything but a confused and poorly managed organization. After a typically ineffective advertising campaign to accompany the launch of the Amiga, Commodore advertised it only in fits and starts and almost always poorly (at least in North America). Corporate strategies and reorganizations came and went even faster than CEOs, the general pattern being for Commodore to announce a bold new marketing direction for the Amiga—positioning it as a business tool, an ideal home computer, or a multimedia workstation—and to indulge in a brief flurry of advertising. When this advertising failed to make an immediate impact on sales and on the following quarterly statement, the approach would be unceremoniously dropped and replaced at some future date by another approach that effectively undercut everything Commodore had said about the Amiga in the previous campaign. These constant changes in message created the impression to the outsider that Commodore itself had no idea what the Amiga really was or what it was good for.

Such an impression was perhaps not far from the truth. Gifted with the most revolutionary computer of its era, Commodore failed to put its full corporate weight behind the Amiga until, all other revenue streams having dried up, there literally was no other choice. Commodore instead tried to hedge its bets, putting considerable resources into designing and marketing unexceptional Intel-based PC-clone computers. (To understand the full extent of Commodore's muddled thinking here, imagine Apple, after having developed the iPod, choosing to make handheld CD players a vital part of its corporate strategy.) An even more incredible Commodore decision was to continue into the 1990s to invest money and engineering effort into developing a new iteration of the Commodore 64, dubbed in-house "the 65." Engineer Fred Bowen wrote of the planned Commodore 65 in a preliminary manual: "The C65 microcomputer is a low-cost, versatile, competitive product designed for the international home computer and game market. The C65 is well suited for first time computer buyers, and provides an excellent upgrade path for owners of the commercially successful C64. . . . The purpose of the C65 is to modernize and revitalize the 10 year old C64 market."[5] One might of course reply that Commodore already had a computer that met all of those criteria, and it was called the "Amiga 500." The 65 fortunately was canceled before Commodore squandered more resources attempting to market it. Yet when one considers that these words were written in March 1991 and that the costly and distracting project itself persisted to the end of that year, a time when even the Amiga 500 was beginning to look aged and Commodore was already encountering serious financial problems, one wonders whether anyone involved with Commodore's management was even aware of the state of the computer industry in the early 1990s. This quaint machine had no chance against the first wave of CD-ROM- and Windows-equipped multimedia PCs then beginning to flood the market. Like Commodore itself, the 65 seemed in 1991 a relic of another computing age. Such distractions as the 65 project undoubtedly funneled precious research-and-development funding, already in short supply at Commodore, away from badly needed improvements to the Amiga line.

Miner's team had been keenly conscious that the Amiga should be continually improved and had begun working on a new generation of custom chips for the "next" Amiga, dubbed the "*Ranger* project," even as the Amiga 1000 was just coming to market. Information on Ranger's exact specifications is incomplete, but at least one Miner interview from 1988 indicates that the project made considerable progress indeed: "Commodore now has a high resolution chip set of Amiga chips that I worked on when we were with Amiga in Los Gatos. These chips use video RAM and can produce a very high resolution ten twenty four display along with the present Amiga display simultaneously. They increase the display address range to two megabytes. These chips are completed and tested and require only a computer and memory to hold them together."[6]

If the Ranger chips were indeed delivered to Commodore in such an advanced state prior to the dismissal of Miner and his team, they never found their way into a completed Amiga. For years afterward, Commodore contented itself with tinkering at the edges of the Amiga's technology, cost reducing and repackaging it in the form of the 500 and 2000 and making modest architectural improvements such as slowly increasing available chip RAM, incorporating faster processors, and adding some of the most widely requested software features to AmigaOS. The platform's core capabilities—its 4,096 colors, its basic display resolutions, its sound capabilities, its blitter and copper—meanwhile remained stagnant until the introduction of the AGA chip set in 1992, which brought the Amiga, once so far ahead of the field, only up to rough parity with standard offerings on other platforms. It is tempting to lay responsibility for this stagnation entirely at the feet of Commodore's management, especially when one considers that Commodore's engineering group initiated the *AAA* chip set in 1988.[7] If completed in a timely fashion, AAA would likely have marked as big a leap over the then-current state of the art in PC graphics as the original Amiga had in 1985. It even included simple 3D acceleration to support games exactly like those that would eventually undo the Amiga as a viable game machine. AAA, however, remained chronically under-funded, and, like the Ranger chip set, it ultimately went unreleased in favor of the somewhat stopgap AGA solution.

Even in repackaging the Amiga technology, Commodore was often negligent. As a multimedia machine ideal for presentations and designed to integrate with video systems, the Amiga was positively crying out for a portable or laptop variant, and yet the idea seems never to have received any real consideration at Commodore, even as such models became increasingly common among the PC clones and as Amiga users lobbied for one of their own. And so the kids of the demoscene were forced to lug complete desktop systems with them to the demoparties, and Johns Hopkins professor Daniel J. Barrett, as described in chapter 5, was forced to content himself with recording his Amiga presentations onto videotape and showing them to his students that way, when what he really craved was the spontaneity of an interactive presentation.

Other aspects of Commodore's business were run equally poorly. Familiar with selling inexpensive home and game computers through mass-market outlets such as Sears and Toys 'R' Us, the company failed to cultivate or support the strong dealer network necessary for many professionals to take its higher-end machines seriously. Meanwhile, its customer support in general was almost uniformly abysmal. If companies such as Apple, IBM, and Microsoft publically treated Commodore's computers as toys unworthy of their attention, this was perhaps because Commodore seemed to have a toy manufacturer's attitude toward its products and its customers. The Bandito, an anonymous author who wrote about Commodore, the Amiga, and the computing industry in general with depth and insight through a long-running column in *Amazing Computing*, had this to say about Commodore in late 1993:

> Commodore International's roots are in manufacturing, not comput-
> ing. . . . Commodore International isn't really a computer company;
> they're a company that happens to make computers. They have no
> grand vision of computing in the future. . . . Commodore International
> merely wants to make products that sell. Right now, the products
> they're set up to sell happen to be computers and video games. Next
> year, it might be bicycles or fax machines. . . . Commodore Interna-
> tional won't do what's good for the future of computing, it will do
> what's good for the bottom line.[8]

Although doing "what's good for the bottom line" is of course what all for-profit companies presumably attempt, Commodore's lack of computing vision and its congenital inability to see beyond the next financial quarter were ultimately fatal to it and to the Amiga. There is something both particularly pathetic and all too typical about Commodore's attempts to market the Amiga in the early 1990s by jumping aboard the "multimedia computing" bandwagon that it had allowed more visionary companies such as Microsoft and Apple to launch. It is debatable whether Commodore's management even realized that Miner's team had created the first multimedia computer years before the term entered common usage. Such promotion now just gave the Amiga the aura of an aging also-ran. Even as early as 1988 Miner himself felt that Commodore had likely mismanaged the Amiga into oblivion: "Amiga is so far behind Macintosh and IBM now [in public recognition and industry acceptance], and they've lost so much momentum and position, that I think it's going to be almost impossible to recover."[9]

I wish to make clear even as I criticize, however, that the failures I have just unspooled were entirely the result of poor management decisions, not of technical incompetence on the part of Commodore's engineering staff. In fact, engineers such as Dave Haynie, the chief designer of the Amiga 2000 and 3000 who in effect if not in title filled Jay Miner's shoes after the ouster of the original Amiga team, accomplished remarkable feats in the face of scarce resources, confused directives, and constant layoff and hiring cycles that kept the whole engineering division perpetually on edge.[10] If the Amiga never evolved as it should have because of poor management decisions, it also, thanks to Haynie and his colleagues, advanced much more than one would have any right to expect under the conditions that Commodore's management created.

And it is also true that the difficulties that engineers such as Haynie faced in substantially upgrading the Amiga were considerable indeed due to factors inherent in the platform's design. These difficulties do not absolve Commodore of responsibility for its inaction and lack of vision, but they are considerable enough to beg the question whether the platform would be with us in recognizable form today even if it had a better parent.

Limitations of the Amiga's Design

Miner and his team designed the Amiga at a time when raw processing power was, at least by today's standards, expensive and hard to come by. They therefore replaced brute power with elegance and efficiency through the tightly coupled network of specialized custom chips that is the Amiga platform's defining hardware characteristic. Yet such a design comes with a major drawback: it is very difficult to upgrade, very difficult to extract one piece of the system and replace it with an improved version, without breaking the entire design. Thus, even as the Amiga anticipated computing's rich multimedia future, it was not well designed to grow along with that future. It was a fundamentally closed system. This fact must be recognized just as much as Commodore's mismanagement in considering the reasons that the Amiga did not survive to dominate the future that its launch promised.

As demonstrated by the Ranger project, Miner and his team were thinking about future improvements to their design even when the Amiga 1000 was still a shiny new product. There was room for growth built into AmigaOS from the start. The graphics libraries, for instance, are designed to support screens of up to eight bitplanes of depth, even though no possible configuration on the original hardware could support more than six. And the designers' main motivation in requesting that programmers use proper OS calls rather than coding to the bare metal was their consciousness that programs built around the former had a good chance of continuing to work on future models and configurations, whereas changes to the hardware registers and other elements necessitated during major upgrades were almost guaranteed to cause programs which worked with the bare metal to fail. But programmers—including at times the designers themselves—did bypass AmigaOS, whether partially or entirely, in the name of speed and efficiency. This practice was most common in the world of games and in the underground scenes, but it was by no means confined to those areas. Thus, Commodore had to consider the fact that any major upgrade to the Amiga's core capabilities would inevitably break compatibility with a huge swathe of its existing software base, including many of the games that were the machine's bread and butter in Europe, by far its most successful market. And this break was exactly what happened when the AGA-based Amiga 1200 and 4000 finally arrived in 1992. Commodore essentially had to ask Amiga owners heavily invested in games to start over, to build their libraries anew on a brand-new platform, and at the same time convince developers to support this new platform with its limited user base. The degree to which these requests were acquiesced to was in both cases actually more considerable than one might have expected, which perhaps serves as a testament to the original Amiga's lingering reputation as a great game machine, but even in Europe the Amiga 1200 never came close to matching the 500's popularity. In North America, meanwhile, the 1200 and 4000 barely made a blip on the general computing industry radar. Even had Commodore survived to complete and bring to market the AAA chip set, it would once again have had to ask its users to buy an entirely new machine that was at least partially incompatible with the old in order to reap the benefits of the new chip set.

The root causes of these problems lay not just in the hardware design, but also in the beloved AmigaOS itself. Modern OSs simply do not allow their application programmers direct access to the hardware. AmigaOS, however, does while only *asking* that they resist the temptation of the bare metal. In giving its programmers such unfettered access to the underlying hardware if they insist on taking it, AmigaOS doubtlessly enabled many creations that would have been impossible through interfering layers of OS abstraction. Nevertheless, this facet of AmigaOS proved to be a double-edged sword as time went on. Thus, some of the very qualities that made AmigaOS so beloved were key factors in the Amiga's decline.

By 1992, the buzz in the computer and graphics-design industries was about 24-bit graphics, in which 24 bits are used to define each pixel on the screen, allowing it to be any of 16.7 million colors. In other words, the RGB value of each pixel is stored in the playfield itself, consuming three bytes there, with no separate table of color registers and no restriction on the total number of colors allowed on screen at once. The Amiga, mean-while, remained absolutely bound, even in the new HAM8 mode that arrived with AGA, to storing its on-screen colors in a color table that had to be referenced to find the actual color for each pixel, a system that made sense in the 1980s when memory was expensive and processing power sharply limited, but that was becoming increasingly cumbersome by 1992. Of course, one might reply with some justification that the 256 color reg-isters provided by AGA represent a pretty fair number to be allowed on screen at once, certainly more than the average painter working with oil and canvas has in her palette. Yet such a statement does not account for the subtle shading and blending such a painter does as she overlays colors on the canvas—techniques computer artists were always keen to emulate—nor does it address the annoyance of having to constantly define and place colors and ranges of colors within the palette before one can make use of them. Further, computer-aided graphics design and image processing were moving farther and farther upscale. Having conquered the fields of home and low-cost video production and onsite presentations and having made significant inroads into television, they were now entering the realms of film and professional photo processing. High-fidelity output was absolutely essential in these fields. For many working in them, even the compromises of HAM8 mode were unacceptable. The Amiga thus looked likely to be shut out of the very computing niches it had created, at least at the high end.

And so the Amiga aftermarket, always more creative and energetic than Commodore itself, did its best to respond. Nevertheless, in doing so it was battling difficulties that stemmed from the very nature of the Amiga platform itself. The Macintosh and especially the Intel-based PCs that ran Microsoft Windows were possessed of a fairly modular, open architecture that used *retargetable graphics*. In other words, their graphics subsystems were contained on separate boards that could be swapped as needs or technology changed, a far less efficient design than the Amiga's, but also a far more flexible one. The aftermarket graphics boards that began appearing in quantity for the Amiga in 1992 had to rely on various hacks and trickery to bypass the Amiga's tightly coupled custom chips, often by trying to intercept and reroute the CPU's communications with its attendants. Such solutions were often unstable and generally failed to work entirely with software that programmed the custom chips directly. To properly explain just what a morass this situation could become, I would like to return one more time to the Deluxe Paint series, specifically the last in the line released in early 1995, DPaint V.

DPaint V's programmers, Lee Ozer and Dallas Hodgson, were faced with quite a dilemma. Twenty-four-bit graphics were increasingly regarded as a necessity, yet DPaint, more so even than most Amiga software, depended on being able to know the exact characteristics of its display so it could provide the user with appropriate palette requestors and perform such operations as blends and shades in a way that maximized that display's potential. Further, since its 1985 DPaint I incarnation, DPaint had relied heavily on the unique properties of the Amiga's custom chips for its operation. Trying to build in customized, individual support for each of the viable graphics boards was a lost cause, especially considering that the older boards were constantly being updated and new ones constantly released. Ozer and Hodgson therefore chose not to attempt it, designing DPaint V to work only with the Amiga's normal chip set. They also chose, however, to give the user the option of working with 24-bit images by abstracting the data that make up the images from the physical screen and the playfields used to display them.

The IFF standard had been updated to support 24-bit images, stored as a rather staggering collection of 24 separate bitplanes, a considerable time before DPaint V appeared. In fact, even DPaint IV is capable of reading these images, although upon its doing so they are condensed to a format the host machine can deal with, with the inevitable accompanying loss of quality. Nor can DPaint IV convert the images back to 24 bit. If the DPaint V user chooses the option of something called a "24-bit backing store" on that program's initial menu, though, a 24-bit image can be loaded and held in the Amiga's memory in its original form, with no loss of fidelity. Holding or even manipulating these data is not a problem for any machine with sufficient memory and speed. Displaying them is a problem, though. DPaint V therefore abstracts the palette of the original, stored in fast RAM, into the normal master and working copies stored in chip RAM and allows the user to edit and paint on the image as usual. The new HAM-mode color-mixer gadget introduced with DPaint IV becomes even more useful here; the user can choose absolutely any of AGA's possible 16.7 million colors, then use it to paint onto the image. If that color is not available in the color table of the playfield used to store the on-screen version of the image, though, it will instead show up as the closest possible approximation. Thus, the artist can paint in absolutely any color onto the 24-bit image in the backing store, with the notable wrinkle that she may not be able to *see* exactly what she is doing. A brief example may clarify the whole process.

Let us say that we wish to edit the 24-bit image shown in the left part of figure 9.1, which we perhaps captured using one of the 24-bit scanners or frame grabbers that were widely available by 1995. We load it into DPaint V, choosing in the process the option of using the 24-bit backing store. We are running DPaint V in AGA's 256-color mode, so the image we see on screen is not the original, but rather the best approximation of the original that DPaint V can manage, given just 256 colors to work with. Because we are using a resolution of 640 × 400, although the image was captured at 800 × 600, we also cannot see the image in its entirety, but must scroll around within it.

We now draw a red X over the top of the image (figure 9.2). The color-mixer bar we have brought up shows that we will be drawing in a bright red. The screen that holds the image itself, however, has no such color available in its limited palette, so it makes the best approximation it can, resulting in a brownish green instead. Only when we have saved the image again and displayed it (perhaps using the specialized software that accompanied our 24-bit display board) can we see that the X is in fact the red that we intended.

Of course, requiring the artist to go through such permutations and to paint by faith rather than sight hardly makes things easy on her and seems far removed from Dan Silva's intuitive early versions of DPaint. To add salt to Amiga loyalists' wounds, 24-bit image editing was a painless process on contemporary Macintosh or Windows machines equipped with modern graphics cards. Even the 24-bit display boards that were available for the Amiga were based largely on chips developed for other computer lines and relegated the Amiga's hardware, once so unique and

9.1 To the left is a true 24-bit image. To the right, the same image loaded into Deluxe Paint V's 256-color mode, with backing store enabled

9.2 To the left, drawing onto a 24-bit image in Deluxe Paint V; to the right, the end result, displayed again in its full 24-bit glory. Color versions of these images are available on this book's Web site and may illustrate this example more clearly.

revolutionary, to little more than a fairly generic machine, albeit one saddled with the host of annoyances and problems that arose from bypassing the original custom-chip-based hardware. The Amiga, once the artist's computer, was simply no longer able to provide the image quality that so many professionals felt they needed, and it had already lost its leadership position in many areas of the graphic arts to the latest generation of the Macintosh, now reaching out from the desktop-publishing niche that had made its name and kept it alive and becoming a tool for other creative endeavors. The Amiga had little outside of the admittedly elegant AmigaOS to recommend it over a Macintosh or, indeed, an everyday Intel-based machine. And here we come to one of the greatest ironies regarding the Amiga: the clunky Intel-based architecture designed by IBM in 1980, so inefficient and aesthetically ugly, butt of countless jokes from Amiga users, had exactly the open, modular architecture that let it take advantage of new technologies without breaking compatibility with previous iterations of itself. This simple and easily copyable architecture also enabled an entire industry of PC-clone manufacturers, thus separating the platform from the fate of its corporate parent—albeit unintentionally and much to IBM's chagrin. By the early 1990s, new processors had brought with them such huge increases in available computing power that the Intel-based machines could easily overcome the inefficiencies of their design by, in computer science jargon, "just throwing more CPU at the problem."

The Amiga did not have access to the computing power of the Intel-based machines, thanks to a Motorola decision that, perhaps more than any other, sealed the Amiga's fate. The last 68000-series processor that Motorola released was 1994's 68060. By the time the 68060, little more than an afterthought in the 68000 line, appeared, Motorola had long since entered into a partnership with IBM and Apple to develop a brand-new processor to replace the 68000-line, the PowerPC. Unlike Intel, which scrupulously made certain every new processor generation was compatible with the previous, accepting the inelegances and inefficiencies that entailed, Motorola and its partners chose to make the PowerPC a "cleanroom" design, with no relation to or compatibility with the 68000 line. If Commodore wished to continue the Amiga with Motorola's latest processors, it thus faced not only designing an entirely new architecture around the PowerPC, but also rewriting AmigaOS to run on that new processor; it would have to make an entirely new Amiga from scratch and to accept that the end result would have compatibility with its predecessors, if at all, only through software emulators. Apple was of course faced with the same dilemma for its Macintosh line, but it had the resources and the entrenched status to execute this immense change successfully, albeit not without much grumbling from and inconvenience to its users. Commodore was in no position to do likewise, as indeed were few other manufacturers. Even in the absence of the Commodore bankruptcy, the Amiga had thus reached a very real end of the road in 1994. Even had Commodore's financial situation been different and its management more competent, one might still ask how much this hypothetical PowerPC Amiga, with retargetable graphics and sound, with an entirely rewritten OS, and with no software compatibility with its predecessors, could really be considered an Amiga at all.[11]

Although Miner's team gave the computing world a vision of its multimedia future, it had to do so with the technology that was available to it in its present. Thus, the Amiga, for all its vision, contains elements that would be of little use in that future, elements that echo the early eight-bit computing era of the late 1970s and early 1980s rather than the computing eras to come. Hardware sprites, planer graphics, and of course the Amiga's very tightly coupled, closed design are only some of the most prominent among these elements. Of course, they are also the very elements that enabled the Amiga to be a true multimedia computer using the technology of 1985. These contradictions and ironies are inherent to any understanding of the platform. To ask whether the Amiga or the Intel architecture was ultimately "better" only invites further qualification. The Amiga was better at countless things in its time, but the Intel architecture was pioneering in its openness and modularity and better suited to realize the future the Amiga previewed.

The Beloved Underdog

There is a sense in which Commodore's neglect and the Amiga's lack of industry acceptance can be construed as a positive, for the platform's perpetual underdog status was somehow vital to the culture and community that sprang up around it. It is difficult to imagine the most devoted members of this community clinging to the Amiga—some even to this day—had it been just another well-funded and well-supported commercial platform. The leadership vacuum left by Commodore created the space for its users to take de facto ownership, thus empowering creative, generous, and visionary communities who learned from and shared with one another. Perhaps nowhere is their spirit more evident than in the Fred Fish public-domain software collection.

Fish was[12] an experienced computer programmer who, fascinated by the Amiga's support for multitasking and its graphics hardware, purchased his first machine very early:

When I got my machine just after Thanksgiving 1985, there was virtually no software anywhere. All I had was the normal Commodore disks that came with the Amiga and a few demo disks that I had managed to con my dealer into letting me take home to play with. I said to myself, "I have to do *something* with this machine," so I started looking around to see what I could find in terms of public domain software that I could port. . . . At the time, I was working at a Unix company and had a fair amount of public domain software on disks that had come through Usenet, so I started porting that. I had gotten two or three disks of useful stuff done when I heard about this user group called The First Amiga Users Group. . . . Well, the users there went kind of crazy because, of course, they didn't have much software either. That's basically how it all got started.[13]

Like many early Amiga users willing to buy the machine on the basis of its raw potential in this period when very little polished commercial software was available, Fish had been reared in the world of institutional computing, which was possessed of a long tradition of cooperation and sharing as opposed to the more cutthroat, commercialized world of PC software development. He brought this ethic to the Amiga, collecting the best and most interesting available free software onto disks, which he distributed for only a nominal shipping-and-media charge to individuals, user groups, magazines, and dealers for further duplication and distribution. It may seem an awkward method of distribution today, but in this era when the Internet did not yet exist in its modern form and telecommunications of any stripe were unreliable and often expensive, the Fish disk collection, along with various others that sprang up in its wake, provided the only access to quality free software for many Amiga users. The Fish collection reached a staggering 1,000 volumes before he turned to CD-ROM as his medium of distribution in 1994, producing bimonthly disks in this format until the slowing rate of new free-software releases following the Commodore bankruptcy and the burgeoning availability of the Internet as a means of wide-scale distribution helped him finally decide to stop in late 1995. The network remained throughout an entirely non-profit operation, a pure creation of the hacker ethic of sharing and open communication that absorbed roughly 20 to 30 hours of Fish's free time per week for a decade.[14]

The Fish collection today provides a veritable history lesson in the evolution of the Amiga free-software community. The early disks are filled with many frankly trivial exercises and code snippets, some provided by the original Amiga developers themselves, as a community of hackers and early adapters struggled to learn just what the machine they purchased was capable of and how it could be programmed. Later volumes contain full-fledged applications of often surprising complexity: word processors, spreadsheets, databases, games, art and multimedia demos of various stripes, music trackers, and of course countless tools small and large to aid in all aspects of graphics, animation, and desktop video. Fish was tremendously respected in the Amiga community for his fairness and dedication, but he did admit to "a general bias towards material that comes with source code," saying that "if two programs come to me and one of them has source and the other doesn't, and there's only room for one on the disk, then, of course, the one with source gets put on." He also admitted to "a bias towards developers."[15] Thus were the Fish disks particularly rich in tools for programmers, including debuggers, system monitors, editors, and a variety of full-fledged compilers and development environments for various programming languages, from the ubiquitous C, Pascal, and BASIC to obscurities such as Oberon-2 and Cleo. These biases reflect the ideals of a hacker who believed not just in providing users with functional software, but also in empowering them with information, tools, and source code that they could build on to create software for themselves—and, it was hoped, to pass on the results to others within the Amiga community. Although Fish did publish some semicommercial "shareware" software—programs that were distributed freely, but in a crippled state, with the user requested to send the programmer a payment to receive the full version—Fish "discouraged" their submission, preferring to adhere as much as possible to the hacker ideal of completely free software exchange.[16]

In *The Cathedral and the Bazaar*, the classic philosophical text of the modern open-source movement, Eric Raymond divides software development into two models: the cathedral model, in which software is "carefully crafted by individual wizards or smalls bands of mages working in splendid isolation," bestowing the product upon the eager users only when it is perfected and polished; and the bazaar model, in which the development process is "open to the point of promiscuity," with all invited to share and participate in a community effort that benefits all.[17] In the latter, the users of software are also its creators and vice versa. With Commodore having abdicated its expected role as high priest of the Amiga community, and with the heavy hitters of the commercial software world (a few exceptions and niche markets aside) also having chosen to ignore the Amiga, the way was open for the bazaar of the Fish collection. Here we see yet another foreshadowing of digital culture's future, of the collaborative development communities that would coalesce around the open-source Linux OS in the 1990s and that are responsible today for such widely used, free, yet powerful applications as the Mozilla Firefox Web browser and the Openoffice.org office suite.

Unfortunately, there were inevitable limits to what the Amiga's free-software community could accomplish in the face of the Amiga's proprietary hardware design and the closed-source AmigaOS. Motivated as they may have been to improve and evangelize for the platform, they could neither design new models and market them nor make needed improvements to the software on the Kickstart ROM chips. Their efforts were likewise limited by the poor state of telecommunications throughout much of the Amiga's run, which made difficult the large-scale, well-coordinated cooperation common in the modern open-source community. Nevertheless, the Amiga's free-software community was certainly the most sophisticated and active in the world of personal computing prior to Linux. It should not be a surprise that countless Amiga users migrated to Linux and other open-source OSs as the Amiga's necessary ultimate fate became clear, for much of the spirit of the Amiga free-software community persisted in these communities without being tied to a single corporation's decisions and fate. Indeed, the Amiga's fate serves as an object lesson for the modern open-source movement, speaking to the way that even excellent hardware and software can wither when said excellence is proprietary and closed source.

In one of the more remarkable examples of passion and sheer stubbornness in the history of computing, some Amiga users have continued to cling to the platform for the past 15 years, even as the Amiga intellectual property has changed hands multiple times and gone through countless alleged rebirths and the inevitable trailing disappointments. There have even been modest successes as well. New Amigas have been manufactured at various times under various licenses, and a small but extant network of dealers and manufacturers persists to this day, selling equipment to upgrade and repair machines now in many cases 20 years old, even providing a trickle of new commercial applications and, yes, games. The spirit of the Fish collection meanwhile migrated to the Internet. Founded in 1991 by a club of Swiss computer science students, an online archive known as "Aminet" quickly evolved into a huge repository of public-domain and open-source software for Amiga computers, with mirrors all over the world. On May 16, 1996, Aminet hit the 30,000 file mark and could declare itself "the largest collection of freely distributable software for any computer system."[18] That distinction inevitably gave way in the wake of the explosion in Internet usage and the increasing popularity of Linux-driven open-source initiatives in the late 1990s, but Aminet remains vital to the Amiga community of today, both as a voluminous archive of the platform's rich past and as a source of new free games, demos, applications, tools, and information. It still receives several new submissions almost every day.

Another impressive achievement of this Amiga community that refuses to die was the completion of AmigaOS 4.0 by Belgian software company Hyperion Entertainment in 2006. Version 4.0 is a complete rewrite of AmigaOS that, although based to a large extent on earlier versions' source code, runs on PowerPC processors that either have been retrofitted into the classic Amiga models or have come as part of new "Amiga" systems from boutique manufacturers. Such systems have of course long since abandoned the custom-chip design that made the original Amiga so unique—thus, my use of quotation marks around the name. AmigaOS 4.0 itself is compatible with software written for older Amigas only through emulation. The number of active Amiga users remaining today is miniscule by the standards of the general computing industry, but their community is a refreshing echo of an earlier era in computing; one is reminded of the Homebrew Computer Club of the 1970s soldering together their systems in garages and sharing knowledge and software simply for the love of hacking.

Although the Amiga's original hardware design has little remaining relevance in the modern world of multigigahertz processors, AmigaOS in fact remains a fecund source of inspiration to many. Two open-source OSs, MorphOS and AROS, are based on AmigaOS's look and feel and design philosophy while running on generic modern hardware. Nor have designers of commercial OSs been oblivious to the Amiga lure, as demonstrated by BeOS, a creation of the startup Be Incorporated in the 1990s. BeOS bears obvious marks of its AmigaOS inspiration, but in a story all too familiar to Amiga users it ultimately failed to attract sufficient users to survive in the face of competition from Apple and Microsoft. Ironically in that light, perhaps the most Amiga-like mainstream OS of today is Apple's OS X, with its slick interface and multimedia orientation built on a solid Unix-like foundation.

And then, of course, the Amiga remains a favorite of the Internet's retrogaming communities. Virtually all of the old games are available through huge legal and illegal archives on the Internet and are playable through emulators such as the UAE. Partially prompted by nostalgia for their adolescence, but also by the very real qualities of many of the best Amiga games, considerable numbers of people continue to play on their modern computers the games from Cinemaware, Psygnosis, and other publishers that were developed during the Amiga's heyday.

But there is no avoiding the fact that the Amiga's significance to modern computing is rooted in its past, not its present. Rather than lamenting the history of the Amiga as a series of tragic might-have-beens and dreaming of a revival, we should perhaps view it as a technology that simply ran its course and ceded the field to those better prepared to build on its innovations. We certainly can do so while also recognizing the elegance and panache that made so many people fall in love with the machine in its day and that still put stars in the eyes of many a hacker, artist, and gamer when the name is mentioned today. Some words written by the Bandito amid the chaos and confusion of the Commodore bankruptcy seem especially wise: "In a few years, no doubt, you'll be able to buy a computer, software, and operating system that will match the capabilities of your current Amiga at about the price you paid for the Amiga way back when. But you can smile to yourself, knowing that you were touching the future years before the rest of the world. And that other computers and operating systems will do with brute force what the Amiga did years before with grace, elegance, and style."[19]

One must search long and hard to find a for-profit corporation willing to sing the praises of a competitor's product; one certainly will not find a record of Microsoft, Apple, IBM, or any other big computer industry player publicly discussing the Amiga's innovations. If one looks to these competitors' actions, though, one can see that they were watching the Amiga. IBM and Microsoft began developing in partnership a multitasking OS of their own in the immediate wake of AmigaOS, OS/2, and Apple began a serious push to bring quality color graphics and sound to the Macintosh. As Jay Miner observed in 1988, "There's a lot of the Amiga in the Mac II [released in 1987], though not done as well, of course."[20] Such developments would have come eventually in the absence of an Amiga, just as they would have in the absence of an IBM or a Macintosh, but the Amiga innovators nevertheless deserve recognition for their vision. The Amiga's unique design makes it a fascinating study in elegant engineering, and the communities of practice that sprang up around it—from artists to game players to video producers to free-software hackers to the scruffy kids of the demoscene—are equally compelling. Yet a study of the platform is also more than an abstract lesson in technology or sociology, for although the technology itself is dead and most of the communities have moved on, the vision of computing that this machine and its disparate users represented permeates our lives today. In another 1994 column that reads like a eulogy, the Bandito tells us that the Amiga "is the [first] computer that made multimedia and multitasking meaningful, that made beautiful music and astounding animations possible."[21] The Amiga's most long-lived and effective marketing slogan, "Only Amiga makes it possible," is of course no longer true. It is true, however, that the Amiga made many things possible *first* and in doing so gave the world a rough draft of its future.

Glossary

3D modeling The process of generating the mathematical description of a 3D scene, whether entirely by hand or via a GUI application, to be turned into an image via a 3D renderer.

3D rendering The process of converting a collection of data that describes a 3D scene into a 2-D image on a computer screen.

AAA Amiga Advanced Architecture. A proposed Amiga chip set with capabilities far beyond even those of AGA. Begun in 1988, before AGA, but never completed due to lack of funding.

ADC Analog-to-digital converter. An electronic circuit that converts a continuous, analog signal into a stream of discrete, digital numbers.

address The unique location of a single byte in memory. Addresses are numbered from 0 up to the total number of bytes in the computer's memory.

AGA Advanced Graphics Architecture. A new version of the Amiga chip set released in 1992, with dramatically improved display capabilities over the OCS and ECS.

Agnus On pre-AGA Amigas, the custom chip that acts as a gatekeeper to prevent chip–RAM conflicts among the other two custom chips and the CPU and that fetches data from memory and feeds them to Denise and Paula as needed. Also houses the blitter and the copper.

Amiga 500 A cost-reduced home-computer version of the Amiga released in 1987. The best-selling Amiga model by far.

Amiga 500+ A new version of the Amiga 500 briefly sold in early 1992, which included AmigaOS 2.0 in ROM and the ECS in place of the OCS.

Amiga 600 An odd Amiga model released in 1992 as a successor to the 500 and 500+ in the low-end market. Despite featuring the ECS and one MB of RAM standard, it was so cost reduced as to be in many ways less desirable than its predecessor.

Amiga 1000 The original Amiga developed by Jay Miner and team and released by Commodore in 1985. Discontinued with the arrival of the 500 and 2000 in 1987.

Amiga 1200 The home-computer AGA Amiga, with a 68020 CPU. Released in 1992.

Amiga 2000 A professional-level Amiga model, with a large case offering ample room for expansion. Released in 1987.

Amiga 2500 An Amiga 2000 with a more powerful 68020 or 68030 CPU. Released in 1989.

Amiga 3000 A significantly improved version of the original Amiga design and the logical successor to the 2000, featuring the ECS, AmigaOS 2.0 in ROM, and a 68030 CPU, among other improvements. Released in 1990.

Amiga 4000 The professional-level AGA Amiga, with a 68040 or 68060 CPU. Released in 1992.

AmigaBASIC A version of the BASIC programming language that shipped with versions of AmigaOS prior to AmigaOS 2.0.

AmigaDOS The disk- and file-management layer of AmigaOS, licensed from Metacomco. Also frequently used by Commodore and others to refer to AmigaOS as a whole.

AmigaOS The Amiga's standard OS. Frequently also referred to as "Amiga-DOS" or "Amiga OS."

analog Data as they are often found in the real world, a continuous stream or curve.

application software A fairly large, complex, interactive program meant for some serious task. A word processor and a paint program are examples.

assembly language The lowest level at which it is normally practical to program a computer. Consists of a system of mnemonics, each representing a single operation that the CPU can natively understand. These are translated into executable code via an assembler. By far the most efficient method of programming, but also be extremely tedious and difficult to work with for all but the smallest programs because it lacks the data structures and logical abstractions of high-level languages. Was often used in the 1980s to coax as much as possible from the era's limited machines, but with the explosion in computing power and program complexity that followed, it is now commonly used only for certain very specialized tasks today. Often also called *machine language*.

bare-metal programming   Coding directly to a computer's underlying hardware, using no support libraries or OS calls.

BASIC   Beginner's All-Purpose Symbolic Instruction Code. A high-level programming language developed for teaching purposes at Dartmouth College in the 1960s. Often derided by experienced programmers for its lack of structure and inefficiency, it was nevertheless ubiquitous on PCs of the 1980s.

batch processing   A model of computing in which a series of noninteractive programs are funneled through the machine, usually to process large amounts of data. An example might be a payroll cycle that accepts input data describing employees and the hours they have worked and outputs their paychecks.

BBS   Bulletin-board system. An online community, generally running on a PC, that users accessed by dialing in using their own computers. Most allowed just one user to be online at any one time.

binary   The base-2 number system used by a computer. Each binary digit corresponds to a single bit.

bit   A single on/off switch, the lowest level of computer storage. Corresponds to a single binary digit. Can be combined together to form bytes, words, or long words representing numbers, symbols, or other data.

bitplane   A part of a playfield consisting of one bit for every pixel. Combined with its siblings when the display is painted to the screen to create the final image. The more bitplanes that constitute a playfield, the more colors it can contain.

blitter   One of the Amiga's two custom coprocessors. Can copy blocks of memory very quickly and can, if desired, logically combine several sources in the process. Very important for animation.

BOB   Blitter object block. On the Amiga, an on-screen object that is superficially similar to a sprite, but that is created by drawing into the playfield on which it appears. Facilitated by the blitter, thus its name.

boot sector The first sector of an Amiga floppy or hard disk, which contains a small bit of code used to boot the machine. A favorite home of viruses. Often also referred to as the *boot block*.

busy wait The process of a program checking for user input by continually looping, thus using CPU cycles, instead of sleeping and waiting for a notification of activity. Very bad programming practice in a multitasking environment.

byte Equal to eight bits. Capable of storing any unsigned number from 0 to 255.

C A hugely popular general-purpose, high-level programming language that corresponds more closely to its underlying technology than most languages do, to the extent that it is sometimes called a "midlevel" language. Although C is still slower than assembly, this correspondence makes it faster and more efficient than most other high-level languages. Was developed in tandem with Unix but spread to many platforms thereafter. Most of AmigaOS is programmed in C, and C was by far the most commonly used high-level language for serious programming on the Amiga platform in general.

CD32 A CD-ROM-based game console that was actually an AGA Amiga internally. Released in 1993 and the last significant new product to come from Commodore.

CDTV Commodore Dynamic Total Vision. A CD-ROM-based "multimedia appliance" introduced by Commodore in 1991. Was an Amiga internally.

CGI Computer graphics imaging. A method of accomplishing special effects in film or video using computer-generated imagery that is superimposed onto real-world footage.

chip RAM The Amiga memory that is accessible by the custom chips. Was the first 512 KB in early models; later expanded to the first MB with the release of Fatter Agnus and finally the first two MBs with the arrival of the ECS. A CPU that is faster than the Amiga's original 68000 must slow down to the 68000's speed when accessing chip RAM. Further, the CPU can access chip RAM only at Agnus's pleasure.

chroma-key compositing A method for mixing live video with other sources in which all areas of the live feed that are of a certain color are replaced with the alternate source. A television weather report is the classic example of this technique in action.

chunky method / chunky graphics A method of storing a playfield in memory as a single contiguous chunk of data. Used by virtually all modern PCs.

CLI Command-line interface. A command-line-driven AmigaOS interface that is similar to the MS-DOS or Unix command prompts.

code space Memory used to store actual code to be executed by the CPU.

cold start Booting a computer from a powered-off state.

collision detection The process, particularly important in games, of identifying collisions between on-screen components. Collisions involving sprites are automatically detected by the Amiga's hardware.

CoolCapture vector A feature of AmigaOS that can allow some code or data to survive a warm start. Frequently exploited by viruses.

cooperative multitasking Multitasking that relies on individual applications to cooperate with one another by politely yielding the CPU to other processes that might be waiting. The OS, in other words, has no authority to seize control preemptively from a process that does not yield it voluntarily.

copper One of the Amiga's two custom coprocessors. Can be programmed to make changes to the display settings at arbitrary points as the display is being painted.

coprocessor A processer that can be programmed, at least within a limited sphere, and can operate semiautonomously but is ultimately subservient to the CPU.

CPU Central processing unit. A computer's programmable brain.

cracker One who cracks protection schemes, whether on commercial software or on larger technical structures such as the phone system or computer networks. Often referred to as a *hacker* by the nontechnical media.

cracktro Crack intro. A multimedia introduction placed at the beginning of cracked games by the pirate group who did the cracking to claim credit for their work and to show off their coding skills. The forerunner of the demoscene demo.

CRT Cathode-ray tube. The standard display technology used for both televisions and computer monitors prior to the advent of liquid-crystal display (LCD) and plasma flat screens.

custom chip A specialized chip designed for a certain computer model, as opposed to more common general-purpose components. A trio of special-purpose chips made the Amiga's hardware design unique. Prior to the

AGA era, these chips were named "Paula," "Denise," and "Agnus"; on the AGA machines, they were named "Paula," "Lisa," and "Alice."

DAC Digital-to-analog converter. An electronic circuit that transforms a stream of discrete, digital numbers into a continuous, analog wave.

data space Memory used to store data that are acted upon by code.

demo In the context of the demoscene, a generally noninteractive piece of computer-based multimedia art incorporating graphics, animation, and music and almost always coded from scratch in assembly language.

Denise On pre-AGA Amigas, the custom chip responsible for doing most of the work of generating the display.

digital Data stored as a series of discrete numbers; the only type of data a computer can deal with.

digitization The process of converting analog data into digital data by sampling it repeatedly at fixed intervals.

digitizer In the abstract, any device that digitizes an analog signal into digital data. In the 1980s and early 1990s, this term was normally used to refer to a device that captured an analog image such as a photograph for storage and display on the computer.

DMA Direct memory access. A device that directly accesses its host computer's memory rather than passing requests through the CPU.

double buffering A method of performing animation in which two playfields are used. While one is the active one being painted to the screen, the next frame of the animation is prepared in the inactive one; the inactive one then becomes the active one, and vice versa.

dual-playfield mode A unique Amiga video mode in which two playfields, each up to three bitplanes deep, can be on the screen at once. The background playfield shows through wherever the foreground playfield is transparent (signaled by color 0).

ECS Enhanced Chip Set. Chip set introduced on the Amiga 3000 in 1990, which increased available chip RAM to two MB and introduced some other modest improvements to the OCS.

EHB mode Extra-Half-Brite mode. A special mode in which the Amiga uses six bitplanes to display up to 64 colors at once on a low-resolution screen, with the last 32 colors being the first 32 at half intensity.

event-driven programming A programming model in which an application is driven by events generated by the user from many options available to her rather than running as a continuous linear stream. These events include such actions as typing a key on the keyboard, clicking a gadget or menu, and so on. An application should ideally sleep when there is no processing to be done between these events, yielding the CPU (under a multitasking OS) to other tasks. A natural fit for a GUI application and for a multitasking OS.

Exec The Executive. The microkernel heart of AmigaOS, which performs the most essential tasks of process management and resource allocation.

executable A program that has been translated from human-readable source code into the CPU's native language of os and 1s, and thus can be executed by the computer.

fast RAM Memory that is accessible to the Amiga's CPU but not to the custom chips. Can always be accessed by the CPU at full speed.

Fat Agnus The version of the Agnus chip developed for the Amiga 500 and 2000. Identical in functionality to the version in the Amiga 1000, but more compact and less expensive to manufacture.

Fatter Agnus A new version of the Agnus chip that Commodore released in 1989 and that increases chip RAM to a maximum of one MB.

frame grabber A device capable of instantly capturing and holding a full digital image in its memory.

free software Software that is entirely free to use and distribute to others, with no fees, onerous restrictions, or licensing requirements. The term has come to imply software that is open source thanks to the efforts of the Free Software Foundation, but this implication was not as prevalent in the 1980s and early 1990s as it is today.

genlock Generator lock. A device that allows the Amiga to interface with and mix its video signal with other analog video sources.

GUI Graphical user interface. A method of controlling a computer using a pointing device such as a mouse, a desktop metaphor, and graphical windows, icons, and menus. Has supplanted and in many cases replaced older CLIs.

Guru Meditation Error The whimsical error message that signals a full system crash under certain versions of AmigaOS. Equivalent to the Microsoft Windows "Blue Screen of Death."

hacker A computer programmer or technician with a certain system of ethics and a certain idealized view of the way that technology and even society ought to function—that is, with complete openness and transparency to all. Associated with the open-source methodology of development;

generally opposed to most proprietary software. A term often used by the nontechnical media to refer to computer criminals, but the term *cracker* is more appropriate in the latter case.

HAM mode Hold-and-Modify mode. A special Amiga mode available in low resolution only in which most pixels are a modified version of the color of the previous pixel. Allows all 4,096 colors on screen at once, but with only a limited number of sharp color transitions. Ideal for digitized photographs.

HAM6 mode See *HAM mode*.

HAM8 mode A version of HAM mode possible on the AGA chip set that allows any of the 16.7 million colors of the AGA palette on screen, subject to the same basic restrictions as the older HAM6 mode.

hexadecimal A base-16 numbering system favored by programmers because it corresponds much more neatly than decimal to the way a computer stores numbers. It consists of the decimal digits 0 through 9 as well as A through F, referring to the decimal numbers 10 through 15, respectively. Thus, four bits will always consist of exactly one hexadecimal digit, and a byte (eight bits) will consist of two. Often shortened to *hex*.

high-level language A language that is somewhat abstracted from the technical details of the computer so as to allow the programmer to design her logic in a more human-comprehensible way. Must either be translated into natively executable code via a compiler or run with the aid of an assisting application known as an "interpreter." Both bring a penalty in speed and efficiency over assembly language, the latter technique much more so than the former. Some high-level languages are specialized and designed to excel at creating a certain category of program such as scientific applications or text–adventure games, whereas others are more general purpose.

IFF Interchange File Format. A standard set of file formats developed at Electronic Arts to allow Amiga users to exchange images, music, and animations among applications.

institutional computer A large mini- or mainframe computer that costs a great deal of money and is shared by many users. Prior to the arrival of the first PCs in the mid-1970s, all computers were institutional computers.

interlace A method of sending video to a television or monitor in which only every other line is sent with each successive paint of the screen. Because each line is refreshed only half as frequently, a visible flickering effect can result, but interlace allows a device to interface easily with standard analog video hardware of the 1980s and early 1990s.

interrupt A signal sent by a piece of hardware or a software component to notify the system that an event has occurred: a key has been pressed, a disk read has finished, one sprite has struck another, and so on. A large suite of interrupts is essential to the event-driven programming model and to multitasking because it allows an application to sleep and wait for interrupts to which it should respond rather than having to poll the hardware again and again.

Intuition AmigaOS's GUI library, which allows the programmer to build windows, gadgets, screens, and other components easily.

KB Kilobyte. Equal to 1,024 bytes.

kernel The core of an OS.

Kickstart The most essential parts of AmigaOS, stored either on disk (in the case of the Amiga 1000) or on a ROM chip (in the case of all other models released during the Commodore era).

library A collection of programming routines that carry out common tasks and that can be called by programs.

long word Equal to four bytes (32 bits). Can hold any unsigned number from 0 to 4,294,967,295.

mainframe computers The physically largest computers, normally found only in large businesses and government. They excel at batch processing but are generally viewed by hackers as rather unimaginative and uninteresting.

MB Megabyte. Equal to 1,024 KB.

memory leak Memory allocated by a process but never properly deallocated, thus becoming inaccessible and shrinking the available total memory pool.

memory protection An OS's ability to protect itself and other processes from a "rogue" process that attempts to access memory it has not properly allocated to itself. See *virtual memory*.

MHz Megahertz. The standard measurement of CPU speed in the 1980s and early 1990s. Each megahertz represents one-million clock cycles per second. Although the term offers some idea of a computer's relative speed, it must be used only with care as a guide to the overall throughput of disparate architectures. Equally important are many other architectural details of the CPU and the computer as a whole.

microcomputer See *PC*.

microkernel A kernel that contains only the most essential functions of the OS. Other functions are loaded in and out as separate modules as needed.

MMU Memory-management unit. A component in a CPU that makes it quick and easy to translate virtual-memory addresses into physical addresses and vice versa. Key to the implementation of virtual memory in an OS.

MOD Modular music file. A system of music storage that consists of a set of instrument samples and a score, the latter being a series of instructions on when and how to play those samples and thus form a song.

monolithic kernel A kernel that contains virtually the entirety of the OS within itself.

MS-DOS Microsoft Disk Operating System. The simple command-line-driven OS found on the original IBM PC (1981) and the many PC clones that followed it. Later served as the base of many versions of Windows; was not phased out of this role until the release of Windows XP in 2001.

multimedia The integration of data, text, images, and sound within a single digital environment.

multitasking Running more than one program at the same time on a single computer.

NTSC standard National Television System Committee standard. The standard format for television and video in the United States, Canada, and scattered other countries from the birth of television until the recent (2009 in the United States, 2011 in Canada) transition to a digital format.

OCS Original Chip Set. Retroactive name for the chip set found in the Amiga 1000, 500, 2000, and 2500.

open source Software for which the source code, as opposed to just the executable code, is made available. Makes it easy for others to analyze, modify, and improve the software as well as to port it to other architectures beyond the one on which it was written.

OS Operating system. The most fundamental piece of enabling software on a computer, it manages resources, provides a user interface, provides programmers with libraries that they can call upon to accomplish many tasks, and often forms a buffer between applications and the underlying hardware.

overscan mode A special Amiga resolution mode that uses the overscan area, which usually contains a border, as additional screen area, yielding resolutions as high as 704 × 480. Very important to video production, where borders around the screen are unacceptable.

paint program A program in which a user manually creates images by coloring the on-screen pixels, usually using painting and drawing metaphors such as a pencil, a brush, and an eraser.

PAL standard Phase Alternate Line standard. The legacy standard format for television and video in Europe and many other regions. In the process of being replaced by digital systems in most regions as of 2011.

parallax scroll A scrolling background that consists of two or more levels, each scrolling at different speeds. Simulates the visual property of parallax.

Paula The Amiga custom chip responsible for sound and miscellaneous input/output tasks.

PC Personal computer. A computer small enough to sit on or under a desktop and that is generally used by only one person at a time. Was frequently referred to as a *microcomputer* from its birth in the 1970s until the early 1990s, but this term has fallen out of fashion in more recent times.

planar method / planar graphics A method of storing a playfield in memory as a series of bitplanes rather than as a single contiguous chunk of data. Used by the Amiga and many other early PCs.

playfield A representation of a screen stored in memory, to be painted onto the monitor by the display hardware. On the Amiga, it is made up of one or more bitplanes.

preemptive multitasking Multitasking under the OS's complete control, in which the OS is the final authority that decides which processes receive CPU time and when.

priority The relative importance of a process running under a multitasking OS. Used by the OS to decide when and how much CPU time should be granted to the process.

procedural programming A programming model in which the program runs as a linear or semilinear stream, either entirely noninteractively or with only occasional branching in response to user input. Was the norm prior to the rise of GUIs and the accompanying event-driven model.

process On a multitasking OS, any instance of running code. Can be an application, a device driver, or some part of the OS itself, among many other possibilities.

progressive scanning A method of sending a signal to a television or monitor in which the entire screen is painted every time. Standard for most computers, but not for analog television and video equipment. See *interlace*.

RAM Random-access memory. Memory that can be written to as well as read and that is erased when the machine is powered off.

Ranger A more advanced version of the Amiga chip set that Jay Miner and the original design team were developing before being laid off by Commodore in 1986. Never completed.

raster Another term for a playfield, one most commonly used on platforms other than the Amiga.

raster graphics A system of storing an image as a grid of colored pixels.

raster-graphics editor See *paint program*.

rasterization The process of converting the data that make up a vector-graphics image into a grid of pixels suitable for display on raster-graphics hardware.

ray tracing A form of 3D rendering that determines the color of each pixel by tracing the path of the light that strikes it through the scene.

refresh rate The number of times a video screen is repainted per second. A faster refresh rate results in a more stable image less prone to flicker. Given in hertz (Hz), which simply means "cycles per second."

register A unique memory address that has a specialized purpose, controlling some fundamental aspect of the computer's operation.

retargetable graphics A design scheme in which a computer's display functions are separated from its core components and placed onto a card that can be swapped and upgraded as needed without the necessity of replacing the entire machine.

RGB value Red green blue value. A method of representing any color as a ratio of these three primary colors.

ROM Read-only memory. Memory that can be read but not written to and that survives even when the machine is powered off.

sample A digital recording done by sampling an analog signal repeatedly at a fixed interval of time. If done frequently enough and on an amplitude scale great enough to allow enough resolution, it is effectively indistinguishable from its analog antecedent.

sample rate In sound sampling and playback, the number of times a sound is sampled per second. Along with the sampling resolution, it largely determines the fidelity of the recorded sound to its real-world antecedent. A CD is recorded at 44,100 samples per second; sample rates on the Amiga can be varied but are always much lower than the CD rate.

sample resolution In sound sampling and playback, the range of values to which a sample is mapped. Along with the sample rate, sample resolution largely determines the fidelity of the recorded sound to its real-world antecedent. The Amiga uses 8-bit sound samples, meaning each value in the sample can range from 0 to 255. A CD player uses 16-bit resolution, with the expected increase in fidelity.

SCSI Small Computer Systems Interface. A longstanding interface standard used for hard disks, CD-ROMs, and other types of storage devices on many PCs, including many Amigas, many models of the Macintosh, and some Intel-based machines.

SEG Special effects generator. A specialized and expensive device used to manipulate video either live or in postproduction. A TV station might use an SEP, for example, to superimpose the image of a meteorologist over a graphical display using chromo-key compositing. Amigas—particularly Video Toaster-equipped Amigas—could perform many traditional SEG functions at a fraction of the cost.

source code A human-readable description of a program's logic written in a high-level language such as C. Translated into executable code via a compiler.

sprite A graphical object that exists independently of any playfield and that can be easily moved about without modifying the on-screen playfield over which it appears. Found on the Amiga and many earlier PCs. Not found on modern PCs, where this functionality is achieved through software only.

TBC Time-base corrector. A device that synchronizes the output of several video sources.

terminal A device that is superficially similar to a PC's monitor and keyboard, but that is not a stand-alone computer. It is instead a "dumb" device that connects its user to a larger computer that she most likely shares with many other users.

tile-based graphics A method of building up screens from a set of tiles that are larger than individual pixels but much smaller than the screen as a whole. Frequently used to build backgrounds and maps for videogames.

time sharing The process of dividing a computer's CPU time and other resources among more than one user at the same time. Implies multitasking capability.

tracker—A music composition tool in which the user arranges musical notes, sound effects, and other events such as a change from one instrument to another along a linear "track" or timeline for each available sound channel. Completed songs can be stored in the MOD format for playback and incorporation into other productions. Tracker-produced music was ubiquitous in Amiga games and demos.

UAE Ultimate Amiga Emulator. The most long-standing and accurate Amiga software emulator currently available. Free, open source, and available for many platforms (including the newest incarnations of the Amiga itself).

Unix A powerful and flexible OS first developed at Bell Labs in the late 1960s and refined and expanded for decades afterward by universities, corporations, and individuals. For years a favorite of hackers working in institutional computing environments and the model for Linux, which operates almost identically.

vector graphics A system of storing an image by the locations and definitions of the shapes that make it up.

viewport On the Amiga, a software and logical construct that defines many aspects of the view that will be painted to the monitor screen: the number of bitplanes, the starting address of each bitplane, the size of the playfield, and so on. Can be thought of as the camera lens aimed at a certain part of memory and transmitting what it finds there to the monitor.

virtual memory Memory that is abstracted from the actual physical memory in the machine. Allows the OS to protect itself from programs that attempt to access memory that they have not properly allocated to themselves; also allows the OS to use a hard drive as a temporary storage space to accommodate programs that request more memory than is currently available in RAM.

virus A program that, unknown to the computer user, attempts to infect its host computer system and from there to spread to other computers. May or may not attempt to engage in other secret or destructive behaviors or both in the process.

warm start A reboot that does not involve powering off the machine.

word Equals two bytes (16 bits). Can hold any unsigned number from 0 to 65,535.

Workbench The Amiga's standard GUI workspace, similar to the Macintosh OS's Finder or to the Windows desktop.

workstation During the 1980s, a small, often single-user computer that is superficially similar to a PC but is more powerful, expensive, and specialized in its application. Often runs a complex OS such as Unix rather than a consumer-grade OS. With the enormous growth in power of the everyday PC since the 1980s, the relevance of this term and the distinction it implies in contrast with more plebian PCs has largely disappeared.

wrap scroll A scrolling background that appears to be infinite but that is actually a smaller playfield wrapped around again and again.

Notes

Chapter 1

1. Hertzfeld, "The End of an Era."
2. Commodore in fact initially referred to this machine simply as the "Commodore Amiga" and added the "1000" designation in 1987 when the debut of two new Amigas, the Amiga 500 and the Amiga 2000, necessitated a way of distinguishing the older machine from its younger siblings. I refer to the original Amiga model as the 1000 in this book for essentially the same reason that caused Commodore to give it that designation retroactively: a desire to avoid confusion.
3. Williams, Edwards, and Robinson, "The Amiga Personal Computer," 100.
4. Anderson, "Amiga," 42.
5. Halfhill, "The Amiga," 16.
6. Electronic Arts, "Why Electronic Arts Is Committed to the Amiga," 7.
7. Morabito, "A First Look at the Amiga," 24.
8. Bert Helfinstein of Entré Computer Centers, quoted in Hoban, "Looks Great, Manny, but Will It Sell?"15.
9. Quoted in Wallace, *AmigaWorld Official AmigaVision Handbook*, 17.
10. Feldman, *Multimedia*, 4.
11. Wise, *Multimedia*, 2.
12. The Ultimate Amiga Emulator (UAE) is a long-standing open-source project that now offers almost 100 percent exact emulation of virtually the whole range of Amiga models. Versions are available for Microsoft Windows, Apple Macintosh, and Linux among other platforms. See http://www.amigaemulator.org and http://www.winuae.net for more information and downloads. Note, however, that the original AmigaOS software is still under copyright and is not freely distributable. The British company Cloanto offers this software for purchase and download at a fairly reasonable price in a bundle with a preconfigured UAE that makes getting started quite easy, particularly for those who are not already familiar with the Amiga. See http://www.amigaforever.com.

Chapter 2

1. The 264 was slightly revised and eventually released as the Plus/4. Although not a terrible machine in itself, the Plus/4 was a sales disaster, largely due to its incompatibility with the similarly priced Commodore 64.
2. Bagnall, *On the Edge*, 411.
3. Graetz, "The Origin of *Spacewar*," 58–59.
4. Bagnall, *On the Edge*, 131–132.
5. Miner died from kidney failure in 1994.
6. Another volume in the Platform Studies series, Nick Montfort and Ian Bogost's *Racing the Beam*, focuses on the Atari VCS.
7. A similar design philosophy dominates the modern PC world. Virtually every PC now sold comes equipped with some sort of graphical processing unit (GPU) to ease the burden on the CPU when running graphically intense programs such as games as well as with various other supporting hardware capable of operating at least semiautonomously in parallel with the CPU.
8. Fulton, "Atari."
9. Reimer, "Total Share."
10. The original Sun 1 workstation, conceived while designer Andy Bechtolsheim was still a student at Stanford University, was in fact designed largely around the 68000's capabilities. Bechtolsheim, Baskett, and Pratt, *The SUN Workstation Architecture*, 5–7.
11. Beginning with the 68020, later processors in the 68000 series are true 32-bit CPUs. These more powerful CPUs found homes in many Amigas as well, both as retrofits to the earlier models and as the standard processors in later models.
12. Epstein, "A Peek at the 68000."
13. Bagnall, *On the Edge*, 398.
14. Conroy and Crotty, *The History of the Amiga* (video).
15. Ibid.
16. Ibid.
17. Ibid.
18. Bagnall, *On the Edge*, 405.
19. Conroy and Crotty, *The History of the Amiga*.
20. These custom chips are the very core of the Amiga design and the key to virtually all of its unique multimedia capabilities. Significant as they are, however, their capabilities are often not well understood and, perhaps as a result, are exaggerated. In his book *On the Edge: The Spectacular Rise and Fall of Commodore*, Brian Bagnall's description of the Amiga's design is dismayingly typical: "Each of these chips was, in effect, a microprocessor. Many call the Amiga a multiprocessor system, since each chip handles its own load of specific processing tasks in a specific domain" (399). In reality, Paula, Denise, and Agnus are in no sense processors because they cannot be programmed. Like many other parts of the Amiga, they are "simply" electronic circuits performing specific tasks. Agnus does *house* two coprocessors, the copper and the blitter, and they can be programmed within a limited sphere to perform some very useful tasks while the CPU is busy elsewhere. Calling the Amiga a "multiprocessing system" on this basis, however, is a huge stretch. The term *multiprocessing* implies multiple CPUs working in autonomous partnership, which is most assuredly not the case in the

Amiga, where the coprocessors are subservient to and sharply limited in comparison to the CPU.

21. Through much of the Amiga's early development, Paula was known as "Portia" and Denise as "Daphne." Later revisions of the chips were sufficiently changed that the design team chose to give them new names entirely. To avoid confusion, however, I refer to the chips by their final production names throughout this chapter.

22. Luck, interviewed in Conroy and Crotty, *The History of the Amiga*.

23. Bateman, "Software Power!," 34.

24. Bagnall, *On the Edge*, 404.

25. I have to some extent surmised this development process, but I believe I have done so on firm grounds. David W. Erhart was recently given an Amiga development system dating from September 1984 that consists of both a SAGE IV machine and the prototype Amiga hardware. He has provided a picture per page of the documentation for this system at http://entertainment.webshots.com/photo/2098298130102595274axoGbF. The documentation gives clear instructions for compiling and transferring C programs from the SAGE to the prototype. And although the original source of the Boing demo has apparently been lost, all extent versions of the executable bear the telltale traces of being compiled C programs.

26. Luck, interviewed in Conroy and Crotty, *The History of the Amiga*.

27. Commodore-Amiga Inc., *The Launch of the Amiga* (video).

28. Nichols, "Amiga and Atari" (television program).

29. Knight, "Amiga Imagery."

30. On a little-endian processor, 1101 would represent (128 + 64 + 16) 208 instead.

31. Modern PCs frequently use alternate encoding schemes collectively known as "Unicode" that allow the representation of non-English glyphs. This representation, however, is facilitated at the OS or application level; at power-on, even a modern PC still speaks ASCII.

32. This excellent analogy is courtesy of Joe Decuir.

33. One can see an artifact of the display's technical underpinning when selecting the screen mode on a modern computer. Microsoft Windows, for instance, offers a choice of 256-color (8-bit), 16-bit, or 32-bit color qualities. All of these choices line up nicely along byte boundaries, devoting exactly one, two, or four bytes to each pixel, respectively. However, 32-bit color is actually only 24-bit color, with one byte being left unused for each pixel to avoid dealing with data in odd installments of three bytes at a time.

34. Detore and Wood, *Jay Miner Speech* (video).

35. I again owe this analogy to Joe Decuir.

36. Detore and Wood, *Jay Miner Speech*.

Chapter 3

1. Wright and Suokko, "Andy Warhol."

2. Quoted in Reifsnyder, "Artists and the Amiga," 29.

3. Skelton, "Rodney Chang," 45.

4. Laughner, "Computer Art," 27.

5. S. Wright, "The Personal Art of a Personal Computer," 42.

6. Conroy and Crotty, *The History of the Amiga* (video).
7. The name "Deluxe Paint" often appears in print as a single-word italicized title of the sort fashionable in the computer industry both then and now: *DeluxePaint*. EA itself used both forms of the name in different versions and different promotional materials.
8. Means and Means, "Inside the Making of *Deluxe Paint III*," 27.
9. Electronic Arts, "Can a Computer Make You Cry?"
10. Ibid.
11. Such practices have not completely left us even today. Microsoft, for example, is frequently accused of obfuscating and constantly altering its Office file formats to force users to buy new versions of its products.
12. IFF lives on even today in the Macintosh, whose audio-interchange file format (AIFF), developed by Apple in 1998 for the storage of sound samples, is a variation on the original IFF format. The Quetzal and Blorb formats used by modern textual interactive-fiction interpreters are also IFF formats.
13. Hiltzik, *Dealers of Lightning*, 342.
14. SuperPaint's design and history are described in Shoup, "*SuperPaint*."
15. Johnson, Roberts, Verplank, et al., "The Xerox Star," 23.
16. Means and Means, "Inside the Making of *Deluxe Paint III*," 27.
17. Foust, "*Amazing* Previews *Deluxe Paint II*," 23.
18. Foust, "Is IFF Really a Standard?" 50.
19. LucasArts, for instance, did the graphics for its early adventure games using DPaint. The name of the main character in its hugely successful *Monkey Island* series was named "Guybrush" after the writers saw the name of the DPaint file used to hold the character—"guy.brush." The first two *Monkey Island* games did receive an Amiga release, but fully one year after the more important MS-DOS versions. See http://www.scummbar.com/resources/faq.
20. Pandaris, "Cynicism and Seduction, Speed and Software."
21. Wray, "Reflections of a Mac User."
22. Bagnall, *On the Edge*, 463–465.
23. Knox, "A New Strategy May Be Needed for Commodore."
24. Bagnall, *On the Edge*, 458–462.
25. G. Wright, "Zeitgest," *AmigaWorld* 2 (5).
26. A central thesis of this book is of course that the Amiga *did* conquer the world in another way, by pointing to the future.
27. The Amiga's histories in North American and Europe are quite distinct. I chart its European history in chapters 7 and 8.
28. G. Wright, "How Many Is a Million?"
29. Means and Means, "Inside the Making of *Deluxe Paint III*," 28.
30. Video production was in fact the most long-lived and important niche of all for the Amiga, as important as desktop publishing was to the early Macintosh. Chapter 5 addresses this topic in much greater detail.
31. Commodore-Amiga Inc., *Amiga Hardware Reference Manual*.
32. The original Agnus chip designed by Jay Miner and his team was present only on the Amiga 1000. Commodore engineer Bob Welland redesigned it in 1987 for the Amiga 500 and 2000, making it smaller and less expensive to manufacture. This redesign was especially critical to the Amiga 500 because that machine retailed for only about half the price of the original 1000. Welland's redesign was dubbed the "Fat Agnus," and, thus, the Fatter Agnus followed in 1989.

33. Smith, "Digital Paint Systems," 9.

34. Barney, "Chief Concerns," 6.

35. G. Wright, "Zeitgeist," *AmigaWorld* 1 (1).

36. Fleming, "We See Farther."

37. Detore and Wood, *Jay Miner Speech* (video).

38. Silva's work as a computer graphics pioneer was, however, far from over even if his days as an Amiga developer were. His next stop was the Yost Group, where he worked on the 3D Studio 3D-modeling application that revolutionized video-game development in the 1990s.

39. Commodore-Amiga Inc., *Amiga Hardware Reference Manual*, 14.

40. Ibid., 15.

41. Microsoft Windows–based PCs also support multiple screens, although they cannot be displayed on the same physical display at the same time. Microsoft's DirectX game libraries, for instance, generally open a new, custom screen on the user's monitor with its own resolution and color depth separate from the screen of the standard Windows desktop. Windows also supports multiple desktops, each running on its own screen, but the user must have two (or more) physical monitors to allow this configuration.

42. The chip set introduced with the Amiga 1000 in 1985 was retroactively labeled the Original Chip Set (OCS) in 1990, when the Amiga 3000 with its modestly improved Enhanced Chip Set (ECS) was introduced. At the time of Commodore's 1994 bankruptcy, work was officially still continuing on the greatly enhanced Amiga AdvancedArchitecture (AAA). In actuality, however, the company's financial straits were so dire during its last year that little was accomplished.

43. Bagnall, *On the Edge*, 543.

44. The Bandito, "Roomers," *Amazing Computing* 8 (9), 69.

45. See note 12, chap. 1, and chapter 9 for more information on the Ultimate Amiga Emulator.

46. Skelton, "Rodney Chang," 45–46.

47. Quoted in Pane, "Color Crunching," 46.

48. Danto, de Salvo, Defendi, et al., *Andy Warhol Prints*, 34.

49. Ibid., 18.

50. George Christianson, quoted in Albert, "Measure of the Man," 32.

51. Skelton, "Rodney Chang," 46.

Chapter 4

1. E. Graham, "Graphics Scene Simulations," 24.

2. E. Wright, "Amiga Juggler Animation."

3. Quoted in Laser, "Osaka and the Turbo SIG," 31.

4. Graham, quoted in E. Wright, "Amiga Juggler Animation."

5. E. Graham, "Graphics Scene Simulations," 18.

6. Sutherland, "*Sketchpad*," 63.

7. Many early graphical tools did not go through this intermediate step, for they did not store a raster image at all in memory. They instead directly controlled the electron beam behind the monitor screen to paint their shapes onto the screen rather than into memory. Such an approach could save a great deal of memory, which was precious and expensive in this era, and could also be more efficient in asking the computer to paint only those pixels that were actually in use, but it

was cumbersome and demanding to program and required specialized display hardware. Nevertheless, it persisted in certain applications almost into the Amiga era; many early stand-up arcade machines used this type of display, as did one early home videogame console, the appropriately named Vectrex.

8. Eric Graham, email to the author, April 2, 2010.
9. Ibid. Graham himself does not remember what SSG actually stands for; "spherical solid geometry" represents his best guess.
10. Graham, email to the author, April 2, 2010.
11. O'Rourke, *Principles of Three-Dimensional Computer Animation*, 84.
12. Graham, email to author, April 2, 2010.
13. E. Graham, "Graphics Scene Simulations," 20.
14. Ibid.
15. Ibid.
16. Ibid.
17. Whitted, "An Improved Illumination Model for Shaded Display."
18. Graham, email to the author, April 1, 2010.
19. E. Graham, "Graphics Scene Simulations," 20.
20. Ibid., 21.
21. Introductory screen of the Juggler demo.
22. Scott, "The Render Junkie."
23. Graham, email to the author, April 2, 2010.
24. Excerpt from "simple1.dat," a sample scene file included with DKBTrace 2.01.
25. Leemon, "Depth-Defying Graphics," 34.
26. Graham, email to the author, April 1, 2010.
27. E. Wright, "Amiga Juggler Animation."
28. Graham, email to the author, July 18, 2010.
29. E. Wright, "Amiga Juggler Animation."
30. Leemon, "Depth-Defying Graphics," 38.
31. Wallace, "Forms in Flight," 68.
32. Originally developed by Bui Tuong Phong for his 1973 PhD dissertation, Phong shading remains in widespread use today.
33. Graham, email to the author, April 25, 2010.
34. Blaize, "3-D Keys to Animation Design," 45.
35. Valich, "World's First Ray-Traced PC Game and Movie to Arrive in 2012."

Chapter 5

1. Skelton, "End User Makes Good!" 28.
2. Jacobs, "Flying Toasters."
3. Quoted in De Jong and Dinkins, "Exploring NewTek," 20.
4. Sands, "Sync Tips," 51.
5. The liquid-crystal display (LCD) monitors that have almost completely replaced CRT monitors today, at least in sales of new units, of course operate on completely different principles. With them, a refresh rate of 60 Hz is not only acceptable but recommended.
6. Video professionals loath NTSC for its poor color separation and resulting unpredictable and often washed-out appearance; a common joke says that the acronym NTSC stands for "Never the Same Color Twice." PAL, being a slightly

later standard that presumably learned some lessons from NTSC, is superior in this respect—and in fact in most respects, although not dramatically so.

7. Joe Decuir, email to the author, July 16, 2010.
8. Joe Decuir, email to the author, September 10, 2010.
9. European Amigas ran at a slightly slower clock speed, 7.09 MHz, to accommodate the slightly different timing of the PAL standard.
10. To be strictly correct, NTSC actually specifies a 525-scan-line screen. The extra 41 scan lines, however, either are left blank or carry nonvisual information. These scan lines are sent at the end of each cycle (20 at the end of one, 21 at the end of the other in an alternating sequence), giving the electron gun time to return to the top left of the screen to begin the next cycle.
11. Virtually all modern computers operate almost exclusively in resolution modes that lead to exactly square pixels in order to avoid this sort of frustration. Typical resolutions of 640 × 480, 800 × 600, and 1,024 × 768, for instance, share the same four-to-three width-to-height ratio as a standard monitor (or television, for that matter). Widescreen resolutions obviously follow different ratios but strive toward the same goal.
12. Although using a television as a monitor was possible and even common for early inexpensive computers such as the Commodore 64, it was not a recommendable option for the Amiga. Televisions of the time were adequate for the Commodore 64's 40-column text screen, but they were neither designed for nor good at displaying the detail required for the 80-column text screen typical of the Amiga. In fact, although the Amiga's interlaced video output format may align with NTSC, its actual physical connectors are of a custom design used only by Amigas.
13. Kirsch, "SEAC and the Start of Image Processing," 9.
14. For a useful survey of the state of digitizers at the time of the Amiga's launch, see Linzmayer, "Digital Image Processors.".
15. Leeds, "Success Story," 27–29.
16. Brannon, "*MacVision* for Apple Macintosh," 61.
17. Foust, "A-Squared and the *Live!* Video Digitizer," 31–32.
18. The Bandito, "Roomers," *Amazing Computing* 4, (9), 67.
19. I owe the very apt comparison between Digi-View digitizing and daguerreotyping to Foust, "What *Digi-View* Is . . . or, What Genlock Should Be!" 19.
20. Jacobs, "Flying Toasters."
21. Ibid.
22. Quoted in Reifsnyder, "Artists and the Amiga," 29.
23. I owe the details of the three typical desktop video setups broadly to Sands, "Video."
24. Barrett, "Classroom Video."
25. Ibid., 29.
26. Albert, "Video Victorious."
27. Grime, "Master the Raster," 20.
28. Tessler, "Super Bowl Amiga Show."
29. Foust, "*Amazing Stories* and the Amiga."
30. Foust, "*Max Headroom* and the Amiga"; Herrington, "Graphics to the Max."
31. Gifford, *The Max Headroom Chronicles*.
32. Humphreys, "Max Headroom."
33. This claim is stated as fact on certain Internet sites, but I have not been able to trace it back to a firm, reliable source from the era of the actual show. I am also

somewhat reluctant to accept these claims completely because I can see no substantial difference in the background of the first season of *Max Headroom*, when Amigas definitely were not involved in the production, from the background of the second season. This lack of difference might mean that the producers had a working, non-Amiga-based solution already in place and simply chose to stay with it. But it might also mean, of course, that they simply did a very good job of converting the process seamlessly to the Amiga. Unlike the foreground animation of Max himself, such simple, abstract animations were well within the Amiga's capabilities.

34. Quoted in Foust, "*Max Headroom* and the Amiga," 14.
35. Martin, "Amiga on Location with *Robocop*."
36. Skelton, "End User Makes Good!" 27.
37. Ibid., 70; Jacobs, "Flying Toasters."
38. Jacobs, "Flying Toasters"; Keith Doyle to Usenet, June 20, 1987, at http://groups.google.com/group/comp.sys.amiga/msg/768bd517bf30e897.
39. For examples of such coverage, see Dunnington, "*Info* Visits the Magic Land of NewTek," and Ryan, "The Brave Now World of Video."
40. De Jong and Dinkins, "Exploring NewTek," 19.
41. Early models of the Toaster did not support chroma keying but did allow for luminance keying. In the latter technique, the background image is separated from the foreground subject not by color, but by brightness. Luminance keying is somewhat more difficult to control than chroma keying, but perfectly satisfactory results can be obtained from it with a bit of trial and error. Later revisions of the Toaster did add chroma-keying support.
42. "Video Toaster at the Ballpark," 90.
43. Robley, "*Babylon 5*," 73.
44. Ibid., 73–74.
45. Leeds, "Allen Hastings," 58.
46. Crotty, "Amiga Goes Hollywood," 44.
47. Ibid., 46.
48. Ibid.
49. Ibid.
50. Quoted in Hicks, "Editorial Content," 6.
51. Quoted in Jacobs, "Flying Toasters."
52. The Bandito, "Roomers," *Amazing Computing* 9 (4), 70.
53. Knight, "The Mighty Amiga 2000 and Video Toaster 3.1 Combo."
54. Becker, "An Interview with Mojo."
55. The Bandito, "Roomers," *Amazing Computing* 9 (5), 68. Montgomery died at a very young age in 1999.

Chapter 6

1. AmigaOS has not always been known as "AmigaOS." The Amiga was released at a time when PC OSs were often discussed only in tandem with the hardware that ran them. The OSs (such as they were) of early 8-bit computers such as the Commodore 64 and Apple II, for example, existed only on ROM chips built into the computers themselves and thus were inseparable from their hosts. These systems were the only types that Commodore had experience with at the time it acquired

Amiga, so it is perhaps not surprising that the company seems to have had difficulty conceiving, even internally, of the concept of a holistic AmigaOS. Commodore instead used a variety of names to refer to either various parts or to the entirety of the Amiga's systems software, such as "Kickstart," "Workbench," and "AmigaDOS," in a frustratingly inconsistent way and without always seeming to have a clear notion of which names represented which components even within a individual publication. Only toward the end of the Commodore era did the company begin referring to an "Amiga OS," years after users had adopted the term. Amiga users often contracted "the Amiga OS" into the more stylish "AmigaOS," which was finally made the OS's official name when version 4.0 was developed after the millennium by Hyperion Entertainment. For reasons of simplicity and clarity, the admittedly often anachronistic name "AmigaOS" is the one I have chosen to employ throughout this chapter and this book.

2. Correspondence between Joe Decuir and the author following Decuir's review of an earlier draft of this book.

3. Detore and Wood, *Jay Miner Speech* (video).

4. Ibid.

5. Quoted in Donner, *Workbench Nostalgia*.

6. It is an unfortunate reality that the word *hacker* has acquired two disparate meanings, one positive and one negative, within different segments of society. Within digital culture, a hacker is an heir to a long computing tradition of creating and sharing good work. The hacker is an idealist, one who believes, as Bruce Sterling writes in *The Hacker Crackdown*, that "beauty can be found in computers, that the fine aesthetic in a perfect program can liberate the mind and spirit" (51). See Steven Levy's *Hackers* for the definitive history of this branch of computing culture. In the mainstream media, however, the word *hacker* is generally used in reference to one who commits computer crime: pirating software, breaking into networks, and so on. True hackers would say that the latter individuals should be referred to as *crackers*, but at this point the negative connotations of the label *hacker* in mainstream society seem unlikely to change. Nevertheless, wherever I use the word *hacker* in this chapter and in this book, I am using it in the positive sense.

7. One can in fact make the argument that MS-DOS is so simplistic as to not be a true OS at all, but merely a bootstrap and a collection of basic input/output function calls and interrupts. Indeed, Microsoft built early versions of Windows right on top of MS-DOS, using it as a foundation on which to erect a proper, full-fledged OS.

8. Macintosh System 5, introduced in October 1987, did offer limited *cooperative multitasking* for the first time. It was not until the release of OS X in 2001, however, that Macintosh users at last got a true preemptive multitasking OS.

9. "Nearly" unprecedented because OS-9, developed by Microware Systems Corporation, did in fact feature true multitasking in the astonishingly early year of 1979. Like AmigaOS, OS-9 was heavily inspired by Unix; unlike AmigaOS, it never gained significant commercial-software support, remaining largely a hobbyist toy in its early years. Since then, though, OS-9 has become popular for use in embedded systems and is still actively developed for that purpose today.

10. The debate over which design is "best" continues to rage, and its details are necessarily outside the scope of this book. A fascinating 1992 Usenet debate on

the subject between Andy Tanenbaum, developer of an early "Unix-like" PC OS known as "Minix," and Linus Torvalds, the originator of Linux, can be found either online at http://groups.google.com/group/comp.os.minix/browse_ thread/thread/c25870d7a41696d2/f447530d082cd95d?q=Tanenbaum+group% 3Acomp.os.minix&lnk=ol& or in appendix A (221–252) of DiBona, Ockman, and Stone, eds., *Open Sources*. Minix uses a microkernel, Linux a monolithic kernel, and both gentlemen argue their cases persuasively enough. As for the major OSs in use today, Linux retains its monolithic kernel (albeit with support for loading and unloading certain functionality via modules), the Macintosh's OS X is built around a microkernel, and Microsoft's Windows uses a hybrid design that is not quite monolithic, but also not quite micro.

11. Conroy and Crotty, *The History of the Amiga* (video).

12. According to AmigaOS's preferred terminology, a "process" is actually a superset of a "task," being a task spawned by the user rather than by an application or by the OS itself. Processes have access to libraries and resources that tasks do not. The distinction is, however, rather fine grained and not terribly germane to this higher-level overview of the Exec's functions. I have therefore chosen to employ the more traditional computer science term *process* throughout.

13. Stuart, *Principles of Operating Systems*, 81.

14. Some modern PCs do have dual (or more) CPU architectures, and many modern CPUs now contain circuitry to execute more than one instruction simultaneously; such designs are effectively two or more CPUs, each known as a *core*, built into the same chip. Although modern OSs are built to support such architectures, the fact remains that at any given time they will still have many more processes competing for attention than they do physical CPUs on which to run them; thus, task switching must continue.

15. The one fixed address is the second four bytes of memory, which contain a pointer to the location of the Exec itself in memory.

16. Bagnall, *On the Edge*, 416.

17. Ibid.

18. Ibid., 430; Finkel, "In the Beginning Was CAOS."

19. Perhaps *"extremely* short order" would be a better description here. As pointed out on the blog pagetable.com (http://www.pagetable.com/?p=193), the first edition of the *AmigaDOS Manual* was little more than a reprint of the already extant *TRIPOS Programmer's Reference Manual*, excising those chapters relating to parts of TRIPOS not incorporated into AmigaOS.

20. Detore and Wood, *Jay Miner Speech*.

21. Knight, "Amiga Joyboard."

22. Conroy and Crotty, *The History of the Amiga*.

23. AmigaOS was in such a state of flux at the time of the Amiga 1000s release that Commodore did not feel comfortable burning it into permanent, unchangeable ROM on that machine. It was therefore provided on a floppy disk labeled "Kickstart," and when the 1000 was powered on, the OS had to be read from there into a special bank of memory that effectively acted like ROM after that point—going unchanged during machine resets and so on. Beginning with the Amiga 500 and 2000 in 1987, all Amigas included KickStart in ROM. One benefit of the Amiga 1000 approach was that 1000 users did not have to swap chips physically with every OS upgrade; the main drawback, of course, was the additional wait for

KickStart to be read into memory at every power-on as well as the theoretical danger of losing access to the machine entirely if one lost or all of one's Kickstart disks or they failed.

24. Programmers could also effectively add to AmigaOS by designing new libraries of their own; ARexx (described later in this chapter) operated in this way, as did many other common utilities such as the very popular AmigaDOS Replacement Project (ARP) library that eased many of the shortcomings of AmigaDOS by the simple expedient of replacing much of it entirely.

25. Commodore-Amiga Inc., *Amiga ROM Kernel Reference Manual: Libraries*, 2.

26. Commodore Business Machines, *Commodore 64 Programmer's Reference Guide*, 23.

27. I have seen at least one instance of a program going into an endless, uncontrolled loop in which it wrote from memory address 0 on up to some unknowably high upper bound again and again. As the program cycled through the loop, the screen filled with cycling garbage as the program wrote random numbers into those memory locations, the power light blinked on and off as the register that controlled it was changed, and even the disk drives thrashed about randomly.

28. For a very simplistic example of how this can happen, we can revisit yet again our hypothetical word processor. Let us say we read from disk a document of 30,000 bytes. Through the Exec, the program allocates that much memory to that document as well as an additional 5,000 bytes to contain additions the user might make. If the user types enough additional text that the total size exceeds 35,000 bytes, the program must then return to the Exec to request additional memory. If it fails to make this request and simply keeps adding to the end of memory already allocated, its data will spill over into memory potentially allocated to something else, and the end result will likely not be a pretty one. This sort of programming error is so common that it has a name: "bounds violation." Of course, most memory-management bugs of this type and others are much more subtle and difficult to track down.

29. Although early versions of both Microsoft Windows and MacOS do implement virtual memory, these implementations are incomplete, allowing applications access to certain memory addresses outside their sandboxes. Only with Windows XP and OS X did true memory protection appear on the consumer versions of these OSs. This fact accounts largely for the general instability of both systems prior to around 2000.

30. Commodore-Amiga Inc., *Amiga Hardware Reference Manual*, 9.

31. Ibid.

32. Quoted in Bagnall, *On the Edge*, 450.

33. Steven Levy uses the term *priesthood* to refer to mainframe technicians in his classic history *Hackers*, while also detailing in considerable depth the differences between the classic hacker culture found at institutions such as MIT and the all-business IBM approach to computing. It should be noted, however, that Levy sometimes exaggerates this conflict for dramatic effect. The creation of an innovative, friendly program such as REXX certainly proves that not everyone at IBM embraced the priesthood stereotype or its associated hierarchical structure and hostility to the idea of empowering everyday computer users.

34. MVS and VM have in recent years been rebranded "z/VM" and "z/OS," respectively.

35. Woehr, "A Conversation with Mike Cowlishaw."

36. Goldberg, "The Man behind REXX."
37. I drew the basic concept of this project, if not many of its implementation details, from Gillmor, "Adventures in ARexx."
38. Levy, *Hackers*, 124.

Chapter 7

1. Brown, "Virus!" 22.
2. See note 6, chapter 6, for more on the distinction between a *hacker* and a *cracker*.
3. Zetter, "Nov. 10, 1983." In an ironic twist, Skrenta later worked on the Amiga for Commodore from 1989 to 1991.
4. Cohen, "Computer Viruses—Theory and Experiments."
5. McLellan, "Computer Systems under Siege."
6. Brown, "Virus!" 22.
7. Beginning with the release of AmigaOS 1.3 in 1988, it also became possible to boot directly from a hard drive, a much-needed feature; before that time, some hard-disk manufacturers had enabled this ability with hacks and workarounds, but it was not officially supported.
8. Email correspondence from the SCA virus's creator (who wishes to remain anonymous) to the author, August 20, 2010.
9. Ibid.
10. Ibid.
11. Brown, "Virus!" 22.
12. Yarbor, "Commercial Software Carries Virus."
13. Email correspondence from the SCA virus's creator to the author, September 4, 2010.
14. Ibid.
15. Wallace, "Vanquishing the Viruses," 50.
16. Ibid.
17. Gustaffson, *The Amiga Virus Encyclopedia*, http://www.teyko.com/Index.aspx.
18. Wallace, "The Help Key: Warning!"
19. Maciorowski, "Put on the Hex," 45.
20. Beginning with the ECS-equipped Amiga 3000 of 1990, it became possible to switch an Amiga to and from PAL and NTSC via software, assuming of course that the monitor connected to the machine supported both video modes.
21. The Bandito, "Roomers," *Amazing Computing* 6 (4), 62.
22. Polgár, *Freax*, 64.
23. Ibid., 84.
24. Ibid., 167.
25. Ibid., 63.
26. Ibid., 93.
27. Polgár, *The Full History of the Demoscene* (video).
28. Carlsson, "The Forgotten Pioneers," 18, emphasis in original.
29. Gruetzmacher, "PC Demoscene FAQ."
30. Spaceballs, "Woman of *State of the Art*."
31. Lone Starr, "Making of *State of the Art*."
32. Quoted in ibid.
33. Chaos, quoted in Spaceballs, "Best Demos of 1992."

34. Dr. Jekyll, quoted in ibid.
35. Laxity, quoted in ibid.
36. Hannibal, quoted in ibid.
37. Lone Starr, "Making of *State of the Art*".
38. Polgár, *Freax*, 220.
39. The Amiga Music Preservation site is at http://amp.dascene.net.
40. The SID chip is nevertheless capable of some very impressive feats. In fact, so-called SID music is still created, traded, and occasionally even sold today. See the High Voltage SID Collection at http://www.hvsc.c64.org for a plethora of examples.
41. Crown and Curt Cool, "Karsten Obarski Interview."
42. Dahlberg, "Interview with Karsten Obarski."
43. M. Wright, "Retrospective: Karsten Obarski."
44. Kotlinski, "Amiga Music Programs 1986–1995."
45. I owe the outline of this sample project to Andy Nuttall's article "Keep on Trackin'" in *Amiga Format*, no. 48. The samples I employ as well as the version of Pro-Tracker itself are drawn from one of that issue's cover disks.
46. It was possible to connect an Amiga to a MIDI-capable synthesizer or drum machine and in so doing to leave behind most of the basic hardware's sound limitations. Many Amiga music applications, including Deluxe Music and some trackers, offered support for MIDI, and some, such as Blue Ribbon Soundworks' still-beloved Bars and Pipes, were designed to interface exclusively with MIDI.
47. Polgár, *Freax*, 282.
48. G. Knight, "The Twists and Turns of the Amiga Saga."
49. Mop, "Age: A Major Concern?"
50. Spaceballs, "A Visit at Funcom!"
51. Zike, "Interview: Animal."
52. Mop, "The Games Industry Is Destroying Our Scene!"
53. Quoted in Menkman, "Chip Music and the 8-Bit Demoscene."
54. Heikkilä, "Putting the Demoscene in Context."
55. Raymond, *The Cathedral and the Bazaar*, 89.
56. I drew these points from Linus Walleij's reply to Raymond, "A Comment on 'Warez Doodz' Culture."
57. Raymond, *The Cathedral and the Bazaar*, 82.
58. Sterling, *The Hacker Crackdown*, 57.

Chapter 8

1. Electronic Arts, "Why Electronic Arts Is Committed to the Amiga," 7.
2. Hull, "*Amazing* Interviews . . . Jim Sachs," 12.
3. Hoban, "Looks Great, Manny, but Will It Sell?" 15.
4. Eskelinen, "The Gaming Situation."
5. Barton, "Interview: Bob Jacob."
6. Ibid.
7. Ibid. The company was officially known as "Master Designer Software" and published Cinemaware games as a marketing label. Today, however, the company is universally remembered, even by its founder Bob Jacob, as simply "Cinemaware." In the interest of simplicity, I have also chosen to refer to it by the latter name throughout this chapter.

8. Ibid.

9. Katz, "The Cinemaware Story," 83.

10. Quoted in Spanner, "Cinemaware," 15.

11. Barton, "Interview: Bob Jacob."

12. Ibid.

13. "Jim Sachs," 55.

14. Hull, "*Amazing* Interviews . . . Jim Sachs," 10–11.

15. Bagnall, *On the Edge,* 476.

16. Hull, "*Amazing* Interviews . . . Jim Sachs," 11.

17. I am indebted to the first chapter of Noah Wardrip-Fruin's *Expressive Processing: Digital Fictions, Computer Games, and Software Studies* for the basis of the distinctions I make here.

18. For a full development history of *Elite* and a description of the inventive programming that made it possible, see chapter 3 of Spufford, *Backroom Boys*.

19. Barton, "Interview: Bob Jacob."

20. Ibid.

21. Juul, *A Casual Revolution,*30–50.

22. Bagnall, *On the Edge,* 475.

23. Quoted in Bercovitz, "Jez San," 45.

24. Anderson, "The Battle for Santa's Software" (television special).

25. Kean, "The Biggest *Commercial Break* of Them All."

26. Monteiro, "Behind the Scenes,"33.

27. Grannell, "Painting Worlds," 82.

28. Ibid., 83.

29. Nichols, "The New Amigas" (televisionepisode, 1989).

30. Bercovitz, "Jez San," 46.

31. This C adaptation to some extent puts the lie to the European demoscene and game industry's insistence on pure assembly as the only viable approach to high-performance Amiga programming. Although the performance of my C adaptation does show occasional hints of jerkiness, it is quite acceptable in my view. Perhaps more significant than the language chosen is the eschewing of AmigaOS libraries in favor of coding directly to the hardware, a tradition that I for the most part continue in my own adaptation.

32. Commodore-Amiga Inc., *Amiga Hardware Reference Manual,* 62.

33. Neither the Intel PC architecture nor the Macintosh utilizes hardware sprites like those described here because at the time of their introduction both were envisioned purely as "serious" machines for business and productivity uses and were thus judged to have little need for such features. Today many libraries and tools nevertheless do allow programmers to code "sprite-based" games on these machines with many of the same conveniences that were enjoyed by programmers on the Amiga. These "sprites" are, however, an illusion manufactured entirely through additional layers of software abstraction—abstractions that were not a practical option on the Amiga's limited hardware.

Chapter 9

1. Barton, "Interview: Bob Jacob."

2. O'Keane, "Microsoft CD-ROM Conference," 59.

3. Spanner, "Cinemaware," 17.
4. Walker, *The Sims* Overtakes *Myst*."
5. Quoted in Bagnall, *On the Edge*, 519.
6. "Jay Miner," 21.
7. Bagnall, *On the Edge*, 541.
8. The Bandito, "Roomers," *Amazing Computing* 9 (1), 69.
9. Skelton, "*Info* Interviews Jay Miner," 25.
10. See Bagnall's *On the Edge* for a complete history of Commodore told largely from the perspective of engineers such as Haynie, who managed to do great work with scant resources for years. Their frustration with management far exceeded even that of the typical Amiga user because they were in a position to see bad decision after bad decision being made yet were powerless to change it.
11. One might of course ask the same question about the Macintosh. That said, it is also true that the Macintosh was defined in the beginning more by the look and feel of its OS than by its (rather unexceptional) hardware and that this look and feel were retained in the newer PowerPC-based machines. The Amiga's identity, meanwhile, was—innovative as AmigaOS was—much more caught up in its custom-chip-enabled hardware design that gave it such unprecedented multimedia capabilities.
12. Fish died in 2007 of a sudden heart attack.
13. Bercovitz, "Hooked on the Amiga with Fred Fish," 31, emphasis in original.
14. Ibid., 32.
15. Ibid., 34.
16. Ibid., 35.
17. Raymond, *The Cathedral and the Bazaar*, 21.
18. Müller, "Aminet Is the World's Largest Archive."
19. The Bandito, "Roomers," *Amazing Computing* 9 (7), 50.
20. Skelton, "*Info* Interviews Jay Miner," 25.
21. The Bandito, "Roomers," *Amazing Computing* 9 (8), 70.

Bibliography

Texts

Abbott, Edwin A. *Flatland: A Romance of Many Dimensions*. Amherst, MA: Prometheus, 1884.

Ahl, David H., and Sheldon Leemon. "1984 Winter Consumer Electronics Show." *Creative Computing* 10 (4) (April 1984): 132–149.

Albert, Sue. "Measure of the Man." *Info* 34 (November 1990): 30–32.

Albert, Sue. "Video Victorious." *Info* 39 (May 1991): 30–32.

Anderson, John J. "Amiga: The Message Is the Medium." *Creative Computing* 11 (9) (September 1985): 32–42.

Anderson, John J. "Amiga Lorraine: Finally, the 'Next Generation Atari'?" *Creative Computing* 10 (4) (April 1984): 150–153.

Anderson, John J. "Apple Macintosh: Cutting through the Ballyhoo." *Creative Computing* 10 (7) (July 1984): 12–17.

Anderson, Rhett, and Randy Thompson. *Mapping the Amiga*. 2nd ed. Greensboro, NC: Compute, 1993.

Antonakos, James L. *The 68000 Microprocessor: Hardware and Software Principals and Applications*. 4th ed. Upper Saddle River, NJ: Prentice-Hall, 1999.

Babel, Ralph. *The Amiga Guru Book: A Reference Manual*. Taunusstein, Germany: Ralph Babel, 1993.

Bagnall, Brian. *On the Edge: The Spectacular Rise and Fall of Commodore*. Winnipeg: Variant, 2005.

The Bandito. "Roomers." *Amazing Computing* 4 (9) (September 1989): 67–70.

The Bandito. "Roomers." *Amazing Computing* 6 (4) (April 1991): 61–66.

The Bandito. "Roomers." *Amazing Computing* 8 (9) (September 1993): 69–73.

The Bandito. "Roomers." *Amazing Computing* 9 (1) (January 1994): 69–71.

The Bandito. "Roomers." *Amazing Computing* 9 (4) (April 1994): 67–70.

The Bandito. "Roomers." *Amazing Computing* 9 (5) (May 1994): 68–71.

The Bandito. "Roomers." *Amazing Computing* 9 (7) (July 1994): 50–54.

The Bandito. "Roomers." *Amazing Computing* 9 (8) (August 1994): 68–71.

Barney, Doug. "Chief Concerns." *AmigaWorld* 8 (2) (February 1992): 6.

Barney, Doug, Dan Sullivan, and Louis R. Wallace. "Welcome to a New Generation!" *AmigaWorld* 6 (6) (June 1990): 18–28.

Barrett, Daniel J. "Classroom Video." *Info* 38 (April 1991): 28–29.

Barton, Matt. "Interview: Bob Jacob on the Cinemaware Era." *Gamasutra*, January 5, 2010. http://www.gamasutra.com/view/news/26583/Interview_Bob_Jacob_On_The_Cinemaware_Era.php.

Bateman, Selby. "Commodore's New Computer Family: News from the Winter Consumer Electronics Show." *Compute!'s Gazette* 2 (4) (April 1984): 16–24.

Bateman, Selby. "Software Power!" *Compute!* 6 (8) (August 1984): 32–41.

Bechtolsheim, Andreas, Forest Baskett, and Vaughn Pratt. *The SUN Workstation Architecture*. Technical Report no. 229, March. Stanford, CA: Stanford University, 1982.

Becker, Chuck. "An Interview with Mojo." *The Lurker's Guide to Babylon 5*, October 16, 1995. http://www.midwinter.com/lurk/making/mojo.html.

Bercovitz, Ed. "Hooked on the Amiga with Fred Fish." *Amazing Computing* 3 (2) (February 1988): 31–38.

Bercovitz, Ed. "Jez San." *Amazing Computing* 2 (11) (November 1987): 44–48.

Blaize, Steven. "3-D Keys to Animation Design." *AmigaWorld* 8 (12) (December 1992): 45–48.

Blaize, Steven. "*Imagine* Animation." *AmigaWorld* 7 (10) (October 1991): 33–38.

Blume, Jeffrey W. "ARexx: New Kingpin of Multitasking?" *AmigaWorld* 4 (11) (November 1988): 55–62.

Borzyskowski, George. "The Hacker Demo Scene and Its Cultural Artifacts." Curtin University of Technology. http://www.scheib.net/play/demos/what/borzyskowski.

Brannon, Charles. "*MacVision* for Apple Macintosh." *Compute!* 7 (5) (May 1985): 60–61.

Brawn, Gene. "Great Graphics, Godzilla, It's *DPaint IV*!" *AmigaWorld* 8 (2) (February 1992): 24–28.

Brown, Mark R. "Virus!" *Info* 18 (January–February 1988): 22–23.

Brown, Mark R. "Virus Update." *Info* 19 (March–April 1988): 29.

Burgard, Mike. "More Than a Toy but No Bargain." *UnixWorld* 8 (12) (December 1991): 75–77.

Calloway, Merrill. "Demystifying ARexx: What Is It? Should I Learn It? Is ARexx Hard to Learn?" *Amazing Computing* 8 (2) (February 1993): 53–56.

Calloway, Merrill. "Inside ARexx." *Amazing Computing* 8 (9) (September 1993): 59–63.

Carlsson, Anders. "The Forgotten Pioneers of Creative Hacking and Social Networking: Introducing the Demoscene." In *Re:live 2009 Conference Proceedings*, ed. Sean Cubitt and Paul Thomas, 16–20. Melbourne: University of Melbourne and Victorian College of the Arts and Music, 2009.

Cashman, Mark. "Deluxe Paint IV" (review). *AmigaWorld* 8 (2) (February 1992): 18–19.

Cawley, John. *The Animated Films of Don Bluth*. New York: Mulgrave Image, 1991.

Clements, Alan. *Microprocessor Systems Design: 68000 Hardware, Software, and Interfacing*. 3rd ed. Boston: PWS, 1997.

Cohen, Fred. "Computer Viruses—Theory and Experiments." In *Proceedings of the 7th DoD/NBS Computer Security Conference 1984*, 240–263. Gaithersburg: Department of Defense, 1984.

Commodore-Amiga Inc. *The AmigaDOS Manual*. New York: Bantam, 1986.

Commodore-Amiga Inc. *Amiga Hardware Reference Manual*. 3rd ed. Redwood City, CA: Addison-Wesley, 1991.

Commodore-Amiga Inc. *Amiga ROM Kernel Reference Manual: Devices*. 3rd ed. Redwood City, CA: Addison-Wesley, 1991.

Commodore-Amiga Inc. *Amiga ROM Kernel Reference Manual: Libraries*. 3rd ed. Redwood City, CA: Addison-Wesley, 1991.

Commodore Business Machines. *Commodore 64 Programmer's Reference Guide*. West Chester: Commodore Business Machines, 1982.

Cottle, James G. "Microprocessors." In *The Electronics Handbook*, ed. Jerry C. Whitaker, 712–722. Beaverton, OR: Technical Press, 1996.

Crotty, Janice. "Amiga Goes Hollywood." *AmigaWorld* 9 (11) (November 1993): 43–48.

Crown and Curt Cool. "Karsten Obarski Interview." The Amiga Music Preservation Web site, http://amp.dascene.net/detail.php?view=3982&detail=interview.

"CRT Monitors." *P.C. Tech Guide*. n.d. http://www.pctechguide.com/42CRTMonitors.htm.

Current, Michael D. "Atari 8-Bit Computers Frequently Asked Questions List." September 26, 2009. http://faqs.cs.uu.nl/na-dir/atari-8-bit/faq.html.

Dahlberg, Mattias. "Interview with Karsten Obarski." *AM/FM Disk Magazine* 11 (1993).

Danto, Arthur, Donna de Salvo, Claudia Defendi, Frayda Feldman, Jorg Schnellmann, and Andy Warhol. *Andy Warhol Prints: A Catalogue Raisonné*. 4th ed. New York: Distributed Art Publishers, 2003.

De Jong, Dick, and Molly Dinkins. "Exploring NewTek: Strategic New Directions." *New Tekniques* 2 (1) (February–March 1998): 18–23.

DiBona, Chris, Sam Ockman, and Mark Stone, eds. *Open Sources: Voices of the Open Source Revolution*. Sebastopol, CA: O'Reilly, 1999.

D'Ignazio, Fred. "Apple's Macintosh Unveiled." *Compute!* 6 (4) (April 1984): 44–47.

Dittrich, Gelfand. *Schemmel: Amiga System Programmer's Guide*. Grand Rapids, MI: Abacus, 1988.

Dittrich, Stefan. *Amiga Machine Language*. Grand Rapids, MI: Abacus, 1989.

Donner, Gregory. *Workbench Nostalgia: History of the AmigaOS GUI*. October 5, 2009. http://www.gregdonner.org/workbench.

Duberman, David. "*Deluxe Paint III* Review." *Amazing Computing* 4 (5) (May 1989): 14–16, 74.

Dunnington, Benn. "*Info* Visits the Magic Land of NewTek." *Info* 20 (May–June 1988): 44–45.

"DVD-Audio Tutorial." June 5, 2002. http://www.timefordvd.com/tutorial/DVD-AudioTutorial.shtml.

Electronic Arts, Inc. "Can a Computer Make You Cry?" Chris Hecker's Website, December 23, 2007. http://chrishecker.com/Can_a_Computer_Make_You_Cry%3F.

Electronic Arts, Inc. "Why Electronic Arts Is Committed to the Amiga." *AmigaWorld* 1 (1) (1985): 6–7.

Epstein, Brian. "A Peek at the 68000." *AmigaWorld* 1 (1) (1985): 76–79.

Erhart, David W. "Sage and Stride." October 13, 2006. http://www.sageandstride.org.

Erzinger, E. E. "Desktop Video." *AmigaWorld* 3 (1) (January–February 1987): 16–21.

Eskelinen, Markku. "The Gaming Situation." *Game Studies* 1 (1) (July 2001). http://www.gamestudies.org/0101/eskelinen.

Farquharson, J. Allan. "OS-9 Multitasking: Repartee." *AmigaWorld* 2 (3) (May–June 1986): 12.

Feldman, Tony. *Multimedia*. London: Chapman and Hall, 1994.

Finkel, Andy. "In the Beginning Was CAOS." *Amiga Transactor* 1 (1) (April 1988): 41–43.

Fleming, Jeffrey. "We See Farther: A History of Electronic Arts." *Gamasutra*, February 12, 2007. http://www.gamasutra.com/view/feature/1711/we_see_farther_a_history _of_.php.

Forbes, Jim. "Microsoft Calls March Seminar to Promote CD-ROM Technology." *InfoWorld* 7 (49)(December 9, 1985): 5.

Forbes, Jim. "Stimulating Simulations: Electronic Arts Gets Involved with the Amiga." *AmigaWorld* 1 (1) (1985): 56–63.

Foust, John. "*Amazing* Previews *Deluxe Paint II* from Electronic Arts." *Amazing Computing* 2 (1) (January 1987): 23–28.

Foust, John. "*Amazing Stories* and the Amiga." *Amazing Computing* 2 (7) (July 1987): 55–57.

Foust, John. "Amiga 3-D: Past, Present, and Future." *Compute!'s Amiga Resource* 2 (1) (February 1990): 30–37.

Foust, John. "A-Squared and the *Live!* Video Digitizer." *Amazing Computing* 2 (7) (July 1987): 31–32.

Foust, John. "Is IFF Really a Standard?" *Amazing Computing* 2 (7) (July 1987): 47–54.

Foust, John. "*Max Headroom* and the Amiga." *Amazing Computing* 2 (10) (October 1987): 10–14.

Foust, John. "What *Digi-View* Is . . . or, What Genlock Should Be!" *Amazing Computing* 2 (1) (January 1987): 17–22.

Friedman, Dean. "Sizzling Sounds." *AmigaWorld* 5 (10) (October 1989): 48–56.

Fulton, Steve. "Atari: The Golden Years—a History, 1978–1981." *Gamasutra*, August 21, 2008. http://www.gamasutra.com/view/feature/3766/atari_the_golden_years_a_ .php.

Fulton, Steve. "The History of Atari: 1971–1977." *Gamasutra*, November 6, 2007. http://www.gamasutra.com/view/feature/2000/the_history_of_atari_19711977. php?page=1.

Gates, Bill. "An Open Letter to Hobbyists." *Homebrew Computer Club Newsletter* 2 (1) (January 31, 1976): 2.

Gibson, William. *Neuromancer*. New York: Ace, 1984.

Gifford, James. *The Max Headroom Chronicles*. December 22, 2009. http://www.max headroom.com/mh_home.html.

Gillmor, Steve. "Adventures in ARexx." *Amazing Computing* 4 (6) (June 1989): 18–22.

Glassner, Andrew S. "An Overview of Ray Tracing." In *An Introduction to Ray Tracing*, ed. Andrew S. Glassner, 1–32. San Francisco: Morgan Kaufmann, 1989.

Goldberg, Gabe. "The Man behind REXX: *z/Journal* Visits IBM Fellow Mike Cowlishaw." *z/Journal* (August–September 2004): 26–29.

Goldwasser, Samuel M. "TV and Monitor (CRT) Picture Tube Information." September 24, 2008. http://www.repairfaq.org/sam/crtfaq.htm.

Goode, Roger. "Deluxe Paint II" (review). *AmigaWorld* 3 (3) (May–June 1987): 62–66.

Graetz, J. M. "The Origin of *Spacewar*." *Creative Computing* 7 (8) (August 1981): 56–67.

Graham, Cathryn E. F. "Ray Tracing Fundamentals: The Theory behind the Magical Images." *Transactor for the Amiga* 1 (3) (December 1988): 26–31.

Graham, Eric. "Graphic Scene Simulations." *AmigaWorld* 3 (3) (May–June 1987): 18–24.

Grannell, Craig. "Painting Worlds: An Interview with Roger Dean." *Retro Gamer* 50: 80–85.

Grime, Derek. "Master the Raster: The Seduction of the Production Houses." *Transactor for the Amiga* 3 (1) (October 1989): 20–23.

Grote, Gelfand, Abraham. *Amiga Disk Drives: Inside and Out.* Grand Rapids: Abacus, 1988. Gruetzmacher, Thomas. "PC Demoscene FAQ." June 16, 2004. http://tomaes.32x.de/text/faq.php.

Gustaffson, Mario. n.d. *Amiga Virus Encyclopedia.* http://www.teyko.com/Index.aspx.

Hagen, Joel. "Not Just a Paint Job." *AmigaWorld* 5 (7) (July 1989): 49–54.

Halfhill, Tom R. "The Amiga: An In-Depth Review." *Compute!* 7 (9) (September 1985): 16–29.

Haynie, Dave. "What You Should Know about the 680 × 0 Processor Family." *Info* 49 (April 1992): 52–58.

Heikkilä, Ville-Matias. "Putting the Demoscene in Context." *Countercomplex*, July 11, 2009. http://www.pelulamu.net/viznut/blog/putting-the-demoscene-in-a-context.

Herrington, Peggy. "Designing Amiga's Sound." *AmigaWorld* 2 (4) (July–August 1986): 24–31.

Herrington, Peggy. "Digital Sound Samplers." *AmigaWorld* 3 (1) (January–February 1987): 29–32.

Herrington, Peggy. "Graphics to the Max." *AmigaWorld* 3 (7) (December 1987): 76–77.

Herrington, Peggy. "Music Synthesis and the Amiga." *AmigaWorld* 2 (4) (July–August 1986): 15–23.

Hertzfeld, Andy. "The End of an Era." http://www.folklore.org/StoryView.py?project=Macintosh&story=The_End_Of_An_Era.txt.

Hertzfeld, Andy. "*MacPaint* Evolution." http://www.folklore.org/StoryView.py?story=MacPaint_Evolution.txt.

Hicks, Dan. "Editorial Content." *Amazing Computing* 8 (11) (November 1993): 6.

Hiltzik, Michael. *Dealers of Lightning: Xerox PARC and the Dawn of the Computer Age.* New York: Harper Collins, 1999.

Hoban, Phoebe. "Looks Great, Manny, but Will It Sell?" *New York* 18 (30) (August 5, 1985): 15–17.

Hodgson, Dallas. "Whatever Happened to *Deluxe Paint*?" *Dallas Hodgson's Private Island*, January 19, 2008. http://dallashodgsonInfo/articles/dpaint.htm.

Hood, Scott. "The NTSC/RS-170A Video Standard." *AmigaWorld Tech Journal* 1 (2) (June–July 1991): 30–34.

Hull, Steve. "*Amazing* Interviews . . . Jim Sachs." *Amazing Computing* 2 (4) (April 1987): 9–14.

Humphreys, John. "Max Headroom." *John Humphreys Sculpture.* http://www.john-humphreys.com/page14/page3/page3.html.

Hunter, William. "Player 4 Stage 4: But Is It Arts?" *The Dot Eaters: Videogame History 101*, November 23, 1999. http://www.emuunlim.com/doteaters/play4sta4.htm.

Hurteau, Fred. "Deluxe Paint IV AGA" (review). *AmigaWorld* 9 (6) (June 1993): 68–89.

IBM Corporation. *The Birth of the IBM PC*. IBM Archives. n.d. http://www-03.ibm. com/ibm/history/exhibits/pc25/pc25_birth.html.

Jacobs, Stephen. "Flying Toasters." *Wired* 2 (5) (May 1994). http://www.wired.com/ wired/archive/2.05/flying.toasters.html.

Jakober, Edward. "Digi-View" (review). *Amazing Computing* 2 (1) (January 1987): 9–13.

"Jay Miner: The Father of the Amiga." *Amiga User International* 2 (6) (June 1988): 20–21, 64.

"Jay Miner Interview." *Metroplex Commodore Computer Club News* 12 (9) (October 1994): 2–6.

Jennrich, Massmann Schulz. *Amiga 3D Graphic Programming in BASIC*. Grand Rapids, MI: Abacus, 1989.

"Jim Sachs: Amiga Artist and Game Developer." *Amazing Computing* 9 (4) (April 1994): 55–57.

Johnson, Jeff, Teresa L. Roberts, William Verplank, David C. Smith, Charles H. Irby, Marian Beard, and Kevin Mackey. "The Xerox Star: A Retrospective." *IEEE Computer* 22 (9) (September 1989): 11–29.

Jones, Dave. "The Whole Truth about Games Programming." *Amiga Format* 7 (February 1990): 63–68.

Jones, Dave. "The Whole Truth about Games Programming: 2 (Scrolling)." *Amiga Format* 8 (March 1990): 63–67.

Jones, Dave. "The Whole Truth about Games Programming: 3 (Designing the Main Ship)." *Amiga Format* 9 (April 1990): 63–67.

Jones, Dave. "The Whole Truth about Games Programming Part 4: Aliens." *Amiga Format* 10 (May 1990): 85–89.

Jones, Dave. "The Whole Truth about Games Programming Part 5: Aliens 2." *Amiga Format* 11 (June 1990): 119–121.

Jones, Dave. "The Whole Truth about Games Programming Part 6: Collision Detection." *Amiga Format* 12 (July 1990): 155–158.

Jones, Dave. "The Whole Truth about Games Programming Part 7: The Guardian." *Amiga Format* 13 (August 1990): 127–130.

Jouppi, Ville. "The Lorraine." *Secret Weapons of Commodore*, December 29, 2004. http://www.floodgap.com/retrobits/ckb/secret/lorraine.html.

Jump, Maria E. "Design and Implementation of an Interactive Ray Tracer." Department of Computer Science, University of Maryland, September 14, 1998. http:// www.cs.umd.edu/~mount/Indep/MJump/report.html.

Juul, Jesper. *A Casual Revolution: Reinventing Video Games and Their Players*. Cambridge, MA: MIT Press, 2010.

Kaiser, Cameron. "The Commodore 65." *The Secret Weapons of Commodore*, July 1, 2007. http://www.floodgap.com/retrobits/ckb/secret/65.html.

Kalisher, Stan. "Digi-View" (review). *AmigaWorld* 3 (1) (January–February 1987): 76–78.

Katz, Arnie. "The Cinemaware Story: Master Designer Software Charts New Directions in Computer Entertainment." *ST-Log* 18 (April 1988): 81–84.

Kean, Roger. "The Biggest *Commercial Break* of Them All." *Crash* 12 (1984): 60–64.

Kirsch, Russell A. "SEAC and the Start of Image Processing at the National Bureau of Standards." *IEEE Annals of the History of Computing* 20 (2) (April–June 1998): 7–13.

Knight, Chris. "The Mighty Amiga 2000 and Video Toaster 3.1 Combo." *The Knight Shift*, June 21, 2006. http://theknightshift.blogspot.com/2006/06/mighty-amiga-2000-and-video-toaster-31.html.

Knight, Gareth. "Amiga Gallery." *Amiga History Guide*, April 8, 2006. http://www.amigahistory.co.uk/rareitem.html.

Knight, Gareth. "Amiga Imagery: The Meaning behind the Amiga's Changing Image." *Amiga History Guide*, February 23, 2002. http://www.amigahistory.co.uk/logo.html.

Knight, Gareth. "Amiga Joyboard." *Amiga History Guide*, June 14, 2002. http://www.amigahistory.co.uk/joyboard.html.

Knight, Gareth. "The Twists and Turns of the Amiga Saga." *Amiga History Guide*, February 23, 2003. http://www.amigahistory.co.uk/ahistory.html.

Knox, Andrea. "A New Strategy May Be Needed for Commodore." *Philadelphia Inquirer*, May 4, 1987.

Koester, Bill. "The Amiga VIRUS." *The Risks Digest* 5 (71) (December 7, 1987). http://catless.ncl.ac.uk/Risks/5.71.html#subj1.

Kotlinski, Johan. "Amiga Music Programs 1986–1995." GOTO80, August 20, 2009. http://goto80.blipp.com/wp-content/themes/goto80/datafoder/kotlinski%20%282009%29%20amiga%20music%20programs%2086-95.pdf.

Kushner, David. *Masters of Doom: How Two Guys Created an Empire and Transformed Pop Culture*. New York: Random House, 2003.

Laser, Harv. "Osaka and the Turbo SIG." *Info* 36 (February 1991): 31–33.

Laughner, Vinoy. "Computer Art: Is It Really Art?" *AmigaWorld* 2 (1) (January–February 1986): 24–27.

Leeds, Matthew. "Allen Hastings: Film Maker." *Commodore Magazine* 9 (12) (December 1988): 58–59, 66.

Leeds, Matthew. "How the Amiga Creates a Display." *AmigaWorld* 2 (2) (March–April 1986): 30.

Leeds, Matthew. "IFF: A New Standard." *AmigaWorld* 2 (3) (May–June 1986): 68–72.

Leeds, Matthew. "Success Story: A-Squared Systems and the Amiga Digitizer." *AmigaWorld* 2 (2) (March–April 1986): 26–32.

Leemon, Sheldon. "24-Bit Graphics Boards Revisited." *AmigaWorld* 10 (5) (May 1994): 20–26.

Leemon, Sheldon. "Depth-Defying Graphics: 3-D Programs for the Amiga." *AmigaWorld* 4 (1) (January 1988): 34–42.

Leemon, Sheldon. "Devices and Desires." *AmigaWorld* 9 (2) (February 1993): 30–38.

Levy, Steven. *Hackers: Heroes of the Computer Revolution*. 2nd ed. New York: Penguin, 1994.

Levy, Steven. *Insanely Great: The Life and Times of Macintosh, the Computer That Changed Everything*. New York: Penguin, 1994.

Levy, Steven. "Okay, Mac, Make a Wish." *Newsweek*, February 2, 2004.

Linzmayer, Owen W. "Digital Image Processors: Give Your Computer the Gift of Sight." *Creative Computing* 11 (7) (July 1985): 65–77.

Lone Starr. "Making of State of the Art." *R.A.W. Disk Magazine* 5 (May 1993).

Luk, Joseph. "What Are Chunky and Planar Displays?" *Amiga-FAQ*, December 5, 1994. http://oldwww.nvg.ntnu.no/amiga/amigafaq/AmigaFAQ_16.html.

Maciorowski, Jim. "Put on the Hex." *AmigaWorld* 9 (7) (July 1993): 43–46.

Mannock, Major Edward. *The Personal Diary of Major Edward "Mick" Mannock*, ed. Frederick Oughton. London: Spearman, 1966.

Martin, David W. "Amiga on Location with *Robocop*." *Info* 30 (January–February 1990): 30–32, 73.

Martin, David W. "Who Are You, Mr. Guru?" *Amazing Computing* 4 (5) (May 1989): 97–101.

McClellan, David T. "Executive Control: Introduction to the Amiga's Kernel." *AmigaWorld*, special issue (1987): 82–95.

McClellan, David T. "Graphics That Won't Stand Still." *AmigaWorld* 3 (5) (September–October 1987): 56–60.

McLellan, Vin. "Computer Systems under Siege." *New York Times*, January 31, 1988.

McMahon, Frank. "NewTek's Video Toaster: A New Era in Amiga Video." *Amazing Computing* 6 (3) (March 1991): 49–62.

Mealing, Stewart. *Computers and Art*. Exeter, UK: Intellect, 1997.

Means, Ben, and Jean Means. "Inside the Making of *Deluxe Paint III*: An Interview with Dan Silva." *Amazing Computing* 4 (9) (September 1989): 27–32.

Menkman, Rosa. "Chip Music and the 8-Bit Demoscene: Hacking, Open Source, and Remixing." *Masters of Media* (University of Amsterdam), December 15, 2008. http://mastersofmedia.hum.uva.nl/2008/12/15/chip-music-and-the-8bit-demoscene-hacking-open-source-and-remixing.

Millerson, Gerald. *Video Camera Techniques*. 2nd ed. Oxford, UK: Focal Press, 1994.

Monteiro, Richard. "Behind the Scenes: An Interview with Psygnosis Artists." *STart* 4 (11) (June 1990): 30–40.

Montfort, Nick. "Spawn of Atari." *Wired* 4 (10) (October 1996). http://www.wired.com/wired/archive/4.10/atari_pr.html.

Montfort, Nick, and Ian Bogost. *Racing the Beam: The Atari Video Computer System*. Cambridge, MA: MIT Press, 2009.

Mop. "Age: A Major Concern?" *R.O.M. Disk Magazine* 4 (June 1995).

Mop. "The Games Industry Is Destroying Our Scene!" *R.O.M. Disk Magazine* 1 (August 1994).

Morabito, Margaret. "A First Look at the Amiga." *AmigaWorld* 1 (1) (1985): 14–24.

Mortier, R. Shamms. "*DPaint AGA*." *Amazing Computing* 8 (7) (July 1993): 85–87.

Müller, Urban D. "Aminet Is the World's Largest Archive." *Aminet*, May 16, 1996. http://fi.aminet.net/docs/misc/30000.txt.

Nuttall, Andy. "Keep on Trackin'." *Amiga Format* 48 (July 1993): 17–19.

O'Keane, Jim. "Microsoft CD-ROM Conference." *Amazing Computing* 1 (4) (May 1986): 59–61.

O'Rourke, Michael. *Principles of Three-Dimensional Computer Animation*. 3rd ed. New York: Norton, 2003.

Pandaris, John. "Cynicism and Seduction, Speed and Software." *AmigaWorld* 1 (1) (1985): 26–31.

Pane, Patricia J. "Color Crunching." *InfoWorld* 12 (20) (May 14, 1990): 43–48.

Parent, Rick. *Computer Animation: Algorithms and Techniques*. San Francisco: Morgan Kaufmann, 2002.

Paterson, Tim. "An Inside Look at MS-DOS." *Byte* 8 (6) (June 1983): 230–255.

Paterson, Tim. "The Roots of DOS." *Softalk PC* 1 (10) (March 1983): 32–41.

Paterson, Tim, and John Wharton. "From the Mailbox: The Origins of DOS." *Microprocessor Report* 8 (18) (October 3, 1994): 1–3.

Patterson, David, and John L. Hennessy. *Computer Organization and Design: The Hardware / Software Interface*. Burlington, VT: Morgan Kaufmann, 2009.

Phong, Bui Tuong. "Illumination of Computer-Generated Images." PhD diss., University of Utah, 1973.

Pickert, Kate. "A Brief History of the Consumer Electronics Show." *Time*, January8, 2009. http://www.time.com/time/business/article/0,8599,1870067,00.html.

Polgár, Tamás. *Freax: The Brief History of the Computer Demoscene*. Vol. 1. Winnenden, Germany: CSW, 2008.

Proven, Liam. "The Amiga Is Dead. Long Live the Amiga!" *The Inquirer: News, Reviews, Facts, and Friction*, January 3, 2007. http://www.theinquirer.net/inquirer/news/1025786/the-amiga-dead-long-live-amiga.

Raymond, Eric S. *The Cathedral and the Bazaar: Musings on Linux and Open Source by an Accidental Revolutionary*. Sebastopol, CA: O'Reilly, 2001.

Redant, John. "The Contributions and the Downfall of the Xerox Star." August 2001. http://xeroxstar.tripod.com/index.html.

Redmond, Kent C., and Thomas M. Smith. *Project Whirlwind: The History of a Pioneer Computer*. Bedford, MA: Digital Press, 1980.

Reifsnyder, Abigail. "Artists and the Amiga." *AmigaWorld* 2 (1) (January–February 1986): 28–34.

Reifsnyder, Abigail. "Deluxe Paint" (review). *AmigaWorld* 2 (2) (March–April 1986): 72–75.

Reimer, Jeremy. "A History of the Amiga." *Ars Technica*, August 1, 2007. http://arstechnica.com/hardware/news/2007/07/a-history-of-the-amiga-part-1.ars/1.

Reimer, Jeremy. "Total Share: Personal Computer Market Share 1975–2005." *Jeremy Reimer: Writer, Technologist, and Futurist*, November 2, 2009. http://jeremyreimer.com/postman/node/329.

Robley, Les Paul. "*Babylon 5*: An Interview with the Show's Creators and a Look at the Video Toaster's Role in Production." *Amazing Computing* 8 (3) (March 1993): 73–76.

Rokicki, Tomas. "The Complete Guide for the Blittering Idiot: How (and When) to Control the Blitter." *AmigaWorld Tech Journal* 1 (4) (October 1991): 2–8.

RTSI (Real-Time Services, Inc.). "OS-9: Frequently Asked Questions." June 6, 2001. http://os9archive.rtsi.com/os9faq.html.

Ryan, Bob. "The Brave Now World of Video." *AmigaWorld* 5 (2) (February 1989): 24–30.

Ryan, Bob. "Bringing It All Back Home." *AmigaWorld* 3 (3) (May–June 1987): 27–30.

Ryan, Bob. "*Defender of the Crown*" (review). *AmigaWorld* 3 (2) (March–April 1987): 80–82.

Sands, Oran J., III. "Sync Tips: Interlace." *Amazing Computing* 4 (5) (May 1989): 51–53.

Sands, Oran J., III. "Video." *Info* 43 (October 1991): 34–40.

Sands, Oran J., III. "Video and Your Amiga." *Amazing Computing* 2 (7) (July 1987): 13–16.

Schaun, Dirk. *Amiga C for Beginners*. Grand Rapids, MI: Abacus, 1987.

Scott, Jason. "The Render Junkie." ASCII, October 19, 2007. http://ascii.textfiles.com/archives/1240.

Scott, Sir Walter. *Ivanhoe*. New York: Barnes and Noble, 2005.

Sears, David, and David English. "The Making of *Babylon 5*." *Compute!* 16 (7) (July 1994): 68–73.

Shoup, Richard. "*SuperPaint*: An Early Frame Buffer Graphics System." *IEEE Annals of the History of Computing* 23 (2) (April–June 2001): 32–37.

Skelton, Mindy. "End User Makes Good! Works in Big Computer Company!" *Info* 17 (November–December 1987): 27–28, 69–72.

Skelton, Mindy. "*Info* Interviews Jay Miner." *Info* 21 (July–August 1988): 23–25.

Skelton, Mindy. "Rodney Chang: Artist on the Edge." *Info* 25 (March–April 1989): 44–46.

Smith, Alvy Ray. "Digital Paint Systems: An Anecdotal and Historical Overview." *IEEE Annals of the History of Computing* 23 (2) (April–June 2001): 4–30.

Solomon, Barry. "Animation for Everyone, or: Animation Can Be a Moving Experience!" *Amazing Computing* 5 (1) (January 1990): 47–50.

Spaceballs. "Best Demos of 1992: *State of the Art*." *R.A.W. Disk Magazine* 5 (May 1993).

Spaceballs. "A Visit at Funcom!" *R.A.W. Disk Magazine* 6 (December 1993).

Spaceballs. "Woman of *State of the Art*." *R.A.W. Disk Magazine* 5 (May 1993).

Spanner. "Cinemaware: Games on Film." *retro:bytes Lite* 1 (December 2005–February 2006): 14–17.

Spufford, Francis. *Backroom Boys: The Secret Return of the British Boffin*. London: Faber and Faber, 2003.

Sterling, Bruce. *The Hacker Crackdown: Law and Disorder on the Electronic Frontier*. New York: Bantam, 1992.

Sting and Mop. "Remembering 1994." *R.O.M. Disk Magazine* 3 (March 1995).

Stuart, Brian L. *Principles of Operating Systems*. Boston: Course Technology, 2009.

Sutherland, Ivan Edward. "*Sketchpad*, a Man-Machine Graphical Communications System." PhD diss., MIT, 1963.

Tessler, Joel. "Super Bowl Amiga Show: Animating Miami Stadium's 40-Foot 'Jumbotron.'" *Amiga Plus* 1 (1) (April–May 1989): 51–53.

Todd, Brett, with Brian Ekberg, Bob Colavco, Alex Navarro, and Jeff Gerstmann. "The History of Football Games." *GameSpot*, August 14, 2005. http://www.gamespot.com/features/6130897/index.html.

"Tripos, the Roots of AmigaDOS." pagetable.com (blog), May 19, 2009. http://www.pagetable.com/?p=193.

Valich, Theo. "World's First Ray-Traced PC Game and Movie to Arrive in 2012." *Bright Side of News*, September 21, 2009. http://www.brightsideofnews.com/news/2009/9/21/worlds-first-ray-traced-pc-game-and-movie-to-arrive-in-2012.aspx.

"Video Toaster at the Ballpark." *AmigaWorld* 9 (9) (September 1993): 90.

Wagner, Brian. "The Basics of Ray Tracing." *AmigaWorld Tech Journal* 1 (3) (August–September 1991): 25–30, 63.

Wagner, Brian. "Building a 3-D Object Viewer." *AmigaWorld Tech Journal* 1 (2) (June–July 1991): 15–20.

Walker, Trey. "*The Sims* Overtakes *Myst*." *GameSpot*, March 22, 2002. http://www.gamespot.com/pc/strategy/simslivinlarge/news_2857556.html.

Wallace, Lou. "The A1200: A New Mainstream Amiga?" *AmigaWorld* 9 (1) (January 1993): 30–32.

Wallace, Lou. "The Amiga 4000." *AmigaWorld* 8 (11) (November 1992): 30–34.

Wallace, Lou. "Amiga Video: Done to a 'T.'" *AmigaWorld* 6 (10) (October 1990): 21–28.

Wallace, Louis R. *AmigaWorld Official AmigaVision Handbook*. San Mateo, CA: IDG, 1991.

Wallace, Louis R. "Double for Nothing." *AmigaWorld* 4 (6) (June 1988): 89–93.

Wallace, Louis R. "Forms in Flight" (review). *AmigaWorld* 4 (1) (January 1988): 68–72.

Wallace, Louis R. "The Help Key: Warning!" *AmigaWorld* 5 (4) (April 1989): 90.

Wallace, Louis R. "Vanquishing the Viruses." *AmigaWorld* 4 (11) (November 1988): 49–52.

Walleij, Linus. "A Comment on 'Warez Doodz' Culture." n.d. http://www.df.lth. se/~triad/papers/Raymond_Doodz.html.

Walters, E. Garrison. *The Essential Guide to Computing: The Story of Information Technology*. Upper Saddle River, NJ: Prentice-Hall, 2001.

Wardrip-Fruin, Noah. *Expressive Processing: Digital Fictions, Computer Games, and Software Studies*. Cambridge, MA: MIT, 2009.

Waters, Harry F., Janet Huck, and Vern E. Smith. "Mad about M-M-Max." *Newsweek*, April 20, 1987.

Watson, Lonnie. "Animation with *Sculpt-Animate 4D*." *Amazing Computing* 5 (1) (January 1990): 51–53.

Weltner, Trapp. *Jennrich: Amiga Graphics Inside and Out*. Grand Rapids, MI: Abacus, 1988.

Whitted, Turner. "An Improved Illumination Model for Shaded Display." *Communications of the ACM* 23 (6) (June 1980): 343–349.

Williams, Gregg, Jon Edwards, and Phillip Robinson. "The Amiga Personal Computer." *Byte* 10 (8) (August 1985): 83–100.

Wise, Richard. *Multimedia: A Critical Introduction*. New York: Routledge, 2000.

Woehr, Jack. "A Conversation with Mike Cowlishaw." *Dr. Dobb's: The World of Software Development*, March 1, 1996. http://drdobbs.com/184409842.

Wolf, Daniel, and Douglas Leavitt Jr. Compute!'s *Amiga Machine Language Programming Guide*. Greensboro, NC: Compute, 1988.

Wray, Bruce. "Reflections of a Mac User." *AmigaWorld* 2 (1) (January–February 1986): 91–92.

Wright, Ernie. "Amiga Juggler Animation." *Ernie Wright*, May 14, 2008. http://home. comcast.net/~erniew/juggler.html.

Wright, Guy. "How Many Is a Million?" *AmigaWorld* 5 (6) (June 1989): 6.

Wright, Guy. "Zeitgeist." *AmigaWorld* 1 (1) (Premiere, 1985): 10–11.

Wright, Guy. "Zeitgeist." *AmigaWorld* 2 (5) (September–October 1986): 4.

Wright, Guy, and Glenn Suokko. "Andy Warhol: An Artist and His Amiga." *AmigaWorld* 2 (1) (January–February 1986): 16–21.

Wright, Mark. "Retrospective: Karsten Obarski." *textfiles.com*, March 1, 1998. http:// www.textfiles.com/artscene/music/information/karstenobarski.html.

Wright, Scott. "The Personal Art of a Personal Computer." *AmigaWorld* 2 (1) (January–February 1986): 37–42.

Yarbor, Bruce. "Commercial Software Carries Virus." *Info* 19 (March–April 1988): 30.

Zamara, Chris, and Nick Sullivan. *Using ARexx on the Amiga*. Grand Rapids, MI: Abacus, 1992.

Zetter, Kim. "Nov. 10, 1983: Computer 'Virus' Is Born." *Wired*, November 10, 2009. http://www.wired.com/thisdayintech/2009/11/1110fred-cohen-first-computer -virus.

Zettl, Herbert. *Television Production Handbook*. 7th ed. Belmont, CA: Wadsworth, 2000.

Zike. "Interview: Animal." *In Medias Res*, September 16, 1997. http://imr.ip-design. com/imr/zimr.htm.

Video

Anderson, Paul. "The Battle for Santa's Software." *Commercial Breaks*, BBC2 TV, 1984.

Commodore-Amiga Inc. *The Launch of the Amiga*. Commodore-Amiga Inc., 1985.

Compton, Richard. "The Gathering." Episode of *Babylon 5*. Prime Time Entertainment Network, 1993.

Conroy, Chris, and Janice Crotty. *The History of the Amiga*. TechMedia Video, 1992.

Detore, Jack, and Brent Wood. *Jay Miner Speech, 1989*. Metroplex Commodore Computer Club, 1996.

Hastings, Allen. *Infinite Loop*. 1986.

Hastings, Allen. *Verx*. 1986.

Haynie, Dave. *The Deathbed Vigil and Other Tales of Digital Angst*. Intangible Assets, 1994.

Lakis, Ronald K. "Mainframes to Micros to Minis." *The Computer Chronicles*, KCSM TV, 1984.

Max Headroom. ABC TV, 1987.

Nichols, Peter. "Amiga and Atari." *The Computer Chronicles*, KCSM TV, 1985.

Nichols, Peter. "The New Amigas." *The Computer Chronicles*, KCSM TV and WITF TV, 1988.

Nichols, Peter. "The New Amigas." *The Computer Chronicles*, KCSM TV and WITF TV, 1989.

O'Neil, Roger. "Revenge of the Nerds." *NBC Nightly News*, NBC TV, June 10, 1992.

Polgár, Tamás. *The Full History of the Demoscene*. Assembly Demoparty, 2008.

Schein, Dan. *Inside Commodore-Amiga*. Commodore-Amiga Inc., 1988.

Wellman, William A. *Wings*. Paramount, 1927.

Index

C compiler, 18
CD-ROM (CD read-only memory), 5, 250–252
CD32 console, 251, 274
CDTV (Commodore Dynamic Total Vision) drive, 251, 274
CES (Consumer Electronics Shows), 11–12. *See also* Boing demo
Winter CES show, 11–12
CGI (computer graphics imaging), 136, 140, 274
Chang, Rodney, 44, 79, 81
Chroma-key compositing, 131, 274
Chunky graphics, 24, 275
Cinemaware, 207, 210, 214, 220–221, 250
games produced, 215–217, 222 (*see also Defender of the Crown*)
interactive movies, 217–220
C language. *See also* SSG ("spherical solid geometry")
Amiga programmed mostly in, 88, 153, 159, 226, 274
programming with, 88, 153, 159, 226, 274, 283
TRIPOS (Trivial Portable Operating System) and, 152–153
CLI (command-line interface), 152, 156
Cohen, Fred, 171
Coleco, Adam, 12
Collision-detection routine, 240–242
Color digitizer, 119, 123. *See also* Digitizers
Color Television Interface Adaptor (CTIA), 13
Commodore
Amiga's corporate parent, 7, 19, 46, 301n10
European subsidiaries, 199, 200
failing to repackage Amiga, 256
financial problems and bankruptcy, 41, 78–79, 200, 251, 263, 268
poor management and marketing cited, 7–8, 41, 43, 55, 77, 165, 253–254, 256–257
slow to implement new technology, 68–69, 154, 250–251, 255
Commodore 64, 2, 115, 119, 183, 208
release, 11, 19

SID (Sound Interface Device) chip, 192, 299n40
Commodore 64 Programmer's Reference Guide, 158
Commodore versions and releases. *See also* Commodore 64
Commodore 65, 254–255
Commodore 264, 12
Compact disc (CD), 11
Compute!, 4
Computer Security Conference, DOD, 171
Computer viruses, 169, 171, 171–172, 284. *See also* SCA (Swiss Cracking Association) virus
"Byte Bandit," 177
Elk Cloner, 171, 176
Lamer Exterminator, 177–178
protective viruses and virus checkers, 178
SystemZ, 178
CoolCapture vector, 174–175, 275
Copper coprocessor, 73–76, 232, 275. *See also* Agnus chip; MOVE function; WAIT function
Coprocessors. *See* Blitter coprocessor; Copper coprocessor
Cowlishaw, Mike, 165, 166
CPU (central processing unit), 13, 148, 150, 159–160, 275, 284, 296n14
Crackers, 181–183, 184, 201, 203, 275, 278, 295n6. *See also* Software piracy
cracktro (cracker's signature), 183, 188, 204, 275
Creative Computing, 3–4
Culture of computing, 7, 8, 133–134, 297n33. *See also* Amiga users; Demoscene; Open-source movement
Amiga commanding respect in, 164, 185, 191, 264
in Europe and global, 181, 182–191
hacker culture, 94, 166, 202–203, 297n33
Internet-based communities, 202, 266, 267
mainframe and institutional culture, 166, 265
Cuomo, Jim, 214

Custom chips. *See* Agnus chip; Denise
  chip; Paula chip
Cutter, John, 214
Cyan Studios, 249. *See also Myst*

DAC (Digital-to-analog converter), 37,
  276
Dean, Roger, 246
Debugging utilities, 157
Decillionix, 37
Decline of the Amiga, 180, 199, 259
  causes (*see* Limitations of the Amiga)
  continuing use after decline, 260,
    267–268
  inherent design issues, 257, 259, 260,
    268–269
  parent corporation policies
    contributing to (*see* Commodore)
Decode exhibition, 204
Decuir, Joe, 144
Defender of the Crown, 209, 210–216, 249
  developed with DPaint, 214
  inspired by *Ivanhoe* (Scott), 212–213
Deluxe Music Construction Set, 193,
  194–195
Deluxe Paint. *See* DPaint (Deluxe Paint)
Demos. *See also* Boing demo; *Megademo*;
  State of the Art; *and by specific name*
  Amiga-based, 12, 26, 39, 125, 144,
    183–185, 191, 200, 273
  the coder demo, 191
Demoscene. *See also* Culture of
  computing; Europe; Scandinavian
  demoscene
  as an aesthetic movement, 186, 203–
    204, 205
  Amiga computing integral to, 185, 191,
    204–205
  based in Europe, 181, 183–185, 188,
    190, 192, 199, 201, 202–205
  parties, 184, 188, 190
Denise chip, 13, 17, 22, 37, 57, 241. *See
  also* Display system on the Amiga
Denmark, demoscene in, 184, 188
De Salvo, Donna, 80
Design and development of the Amiga,
  16, 29, 39–41, 289n25, 290n26,
  295–296n11

design decisions, 1, 2, 25, 114–115,
  156, 257–258, 288n7
  original team (*see* Luck, Dale; Miner,
    Jay; Sassenrath, Carl)
  replacement of original team, 165
Desktop publishing, 140–141
Desktop video. *See also* Video
  production; Video Toaster
  Amiga features facilitating, 124, 125–
    127, *128, 129*, 138
  limitations, 122
Digital art and media, 5, 6, 25. *See also*
  Boing demo; Graphics technology;
  Multimedia capabilities, Amiga
Digital Illusions, 201–202
Digitizers, 119–120, 276
  ADC (analog-to-digital converter), 36,
    121–122, 123, 271
  color digitizer, 119, 123
  Digi-View, 118, *119*, 120–124
  video digitizer(s), *119*
Digi-View, 118, *119*, 120–124
Disk management/input and output,
  152–153
Display system on the Amiga. *See also*
  Demos; Graphics technology;
  Monitors
  Agnus chip and, 16, 23–24, 31, 37,
    38–39, 53, 244
  attributes, 22–25, 34–35, 39–40, 76,
    289n33
  color palette, 21–23, 26–27
  Denise chip and, 13, 17, 22, 37, 57
  frame grabber, 85, 277
  the genlock, 117–118, 124, 277
  HAM mode (*see* HAM [Hold-and-
    Modify] mode)
  Paula chip and, 13, 17, 38–39, 76
  planar system, 24, 25, 31, 32–33,
    34, 39
  resolution mode, 26, 64, 93, 96, 112,
    116, 122, 293n11 (*see also* Resolution)
  retargetable graphics, 260, 282
  screen display rate, 113
  size, 3, 17
  text, 2
  viewport system, 39
  virtual screens, 76